NEIGHBORWORKS WORKS

Practical Solutions from America's Community Development Network

NeighborWorks America
999 North Capitol Street, N.E.
Suite 900
Washington, D.C. 20002

Contributing Editors

Anne Davis Burns
Mary Kate Cary
Gretchen Cook
Paul Frysh
Michele Lerener
Megan Scripps
Joan Shipps

TWITTER, TWEET, RETWEET and the Twitter logo
are trademarks of Twitter, Inc. or its affiliates

Printed in the United States of America

ISBN-13: 978-0-692-78519-5

Dedicated to all those
who work to improve
our nation's communities.

TABLE OF CONTENTS

II   Foreword
Paul Weech, President & CEO, NeighborWorks America

1   Affordable Homes
Section foreword by Peter Carey, former CEO, Self-Help Enterprises

131   Community Building
Section foreword by Tracy Hoover, Chief Executive Officer, Points of Light

269   Cross-Sector Collaboration
Section foreword by David Erickson, Director,
Community Development Department, Federal Reserve Bank of San Francisco

403   Financial Stability
Section foreword by Rodney Brooks, Washington Post Columnist

465   Nonprofit Excellence
Section foreword by Bill Ryan, Kennedy School of Government at Harvard University

543   Place-Based Investments
Section foreword by Mel Martinez, Chairman,
Southeast U.S. and Latin America, JPMorgan Chase & Co.
Former Secretary, U.S. Department of Housing and Urban Development

633   About NeighborWorks America

637   The NeighborWorks Network

642   References

647   Story Index by Author

649   Story Index by Organization

Foreword

Paul Weech, President & CEO, NeighborWorks America

More than 35 years of working in the housing, community development and financial services sectors has taught me that you can learn a lot from those who are actually doing the work to build communities and create opportunities. If you listen closely, you can discern how their sense of purpose and meaning drives their work. You can hear them define practical solutions to the challenges and opportunities they face. They know what works and what doesn't work.

This book tells those leaders' stories in their own words. Heads of 140 of the nonprofit organizations in the NeighborWorks network write about how they have been able to make a difference in the lives of the people and the communities they serve. They share how affordable housing with supportive services provides a home for formerly homeless veterans, and allows low-income seniors to age in place with dignity. Many highlight innovations that are making homes more affordable – through new approaches to manufactured housing, through home sharing models, through community land trusts, or through tiny homes. Others were able to lower the operating costs on homes through energy savings. You'll read of communities' resiliency in the wake of natural disasters like hurricanes, tornados, and floods and unnatural disasters like oil spills and the foreclosure plague. Through them all, the strong nonprofits in the NeighborWorks network help drive recovery.

You'll read about a growing entrepreneurial streak in the nonprofit sector. Non-profits that have adopted a social enterprise ethos are taking a business-like approach to achieving their missions. These social entrepreneurs are building sustainable organizations by identifying new sources of capital, by creating di-versified sources of earned revenue, and by looking for efficiencies that help control their costs – all in the name of making a bigger impact on behalf of the people they serve. Other entrepreneurs in the network developed small businesses – businesses from an olive oil manufacturer to one that sources local seafood for restaurants and grocery stores to another that offers nonprofit loans to low income people as an alternative to those terrible payday loans – all of which provide jobs to residents and generate dollars that can go back into their mission work of supporting services to low-income people and places.

This collection of stories from all across the country teaches us about the power of networks. NeighborWorks America supports a national network of strong, diversified nonprofits that deliver solutions that work because they can draw on their peer organizations to solve problems, share best practices, and spread innovation. This is a book about America's community development network.

Almost every story speaks to the importance of partnerships, collaboration and resident engagement. Community-based nonprofits are bringing economic opportunity to more Americans through cross-sector collaborations, complementary investments, and collective problem solving. Not only do these partnerships allow us to share what works, but to learn together from what doesn't work – an important part of innovation.

These new collaborative approaches are a recognition that community development is about more than housing. Leaders are creating a better quality of life in communities through new partnerships between the housing and community development sector and top organizations working in education, workforce development, public safety, arts and culture, and health care. Many NeighborWorks organizations are positioned as "community catalysts," marshaling public, private and philanthropic sector resources to help build access to education and employment opportunities. We know that these comprehensive approaches are changing lives.

NeighborWorks America is in the community- and opportunity-building business. We've learned that building communities of opportunity requires many "community catalysts." We work hard to support those innovative nonprofits in our network – the breadth and depth of whose work is manifest in these pages – through grants, training, technical assistance, peer exchange, organizational assessments and our signature leadership training programs, Achieving Excellence and Excellence in Governance.

At NeighborWorks, we also deeply believe that building social capital is fundamental to developing places of opportunity. NeighborWorks has a strong history of working with our network organizations to empower residents as agents of change. Community strength comes from encouraging diversity and inclusion – across race, income, and culture. In our nearly 40 years in communities across America, we've learned that strong nonprofit leadership, resident engagement and an inclusive approach are key to creating places of opportunity.

These places of opportunity create growth, well-being and a sense of "neighborness." That's why we want to expand economic opportunity for all Americans – no matter where they live.

We want to make sure that every community in America is a place of opportunity.

Paul Weech
Washington, DC
December 2016

Paul Weech is the president and CEO of NeighborWorks America, a 35-year-old, congressionally chartered nonprofit serving more than 245 of the strongest nonprofits working in housing and community development. Previously, he was the executive vice president for policy and external affairs at the Housing Partnership Network. Prior to that he was the senior vice president for policy for both the Housing Partnership Network and Stewards of Affordable Housing for the Future.

Weech served as chief of staff at the U.S. Small Business Administration; staff director for the Subcommittee on Housing and Community Development for the U.S. Senate Committee on Banking, Housing and Urban Affairs; and senior analyst for Housing and Credit for the U.S. Senate Committee on Budget. He also worked in various positions at Fannie Mae culminating in the role of vice president for mission strategy in the office of corporate strategy there.

Affordable Homes

Peter Carey

Across the nation, local and regional NeighborWorks organizations are finding creative ways to address their community's need for decent affordable housing. Combining creativity, commitment, business skills and financial resources, these organizations are implementing local solutions to meet local needs. This might mean improving or replacing substandard housing, the preservation of existing affordable rental housing or the development of new rental and ownership homes. The need may be affordable financing, homeownership education, or service-enriched rental housing.

In this chapter, you will read a few examples of the work being done throughout the NeighborWorks network. The geography, demographics and approach vary, yet there is a common mission which runs through each. A decent, affordable home is the most basic building block of community, and from childhood on, where we live can affect our entire lives.

NeighborWorks organizations know that community development is not simply building housing but that safe and decent housing is one key element of the big picture – a foundation that can provide the opportunity for people of all income levels, of all backgrounds, to live in a healthy, thriving environment.

Today we are learning even more about the negative individual and societal impacts of poor housing conditions and the value of investing in decent housing. Studies have shown that housing quality can affect the ability to learn and socialize in school. There is growing evidence that growing up in substandard housing can negatively impact healthcare costs, not just during childhood, but into adulthood.

For those in the lower rungs of our economy, housing is often a choice among unsatisfactory alternatives. Housing conditions and affordability pose an obstacle that has far-reaching impacts. The very word "Home" carries connotations of safety and security. Home is the base from which we interact with our community and with society, and increasing evidence suggests that where we grow up has lifetime implications for education, health and income. As Harvard Professor Matthew Desmond states in Evicted, "Without stable shelter, everything else falls apart."

Senior citizens with unsafe wiring or a leaky roof they can't afford to fix. Children who are ashamed to bring their friends home from school, or who have to change schools frequently because there is no affordable housing available. Parents who feel a sense of failure because they can't provide a decent home for their children. Disabled individuals who struggle to maneuver within their own home. These are not theoretical examples- each of these represent real people I've met throughout my career in affordable housing.

Past decades have seen dramatic changes in the housing industry, as the financing for affordable housing has become more complex, construction is more technical and costly, and market pressures create an impediment to affordability. Of necessity, nonprofit housing developers, owners, managers, and funders have kept pace. In the last decade, the collapse of the real estate market threatened the viability of homeownership and has placed even more pressure on rental markets. NeighborWorks America has been in the forefront of efforts to equip and support local organizations in this increasingly complex environment through training, technology and capital.

Perhaps the best way to understand the lasting effect of this work is to look in the eyes of those who have been given the opportunity to live in a decent home, finally enjoying the warmth and security much of this nation takes for granted. Kids who have a safe place to grow up, seniors who no longer have to choose between paying the rent and buying food, parents who can take pride in the home in which they are raising their children. Each one living in a dwelling that is worthy to be called "Home."

The organizations in this chapter are just the tip of the iceberg, representing a broad and diverse network that is creating opportunity for decent, affordable, stable homes across America.

Peter Carey's career in rural housing has spanned more than four decades, including 25 years as CEO of Self-Help Enterprises, a leader in the development and preservation of rental and ownership housing in rural California. Following his retirement in 2014, he served for a period of time as acting COO for NeighborWorks America. He continues to be actively engaged in housing policy at the local, state and national levels.

MONTEVERDE ROWE – BREATHING NEW LIFE INTO A CITY BLOCK

Walter D. Webdale, President & CEO

AHC Inc.

Baltimore's Park Heights neighborhood has been home for generations of west Baltimore families and includes parks and churches as well as residences. The neighborhood has experienced decades of decay and a lack of investment. In 2008, AHC purchased and renovated a 301-unit affordable apartment community for seniors and people with disabilities known as MonteVerde Apartments in the Park Heights neighborhood. The road leading to the apartment complex was full of abandoned, crumbling row houses, so in 2010 AHC decided to build on its commitment to the neighborhood and tackle the blighted block with a homeownership project called MonteVerde Rowe.

The mission of AHC is to produce and preserve quality affordable housing for low- and moderate-income individuals and families. Founded in 1975, AHC focused primarily on Northern Virginia until 2001, when the organization purchased its first property in Baltimore, Greenspring Overlook, a 189-unit property also located in the Park Heights neighborhood. Since then, AHC has invested nearly $60 million in four affordable housing developments in that neighborhood.

"AHC believes we can make a bigger impact in the community by focusing our investment in a specific area," explains Andrew Vincent, director of AHC Greater Baltimore. "Providing opportunities for more quality affordable housing in a concentrated area can help tip the balance in a neighborhood and bring it to life."

CHALLENGE

Baltimore's Park Heights neighborhood has been home to generations of families. But the community of row houses, parks and churches experienced decades of decay that deterred new investments. Revitalization efforts needed a jumpstart, and one particular block of abandoned crumbling homes seemed the perfect place to launch the process.

Renovating a block is a big challenge;
but changing perception of a neighborhood is even harder.

AHC's $30-million investment in the two 13-story buildings at MonteVerde Apartments transformed the run-down property and provided more community space, updated kitchens and baths, new windows and heating and cooling systems. A thriving program for residents improves their physical and mental health and their ability to age in place. However, Violet Avenue, the road leading to the apartments, was an eyesore ridden with boarded-up windows and trees growing out of the sagging roofs of abandoned row houses.

Since 2010, in order to maximize its impact, AHC has focused its attention on one block of Violet Avenue. AHC has purchased 12 homes – about two-thirds of the block. Most have been fully renovated, with more construction projects slated to begin soon.

Each townhome is constructed to accentuate the charm and character of its historic nature while leveraging modern design standards, current technology and today's most desirable finishes. These three-bedroom and two-bedroom with den homes include features such as granite countertops, exposed brick, recessed lighting, energy-efficient appliances and fenced backyards.

Along with interior renovations, AHC is also improving the overall look of the street. We have cleaned up the block extensively, clearing junk piles and fencing yards to prevent dumping. To spruce up the block still more, AHC planted trees and flowers and repaired steps and sidewalks along the street – whether we owned the adjacent homes or not.

AHC is working hard to strengthen ties with the community and has formed partnerships with the local neighborhood association and the City of Baltimore. AHC is working with the Baltimore Vacants to Value program to provide extra incentives to first-time homebuyers. MonteVerde Rowe is on the city's annual tour of homeownership opportunities, which helps boost awareness of the renovated community. Events to gather residents together to build more community cohesion are planned.

The project has been slow going, but AHC is committed to investing the time and effort to make a difference. The dedication is beginning to pay off. So far, four first-time homebuyers, including a nurse and a postal worker, have purchased homes. Several of the individuals grew up in the neighborhood or nearby and are thrilled to become homeowners.

AHC has invested $30 million in the Monte Verde Apartments.

We are making progress with the rest of the block and hope to sell more homes. Three more homes are completely renovated and ready for sale. Two homes are under construction and construction will begin on two more soon.

AHC has learned lessons along the way. Transforming a neighborhood takes time and doesn't happen overnight. Renovating a block is a big challenge, but changing the perception of a neighborhood is even harder. Baltimore has some challenging neighborhoods and a renovated block is just a drop in the bucket. Often, people love MonteVerde Rowe's renovated houses, but are scared away by the neighborhood, even though the block looks very welcoming and safe. Another lesson we've learned is that this type of project takes a village. Working with the city government, community associations, local leaders and other neighbors is critical.

The reward is that the block is beginning to bloom. Last winter, possibly for the first time ever, MonteVerde Rowe sparkled with festive holiday lights. The lights were just the latest indication the block is coming back to life after decades of disinvestment. And, four families so far are putting down roots and stabilizing their families in affordable, high-quality homes.

ABOUT WALTER D. WEBDALE

Walter D. Webdale serves as president and CEO of AHC Inc. Founded in 1975, AHC is a nonprofit developer of affordable housing in the mid-Atlantic region that provides quality homes and education programs for low- and moderate-income families. Based in Arlington, VA, AHC has developed more than 7,000 apartment units in 52 properties in Virginia and Maryland. AHC's Resident Services program reaches 2,000 children, teens, adults and seniors each year through onsite education programs and activities.

COLUMBUS COTTAGE PROGRAM: NEW HOMES ALLOW SENIORS TO AGE IN PLACE

Cathy Williams, President & CEO

NeighborWorks Columbus

Eighty-two year old Mary Jenkins had been living in her rented Columbus, GA, home for over three decades. The house started falling down around her, but Jenkins feared the repairs would increase her rent so she said nothing to her landlord. The bathroom was unusable, extension cords were strung together to provide scant lighting, and she had no refrigerator. "I haven't had one of those in years," she said. The dangerous health and safety conditions seriously threatened the cancer survivor's welfare. When the landlord passed away and his heirs discovered the conditions Jenkins was living in, they approached NWC to help.

Such deplorable living conditions are all too common in Columbus. Many seniors own their homes outright, but cannot afford to maintain and repair them or install desperately needed heating and air conditioning. The choice between eating and fixing a leaking roof becomes a matter of sheer survival. When an elderly woman is wearing everything she owns to keep warm in her shack with no kitchen or bathroom, she should be considered as homeless as the young single mother staying in a shelter. However, in 2012, new federal rules changed the way the homeless were counted, no longer including those who live in "housing that is in such bad condition it is no longer fit for human habitation." In other words, people like Jenkins were no longer included in the homeless count and could not receive assistance.

CHALLENGE

Georgia is one of the poorest states in the country, and many of its elderly residents spend much of their limited income on housing that is often in disrepair and lacking plumbing and appliances. Though living in squalor, these people are not classified as homeless and thus cannot receive public assistance.

The Cottage Program is a sustainable, mortgage-based program that provides safe, affordable housing to many of the city's most vulnerable residents.

NeighborWorks Columbus has uncovered a number of residents falling between these cracks – those who are over 60 and have lived in their mortgage-free homes for decades on fixed or low incomes. To fill their critical needs, NeighborWorks Columbus created a public-private partnership to launch the Columbus Cottage Program (CCP). The program temporarily relocates elderly homeowners living in substandard housing while a new cottage is constructed on their property, placing a modest and affordable mortgage on the new home.

Once qualified under flexible guidelines, the resident is counseled on the financing process and NeighborWorks Columbus approves the loan. The homeowner moves into temporary housing and a new two-bedroom, energy-efficient cottage is built to provide a safe, healthy and dignified environment for the residents to age in place. When the residents move in, they take on an affordable first mortgage costing no more than 30 percent of their income. This first mortgage includes an allowance for utilities, but a second deferred, non-interest bearing loan can cover any costs exceeding the resident's income.

Funding from the federal HOME program provides the capital needed up front for the demolition and construction on a typical two-bedroom cottage, which costs approximately $74,000. Program-related investment, program-related income, and community development financial institutions grants cover any mortgage financing gaps. In one example, a 78-year-old widow living on $20,000 a year in Social Security income can afford $500 a month in housing costs. This will support a $387 mortgage payment and $100 in utilities, so no gap subsidy is required.

The cottage program started as a "give-away" one-off program and the homes were established as life estates that terminated upon the death of the recipient. Today it has evolved into a sustainable, mortgage-based program that provides safe, affordable housing to many of the city's most vulnerable residents. Cottages have been built to house many Columbus seniors, and the program will build on the success achieved through identifying those in need, providing financial counseling and partnering with government and private organizations.

Social security benefits replace just 39% of the average person's income.

ABOUT CATHY WILLIAMS

Cathy Williams is the founding president and CEO of NeighborWorks Columbus, where she has served for 16 years. Williams is also on the board of the local Boy Scouts of America and has served on the local school board and the Columbus Technical College Board of Directors. She was vice chair of the Georgia State Trade Association for Non Profit Developers, and vice chair of the National NeighborWorks Association.

THOUGHTFUL DESIGN ALLOWS AGING IN PLACE

Janaka Casper
President & CEO

Melissa Hammond, Communications Manager

Community Housing Partners

In 2012, the New River Valley (NRV) Planning District Commission in Virginia's southwestern region was awarded a federal grant for a three-year project aimed at developing livability strategies for businesses, community organizations, local governments and individuals. The resulting report, Home in the New River Valley, finds that by 2030 the number of the region's residents aged 65 and older is expected to double and that the area's existing housing stock is aging.

Homes occupied by the elderly often have stairs, inadequate lighting and bathing facilities that are difficult to use and unsafe. Older adults no longer able to drive have few transportation options. By the time they are 85, two of every three people have some type of disability, regardless of income levels. These challenges increase isolation and health risks, which are significant factors that drive premature placement into institutionalized care – an extremely costly housing option for older adults, their families and the public.

In 2013, Community Housing Partners (CHP) facilitated an aging in place workshop with over 80 community members including architects, building contractors, elected officials, aging service providers, community planners, housing professionals, academics and residents. The group discussed the meaning of aging in place and new intentional housing options. The result was a Design Strategies and Implementation Guidebook for

CHALLENGE

80 percent of older people want to remain in their homes as they age, yet many of their houses were built for people who function independently. Older residents are more likely to live in homes that require substantial modifications and are less energy-efficient than newer homes.

> ## "It's clear that they thought about all of my needs – from hand railings and lower cabinets to wheelchair accessibility. There is no instance where I've wished they had done things differently."
>
> ### – Patricia Lewis, Grissom Lane Apartments resident

"lifespan-friendly homes" which ultimately led to the creation of the Grissom Lane Apartments. This affordable rental community for seniors has universal design features to make it usable for residents, regardless of their age, size or disability. To maximize resident health and comfort, CHP employed green design and construction practices that improve each apartment's energy efficiency, air quality and ability to regulate temperature fluctuations.

Grissom Lane Apartments is the first certified EARTHCRAFT Net-Zero development in Virginia, meaning each home produces as much or more energy than it uses with electricity generated by a solar photovoltaic system.

The rental community, managed by CHP Property Management, has four duplex cottages on a 1.25-acre site with a community garden and central gathering area where residents can create an interactive and supportive community.

The community includes these universal design features:
- At least one step-free entrance into the home
- An accessible bedroom, kitchen and full bathroom on the ground floor
- Wide doorways and hallways to allow accessibility
- Controls, switches and outlets that are reachable from either a seated or standing position
- Easy-to-use handles and switches
- Low- or no-threshold stall showers with built-in benches or seats
- Non-slip floors, bathtubs and showers
- Raised toilets
- Appliances installed within the universal reach range of 15" to 48"

"It's so nice that the apartments are all on one level. It's clear that they thought about all of my needs, from hand railings and lower cabinets to wheelchair accessibility," says Grissom Lane Apartments resident Patricia Lewis, adding: "It's also great that I am located so close to everything, from my neighbors to the stores and restaurants downtown. There is no instance where I've wished they had done things differently."

By the age of 85, 2 out of 3 people have some type of disability, regardless of income level.

The development of Grissom Lane Apartments is recognized as a best practice by the region, the town, the residents and CHP. The eight apartments were fully leased months in advance and eligible residents were selected through a lottery. There is currently a one- to two-year wait for a vacancy. Financial contributions include $600,000 in community development block grant funding from the Town of Blacksburg and $400,000 from the NRV HOME Consortium.

The Grissom Lane Apartments allow residents to age in place in a healthy and comfortable environment. Winter drafts have been mitigated through a combination of airtight construction, high-performance windows and super-insulation. The homes are healthier than the average home due to finishes and paints with low to zero volatile organic compounds and the installation of hardwood floors and ceramic tiles instead of carpeting. They feature a ventilation system that expels stale air from the center of the home while bringing in fresh air to areas where the tenants spend most of their time.

The lessons learned through this project include: 1) universal design features enable residents, regardless of age, size, or ability to live safely and comfortably in their homes, even as needs and abilities change, 2) a collaborative planning process harnesses the talents and energies of all interested parties to create and support a plan based on a shared vision that results in real sustainable and transformative community change and, 3) green building techniques increase a home's energy efficiency and therefore its affordability and support healthier and safer living conditions that contribute to successful aging in place.

ABOUT JANAKA CASPER

Janaka Casper, president and CEO of Community Housing Partners (CHP), has over 40 years of experience in housing and community development. He joined CHP in 1976, growing the once all-volunteer organization into a social enterprise that works with private and public partners to design, preserve, construct, manage, and sell healthy, sustainable, and affordable homes in the eastern United States. CHP also offers energy conservation training and services across the nation. During his tenure with CHP, the organization's programs and activities have expanded across seven states and are delivered by almost 400 employees.

MY OWN SPACE: FULFILLING THE NEEDS OF THOSE SEEKING INDEPENDENT LIVING

John Niederman, President & CEO

Pathfinder Services, Inc.

In recent years, more and more seniors and people with disabilities have sought to live independently, a more private option to living in group homes and less costly than institutions such as nursing homes. But many of them don't have the means to live on their own, in part because insurance often covers only the costs of the less desirable alternatives. Increasingly, such residents in Huntington, IN, particularly young people with disabilities moving out of their family homes, have been looking for a viable alternative to provide them with more privacy and independence.

For many years, Pathfinder Services has helped people with physical, developmental or economic challenges move from large institutions to smaller group homes in Huntington. A typical group home provides housing and support services for up to eight residents. More recently, clients – especially younger one with disabilities – have expressed the desire for more privacy and independence than a typical group home could offer.

Pathfinder responded by investigating new housing alternatives. We particularly liked the "motel suite" model, with a sleeping area, bathroom, living area and kitchenette. Careful financial projections revealed that – because each bathroom had to be fully accessible with a roll-in shower – the kitchenette (which was non-essential) would be cost-prohibitive.

An architect drew up a plan for three, 2,000-square-foot fourplexes on land we owned in a residential neighborhood.

CHALLENGE

Seniors and people with disabilities increasingly seek independent living, a more private option to living in group homes and significantly less costly than institutions. But many don't have the means to live on their own, in part because insurance will often cover only the costs of the less desirable facilities.

Residents were thrilled to have their own space —
they could visit with friends and family on their front porch
and could come and go through their own outside door.

The design featured the needed common areas and four efficiency-style rooms, each with a fully accessible bathroom, bedroom-area, and room for a loveseat, desk and television. To increase client independence, each efficiency had two doors, one leading to the common area and one to an individual front porch.

The development was designed to accommodate not only people served through the Medicaid waiver program for people with disabilities, but also low-income seniors who could not live totally independently or who would benefit from on-site support.

The first order of business was financing. Federal Home Loan Bank of Indianapolis supplied $389,000 in Affordable Housing Program funds and NeighborWorks supplied $50,000. This enabled us to break ground on a "front-porch" community in the summer of 2013.

Once open in May of 2014, we had full occupancy in very short order. Residents were thrilled to have their own space – they could visit with friends and family on their front porch and come and go through their own outside door. They also enjoyed being able to decorate their efficiency in any way they wanted.

We had to make adjustments along the way. For example, security concerns led to the installation of cameras facing the front door of each unit, so support staff could monitor any problems. In addition, residents requested a larger covered patio area with picnic tables where they could have a party or cookout with friends. We built one with NeighborWorks America funds, a grant from the Pathfinder Services Foundation and volunteer construction labor.

The success of the project spurred us to plan a new development. But as we planned the second independent living complex along the lines of the first, parents and guardians of some clients objected to what they saw as a potentially dangerous level of openness and independence. After discussions with families and guardians, we made the following changes to the new development:

1. For added security, outside doors face a garden area with a gazebo and fenced yard. The only doors accessible to the public are doors to the common rooms of each building.

2. Emergency call buttons are installed in each bathroom for residents to notify staff if they need assistance.

3. No carpeting. Carpeting added warmth and homeyness to the first development, but impeded walkers and wheel chairs and needed frequent cleaning. We installed laminate-look vinyl strips, which are attractive, wear well and can be replaced piecemeal.

Adults with disabilities, age 21–64, had median monthly earnings of $1,961, compared with $2,724 for those with no disability.

The new units were completed in March of 2016, were rented quickly and residents as well as family members are very happy with the results. One example is Kurtis, who lived at home with his mother his entire life. Once his mother passed away, Kurtis moved into one of our group homes, but did not always get along with all of his housemates. In addition, his room was very small and his family reported the home had an institutional feel.

Both Kurtis and his family are now very happy he has a place to call his own. He can be with friends and housemates in the kitchen and living room, but can also have time to himself whenever he chooses.

"Kurtis had gone through a trauma when his mother passed away. That pushed up a need to find residential services since his mother was his primary caregiver," says Kurtis' father. "The group home he first lived in was too crowded, his room too small and it just didn't feel like home. He has been very happy with this new home and is doing very well."

Pathfinder is meeting an essential need in the community of those with disabilities, but there are challenges. For example, though there is a consistent demand, there are rental gaps, and Pathfinder suffers financial loss when all units are not rented. If residents move out, we are dependent on the state's Medicaid waiver referral process to send us potential residents who can succeed with this level of independence, and those clients have been difficult to identify.

And though we have yet to market the units to senior citizens, we believe it will be difficult to find seniors who will agree to share space with adults with disabilities. Still, Pathfinder continues to work to find solutions for this model because it meets a unique need, and supports our mission of helping those in need to achieve independence, inclusion and stability.

ABOUT JOHN NIEDERMAN

John Niederman is president and CEO of Pathfinder Services, a nonprofit community development organization whose mission is to strengthen communities by enabling people facing physical, developmental or economic challenges to achieve independence, inclusion and stability.

HOMESHARING MEETS CHALLENGES FOR HOMEOWNERS AND RENTERS

Gerard Joab, Executive Director

St. Ambrose Housing Aid Center

Traditional housing assistance programs are unable to respond to the overwhelming need for affordable housing in the Baltimore area. When the waiting list for the Section 8 Housing Choice voucher program opened for a week in October 2014, it was the first time the Housing Authority of Baltimore City had accepted applications since 2003. The housing authority received more than 10,000 applications in the first hour, and more than 60,000 over the course of the enrollment week. In a random lottery, fewer than half were chosen to be added to the waiting list, and it will likely be years before those selected receive a Housing Choice voucher. In the surrounding Baltimore County, where the odds are more favorable, there is still a nine-year wait to receive a Housing Choice voucher.

Fair market rent in our region hovers around $1,000 a month for a one-bedroom apartment, causing many people to fall through the cracks. Other residents have limited options for different reasons, such as a history of bad credit and crushing debt.

Meanwhile, our Baltimore neighborhoods are filled with homeowners who are struggling to afford the costs of mortgage payments, utility bills and necessary upkeep on their homes. These homeowners are looking for a financial solution that doesn't force them to give up their homes and communities.

A successful match-up of these renters and owners can create housing and financial stability. It helps the owner

CHALLENGE

Both homeowners and renters can face financial challenges. For renters on limited incomes, a history of bad credit or evictions can limit options, and high-interest debt can limit housing budgets. Homeowners may struggle with mortgage payments and other expenses. Can there be a shared solution?

NeighborWorks Works: Practical Solutions from America's Community Development Network

Homesharing programs fill a gap where traditional housing assistance has been unable to meet community needs.

pay the bills and provides housing for tenants poorly served by the traditional rental market. "Homesharing" can also help combat feelings of isolation and provides the additional comfort and security of living with a companion.

Since its founding in 1968, St. Ambrose has been committed to providing innovative, comprehensive housing services to vulnerable homeowners, renters and neighborhoods in Baltimore.

Our Homesharing program fills a gap where traditional housing assistance programs have been unable to meet the community's needs and has been working for an expanding demographic of homeowners and renters in the Baltimore area since 1988. It is the only one of its kind in the state of Maryland and has served as a model for homesharing startups in other states.

St. Ambrose Homesharing counselors screen Homesharing applicants through interviews, background checks and personal references before recommending a match. Counselors provide budgeting assistance, home assessments, housing counseling, mediation and referrals to supportive services.

After the initial screening and interview process, Homesharing counselors recommend a match between a home provider and home seeker. The match is finalized at a meeting where parties discuss their expectations and sign a contract.

Matches can be finalized in as little as a week, a stark contrast to other public housing programs. In addition, counselors connect clients with other community resources from St. Ambrose and elsewhere, and are available to serve as mediators if problems arise.

Home seekers pay, on average, $500 a month, including utilities – roughly half of fair market rent in Baltimore. The deal enables renters to reduce debt, pay for education or simply achieve housing stability. The extra monthly income for home providers, which averages $6,000 a year, helps them to pay their bills on time, make necessary home improvements or simply to keep their homes.

36% of home providers in the Homesharing program are older than 65.

Homesharing has adapted and expanded over the years to respond to changing community needs. It was founded to reduce the financial burden on seniors who wanted to stay in their communities. The economic downturn in 2008, however, broadened the demographics of the home providers in the program. Today, 36 percent of home providers are older than 65.

The demographics of home seekers have also expanded. In 2015, with support from the O'Neill Foundation, St. Ambrose launched "Parent-Child Homesharing," a pilot program to explore Homesharing as a housing solution for single parents.

The goal of "Parent-Child Homesharing" is to create an affordable and stable housing option for a single parent and their child, as well as provide case management and other supportive family services. The hope is that this supportive housing model will foster greater family stability and self-sufficiency. The vast demand during the pilot-year solidifies our commitment to make Parent-Child Homesharing a permanent part of our program.

At its core, Homesharing provides income for struggling homeowners and affordable housing for individuals who need it. But it does more than that: by taking such care with each match, it fosters social connections that reflect in the larger community, and help to build strong, safe, supportive and diverse neighborhoods.

ABOUT GERARD JOAB

Gerard Joab began as executive director of St. Ambrose Housing Aid Center in 2011. Since then, Joab has initiated a phased capital improvement plan to improve St. Ambrose's facilities and rental portfolio, restructured divisional leadership and invested in human capital. A former home sharer himself, Joab previously served as executive director for the Local Initiatives Support Corporation's Greater Newark and Jersey City Program and the Donald Jackson Neighborhood Corporation in Newark's Clinton Hill neighborhood.

CREATING NEIGHBORHOODS OF OPPORTUNITY THROUGH AFFORDABLE HOUSING

Julie Bornstein, Executive Director

Coachella Valley Housing Coalition

Agriculture contributes approximately $1.3 billion annually to the Riverside County, California, economy. The value of agricultural crops in the Coachella Valley alone is $650 million, or roughly 50 percent of the county's annual contribution. Given the types of crops grown in the Coachella Valley, agriculture cannot survive without farmworkers. At the same time, the U.S. Department of Labor reports that migrant and seasonal farmworkers are some of the most economically disadvantaged people in the country. Farmworker incomes typically fall within the extremely-low to very-low-income classification.

In fact, more than one in 10 families in the Coachella Valley live below the federal poverty level. The lush golf courses, exclusive resorts and celebrity sightings at the world-renowned western communities – like Palm Springs, Rancho Mirage and Indian Wells – are worlds apart from the unpaved streets, failing septic systems and unauthorized waste dumps of the eastern valley, where roughly 88,000 people live.

The Fred Young Farm Labor Camp was the first permanent farmworker housing development funded by the U.S. Department of Agriculture in Southern California when it was constructed in the 1930s as temporary wood shacks for migrants. The shacks were replaced in the 1960s with 500-square-foot, two-bedroom, cinder block dwellings.

The Coachella Valley Housing Coalition (CVHC) was established as a response to the substandard living condi-

CHALLENGE

Over the years, the 58-acre Fred Young Farm Labor Camp, known as "El Campo" and home to 253 families, had deteriorated into an isolated slum community with the accompanying ills of crime, poverty and hopelessness. In 2007, Coachella Valley Housing Coalition (CVHC) was asked to take it over.

Previously, families endured extreme summer temperatures that regularly exceed 115 degrees Fahrenheit and dropped to below freezing on winter nights.

tions endured by farmworkers. In 1986, CVHC built its first 50-unit apartment community to house farmworkers and their families.

Today, CVHC is one of nine U.S. Department of Agriculture Self-Help Housing Technical Assistance providers in the State of California and is amongst the largest producers of Single Family Mutual Self-Help housing in the country. CVHC has helped more than 1,900 families fulfill their dream of homeownership. CVHC also owns and operates 34 multi-family affordable housing developments, or 2,433 units, including two migrant-farmworker housing facilities.

The history of the relationship between El Campo and CVHC can best be told through the eyes of Juan Rodriguez, whose parents, Juan Antonio and Elizabeth, moved as teenagers with their baby son into a cramped El Campo two-bedroom apartment, joining several generations of family members.

"It was in the 1990s when my parents finally could move into an apartment of their own, a CVHC building called Pie de la Cuesta," recalls Juan. "That was the move that brought CVHC into my life and has been a positive factor ever since, from providing us the opportunity to own our own home to helping me earn my college degree at UC Berkeley."

After arranging financing and beginning its work at El Campo, CVHC replaced 86 of the units, planned the demolition of another 86 and began predevelopment of the final phase of new construction. In addition, CVHC ensured that El Campo's existing residents had functioning air conditioning and heating units, since previously, families endured extreme summer temperatures that regularly exceeded 115 degrees Fahrenheit and dropped below freezing on winter nights.

CVHC then implemented its full community services programs at El Campo, with the replacement units including a free, onsite after-school program, a state-funded preschool, enrichment activities such as nutrition and health classes, an English-as-a-second-language program, summer youth and adult fitness offerings.

As the Rodriguez family developed, they took advantage of the child care program, free tutoring, tennis camp, ballet folklorico, mariachi and even opera appreciation programs. Juan's parents applied to CVHC's self-help program, receiving one-on-one credit and housing counseling and starting the process to become homeowners. The couple worked alongside seven other families to build their home and that of their neighbors. After working all day, they spent evenings and weekends building their dream home under the direction of CVHC staff, funded by the USDA Mutual Self-Help Housing program.

In 2012, there were more than 1 million hired farmworkers in the U.S. labor force.

Juan's parents wanted their children to aspire to a life better than farm work; establishing a stable home of their own was the first step toward that end. "Working in the fields from 6 a.m. to late in the afternoon was the greatest motivator to study, so that I would never have to do such backbreaking work again," Juan explains.

Although he had never left the Coachella Valley except for grape harvests, Juan appreciated the wider world he glimpsed in high school. A good student, he tutored others in math and volunteered as a translator for the faculty. When he was accepted by UC Berkeley, CVHC provided support through its John F. Mealey College Scholarship Fund. Once there, Juan used his knowledge of how affordable housing, or the lack of it, affects family stability, safety and aspiration by majoring in urban planning and architecture. He served as an intern with CVHC in the community services department, assisting in the implementation of programs such as a STEM robotics program and an art appreciation and tennis camp. During a second internship, he worked in the multi-family department learning the process of planning, funding and winning approvals for future developments.

Transforming El Campo into Villa Hermosa, the new replacement housing, is a metaphor for how CVHC transforms lives.

ABOUT JULIE BORNSTEIN

Julie Bornstein is the executive director of the Coachella Valley Housing Coalition, a nonprofit affordable housing development organization that for 34 years has helped low-income families build their own homes, provided safe and decent housing in its rental housing communities, and restored and revitalized their neighborhoods in Riverside, Imperial and San Bernardino counties. Coachella has developed more than 1,700 single-family homes and 2,433 apartments for low-income individuals and families. Bornstein previously served as president and CEO of the Campaign for Affordable Housing and as director of the California Department of Housing and Community Development.

COMMUNITY HOUSING TRUST: KEEPING HOMES FOREVER AFFORDABLE

Alan Hipps, Executive Director

—

HAPEC

Adirondack Park is an expansive and mountainous rural region about the size of neighboring Vermont with only a fraction of its population. The area is a magnet for outdoor recreation and is increasingly attractive to second-home buyers from more affluent areas less than a day's drive away. The increasing demand on land and homes is pushing up the prices, leaving many local residents unable to find affordable housing. Younger adults are forced to leave for more affordable areas as the local workforce – and with it the economy – evaporates. This market-driven gentrification presents an existential crisis for the small, economically challenged communities of the Adirondacks.

The Housing Assistance Program of Essex County (HAPEC) has supported affordable, safe and energy-efficient housing for Adirondack Park residents since 1984. But now they needed to come up with an innovative, financially sustainable way to help local residents meet this growing challenge. HAPEC turned to the Community Land Trust model as a means of keeping at least a subset of Adirondack homes forever affordable.

A Land Trust balances the competing goals of providing a fair return on the owner's investment while assuring that the home is kept affordable for future buyers. It achieves this by retaining ownership of the land on which the homes are built. Homebuyers get a deed to the house and a renewable, 99-year lease to the property, giving them most of the rights of traditional homeowners. They can

CHALLENGE

With its vast forests, mountains, free-flowing rivers, the Adirondacks are a huge draw to those seeking beauty and outdoor recreation. As many of the affluent seek to secure a piece of this land for their own, the costs of homes are skyrocketing and pricing out local long-term residents.

"I don't think we'd ever be able to afford a home without the Trust."

– Emily Goodspeed, Adirondack resident

even pass the home on to their immediate family members. The Trust, however, retains ownership of the land and exercises control over any resale.

In 2007, HAPEC organized the Adirondack Community Housing Trust as an independent, non-profit corporation and recruited community leaders from across the park to serve as the trust's board of directors. HAPEC provides staffing and administrative services under contract, but the board fully controls the trust.

HAPEC Executive Director Alan Hipps worked closely with state Senator Elizabeth "Betty" Little, (R-Queensbury) to form the Adirondack Community Housing Trust (ACHT). With Little's support, New York State provided $1 million to establish the Trust. Two philanthropists provided an additional $240,000.

The ACHT funds are used to reduce the cost of home purchases for income-qualified families across the Adirondacks who make up to 120 percent of the region's median income. Resale limitations on the property require that future sales of these homes be controlled by ACHT so that they will be passed on to other income-qualified families at affordable prices in the years ahead.

To date, the ACHT has helped 17 families find affordable homes, which are now part of the Trust.

"I don't think we'd ever be able to afford a home without [the Trust]," said Adirondack resident Emily Goodspeed. She and her partner Derek now own a modest trust home in North River, where the couple is raising two school-aged children.

Like many Trust homebuyers, the Goodspeeds feel that the resale restrictions are a reasonable part of the arrangement. "We're not going anywhere," Goodspeed said. "And if we did sell the house, I'd want someone else like us to have it," she added.

Trust homeowners pay modest lease fees that combined with transfer fees and property sales provide revenue to offset the cost of running the Trust. HAPEC estimates that to be completely self-sustaining, the Trust will need to expand to at least 50 homes. But that day may not be too far off – there is a substantial waiting list of income-qualified families interested in buying, and New York State recently provided a second $1 million award to continue the program.

By owning the land and regulating purchases, land trusts ensure permanent affordable housing.

Another aspect of home affordability is, of course, the property taxes Trust homeowners are required to pay on both the house and the leased land. The ACHT has worked closely with various agencies to ensure that Trust homes are assessed for their value under their resale restrictions, not the potentially much higher value without the restrictions. This helps keep the tax bill affordable for the homeowner.

The success of the Trust model and its mission to provide affordable homes has had an impact on local decision-making. Leaders in the village of Lake Placid recently approved an "Inclusionary Zoning" ordinance to require that 10 percent of all new subdivision lots in the community will be dedicated to the Land Trust to ensure that at least some newly built homes will remain affordable for local residents. HAPEC has been tapped to help implement the ordinance.

HAPEC learned important lessons through this project. The most critical lesson is that they must respond to the needs of homebuyers. In their sparsely populated, very rural area, the location of the home, and its proximity to employers, is a primary concern. They had a home sit unoccupied for over a year even though it was gifted to them and they could sell it for any price that was affordable to the buyer. Also, to be financially self-sustaining, the Trust will need to approximately triple in size to 50 homes.

ABOUT ALAN HIPPS

Alan Hipps is the executive director of HAPEC, a nonprofit community development organization that partners with local government, residents, businesses, and other organizations to foster viable Adirondack communities. For 40 years, HAPEC has provided homeownership assistance, home rehabilitation assistance, community services, multi-family housing development and rental assistance. In 2015 HAPEC provided housing services to over 1,000 households and generated more than $8.2 million in estimated regional output. HAPEC is a chartered member of the NeighborWorks Network.

SELF-HELP HOUSING REHABILITATION IN RURAL OREGON

Merten Bangemann-Johnson, CEO
Arthur Chaput, Director of Housing Rehabilitation

NeighborWorks Umpqua

According to the American Housing Survey, problems with the quality of housing are most common in rural areas and central cities. That is in large part because poverty is high in rural areas, with 2012 data from the Housing Assistance Council showing that about 17.2 percent of rural residents living below the poverty line in 2012 versus 14.9 percent nationwide.

Meanwhile, funds for rural housing provided by the USDA via the 502 Direct Loan program – one of the primary government aid programs for purchasing or rehabilitating homes in rural areas – have decreased over the past few years, dropping from about $2.1 billion in 2010 to around $828 million in 2013.

Another dynamic is that rural America is "older" than the nation as a whole, with more than one-quarter of all seniors living in rural and small town areas. Most seniors wish to remain and age in their homes as long as possible, but rural elders are increasingly experiencing challenges with housing quality as well as affordability. In far too many rural communities, the only housing options for seniors are their own homes, which are often difficult for them to maintain, or nursing homes, which have their own set of problems (including affordability).

In addition, the vast majority of rural seniors live in single-family units built in earlier decades when there was less awareness of what's required to ensure accessibility

CHALLENGE

Rural Oregon's single-family housing stock has deteriorated in recent decades with the collapse of local industries and depressed rural wages. Traditional housing rehabilitation resources like community development block grants are insufficient to meet demand. However, many homeowners have some of the skills – and the enthusiasm – to perform their own repairs.

Homeowners, empowered by accessible financing and in-person construction training, exit our program not just with a safe and durable home, but with skills for future home repair.

for people with all levels of physical abilities. A recent study published by AARP estimated that more than 1 million older adults with disabilities live in homes that present barriers to meeting their daily needs. Rehabilitation is a way for family members to help them stay at home.

NeighborWorks Umpqua's Self-Help Housing Rehabilitation Program is designed to address these challenges. It is part of USDA Rural Development's 523 Mutual Self-Help initiative, which we have successfully redesigned to address the need for rehab, and financed in part by community development block grants and NeighborWorks America funds. We rehabilitated 70 homes in the last three years, improving the lives and preserving the assets of more than 150 individuals.

Our program provides low- or zero-interest loans to low-income families whose homes need health- and safety-related repairs and who cannot qualify for other financing. Coupled with construction coaching and a tool library, this financing goes a long way; we replace leaking roofs, repair failed septic systems, install adequate heat sources and fix rotted flooring. Our program relies on the homeowners themselves to supply much of the labor; many families put more than 40 hours a week into their rehab projects, often saving tens of thousands of dollars. Without our staff's tools and technical expertise, and without the support of the USDA Rural Development 523 program, these health and safety repairs would not be feasible, and many of these homes would exit the housing market through deterioration. Housing rehabilitation preserves housing affordability.

The bottom line: homeowners, empowered with accessible financing and construction coaching, exit our program not just with a safe and durable home, but with skills and techniques that set them up for success in future home repair and maintenance. Furthermore, they can leverage these same skills in the job market. First-time homebuyers, too, have taken advantage of Self-Help Housing Rehabilitation – often first-time buyers in our area can only afford homes in need of significant repair, and our rehab program enables them to build skills, equity, and a healthy home at the same time.

Mitchell Howard of Gold Beach, Oregon, is an example. "I knew the house needed some work when we bought it, and I had a plan for remodeling the kitchen," he told my team. "But the [termite] damage was so much more extensive than we thought. It was scary. We would have walked away from the house if you hadn't helped [us]." Now, the hidden damage is fixed, the home has new siding, and Mitchell is ready to tackle the kitchen remodel he had planned from the beginning. His new skills and confidence should ensure a smooth construction process.

In 50 years, 50,000 rural homes have been built under the Self–Help Housing program.

Another example is Bill from Roseburg's Green District. NeighborWorks Umpqua helped replace his roof, reframe a rotten wall, replace a foundation wall, and gut and repair a rotten bathroom. The home was completely re-sided and every window was replaced, and Bill's old heat pump was repaired.

"I started walking months ahead to get in shape for this," said 74-year-old Bill. "I lost 20 pounds during the project!"

ABOUT MERTEN BANGEMANN-JOHNSON

Merten Bangemann-Johnson is CEO of NeighborWorks Umpqua. He has worked with the Gilman Housing Trust in Vermont, and served as special assistant to Mayor Mark Begich in Anchorage, Alaska, where he was CEO of the Anchorage Community Land Trust. He is on the board of the National Rural Housing Coalition.

BOSTON'S BARTLETT SQUARE: A CREATIVE VILLAGE IS KEY TO ANTI-GENTRIFICATION EFFORT

David Price, Executive Director
David Bresnahan
Director of Resource Development and Marketing

Nuestra Comunidad

Boston is filled with creative people, but many can't afford to live near their jobs, friends and social activities. The surge of urban renewal around Roxbury may bring many improvements, but it also means those in Boston's geographic heart face the increasing threat of displacement. Nuestra Comunidad, a community development corporation with a 35-year history in the area, has teamed up with the local minority-owned Windale Developers to create an innovative urban-mixed use project to satisfy the growing need for affordable housing and retail and public space.

The new Bartlett Place development is central to the anti-gentrification efforts of Nuestra Comunidad, which has successfully promoted effective renewal in Roxbury and nearby Boston neighborhoods.

Before the project broke ground, Nuestra Comunidad held a mural festival and public space project with local artists to depict their hopes for the neighborhood; it was attended by more than 3,000 people. The eight-acre "creative village" will transform an urban wasteland into a modern, sustainable expanse with affordable rental, for-sale and senior housing, retail and restaurant space and a public square. It is designed to draw creative people from all walks of life – science, technology, arts, business and

CHALLENGE

Roxbury, once a crime-ridden, blighted neighborhood in the center of Boston, is rapidly transforming. But the home to mostly black, Hispanic and Asian communities is also still one of the city's poorest areas and many residents and businesses fear being pushed out in the transition.

The new Bartlett Place development is central to the anti-gentrification efforts of Nuestra Communidad, transforming an urban wasteland into a modern sustainable expanse.

education – by offering better quality and value than in other neighborhoods popular with Boston's young innovators and creators.

Bartlett Place will be made up of 323 homes, including 194 apartments and 129 for-sale homes, affordable to families at a range of incomes. The new homeowners will gain $500 million in equity over 20 years. The project will generate 150 permanent jobs and approximately 900 construction jobs, with more than 60 percent going to workers of color. Construction is slated to begin in 2016 and is expected to be completed in 2021.

A Public Plaza for Fostering the Arts and Commerce
The centerpiece of the new neighborhood will be a large public plaza that taps into Roxbury's richly diverse and artistic community. There locals and the broader community can enjoy art installations and performances throughout the year. Bartlett Place will bring together visual artists, ranging from street sculpture to murals; creations by artists-in-residence for shoppers to view or join in the creative process; rotating visual arts displays; and diverse performance programming encompassing music, singing, theater and dance. Live-work space and the rich arts environment will attract artists and other creative people.

Education
An important component of Bartlett Place's cultural and economic impact will be the Conservatory Lab Charter School. Conservatory Lab Charter School, one of Boston's best performing charter schools, incorporates a music and performance-focused curriculum and will place emphasis on drawing students from Roxbury. The new school at Bartlett Place will include two new performance venues for community use and attract an estimated 4,000 concert attendees per year. The facility will serve 300 local children through an after-school music program and will be open at night and on weekends as a community center offering music rehearsal and performance space

among other programs. The school will help create a vibrant music and arts scene, draw customers for small local businesses, spend significant dollars on local purchasing and support the timely development of promised housing and business opportunities.

A Public Market and Shops

Weekends in Bartlett Place will feature a bustling public market offering diverse goods from artists, craft vendors and farmers. The market will be held outside for three seasons and move indoors during the winter. The development is designed to attract new customers to the local shops in Bartlett Place, which bridges Roxbury's bustling Dudley Square and the adjoining historic Fort Hill and Tommy's Rock communities.

Nearly 20% of neighborhoods with lower incomes and home values experienced gentrification since 2000.

Green Design

In keeping with Nuestra Comunidad's mission, Bartlett Place will be a green neighborhood featuring innovative energy technology and sustainability practices that will draw environmentally-conscious renters, homebuyers and businesses. The homes will be LEED-certifiable for new housing and commercial construction, incorporating passive solar heating, geothermal heat pumps, rain and greywater recycling. Finishes and materials will be environmentally safe and renewable.

Nuestra Comunidad will continue to build on the models of Bartlett Place and its other successful developments. Keys to success in the drive to enhance the physical, economic and social well-being of underserved neighborhoods include: increasing affordable and mixed-income rental housing, encouraging homeownership through education and coaching, and generating wealth by fostering entrepreneurship and grassroots leadership.

ABOUT DAVID PRICE

David Price is the executive director of Nuestra Comunidad, a community development corporation serving Boston's Roxbury community since 1981. Nuestra Comunidad educates first-time homebuyers, counsels homeowners facing foreclosure, strengthens the financial capability of low- and moderate-income residents and advocates for systems and policy change to improve community wealth and health. Price has been a leader in Boston's community development field since 1995, beginning as a volunteer for Mel King's campaigns for mayor of Boston in 1979 and 1983. Price was a real estate attorney at Goulston and Storrs in Boston prior to joining the CDC field.

OVERCOMING ZONING OBSTACLES TO CREATE AFFORDABLE HOMES FOR FAMILIES

Mary Duvall, CEO

Thistle Communities

Boulder, CO has among the highest income and highest housing cost per capita areas in the nation. Boulder's decades-old Open Space preservation ordinance and subsequent planning regulations have created a beautiful and well-planned city, but one with little land available for development or growth. As a result, working families are effectively priced out of this real estate market. In June 2011, the median sales price for a single-family home was $535,000. To qualify for a loan on a home at that price, the buyer would have to earn $210,000 a year, but the median household income in 2011 was $57,112.

Boulder's Inclusionary Zoning was designed to address the problem by providing incentives for affordable housing construction. It requires developers to build 20 percent of their homes as affordable, or make payments of up to $180,000 per unit. But the ordinance allows builders to transfer the portion of their required affordable homes to other entities. As a result, 75 percent of affordable homes developed are one- or two-bedroom condos, and not attractive to families who work and live in and around Boulder.

Thistle Communities is a nonprofit affordable housing supplier in Boulder, and we sought to address the problem by partnering with a developer that had complementary strengths. Thistle provided the financing and Allison Management provided the development expertise. Yarmouth Way was our second project together.

CHALLENGE
Boulder, CO has some of the nation's highest incomes and housing costs per capita. Boulder's decades-old Open Space regulations have resulted in a beautiful and well-planned city, but one that has effectively priced working families out of the real estate market.

Thistle and Allison Management developed 25 homes in a variety of housing types at Yarmouth Way at affordable price points.

In an innovative move, the team transferred another builder's four-unit affordable obligation to our Yarmouth Way site. Adding these units also provided additional financing when the builder paid us approximately $100,000 per unit to complete his affordable requirement. The project included 15 market-rate homes as well. Without the 15 market rate homes and the obligation transfer, Thistle would have been limited to six affordable homes. The transfer increased that number to 10.

All told, Thistle and Allison Management developed 25 homes in a variety of housing types at Yarmouth Way at affordable price points. The site maximized density with townhomes, duplexes and single-family homes, all having at least three bedrooms and garages. A majority also had finished basements. Most were laid out along an arbored lane where pedestrians and cyclists have priority over motorists.

Because it was a "by-right development" (a project permitted under zoning that does not require legislative action), Yarmouth Way was not subject to time-consuming and costly reviews by the Planning Board or City Council. The 1.82-acre site was slated for 25 homes, necessitating efficient and compact use of the space. Both development partners agreed to build homes with three and four bedrooms for larger households that were shut out of the existing market.

Carlyn Carroll was a first-time buyer and teacher at Boulder High. "I needed a three-bedroom home because of the kids," she says. "Now Christian will be able to graduate from Boulder High and Chloe can ride her bike in the neighborhood with other kids. That was missing in the young professional complexes where I lived."

The 10 income-qualified families that bought Yarmouth homes paid between $208,000 and $237,000, about 65 percent of market rate. Six of the purchasing families were employed by the Boulder Valley School District and two were affiliated with the University of Colorado.

David Williams is another affordable buyer at Yarmouth and a writing instructor at the university. "There are limited opportunities for renting in Boulder because of all the students," he says. "Many people work at lesser paying jobs at [the university]; it's beneficial for those people. It's a great program."

Even those who bought the market-priced homes paid only between $275,000 and $450,000 – very low for new residential construction in Boulder.

Using Community Housing Capital and federal CDFI funds for the development loan streamlined the financing process. The transfer of another builder's affordable housing obligation increased the number of low-income housing units in the project. CHC had flexibility in underwriting the loan due to Thistle's NeighborWorks members. The terms of the loan and limited fees kept costs down and helped meet a fast timeline of one year to completion.

The Yarmouth project earned Thistle and Allison Management the 2013 Jack Kemp Workforce Housing Model of Excellence Award.

Community response has been overwhelmingly positive. The site design facilitates resident interaction and frequent social gatherings, and children play in the covered arbor and adjacent alleys. The success of Yarmouth Way demonstrates how nonprofit and for-profit developers can collaborate to accomplish community goals. Thistle hopes to replicate it elsewhere in the Boulder area.

ABOUT MARY DUVALL

Mary Duvall is the CEO of Thistle Communities and has over 25 years of experience in real estate management and affordable housing development. Under her leadership since 2007, Thistle disposed of non-performing real estate assets including 312 rental units and a parcel of land, and added 178 affordable rentals and 51 homeownership opportunities, both market and affordable.

THE CHERRY LEGACY PROJECT: RAISING THE BAR FOR AFFORDABLE HOUSING

William E. Farnsel, Executive Director

NeighborWorks Toledo Region

The center of Toledo, Ohio, boasts some of the grandest old homes in the city, many built at the turn of the 19th century by the leading architects of the time. But the Olde Towne has suffered serious decline in recent decades, with blighted, vacant lots, dilapidated houses, high crime rates and a disaffected community. The 2008 foreclosure crisis deepened that despondency: investments were bottoming out and many believed funding revitalization efforts would be a waste of taxpayers' money. Even the neighborhood's oldest stakeholder was considering relocating, threatening the community's complete collapse. Since it was built in 1855, Mercy St. Vincent Medical Center has been an anchor in central Toledo, but the area's demise was prompting the hospital to think about pulling up stakes.

The mission of NeighborWorks Toledo Region (NTR) is to restore and revitalize neighborhoods, primarily for the benefit of current and future inhabitants, by providing services and programs that renew pride, stimulate reinvestment and restore confidence. In 2010, NTR conducted a survey of Olde Towne to establish a baseline for measuring development progress. The biggest concerns to emerge were community engagement, crime and the properties' improvements in appearance and value. We needed a project that would address all those goals, one that would seamlessly blend compatible architecture, implement a holistic approach using green materials and methodologies and successfully engage disinterested residents and project partners.

CHALLENGE

Toledo, Ohio's Olde Towne has many majestic homes built during the late 1800s and early 1900s, and more than 150 of them are registered as historic. But the neighborhood fell victim to urban blight, with hundreds of abandoned properties, high crime rates, soaring unemployment and failing schools.

Cherry Legacy homes create a new paradigm in developing affordable housing using materials and methodology more typical in a high–value subdivision.

The end result was the Cherry Legacy Project, a 40-unit infill housing project of affordable single-family homes. Completed in 2014, the historically-sensitive designs range from 1,328 to 1,800 square-foot homes, 28 of them with full basements. Rather than building the homes on adjacent sites, they are scattered throughout the neighborhood around the medical center. The low-income renters would be able to purchase the homes after the 15-year tax credit period, and $40,000 has been set aside for down payment assistance. The homes are also designed to allow residents to age in place, with at least one bedroom and one full bath located on the first floor.

The Cherry Legacy Project was an admittedly ambitious goal, but it started out small. It began in 2010, when NTR came up with a plan to build a single-family home on land the Grace Temple Church acquired through Toledo's Land Bank. Real estate values in the neighborhood made the construction project commercially impractical, but federal stimulus funding was secured to build the single home.

Construction was completed in six weeks and the home became the prototype for the future Cherry Legacy Project, which uses unprecedented energy-efficient systems. A third party rater scored all the homes ranging from 40-50, with an overall average of 42 on the Home Energy Rating System. A typical new home today, scores 100 on the index, the lower the score the higher the structure's efficiency. The Cherry Legacy homes create a new paradigm in developing affordable housing using materials and methodology more typical in a high-value subdivision.

During pre-production, NTR purchased more than 70 parcels and dedicated numerous hours in establishing partnerships and educating contractors about our environmental approach. In August 2013, NTR finally broke ground on the $10.4 million project, which was funded through private equity, federal HOME funds and NeighborWorks America. What could be considered an insignificant expenditure proved to be a crucial component in the project's success. The investment far exceeds the local market value, and cost per square foot ranged from a high of $130 to a low of $86, with utility costs expected to be approximately $1,000 a year. Thanks to the high efficiency ratings, NTR became a New Homes Builder Partner and is currently the only Affordable, Site-Built Homes Energy Star Builder Partner in Ohio. In recognition of this achievement, NTR also received the EPA's 2015 Energy Star Award of Excellence in Affordable Housing and other recognitions.

NTR received the EPA's 2015 Energy Star Award of Excellence in Affordable Housing.

Surveys conducted following construction showed a strong increase in the residents' satisfaction with the community. Crime rates are down, schools are thriving and prospects for future investments in Olde Towne are good. And rather than fleeing the neighborhood, Mercy St. Vincent Medical Center is investing $32 million to expand its emergency room facility, providing further economic stimulation and stability to the area.

NTR's Cherry Legacy Project's approach was comprehensive, therefore raising the bar for affordable housing and community development. We discovered that doing our homework in the earliest stages was critical. We invested time and money listening to the community, conducting comprehensive surveys before and after construction. Our cross-sector collaboration introduced financial stability and demonstrated nonprofit excellence. We set standards high while keeping costs down and were able to offer the community high-quality affordable homes with unprecedented energy efficiency.

ABOUT WILLIAM E. FARNSEL

William E. Farnsel has served as a community development leader in Toledo since 1981, and is the executive director of NeighborWorks Toledo Region (formerly Neighborhood Housing Services of Toledo). NTR engages in mortgage lending for homeownership and administers a variety of energy efficiency weatherization programs throughout Lucas County, Ohio.

GAFFNEY PLACE: REHABBING HISTORIC HOMES BRINGS NEIGHBORHOOD BACK TO LIFE

Seila Mosquera, Executive Director

NeighborWorks New Horizons

The exodus of homeowners over the past three decades left a vacuum in Waterbury's Hillside District, degrading its rich historic architecture and its social and economic health. The area is listed on the National Registry of Historic Places and rises above the city's central business district and The Green, one of New England's most beautiful downtown parks. But about 30 years ago many residents began moving to the suburbs and homeowners have become virtually non-existent in Hillside. Plunging property values, negligent landlords and crime devastated the once-vibrant neighborhood. Crumbling streets and sidewalks discouraged foot traffic to the nearby businesses, stalling economic development and job creation.

In an effort to restore the neighborhood, NeighborWorks New Horizons (NWNH) joined forces in 2011 with the Harold Webster Smith Foundation, a local private non-profit, to create the Waterbury Community Investment project. The public-private partnership brought together local residents, business owners, cultural institutions and legal professionals to rehabilitate and convert rental properties for owner-occupancy and revitalize the streetscape.

The program's first endeavor was the Gaffney Place Housing Revitalization project, which included the rehabilitation of four circa 1880's Queen Anne homes and the construction of one new home in the same style. Completed in 2014, the strikingly colorful homes preserve the neigh-

CHALLENGE

The Hillside Historic District is among Waterbury, Connecticut's oldest neighborhoods, home to an impressive collection of diverse 19th and early 20th century architecture. But about 30 years ago, many residents began moving to the suburbs and homeowners became virtually non-existent in Hillside, which spiraled into decline.

The revitalization project serves as a blueprint founded on creating new homebuyer opportunities, preserving historic structures and repairing and beautifying the streets.

borhood's historic integrity while providing homebuyers with modern, energy-efficient amenities. An innovative design creates a more pedestrian-friendly streetscape, where trees and planters improve the traffic flow. Period street lamps and buried utility wires enhance the neighborhood's aesthetics, and a linear park connects the neighborhood to the downtown businesses.

The new homeowners establish stability and pave the way for new homebuyers and other stake-

holders in the neighborhood. The pilot project also preserves historically significant structures and protects the integrity of the area and the larger Waterbury community. Improved streets and walkways ease residents' access to the business district, which has enjoyed an increase in customers and clients, making it an attractive option for new businesses and investment.

The Gaffney Place homes are a stunning visual example of NWNH's mission in Connecticut to offer quality affordable housing and promote economic growth through technical assistance, grants and training. The revitalization project serves as a blueprint for successful urban renewal founded on creating new homebuyer opportunities, preserving historic structures and repairing and beautifying the streets.

Now that the Gaffney Place project is completed, NWNH is looking to identify and create opportunities for development and community action in other Hillside neighborhood areas. This includes the revitalization of Linden Street, near Gaffney Place, where planning is underway for a mixed-income housing development. An abandoned, blighted office building will be demolished to make way for the construction of an apartment building with 30-55 units of quality, affordable housing.

Additionally, NWNH has recently become involved in establishing a YouthBuild chapter in Waterbury. The goal of the program is to develop a community-based alternative education program for at-risk youths. It also seeks to stabilize the neighborhood by advancing affordable housing, education, employment, leadership development and energy efficiency. Participants are offered both academic learning and occupational skills training to prepare them for careers. The youths will join in an NWNH home rehabilitation project on Central Avenue as part of their skills training. The newly renovated home will provide an affordable housing opportunity one block from Gaffney Place. Waterbury YouthBuild has collaborated with a number of stakeholders on the YouthBuild program, including the Northwest Regional Workforce Investment Board, Waterbury Adult Education, YMCA and the Waterbury Police Athletic League.

Since 1975, more than 75,000 properties have been listed in Connecticut's state register of historic places.

Gaffney Place was a success in large part because we recognized the potential of these historic but dilapidated homes to restore the neighborhood's beauty and attract stable homeowners. Improving the streetscape not only enhanced the area's aesthetics, it facilitated the residential-commercial link and boosted the local economy. Collaborating with residents, investors and businesses solidified the collective community's commitment to long-lasting improvements and to future prospects.

ABOUT SEILA MOSQUERA

Seila Mosquera is the executive director of NeighborWorks New Horizons, which was founded in 1992 to build strong communities by providing affordable housing opportunities and revitalizing neighborhoods throughout Connecticut. NWNH manages a portfolio of residential units and retail spaces, serving some 2,000 people annually with affordable housing, leadership seminars, after-school and summer youth programs, one-on-one credit and budget counseling and classes for first-time homebuyers.

STRENGTHENING THE LATINO COMMUNITY THROUGH ENERGY-EFFICIENCY OPPORTUNITIES

Kevin O'Connor, CEO

RUPCO

Homeowners with low to moderate incomes often live in older houses with poor insulation, aging appliances and energy inefficient heating and cooling systems. These residents are the most adversely affected by rising energy costs, but assisting them with effective solutions can be challenging. This is particularly the case in Latino communities, where many have little or no English, speak various dialects and cannot read their native language. Reaching Latino residents in geographically diverse areas when budgets and staff are limited also significantly complicates efforts to provide them with much-needed assistance in lowering their energy costs.

RUPCO, a housing and community development non-profit in the Hudson Valley, specializes in housing for seniors, people with disabilities, working families and artists. One of RUPCO's primary objectives is to assist homeowners with energy-efficient and renewable energy solutions. More than 16 percent of residents in the Mid-Hudson region identify as Hispanic or Latino, and we deployed our Green Jobs-Green New York Program (GJGNY) to connect with them.

GJGNY is New York State's top independent marketing contractor for the New York State Energy Research and Development Authority (NYSERDA). The agency's Home Performance with EnergyStar Program promotes conservation, efficiency and residential energy upgrades,

CHALLENGE

Rising utility costs are beyond the control of the average homeowner and even minor increases can significantly affect those with low incomes. But figuring out how to offer energy efficiency solutions to those homeowners and get them to take action poses challenges, particularly in Latino communities.

To reach low- to moderate-income, non-English speaking residents in Latino communities we hired bilingual staff as program liaisons.

or retrofits. To reach the low- to moderate-income non-English-speaking residents in Latino communities, we hired bilingual staff members as program liaisons. To encourage Latinos to contact the liaisons, GJGNY places an advertisement in the monthly magazine, La Voz. RUPCO also created a step-by-step online video on how to complete applications for the program.

GJGNY prints all its materials in English and Spanish to get its energy message out widely. While many adults in Latino households do not read English or Spanish, their children can usually translate for their parents. Bilingual "door knockers" target the relevant communities, canvassing key neighborhoods door-to-door and leaving doorknob hangers to broadcast their message. RUPCO also engages the Mano-a-Mano community group of Latino-focused agencies in the campaign.

Each month, RUPCO broadcasts its energy program message to 40 county agency and nonprofit representatives. They in turn pass the information on to their constituents, mostly non-English-speaking residents who can benefit from the program. Additionally, by engaging with this group every month, RUPCO is gaining trust among these partners, fortifying its reputation as a willing and helpful service provider. As a result of these efforts, RUPCO received $50,000 from New York State Assemblyman Kevin Cahill to address Latino communities in his district in 2016.

Churches play a pivotal role in bridging the gap to Latino families. RUPCO collaborates with both clergy and key Latino business leaders to disseminate information about energy-efficiency and homeownership opportunities. As facilitators, these leaders introduce RUPCO staff to community members, helping to establish trust and broaden visibility. RUPCO also formalized valuable partnerships with businesses and agencies such as Solarize Hudson Valley, GRID Alternatives Tri-State, government officials, local environmental groups and other community-based organizations.

Green Jobs-Green New York is currently the highest performing of the state's 12 community based organizations (CBOs). In 2015, we performed 22 percent of all CBO retrofits. Between 2011-2016,

GJGNY collected 5972 residential referrals, completed 2182 energy audits, negotiated 433 retrofits, held 492 public outreach events, presented at 509 partner meetings and referred 269 households on to the EmPower NY program, which provides free energy efficiency solutions to low-income homeowners. GJGNY also boosted the local economy. The program spent $4.39 million for completed projects and another $584,000 in NYSERDA subsidies to contractors and installers. As of November 2015, the environmental impact of retrofits reduced CO_2 emissions by 184 metric tons. Put another way, this work saved 20571 kWh (the equivalent of 361 tree seedlings grown for one year) and 3205 MMBTU (4,377 trees planted and grown for a year).

In 2015, Green Jobs–Green New York held 492 public outreach events.

Most significantly, GJGNY's work has paved the way for future collaboration and funding for energy-efficiency projects related to RUPCO's other programs. In 2016, RUPCO received a $1 million NYSERDA Cleaner Greener grant for our E2: Energy Square housing proposal for midtown Kingston. RUPCO also received $750,000 in a community development block grant award for home buying and rehabilitation with a solar focus in Ulster County. RUPCO won a similar grant for Kingston for $100,000 the previous year. NeighborWorks America matched this funding with $25,000 to contribute to 10 solar installations in Kingston for low income households with GRID Alternatives Tri-State, the nation's largest not for profit solar installation company.

From this experience, RUPCO learned how essential collaboration is to meeting ambitious goals. Allowing local affiliates to run with the ball paves the way for reputation building and introductions particularly within the Latino communities. RUPCO also recognized that it had to rely significantly on backend support with bilingual staff and marketing materials. A true partnership effort with groups trusted by the target audience – in this case the Latino community – goes a long way to opening the door to energy-efficiency opportunities. Finally, consistent funding for the long-term yields results and warrants an extended commitment to energy-efficiency programs and incentives for those most in need.

ABOUT KEVIN O'CONNOR

Kevin O'Connor is the executive director and CEO of RUPCO, which has a staff of 61 and an annual operating budget over $6 million. RUPCO, a comprehensive housing and community development service in the Hudson Valley region, has over $15 million of real estate development and five business lines: real estate development, property management, rental assistance, community development and a NeighborWorks HomeOwnership Center. RUPCO provides nearly 2,000 units of rental assistance in Ulster and Greene Counties, and owns/manages 411 affordable housing units.

A UNIQUE COLLABORATION CREATES SAFE, AFFORDABLE HOUSING IN FLOOD AFTERMATH

Brent Ekstrom, Executive Director

CommunityWorks North Dakota

The energy boom in western North Dakota created many new jobs leading to a 17 percent increase in the state's population. Housing costs skyrocketed leaving many low- and middle-income residents financially burdened or homeless. In the midst of this unprecedented growth, a flood devastated Minot destroying more than 4,100 homes. While many homeowners were able to rebuild, low-income residents were left with few housing options. Many residents and construction workers had to find shelter in campers, tents, temporary FEMA housing, relatives' homes or in nearby rural towns.

With thousands of single- and multi-family homes in need of rebuilding, the devastation threatened to break the community. CommunityWorks North Dakota was anxious to help the city rebuild and ensure housing for its most vulnerable citizens.

Located in Mandan, 110 miles south of Minot, CommunityWorks North Dakota and its two nonprofit partners serve low- and middle-income residents across the state. We seek to remove financial barriers to homeownership and to create safe, high-quality multi-family housing. Over its 20-year history, CommunityWorks has partnered with numerous developers to remodel vacant rural schools to provide low-income housing for elderly or disabled residents, to build shelter apartments for women and their children leaving abusive relationships and to develop multi-family neighborhood housing for low and middle-income families.

CHALLENGE

In 2011, the city of Minot, ND, was inundated by a flood that destroyed thousands of homes. Suddenly, the already severe housing shortage became a catastrophe. With thousands of homes in need of rebuilding, how could this community ensure safe and affordable housing for its most vulnerable residents?

With thousands of single and multi-family homes in need of rebuilding, the devastation threatened to break the community.

Since its founding in 1995, CommunityWorks has closed 929 loans totaling more than $30 million in homeownership and multi-family investment. These loans are leveraged with more than $50 million in private sector financing for a total investment exceeding $80 million in housing for low and middle income residents across North Dakota.

In Minot, CommunityWorks developed a two-fold response to address the housing crisis. We removed barriers for single-family homeowners to finance the rebuilding of their homes, and we created new, high- quality, safe and affordable multi-family housing for low and middle-income families.

CommunityWorks partnered with MetroPlains, LLC to develop and build Minot Place Rowhomes. Located on four acres, Minot Place has 30 rental units, some of which are designed for wheelchair accessibility. The units range in size from one to three bedrooms to accommodate families with children and those caring for elderly parents. The townhomes have an open front porch and a private drive with an attached garage at the back. The complex also features a playground and a community room equipped with a kitchen. The layout of the development, the front porch design, playground and community room foster a sense of stability, community and neighborliness – qualities that had been lacking since the devastation of the flood.

The success of Minot Place is due to a unique collaborative partnership between non-profit CommunityWorks North Dakota, for-profit MetroPlains LLC and the State of North Dakota's Housing Incentive Fund. In addition, CommunityWorks' members in NeighborWorks America provided access to financing from Community Housing Capital. Through these efforts, the partnership was able to reduce the cost of the project ensuring that six of the units are reserved for residents below 30 percent of average median income and the remaining 24 units for residents below 60 percent of average median income.

This project reveals how economic development and housing are strongly linked and how fostering unique relationships and creative partnerships can provide vital opportunities that would not otherwise come about. For instance, in this case, without this unusual combination of government, non-profit, and private sector financing and expertise, Minot Place would not have succeeded. And without this collaborative effort, 30 families would not have access to affordable, safe and healthy homes.

Since 1995, CommunityWorks has loaned more than $30 million for homeownership and multi-family investment.

ABOUT BRENT EKSTROM

Brent Ekstrom serves as the executive director of CommunityWorks North Dakota, Lewis and Clark Regional Development Council and Lewis and Clark Certified Development Company. The three organizations have a combined staff of nine and an annual operating budget of $2 million.

HOME AND EQUITY RESTORATION POST-HURRICANE SANDY

Donna Blaze, CEO

Affordable Housing Alliance

In 2012, Hurricane Sandy hit New York and New Jersey hard, causing mass destruction to businesses, homes and communities. According to FEMA, Hurricane Sandy was the second-costliest hurricane in U.S. history, behind only Hurricane Katrina in 2005. An estimated 2.7 million New Jersey residents were left without power, and over 37,000 primary residences were damaged or destroyed.

While homes were uninhabitable and repair funding was yet to be available, many homeowners had to resort to rental options until their primary residences were repaired or rebuilt. With rent in New Jersey averaging $1,344 a month for a one-bedroom apartment, financial difficulties began to overwhelm these dislocated families. They weren't living in their damaged homes, but they still had to make their mortgage payments in addition to paying their rent.

While more than 35 disaster recovery centers opened to provide aid to the astounding number of Sandy victims, the Affordable Housing Alliance (AHA), located in Monmouth County, NJ, was also determined to address the extensive Hurricane Sandy-related needs of the community. In July 2014, AHA opened the Housing Recovery Resource Center (HRRC) in Atlantic Highlands, NJ, with the help of the Hurricane Sandy New Jersey Relief Fund. The resource center would provide HUD-certified

CHALLENGE

Hurricane Sandy caused massive destruction in New York and New Jersey in 2012, damaging businesses, homes and communities.
The super storm was the second-costliest hurricane in U.S. history, behind only Hurricane Katrina in 2005. Many Hurricane Sandy victims had to move to rental units and faced significant financial hardships.

Joyce Uglow felt as many hurricane victims did, as though there would be no return from such a horrific disaster.

housing counselors to help victims find viable, permanent housing solutions by repairing or rebuilding homes or relocating residents. Clients would also receive one-on-one counseling sessions to identify financial aid options including local, state and federal grants.

AHA went a step further in creating the Bayshore Bungalow Program. Under that project, victims can have a new modular home built with the assistance of program managers who handle the entire development process from submitting permits to the certificate of occupancy, all included in upfront consolidated pricing. This program is for New Jersey residents who were approved for the Rehabilitation, Reconstruction, Elevation and Mitigation (RREM) grant but continue to have difficulties getting back into their homes. The five model homes all meet or exceed the New Jersey RREM program guidelines and range from 700 to 1,600 square feet. The AHA's 24 years of housing experience in Monmouth and Ocean counties contributed to the program's success.

The intent of the program is to get families into a home while restoring their pre-storm equity. For many families, their home equity is the largest source of funds for retirement, college tuition or equity lost during the hurricane. The Bayshore Bungalow Program, which allows hurricane victims to avoid hiring expensive private contractors, constructs the model of their choice for a fraction of the cost. In turn, the equity in the home is restored, allowing families to get back on their feet and maintain stability within the community. Upon the completion of the Bayshore Bungalow models, these hardworking homeowners can return to the lives they knew before the storm.

Severe flooding created by the lake just a few yards from Joyce Uglow's home made it uninhabitable and she was forced to rent a mobile home. Uglow felt as many hurricane victims did – that there would be no return from such a horrific disaster. However, in spite of her fear, doubt, anger and insecurity, Uglow refused to give up. Her determination and perseverance led her to a successful recovery during which she used the resources around her, eventually leading Catholic Charities to refer her to AHA's resource center and Bayshore Bungalow Program. "Working with the Housing Recovery Resource Center was the best experience for me. The HRRC was able to help guide me in moving forward during this process," Uglow said.

37,000 New Jersey residences were damaged in Hurricane Sandy.

AHA learned that expanding our assistance through partnerships with modular homebuilders and construction managers and taking advantage of the financial benefits of consolidated pricing enables us to help courageous individuals like Uglow. We look forward to serving more members of the community through our Bayshore Bungalow Program.

ABOUT DONNA BLAZE

Donna Blaze, CEO of the Affordable Housing Alliance, founded the Monmouth Housing Alliance in 1991 to address the paucity of affordable housing for low-income residents in Monmouth County. In 2010, the organization expanded its services to Ocean and Mercer counties and became the Affordable Housing Alliance. The organization's mission is to improve the quality of life for all New Jersey residents by developing and preserving affordable housing, providing housing education and helping communities meet their legal and moral housing obligations. During the past 25 years, Blaze has successfully renovated over 400 affordable housing units and secured over $25 million in state and federal funding for the purchase, construction and renovation of projects. Recently, the AHA received one of the largest tri-state Hurricane Sandy relief grants and became a major relief responder.

RAPIDO: DISASTER RECOVERY HOUSING FOR THE 21ST CENTURY

Nick Mitchell-Bennett, Executive Director

Community Development Corp. of Brownsville

Texas hurricanes Rita in 2005, Ike in 2008 and Dolly in 2008 caused $2 billion in damage and exposed the inadequate disaster recovery response of local, county, state and federal agencies. Many of the victims are from "Colonias," semi-rural subdivisions lacking basic infrastructure, potable water, sanitary sewage systems and adequate roads. More than 40 percent of the 500,000 residents in these Colonias live below the poverty line, while an additional 20 percent live at or just above the poverty line. They could not afford to rebuild their destroyed or severely damaged homes themselves and had to rely on government aid.

The Community Development Corp. of Brownsville (CDCB) is an affordable housing nonprofit devoted to partnering with other organizations to create sustainable communities across the Rio Grande Valley through quality education, model financing, efficient home design and superior construction. We serve one of the poorest regions in the country, the Lower Rio Grande Valley, where one in three people live below the poverty line. Persistent poverty coupled with the threat of natural disasters creates the need for an efficient and affordable way to address disaster recovery.

Our organization created the Rapid Disaster Recovery Housing Program (RAPIDO) with our partners in response to inadequate government aid after Hurricane Dolly. RAPIDO's plan addresses three of the biggest obstacles of the current disaster recovery model: slow transi-

CHALLENGE

Disaster recovery has been a challenge in the Rio Grande Valley in Texas. Six years after Hurricane Dolly hit the valley in 2008, residents were still waiting for assistance, many of them among the poorest in the country. Their semi-rural subdivisions lacked potable water, sanitary sewage systems and adequate roads.

The CORE's pre-fab construction takes three days in a local lumber yard, and can be assembled on site by hand in four days.

tion from disaster response to housing recovery; the need for a designated resource for each family and the lack of pre-disaster planning.

Transition: The transition from disaster response to housing recovery is a lengthy process that can put vulnerable communities at risk. RAPIDO is a temporary-to-permanent solution, providing immediate housing as a first step toward a permanent home. CDCB and the design nonprofit, bcWorkshop, designed and built 21 prototype homes in the Rio Grande Valley to test a scalable solution. The goal is getting families into a home within four to six months rather than the six years it could take under the government system. We shrink the timeframe by providing a

"CORE" on the resident's lot, a simple structure with essential living facilities that can easily be expanded once full recovery is underway. The CORE's pre-fab construction takes three days in a local lumber yard, and can be assembled on site by hand in four days.

Disaster Recovery Design: Disaster recovery requires a focus on community outreach, case management, eligibility and policy. Low-income families affected by a natural disaster find it difficult to navigate the process of receiving assistance. RAPIDO is designed as a comprehensive system that empowers local teams to help families recover. Each family is assigned a "navigator" who acts as the primary contact through the entire recovery process, understands all aspects of the rehousing process and knows the steps required to receive assistance quickly and efficiently. A trained local eligibility team who determines if a family qualifies for assistance works closely with a family's navigator to ensure they are aware of the process and documents needed.

Pre-disaster planning "Pre-covery": The RAPIDO model starts recovery activities prior to a disaster by creating a catalog of homes that residents can use when designing their new home once rebuilding begins. RAPIDO handles pre-procurement of permits from city and county agencies and trains contractors to construct, store and reconstruct CORE units. RAPIDO also trains organizations and individuals as navigators for families so everything is in place to support local jurisdictions and families through the recovery process.

Hurricanes Rita, Ike and Dolly caused $2 billion in damage in Texas over 4 years.

CDCB, bcWorkshop and experts at the Texas Low Income Housing Information Service created a Rapid Disaster Recovery Housing Program technical guide and policy recommendations. This document outlines policy changes to make at the local, state and federal levels to respond to a disaster quickly and effectively. The Texas legislature's committee on Intergovernmental Relations is reviewing the recommendations needed to make RAPIDO the state's disaster recovery solution.

Maria Cordero was just one of the many clients who was glad to be involved in the process. "RAPIDO Design wasn't just a plan that they imposed on us that we just had to accept, they gave us the opportunity to choose details," she says.

We learned that planning and partnering with other organizations could reduce the impact of a disaster on low-income families. The RAPIDO model can be replicated in any location. Construction costs may differ but the process is the same: a state or city must partner with local organizations to create a housing catalog, pre-permit post-disaster building, pre-construct the CORE and store it for accessibility for reconstruction. The technical guide explains required training and can be used to recruit organizations that are close to the community to be navigators during the recovery process, ensuring that low-income disaster victims will have support.

ABOUT NICK MITCHELL-BENNETT

Nick Mitchell-Bennett serves as the executive director of the Community Development Corp. of Brownsville, a community housing development organization that serves the Rio Grande Valley in South Texas. CDCB, one of the largest affordable housing providers in Texas, helps an average of 150 clients a year attain affordable housing. Mitchell-Bennett also serves as the administrator of the Rio Grande Valley MultiBank of which CDCB is the managing partner. Nick has been a community development leader in south Texas for more than two decades as director of the Mennonite Partnership Building Initiative and development director at the United Way of Southern Cameron County.

A SAFE PLACE TO CALL HOME: SUCCESSFUL HOUSING STRATEGIES FOR FORMER INMATES

Peggy Hutchison, CEO

The Primavera Foundation

Some 650,000 men and women are released from state and federal prisons every year across the country. They face many challenges upon their return, including finding a safe place to call home. The lack of affordable housing makes it difficult for them to secure employment, get their lives back on track and become valuable members of the community – causing many of them to re-offend and return to prison. These ex-offenders urgently need affordable, rental housing that welcomes those seeking a second chance, while adding value to the neighborhoods where they are located.

The Primavera Foundation's mission is to provide pathways out of poverty through safe, affordable housing, workforce development and neighborhood revitalization. Located in Tucson, AZ, Primavera serves residents in one of the most economically-distressed large cities in the United States. In Pima County, home of Tucson, one in five people lives below the poverty line and the homelessness rate is the highest in the state. In Arizona, around 13,000 people leave prison every year, and of those, about 2,000 people come home to Pima County.

Formerly incarcerated individuals in Arizona are unable to receive federal cash assistance such as Temporary Aid to Needy Families and are not eligible for Section 8 housing assistance. Those with felony drug convictions are

CHALLENGE

Every year, approximately 650,000 men and women are released from prisons across the nation. These former inmates face few affordable housing options, making it difficult for them to secure employment, get their lives back on track and become valuable members of the community.

People returning to the community following incarceration are motivated to pay their rent on time, to be good neighbors and are grateful for a second chance.

not eligible for the Supplemental Nutrition Assistance Program (SNAP). In addition, most have multiple fines and fees they must pay upon release. Without safe, affordable housing, it is nearly impossible for them to secure employment and build foundations for stable futures. That is one of the main reasons why at least half of formerly incarcerated individuals re-offend and go back to prison, costing millions of taxpayer dollars.

Primavera's strategy is to remove barriers for ex-prisoners seeking a second (or third) chance. Primavera offers high quality, affordable multi-family rental housing to former inmates and their families. Many of these properties participate in a crime prevention program to ensure that these homes and the neighborhoods are safe. Residents in rental housing programs are also offered employment services through Primavera Works, a temp-to-hire staffing social enterprise. The program focuses on employment retention strategies to support local residential customers, employers and the individuals they have hired.

Primavera's Rights Restoration collaborative offers free rights restoration clinics to people with felony convictions seeking to get their civil rights restored. Primavera also works closely with neighborhood groups, police departments and the Second Chance Tucson collaborative, which brings together public and private sector partners. Strategies include helping to educate and inform the general public about the challenges and opportunities for family members and friends returning home from prison.

Ricky Miller is one of our many success stories. He grew up in Pennsylvania with his mother, a garment worker, and his four siblings, in a home without heat, hot water or a bathtub or shower. Miller's father, an alcoholic, left his mother while she was in the hospital delivering their sixth child. The children ended up in foster care. Miller spent his childhood on the streets, in reform school, in the state hospital – and incarcerated. With barely a sixth grade education, mental illness, and an addiction to alcohol and drugs, it's no surprise that Miller spent most of his adult life in and out of prison.

That is until he hit his mid-50's, when he began to turn his life around. Though he had got a job, Ricky initially couldn't find a landlord willing to rent to someone with multiple felony convictions and a poor credit history. But since 2013, Miller and his service dog Muppet have lived in one of Primavera's multi-family rental housing units. "The staff is understanding. It's clean, peaceful, a good, safe environment. And it's affordable," said Miller, who was about to see his mother for the first time since he was 18 years old.

In Arizona, about 13,000 people leave prison every year.

Providing safe, affordable rental housing to people returning from incarceration is a good community and business decision. People re-entering the community are motivated to pay their rent on time, to be good neighbors and are grateful for a second chance.

It is also the law. The U.S. Department of Housing and Urban Development (HUD) recently issued guidance regarding the denial of rental properties to people with criminal records. On April 4, 2016, HUD Secretary Julian Castro said: "When landlords summarily refuse to rent to anyone who has an arrest record, they may effectively and disproportionately bar the door to millions of folks of color for no good reason at all."

Primavera learned many valuable lessons in this process, including: 1) safe, affordable housing is key to the successful return of formerly incarcerated individuals; 2) working with neighborhoods and the public in general is important for generating acceptance and support of these individuals; 3) working closely with employers who hire people with felony convictions improves employment retention; and, 4) partnering with other local organizations helps to create a broad-based web of support for these individuals and their families. These strategies transform lives and make our communities stronger, more inclusive, and more vibrant, which are benefits for all.

ABOUT PEGGY HUTCHISON

Peggy Hutchison serves as the CEO of The Primavera Foundation, a nonprofit community housing development organization whose mission is to provide pathways out of poverty through safe, affordable housing, workforce development and neighborhood revitalization. Primavera has a staff of 80, a volunteer base of 1,400, and a budget of $7.5 million. The organization serves about 8,500 people annually in Tucson and Pima County, Arizona through a variety of programs. Primavera's vision is to promote social and economic justice while working to build a future in which all people are assured basic human rights, a livable income and safe, affordable housing.

FORGIVABLE LOANS: A UNIQUELY-EFFECTIVE STRATEGY IN EXPANDING OPPORTUNITIES FOR WEALTH ACCUMULATION

Susan M. Ifill, Interim Chief Executive Officer

Neighborhood Housing Services of New York City

Real estate prices in New York City have skyrocketed in recent years, forcing residents out of the communities where their families have lived for decades. Between 2000 and 2012, the median value of a single-family home in New York City increased from $225,000 to $450,000, according to a city comptroller report. The median sale price for a home in all five boroughs averaged $540,000, a 5.2 percent increase from 2014 to 2015, according to the New York real estate board. Black and Hispanic residents are particularly vulnerable to the displacement caused by these rising real estate prices.

The spike in prices has attracted investors who view real estate throughout the city as a source of commercial profit. Many have secured financing to purchase substantial quantities of New York City real estate in cash, including single-family homes in low- and moderate-income communities. Such investments eliminate key opportunities for families who rely on wages to obtain the mortgage financing needed to purchase property as a home – not as a commercial asset. An index of single-family mortgages in New York City declined from a baseline measure of 100 in 2004 to 40 in 2012, while mortgage lending in low- and moderate-income census tracts declined by 65 percent, according to the New York University's Furman Center for Real Estate and Urban Policy.

CHALLENGE

Low- and moderate-income New York City residents are getting pushed out of the neighborhoods where their families have lived for decades. The increasing dislocation is particularly acute among black and Hispanic residents, who urgently need help with financing, upkeep and foreclosure prevention.

NHSNYC successfully implements a comprehensive suite of integrated homeownership services that helps low-and-moderate-income families sustainably purchase their first home, prevent a foreclosure, and finance critical home repair or modification projects.

To meet New York City's affordable housing challenge, Neighborhood Housing Services of New York City (NHSNYC) offers integrated homeownership services that help low- and moderate-income families. We assist them with the means to purchase their first home sustainably, prevent foreclosure, finance critical home repairs and better understand their insurance needs and coverage options. One of NHSNYC's most effective programs is providing clients with affordable capital to achieve their homeownership goals, often structured as forgivable loans.

Since 2004, NHSNYC has successfully served as fiscal administrator for the New York City Department of Housing Preservation and Development's HomeFirst program. Through this work, we originate forgivable loans for down payment assistance to first-time home buyers who earn 80 percent or less of the area median income, which cannot exceed $15,000 or 6 percent of their property's purchase price. NHSNYC has enabled 2,480 New York City residents to become homeowners by providing $36.2 million in down payment assistance, which leveraged over $642.5 million in mortgages from our network of bank partners.

In 2013, we significantly expanded this work after NeighborWorks America selected NHSNYC to administer the Wells Fargo CityLIFT initiative throughout New York City's metropolitan area. Through our efforts, we received $9.5 million to originate forgivable loans of $30,000 for down payment assistance to income-eligible families who were purchasing homes in Brooklyn or the Bronx. We also collaborated with another non-profit organization to provide forgivable loans of $15,000 for down payment assistance to families in Newark and Jersey City. By administering this initiative, NHSNYC enabled 351 families – including 280 New York City residents – to achieve homeownership and leveraged $88 million in mortgages from our bank partners.

NHSNYC recognizes the impact of offering forgivable loans in helping to address long-standing disparities in wealth that affect black and Hispanic families, which often far exceed inequality of annual income. According to 2013 data analyzed by the Pew Research, home equity comprised 59 percent of the total wealth accumulated by black families and 66 percent by Hispanic families. In addition, a 2013 Brandeis University report found that the differential in years of homeownership accounted for 27 percent of a $152,000 wealth disparity between white and black families. Forgivable loans represent a uniquely effective strategy for enabling black and Hispanic families to acquire or preserve homeownership as an essential step toward accumulating wealth.

> **1 in 5 New York City residents, and 16% of residents in the state, live below the federal poverty line.**

During 2014 and 2015, 67 percent of the 380 clients who received forgivable loans for down payment assistance through NHSNYC's successful administration of the HomeFirst program and CityLIFT initiative were either black or Hispanic – 36 percent and 31 percent, respectively. We credit the involvement of community residents who guide our work as board members in helping to promote key services, including forgivable loans for down payment assistance among low- and moderate-income residents in the communities of color.

In July 2015, the New York City Council awarded NHSNYC $2 million to help more low- and moderate-income families finance critical home repair projects – such as fixing a leaking roof or replacing a broken boiler. NHSNYC disburses the funds as forgivable loans that cannot exceed $20,000 to families who earn 120 percent or less of the average median income. Recipients will repay our loans in full if they sell their homes within five years of completing a specific repair project or refinance their mortgage with a cash-payout. NHSNYC will then forgive 20 percent of the total loan balance in each of the next five years. As a result of this work, NHSNYC will help more low- and moderate-income families complete essential repair projects that preserve homeownership, without the financial burden of a loan they cannot afford to repay.

ABOUT SUSAN M. IFILL

NHSNYC's Board of Directors formally appointed Susan M. Ifill as interim chief executive officer in September 2015. Ifill is also NHSNYC's chief operating and financial officer, a role she has held since 2010. In these capacities, Ifill oversees all aspects of NHSNYC's work, including: homeownership and foreclosure prevention counseling, resource development, lending services and loan fund operations, accounting and finance, research and planning and information technology. Ifill began her career at the Bank of New England – which was acquired by Bank of America – where she worked for 28 years.

A RAY OF SUNSHINE AT AN UNCERTAIN TIME: PEARLS AND PRIDE

Roy Nash, President and CEO

NeighborWorks Waco

When the housing crisis hit in 2008, foreclosures were taking a toll across the nation, and families, especially in Waco, TX, were having trouble getting mortgage loans. Prior to the crash, NeighborWorks Waco generated most of its revenue through housing sales and mortgage loans. Revenue from these activities was $380,000 in 2006, but by 2010, in large part because of the housing crash, revenue had fallen to $79,000.

NeighborWorks Waco responded to the housing crisis with PEARLS and PRIDE: Purchase-Efficient-Affordable homes, Rehab, Lease and Sell; Purchase-Rehab-Invest-Delight-Enjoy. The program acquires and rehabilitates distressed single-family properties and leases them to clients who are not yet ready to purchase but may want to buy in the future. Local banks helped with seed money and the NeighborWorks network gave unique access to grants and low-cost capital to buy the properties.

Rehabilitation capital has largely been supplied through grants from NeighborWorks America, and loans through NeighborWorks-related capital sources, particularly, the Capital Funding for the Rehabilitation of Affordable Housing, which provided a total of $650,000 for 2010 and 2011.

In 2008, Waco resident Zenia Evans was renting a house just a couple of houses down from her mother. When the

CHALLENGE

The 2008 housing crisis was devastating for Waco, TX. As more houses went into foreclosure, residents were evicted and affordable housing and mortgage loans became difficult to find.

2014

Families, especially in Waco, were having trouble getting mortgage loans. Although there were visible scars of the foreclosure crisis all across the city, Waco's healthy market for affordable housing was a ray of hope.

economy took a downturn, the property she was renting went into foreclosure and she was evicted.

She came to NeighborWorks Waco and went through the program and educational classes required to become a tenant. At around the same time, Neighbor-Works Waco bought the house Evans had rented, completely unaware that she had lived there. Soon, Evans was reunited with her mother in the same house, now owned by NeighborWorks.

As a single mother and head of household, Evans persevered with rent for more than a year before deciding to purchase. At the time of this writing, she was making her mortgage payment without any assistance and happily enjoying her home.

PEARLS and PRIDE is self-sustaining and has grown to a total of 85 homes, all rehabbed, all for low and moderate-income families and individuals. Since one of our goals is to provide income for our organization, we choose the homes for this program very carefully. Rental income has grown from $23,000 in 2008 to $313,000 in 2015. In addition, between 2008 and 2011, PEARLS and PRIDE renters converted to homeowners at a rate of about one tenant per year. Now that number is five to seven per year.

We have learned much along the way: make policies and procedures very clear; m From 2005-2015, the Fahe Network produced more than 51,000 units – valuing more than $1.9 billion.

ake sure to strictly abide by those policies and procedures – particularly when it comes to rent deposits, inspections and tenant selection; and pay attention to the marketplace. For example, we discovered that we needed to maintain a more diverse inventory of single-family homes.

In more general terms, we have learned that as the economy recovers and NeighborWorks Waco continues to grow, we must continue to evolve and improve to best accommodate those in the community looking for assistance as they move toward homeownership. And that's just what we will continue to do.

Through PEARLS and PRIDE, 85 homes have been acquired and rehabbed for low- and moderate-income families to rent or buy.

ABOUT ROY NASH

Roy Nash serves as the president and CEO of NeighborWorks Waco and has over 38 years of experience in the housing and building industry. He serves on the Visibility and Resource Development Committee for NeighborWorks America as well as the NeighborWorks America HomeOwnership Steering Committee and the National NeighborWorks Association. He is the founding and current chair of the NeighborWorks Alliance of Texas, a collaboration of Texas NeighborWorks organizations. Nash is the current vice-chair of the Waco Housing Coalition, and he also serves on the boards of the Heart of Texas Builders Association, the Texas Association of Builders and the Heart of Texas Workforce Solutions.

SAFE RETURN: PREVENTING VETERAN HOMELESSNESS

Robert Corley, Executive Director

NeighborWorks Southern Mass

In the United States, an estimated 100,000 veterans are without a home. Many of the other 12 million veterans can't afford to maintain the homes they do own. Sometimes they live in dilapidated dwellings to avoid becoming homeless. Many are in need of much more than housing, but they lack access to services for mental and physical health care, job training and financial assistance.

Since 1996, NeighborWorks Southern Mass (NWSOMA) has supported this underserved population by developing properties specifically intended to house homeless veterans. We have transformed many vacant, blighted neighborhood eyesores into new, energy-efficient homes and green spaces to support formerly homeless veterans. Unfortunately, the broader solution does not end with providing housing and beautifying neighborhoods. To make any real continuing impact, NWSOMA has had to put significant effort into raising public awareness of the veterans' dire predicaments and to breakdown the stereotypes that act as barriers.

When we began developing housing for homeless veterans, we started with an eight-unit home in Quincy. Since then, we have developed and assisted in the development of 44 homes on the South Shore with a preference for veterans and their families and we have six more veterans' homes under development now. Our partner in this project is Father Bill's & MainSpring, which provides emergency and permanent housing, job skills training and other services in southern Massachusetts.

CHALLENGE

On any given night in the United States, more than 100,000 veterans are without a home. Many of the other estimated 12 million former service members face significant hurdles in maintaining the homes they do own. Sometimes they choose to stay in dilapidated houses to avoid becoming homeless.

Through partnerships with veterans service agencies we are able to extend our mission beyond housing.

Through partnerships with veterans' service agencies, we are able to extend our mission beyond housing. Massachusetts is the only state in the country that provides a veteran's service agent in every city and town. The agents help our veteran clients and their families access physical and mental health care, job placement assistance and financial education services. Quincy's Veterans' Service Director George Nicholson praised the collaboration at a ribbon cutting ceremony for one of our new properties.

"Veterans are living with the depression and despair of not being able to provide adequate, safe housing for their families. Suddenly, out of the darkness of that despair gallops the white knight known as NeighborWorks … and what was no more than a dream is now a reality," he said.

Recently, we were given the opportunity to expand our community partnership to include one of our residents. Several years ago, Dave needed a place to live and was introduced to us by his case manager at Volunteers of America. Dave says he did not fit the stereotype of a homeless veteran. "Most people think of a veteran as someone who is missing a limb or has PTSD, but many of us are not that," he says. "We just need a little push to get us back on our feet."

After Dave's service in the Navy, his personal struggles led him to live on the couch at his brother's, who is also a veteran. It was then that he realized he no longer had a home, a car or any of the other defining aspects of independence. He was finally motivated to reach out for help, even though he did not feel that the help out there was really intended for him. Dave now lives in one of our properties in Weymouth, MA, and works as a case manager for Volunteers of America.

Dave agreed to share his story in a short video intended to raise awareness about the prevalence of homelessness veterans. During the process he decided he wanted to explore other veterans' journeys and now hopes to someday produce a feature length documentary entitled Safe Return.

Homelessness among veterans fell by 36% between 2010-2015.

A retired sergeant and Iraq War veteran named David is another success story. David lives with his wife and four children in a four-bedroom, single-family home that NWSOMA and the City of Quincy purchased and renovated for veterans' housing in 2013. David and his family had been homeless. "I am truly grateful for being able to provide my family with a safe and comfortable home," David says. "My kids love the house, they have friends that sleep over and play in the backyard. It's just been amazing. I could not ask for more."

Among the things we've learned along the way are that experience is what connects us to the community we serve. At NWSOMA, we recognize how important it is to go beyond providing affordable housing and to share the experiences through telling the stories of those we support. Without allies throughout our community, we would be unable to help our veterans grapple with the challenges of day-to-day life and gain the momentum that they need to thrive.

ABOUT ROBERT CORLEY

Robert Corley took over as NWSOMA's executive director in 2009. He first joined the organization in 1997, serving as the director of real estate, overseeing all of the agency's housing development activities. For over 30 years, NWSOMA has worked to meet the critical demand for special needs and affordable housing in our community. In collaboration with social service providers and government agencies, NWSOMA strives to provide housing for the homeless, battered women and their children, people with developmental and physical disabilities and veterans.

SERVING THOSE WHO HAVE SERVED OUR COUNTRY

Jennifer Gonzalez, Executive Director

Alamo Community Group

In 2011, veterans returning to San Antonio from Operation Iraqi Freedom and Operation Enduring Freedom faced an affordable housing shortage, forcing many into "couch surfing" and then into homelessness. HUD reports conclude that veterans are far more likely to experience homelessness than other Americans, in part because of their high rates of post-traumatic stress disorder, injuries and disabilities and other factors that make reintegrating into civilian life and employment difficult. The Department of Veterans Affairs estimates that about 1.5 million U.S. veterans are at imminent risk of homelessness. San Antonio is home to four active military installations and has the second largest veteran population in Texas.

The Alamo Community Group (ACG) provides quality affordable housing to low- and moderate-income families throughout Bexar County, Texas. In addition to providing housing, we believe it is essential to promote resident education, self-sufficiency, leadership and volunteerism and do so with a menu of services and programs. ACG, guided by the most prevalent needs of the community, sometimes focuses on a geographic area where affordable housing is needed for employees of nearby major employers. At other times, certain populations drive ACG's direction, such as focusing on assisting homeless veterans' families.

In 2011, ACG initiated the House Our Heroes Program with the assistance of the Texas Veterans Commission. The program uses a Housing First model that expands our existing resident services to offer homeless veterans and

CHALLENGE

An estimated 1.5 million U.S. veterans are at risk of becoming homeless. San Antonio has the second largest veteran population in Texas. Each year, roughly 132,000 students complete military training here and many veterans make this city their home. In 2011, the Alamo Community Group saw an increase of veterans' families facing homelessness.

About 1.5 million Veterans are at imminent risk of homelessness due to lack of support, poverty, and poor living conditions.

ACG housed more than 500 previously homeless veteran families or families at risk of homelessness throughout its multifamily portfolio.

their families case management and temporary financial assistance. Our efforts are in line with the National Alliance to End Homelessness' view that: "By providing housing assistance, case management and supportive services responsive to individual or family needs after an individual or family is housed, communities can significantly reduce the time people experience homelessness and prevent further episodes of homelessness."

ACG housed over 500 previously homeless veteran families or families at risk of homelessness throughout our multi-family portfolio, with over 80 percent of them maintaining self-sufficiency. Once our veterans and their families move in, our case manager addresses any immediate concerns such as food, clothing and basic necessities. Next, our case manager works with families to create individualized family work plans by outlining short-term goals such as securing veteran benefits, employment or training and educational opportunities. As short-term goals are accomplished, families can move toward longer-term goals such as homeownership. We have found that families are more successful when tasks are broken into smaller manageable goals.

In addition, we have found it imperative to assist many veteran families to create a much-needed support network. Resident programs that encourage constructive relationships with neighbors promote community and support reliance upon each other. Many of our veterans suffer from physical and mental disabilities and often must overcome significant barriers in their everyday lives. "When you have to deal with multiple issues all the time, life gets very overwhelming very quickly and it is hard to not get angry or depressed," says Army veteran Max Sotelo. Having a community support network provides many of our veterans with an opportunity to share their experiences and frustrations with others in similar situations and to help them become more resilient.

For example, one veteran family found that since moving into the Cypress Cove Apartments they are better equipped to deal with events that could have easily thrown their lives into havoc. Steven Barnett has lived with his elementary school-aged daughter at Cypress Cove since 2014. Previously homeless, Barnett and his daughter rode the bus throughout the city since they had no

There are nearly 22 million veterans in the U.S.

home to go to. Since moving in to the apartment, Barnett has secured employment as a car mechanic, owns a vehicle and is saving to purchase a home. He attributes his resilience to a variety of factors, including housing assistance, employment and training resources, as well as a support system. "With the friends I have made and the resources that I know are available I don't feel alone. Things don't trigger my PTSD as quickly. I can now go to my buddies here and talk through things a little better," he says.

This project illustrates two important lessons learned: 1) a multitude of resources are needed to encourage continued family resilience among our previously homeless veteran families, and 2) flexibility is essential since no one system works for everyone. Interventions must be individualized and allowed to evolve. Our future challenge is to demonstrate continuing resilience using data to monitor housing and employment stability, and to look for other outcome measurements that can demonstrate overall upward mobility.

ABOUT JENNIFER GONZALEZ

Jennifer Gonzalez serves as the executive director of Alamo Community Group, a nonprofit affordable housing provider. ACG's mission is to develop, acquire, own and manage affordable housing in an environment that promotes resident education, self-sufficiency, leadership and volunteerism through successful partnerships. ACG owns 1,317 rental units at 10 affordable communities throughout Bexar County, Texas. Gonzalez is also the current chair of the San Antonio Housing Commission to Protect and Preserve Dynamic and Diverse Neighborhoods.

AFFORDABLE HOMES FOR LONG-TERM SUSTAINABILITY

Patricia Garcia-Duarte, President & CEO
Carole Kauffman
Director of Development and Communications

Trellis

Across the nation, the housing crisis that began in 2007-2008 took its toll on communities, homeowners and prospective buyers. It was especially felt in Phoenix, consistently one of the hardest hit areas in the country for foreclosures. But with challenges, come opportunities for those who are willing to take a risk.

Thanks to a loan from one of our financial partners and approval from our Board, Trellis purchased a vacant and abandoned partially-built subdivision at a Trustee sale in 2009 with 10 occupied homes, 16 partially-built homes and 18 vacant lots. We completed the unfinished homes, sold 14, rented out two and patiently waited for the market to recover before building on the remaining lots.

The risk Trellis took on was not insubstantial, given the thousands of vacant lots spread across the Phoenix market. According to an estimate from Nathan and Associates, a residential land brokerage firm based in Scottsdale, at the end of 2009 there were as many as 40,000 unfinished lots in the Phoenix market.

This enforced delay gave us time to assess the future buying market. We recognized that the baby boomer generation wanted to age in place and would look for homes that would allow them to do so. According to a survey from AARP, 71 percent of adults nationally between 50-64 want to age in place. We also learned that the millennial generation would soon be interested in homeownership

CHALLENGE

Across the nation, the 2008 housing crisis took its toll on communities, homeowners and prospective buyers. It was especially difficult for Phoenix, consistently one of the hardest-hit areas in the country for foreclosures.

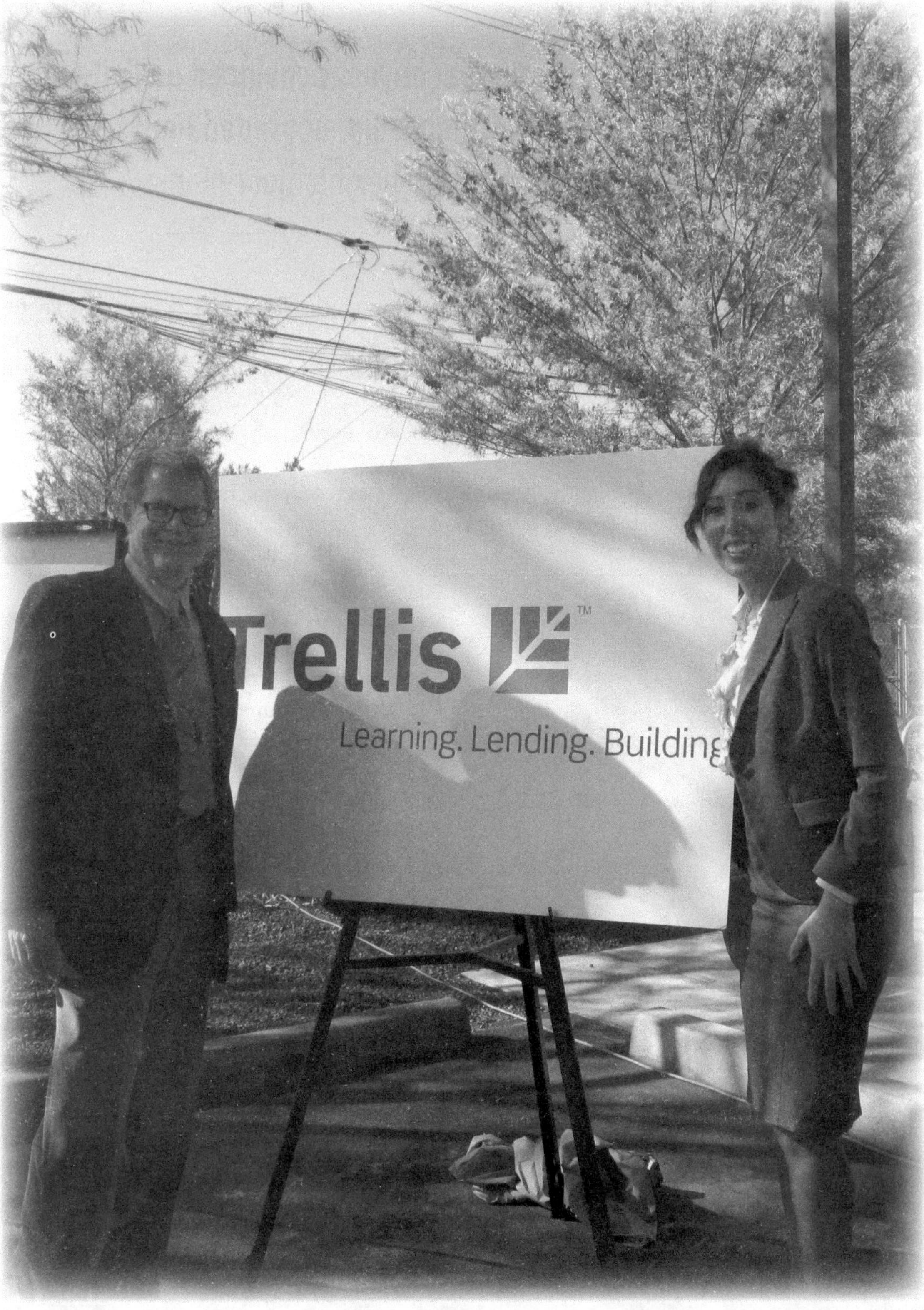
Trellis
Learning. Lending. Building

Positive comments from potential buyers convinced us that we did it right, with quality workmanship, upgraded finishes, energy-saving features and flexible floor plans.

and being "conservation-focused," they'd be interested in sustainable development. Unfortunately, we know that the homeownership dreams of millennials might have to be delayed because of student debt. Various surveys, including one from NeighborWorks America note that student loan debt ranks among the top three obstacles to homeownership by millennials. However, creative multi-generational development might satisfy both cohorts' needs.

Taking our cue from indications that the housing market was recovering in 2012-2013, we set out to plan our new houses to finish out this subdivision.

We developed designs and used computer-based tools to simulate and assess the energy use of a home in order to quantify the savings attributable to the proposed design. By June 2015, we had sufficient capital investment to break ground. By the end of that year we had completed nine homes with three floor plans, all designed to promote maximum maneuverability and control; all with multigenerational options including plans with two master suites and private suites with separate entrances; all energy-efficient with a "silver" certification for green standards. According to the United States Green Building Council, more than half of consumers rank green and energy efficiency as a top requirement for their next homes.

In addition to this standard, all of the homes we built were fully accessible for persons with disabilities which include zero-clearance steps, wider door and hallways and conveniently located electrical outlets. Residents will feel confident that their home is ready for all of life's changes, unexpected or not.

The result of this planning was clear. Within the first month after opening we had hundreds of showings and closed on four contracts. Positive comments from potential buyers convinced us that we did it right. From quality workmanship to upgraded finishes, from energy-saving features to flexible floor plans that can accommodate varied generations, from universal design features that can be modified to accommodate any disability, these affordable homes, currently offered at $175,000 - $195,000, meet the demand for homes that working individuals and families can afford in today's Phoenix market and enjoy for a lifetime.

LEARNING. LENDING. BUILDING.
Trellis services 2,000 clients per year.

As we reflect on our initial risk to purchase this abandoned subdivision, several lessons become clear, including: 1) calculated risks, taken only after assessing the environment, proved critical in being able to move forward when the time was right; 2) thinking about new construction, coming out of the housing crisis, taught us a lesson in patience. We waited until the market had improved before we tackled new builds; 3) the luxury of time that we had to research and model before breaking ground taught us that the upfront investment we put into due diligence paid off in being able to design and construct homes with features that will have a better return-on-investment for our clients in the long term; and 4) despite claims from the homebuilding community to the contrary, we could include green features at the silver level cost-effectively to target entry-level buyers who will reap the cost-savings.

What we've learned will inform us as we get ready to start on completing the final eight homes that will be even more energy-efficient.

ABOUT PATRICIA GARCIA-DUARTE

Patricia Garcia-Duarte is the president and CEO of TRELLIS, formerly Neighborhood Housing Services of Phoenix, a nonprofit organization serving Maricopa County and dedicated to the creation of stable homes and communities by providing housing education and counseling, building and lending. She is responsible for a $3 million operating budget, $14.0 million in assets and 30 employees. Duarte joined Trellis in 2006 with 28 years of experience in community and economic development. Since its inception, Trellis has helped over 2,900 families purchase their first home, built or rehabilitated over 200 homes, and trained or counseled more than 31,000 families in financial management and / or how to buy a home. Based on conservative estimates, Trellis has originated/facilitated over $100 million in mortgage loans during the last twenty years. The three primary lines of business at Trellis are homeownership promotion and preservation, real estate development, and lending and loan servicing. We like to summarize our programs and services by our tag line: learning, lending and building. Trellis serves about 2,000 clients per year primarily in Maricopa County, Arizona.

HELPING PEOPLE, BUILDING DREAMS

Kimberly Miller, Executive Director

Universal Housing Development Corp.

Arkansas is one of the poorest states in the nation and affordable housing is one of its biggest challenges. Many homes are old and rundown, posing serious health and safety risks. This is especially the case for the elderly, the low-income and people with disabilities. These residents may own their homes outright, but their houses no longer provide suitable shelter because they cannot cover the necessary repairs or the cost of moving to better housing. While they may have family or friends who could help them rehabilitate their homes, they still lack the funds for materials and assistance in getting the job done. These homeowners may have realized the American Dream of homeownership, but they risk losing that home if they can't make it livable.

Since 1971, Universal Housing Development Corporation (UHDC) has helped residents in the Arkansas River Valley build their own homes. Our Mutual Self-Help Housing Program allows clients or volunteers to contribute labor for the construction, for which we provide supervision. But that doesn't help those who already own homes that are falling into disrepair and may jeopardize their health and security. Their urgent need prompted UHDC in 2012 to extend our "sweat-equity" approach to home rehabilitation.

Our Self-Help Home Rehabilitation program has homeowners or volunteers provide the labor for repairing their homes, and the savings on labor allows more work to be completed on the project. Sometimes when a needed repair such as a leaking roof has been deferred for years, the scope of the work can grow to include damaged or

CHALLENGE

For more than a decade, the lack of affordable housing has been one of the biggest challenges in Arkansas, one of the poorest states in the nation. The housing stock is among the oldest and many of the houses are dilapidated and pose serious health threats.

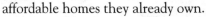

Deferred home maintenance can lead not only to deplorable and unsafe living conditions, but to the loss of one's home and independence.

collapsed ceilings, walls stained with mold or mildew and weakened floors. In such cases, limited funding can make it nearly impossible to do everything that needs to be done. Using contributed labor changes that, making it possible to breathe life into a dream of homeownership that was slowly dying. Tasks that require professional licenses such as plumbing and electrical work are still completed by contractors, but the homeowners are able to get more of the necessary work completed by doing other tasks under the guidance of UHDC's supervisors. This ensures that all the work is completed to the highest standard and that low-income residents can safely stay in the affordable homes they already own.

In one of our projects, Brent Christy and his family lived in a home built in 1938 that was falling into serious disrepair. His Rural Development Housing Preservation Grant (HPG) would only cover a new roof, not the other urgently needed repairs. His bathroom tub leaked, and all of his windows were single-paned aluminum that leaked air badly. His exterior doors were hollow core, which is useless for stopping heat from escaping in the winter – or anyone from breaking in. The hall floors were weak and there was little or no insulation, the wooden siding was rotting and the electrical system wasn't up to code. The gas stove was also leaking and the hot water heater needed to be replaced. We got assistance for some of the work through the Federal Home Loan Bank of Dallas Special Needs Assistance Program (SNAP), but those funds wouldn't have made a dent in the rest of the work needed without Christy's contributed labor.

Christy installed the windows and doors provided by SNAP himself with coaching from a UHDC construction supervisor. Christy was supposed to prep the bathroom for the plumber as well, but there was a breakdown in communication and Christy ended up taking the entire bathroom down to the stud walls! There was enough left in the HPG to buy the materials for Christy to replace the walls and to have a plumber reinstall the toilet and vanity. The Rural Initiative for the Neighbor-Works-Wells Fargo Safe and Sound program provided funding for the rest of the work.

Christy's aging home is now as energy-efficient as a new one, and it is structurally solid enough to last as long. It took funds from three different programs and a lot of hard work, but Christy and his family are living in a decent, affordable home that makes the whole neighborhood proud.

Since December of 2012, UHDC has preserved 52 homes for low and very-low income homeowners through our Self-Help Home Rehabilitation program. The contributed labor has resulted in a total savings of over $274,400 in project costs for these homes. Homeowners have also learned valuable skills that enable them to make future repairs. Often they don't stop at just the health and safety improvements we can fund, and the results are often a more dramatic improvement in living conditions than we had anticipated.

Since 2012, UHDC has preserved 52 homes for low- and very low-income homeowners.

Our motto, "Helping People, Building Dreams," now extends beyond our original mission to make homeownership more than a dream for our residents. We can now help those in need to hang on to their homes and age in place safely and securely. Since launching our Self-Help Rehabilitation program, we have learned three simple keys to success: communication, coaching, and coordinated funding.

ABOUT KIMBERLY MILLER

Kimberly Miller is the executive director of Universal Housing Development Corporation, a non-profit housing development agency serving nine counties in the Arkansas River Valley since 1971. UHDC's mission is to promote quality affordable housing, economic opportunity and a suitable living environment free from discrimination. The organization serves approximately 400 clients each year, providing high quality housing-related assistance in a rural area.

SETTING AND MEETING AMBITIOUS GOALS THROUGH COLLABORATIVE LEADERSHIP

Jim King, President & CEO

Fahe

Appalachia is one of the poorest regions in the country and poses considerable challenges to the nonprofits seeking to improve conditions in the struggling communities. In 2003, Central Appalachia had an estimated 100,000 units of substandard and overcrowded housing. Seventeen percent of homeowners and 33 percent of renters were cost burdened, paying more than 30 percent of their income on housing.

At the time, Fahe, a network of over 50 nonprofits, was producing 2,000 units of housing per year. Fahe President and CEO Jim King realized that while the network's mission was strong, the scale of its production was not adequate to meet the housing challenges within a reasonable timeframe. To address the growing number of subpar housing units, Fahe had to change the way it did business.

Fahe is based Berea, KY, and is dedicated to eliminating persistent poverty in Appalachia. The network serves communities across the Appalachian portion of Kentucky, Tennessee, West Virginia, Virginia, Alabama and Maryland. The organizations use their expertise in finance, collaboration, innovation, advocacy and communication to achieve a more prosperous Appalachian region. Key to attaining this goal is providing leadership, housing, education, health and social services and economic opportunity. Fahe empowers the region's communities of Appalachia with the resources, opportunities and tools needed to build a better life. Their strength in numbers creates positive change in Appalachia, one of the poorest and most difficult regions of the country to serve.

CHALLENGE

Central Appalachia had an estimated 100,000 units of substandard or overcrowded housing. Housing nonprofits serving the area could only produce 2,000 units annually. The organizations thus needed to change the way they did business to meet the challenges in the impoverished region.

The most critical success metric for any collaboration is this: Is it stronger, and does it accomplish more, than would the sum of its parts individually?

One of the challenges of leading a collective organization such as Fahe is that when a difficult change is required, everyone needs to be committed for the effort to be successful. Strong leadership is necessary to convince people of the need and of their potential for success to find a solution that fits the situation. At this time, King was in touch with other national organizations that were similar to Fahe but were achieving greater results. He realized that Fahe needed to find a way to grow through structured reorganization.

King knew that if he told the members that he thought they were failing at their mission, it would cause unnecessary tension and turmoil. Instead, he framed the problem as a question that would invite self-examination. Working with outside advisors and other key Fahe leaders, he asked if members felt that the network's current response to the housing issue had the potential to fix the problem.

Another part of the solution was challenging members to become more productive. The Network committed to increasing the production numbers from 2,000 units per year to 8,000 units annually between 2005 and 2015. While hitting the targeted number would, of course, be a great benefit to the people in Appalachia, setting such an ambitious number also served to show the members what they were truly capable of. Even if they didn't hit the 8,000 mark, it was ambitious enough and it would help members learn that they could achieve more than expected. Attempting to meet the challenge would empower them to push themselves and stop playing so safely.

Finally, a key part of the solution was to establish systems that would support the reach for scale and help ensure success. Fahe created the Berea Performance Compacts framework to provide members with a structure that supported collaboration and the delivery of products and services more efficiently at greater scale. Each participating group in a compact had a strong set of skills, so instead of duplicating services and infrastructure, members would build on one another's strengths. The first compacts focused on loan servicing, manufactured housing, multi-family housing, cooperative purchasing and volunteer management. The compacts also required members to break out of their isolation and work together, which allowed them to share their core competencies, divest administrative functions, decrease costs and increase efficiency without sacrificing impact.

From 2005-2015, the Fahe Network produced more than 51,000 units—valued at more than $1.9 billion.

The challenge and the support of the Berea Compacts was a success. In 2014, a year ahead of the challenge deadline, the Fahe Network produced 8,725 units of housing. During the 10 years of the challenge, over 51,000 units were produced which brought in an additional value of over $1.9 billion.

The experience of successfully meeting this challenge proved to the members that they could accomplish more by working together than apart. Those who initially doubted the ability to conquer such an ambitious goal had their opinions shifted over time as they experienced real progress year after year. Now, with their new goals and strategic plan in place, instead of meeting new challenges with doubt, the members meet these new opportunities with boldness and a desire to push the limits of what they can accomplish for the people of Appalachia.

This project illustrates three important lessons learned: 1) it is possible through planning and collective effort to meet ambitious goals, 2) a leader can ask an organization and its members to do more than they may think is possible, and 3) working together in collaboration greatly strengthens the resources and possibilities for success.

ABOUT JIM KING

Jim King has served as president and CEO of Fahe for 15 years, a period of considerable growth in the organization's impact, lending and geographic reach. Fahe is a network of more than 50 nonprofits serving communities across the Appalachian portion of Kentucky, Tennessee, West Virginia, Virginia, Alabama and Maryland. The network's mission is to eliminate persistent poverty in Appalachia.

A SMALL SOLUTION TO A BIG PROBLEM

Martina Guilfoil, President & CEO

Chattanooga Neighborhood Enterprise

The shortage of affordable housing is on the rise in Chattanooga, TN, but government subsidies continue to fall. Homeownership is at an 18-year low and a large percentage of lower income households are spending more than 30 percent of their income on housing costs. In addition, the neighborhoods of Highland Park and Ridgedale suffer from years of disinvestment and blighted buildings. In an effort to spur revitalization in those neighborhoods, Chattanooga Neighborhood Enterprise (CNE) created a cottage home prototype as an affordable housing option.

Property values in the Highland Park and Ridgedale neighborhoods of Chattanooga, Tennessee have declined since the 1960s when Highland Park Baptist Church demolished blocks of houses to build Tennessee Temple University (TTU), a small seminary. Initially the seminary brought jobs and demand for rental housing into the area along with institutional buildings and parking lots, but as the neighborhood declined, the church lost members and school enrollment declined. In the 2000s the church moved its campus to the suburbs, leaving blighted vacant properties and empty lots.

CNE purchased 34 vacant parcels from TTU with the goal of rebuilding the fabric of the Highland Park and Ridgedale neighborhoods and spurring rental and home-ownership development. CNE's work is revitalizing both areas into safe, affordable and inclusive neighborhoods on par with other urban neighborhoods in the city. The result is renewed market interest in forgotten neighborhoods.

CHALLENGE

While the need for affordable housing continues to grow in Chattanooga, TN, government subsidies continue to dwindle. Homeownership is at an 18-year low and a large percentage of lower income households are spending more than 30 percent of their income on housing.

"We want to provide small homes that will uplift the neighborhood."

— Bob McNutt, real estate manager, Chattanooga Neighborhood Enterprise

Our organization has a history of introducing new housing types as part of a neighborhood revitalization strategy. In the early 2000s, CNE built the first townhouses in the Cowart Place neighborhood and the first narrow-lot houses in the Jefferson Heights neighborhood. Both of these housing types were designed to add density to offset increasingly expensive land costs and offer a smaller housing product. Smaller units are more affordable and additional density provides economic development for emerging neighborhood businesses.

The property acquisition in the Highland Park and Ridgedale neighborhoods gave us an opportunity to create another new housing type in Chattanooga: the "tiny house." Tiny homes are

small, well-designed homes that can be built at a lower price point due to their smaller size. The concept of tiny houses has generated interest in Chattanooga and elsewhere, so we decided to build one in the Ridgedale neighborhood. The strategy had three goals: 1) create a house for a lower income person, 2) establish a homeowner in a neighborhood where rentals dominate, and 3) up the cool factor of the historically underserved neighborhood by building the very first tiny home in Chattanooga.

After researching the phenomenon of tiny homes, CNE developed a 532-square foot cottage on a small truncated gravel lot. Zoning restrictions do not permit tiny homes on wheels so the house was built on a foundation, which means the homeowner owns both the house and the land, which could appreciate in value. The cottage has one bedroom, a full bath, a big kitchen and open dining and living space, 10-foot ceilings and a fenced backyard. The prototype, a small, well-built home that can be sold at an affordable price due to its smaller size, has created interest in the Chattanooga community as an alternative form of housing.

The home's sales price is $79,999, which makes the home affordable for someone earning $12 an hour. As public funding for housing shrinks, CNE has created an alternative way to provide housing for people earning 60 percent of the area median income. Building smaller homes is one of the best ways to meet that need, so we plan to build a cottage home community in the Ridgedale neighborhood to spur more investment in the area.

CNE sold cottages for $79,999, making a home affordable for someone earning $12 an hour.

CNE learned two lessons through this process. First, even the cool factor of a tiny house can't overcome a depressed neighborhood by itself. Building the real estate market where there has been years of disinvestment takes more than a single house. We hired a professional urban designer to design a community of small cottages adjacent to the first cottage. The cottage community will create seven new units of affordable housing and provide outdoor space to promote community for residents.

CNE also learned that it needs to differentiate the cottage product from a tiny house on wheels. Shows like "Tiny House Nation" feature tiny homes on wheels that range from basic to custom cabinetry throughout. We worked with a local homebuilder to build the cottage efficiently and affordably with design standards to fit any neighborhood.

Ultimately, these homes will be an innovative solution to revitalization and affordable housing. These cottage homes are a market-based approach to affordable housing that the private sector can produce without government subsidy.

ABOUT MARTINA GUILFOIL

Martina Guilfoil is the president and chief executive officer of Chattanooga Neighborhood Enterprise (CNE), a community housing development organization whose mission is to create economically diverse neighborhoods filled with financially empowered citizens and housing for all. CNE provides a variety of programs to achieve its mission including homebuyer education, affordable mortgage products, real estate development, and community leadership and engagement. Since its inception, CNE has invested in over 14,000 families, individuals and small businesses. Martina is passionate about creating opportunities for CNE customers that result in heightened prosperity and vibrant communities.

SEATTLE'S TINY HOUSE VILLAGE

Sharon H. Lee, Executive Director

—————

Low Income Housing Institute

In 2015, homelessness in Seattle reached such a critical mass that the city declared a state of emergency. In response, the city council passed an ordinance to permit up to three tent encampments on city-owned or private property. The Low Income Housing Institute (LIHI) stepped in to help. LIHI established three city-sanctioned tent encampments in partnership with Nickelsville, a self managed eco-village for up to a thousand homeless people, and SHARE, self managed communities of homeless people. In January 2016, the Tiny House Village for homeless families, couples and singles was opened, the first of its kind in the Seattle area.

LIHI develops, owns and operates affordable housing for a variety of populations, including homeless families, seniors, immigrants, refugees, low-wage workers, young adults and low-income households. LIHI also provides essential services to support those who are unsheltered, including three "urban rest stops," full-service hygiene centers providing free showers, laundry and restrooms. The Tiny House Village is a step in LIHI's spectrum of interventions that can help move people out of homelessness.

The Tiny House Village is located in central Seattle on land owned by the Lutheran Church of the Good Shepherd. The partnership among LIHI, the Lutheran Church, and Nickelsville is vital to the Village's success, as each organization handles different parts of the operation. Among LIHI's contributions is case management to help residents on the path to securing employment and permanent housing.

CHALLENGE

In November 2015, the number of homeless Seattle residents prompted the city to declare a state of emergency. The shelters were full and the homeless were dying from violence and the dangers of living on the streets. More than 4,500 men, women and children were living without shelter on any given night.

"Housing, four solid walls and a door that can close out the world; this is an essential need for a person's sense of safety, security and stability."

– Kitty DeBerry, current Nickelsville resident

The Village has 14 tiny houses, a toilet pavilion, a kitchen and dining tent, a security booth and a donation shed. A shower on site is in the works. The Village provides safe housing for homeless individuals and families. The Village was developed as an innovative crisis response to homelessness by moving people into tiny houses instead of tents.

The partnership formed to create the Village extended to pre-apprenticeship programs and vocational schools, which built the tiny houses as part of their curriculum. Volunteer groups formed as well to build the tiny houses. The groups include the Tulalip Tribes TERO Training Program, Apprenticeship and Nontraditional Employment for Women, Renton Technical College, Seattle Vocational Institute, the Wood Technology Center out of the Seattle Colleges, Sawhorse Revolution and the Mercer Island Presbyterian Church.

The tiny houses are slightly different in design, but they are all safe, sturdy structures that will help protect many of the homeless otherwise forced to sleep on the streets. The houses cost $2,300 in materials and are eight feet by 12 feet in area, about the size of a bedroom. The houses include electricity, ventilation and insulation.

The Tiny House Village has proved to be incredibly successful. Kitty DeBerry, a current Nickelsville resident, believes that the tiny houses are a good alternative for people experiencing homelessness. "Housing, four solid walls and a door that can close out the world; this is an essential need for a person's sense of safety, security and stability. The recent movement seen here in Washington, and throughout the nation, of supplying homeless populations with small housing units in long-term communities, has shone a large ray of hope upon a population that can use all the hope it can find."

The partnership of the Lutheran Church, Nickelsville, LIHI and the volunteer build groups hosted a Tiny House Construction Review event in February, where they discussed lessons learned from this pilot project. Ultimately, LIHI sees tiny house construction as an effective crisis response to ending homelessness. High-quality, but inexpensive, housing can go from planning to move-in in a matter of months. Seattle's Tiny House Village provides an easily replicated blueprint for creating similar homelessness solutions. There are now three such villages in Seattle and we are regularly helping other communities start their own.

The typical tiny house is 100–400 square feet.

ABOUT SHARON H. LEE

Sharon Lee is the executive director of the Low Income Housing Institute (LIHI), a nonprofit organization she founded in 1991 in Seattle. LIHI develops and operates housing for low-income and homeless people, and also provides a range of supportive service programs to assist tenants in maintaining stable housing and increasing self-sufficiency. Lee oversees a staff of 140 engaged in housing development, management, advocacy and supportive services.

MANUFACTURED HOUSING DONE RIGHT WITH THE NEXT STEP NETWORK

Sherry Farley, President & CEO

Frontier Housing

Historically, manufactured housing has been overlooked as an option for promoting financial security and stimulating wealth through homeownership. The prefabricated homes, constructed in factories and assembled at building sites, are an energy-efficient and readily available solution to housing shortages. But the industry was plagued by stereotypical images of mobile homes, even though the latest generation of homes included modern designs with efficient energy systems. The stigma was compounded by a misunderstood marketing and loan structure.

In 2004, the nonprofit corporation Frontier Housing pledged to cut its building cycle times in half. To meet this challenge, the organization recognized manufactured housing as the obvious choice. But Frontier Housing's president, Stacey Epperson, had viewed manufactured housing as an inferior product rather than as an essential, affordable option for Frontier's customers. In researching the field, however, she discovered that it represented the largest source of unsubsidized affordable housing in the United States. Manufactured housing was home to 22 million Americans with median incomes of about $30,000, while those with median incomes of at least $70,000 lived in traditional site-built housing.

In 2010, after testing a regional pilot in eastern Kentucky, Epperson created Next Step, a subsidiary nonprofit of Frontier Housing. Next Step's mission was to put sustainable homeownership within reach of everyone, while

CHALLENGE
Manufactured houses, once commonly called mobile homes, represent the largest source of unsubsidized affordable housing in the United States. They are an energy-efficient and readily available option for communities experiencing housing shortages. Yet many view the homes as inferior and dismiss them as a viable alternative.

The industry continued to be plagued by stereotypical images of mobile homes, even though the latest generation of homes included modern, energy-efficient home designs.

transforming the manufactured housing industry through consumer education, affordability and energy efficiency.

Next Step became the first place where the elements necessary for Manufactured Housing Done Right came together. That program began training and providing technical assistance to a national network of nonprofits to increase access to affordable housing by following the Next Step System. The system connects responsible financing, comprehensive homebuyer education and a method for delivering high-quality, sustainable factory-built housing at scale.

With Frontier's support, Next Step was launched as an independent social enterprise in 2013. Over the next three years, Next Step's fast-paced infrastructure developments led to unforeseen challenges that became opportunities for innovation. One of Next Step's critical lessons came in 2014, when they examined their impact and realized that their member-centric strategy needed improvements. In order to grow, it would be essential to work more closely with the industry, including manufactured housing retailers, lenders, community owners and manufacturers.

Before pivoting their strategy, they deconstructed the layers of their mission: preparing homebuyers for purchasing the homes, providing quality homes with fair loans and sustainable life-cycle costs and advocating for relevant policies. Next Step realized that all the layers did not need to be in one package as they had been with the original member-centric strategy. Instead, they could be delivered over time through different channels that also drew strength from industry players.

Next Step then launched two industry initiatives in 2015, Retail Direct and SmartMH, to leverage the existing systems to deliver quality factory-built homes, while continuing to sustain their members' strategy. In the Retail Direct program, members partner with Next Step approved retailers to prepare customers who then order homes through the retailer. The member acts as the customer's trusted advisor while the retailer orders homes with a small deposit from the member. The retailer then completes the home, manages the construction and, after closing, assumes the warranty liability.

With SmartMH, Next Step identifies loans that support the purchase of Energy Star manufactured homes incentivized by utilities. The goal of the pilot program is to increase production of Energy Star manufactured homes from one percent to 50 percent in Kentucky over the next two years and provide access to better loans for these purchases.

Manufactured housing accounted for 9% of all new, single-family homes sold in 2015.

Over 10 years, Next Step has created a valuable process by asking businesses to do something different and innovative. To date, the Next Step Network has supported more than 1,400 families who have either bought a new Next Step home or live in a manufactured housing community that is owned and managed by a network member. Next Step has created a field of work where none existed before with a network of 49 members serving 28 states and the District of Columbia, and partnerships with Clayton Homes, Champion Homes, Cavco and regional manufacturers.

Erika Ortiz is a homeowner who worked with a Next Step network member to purchase a new Energy Star manufactured home and replace her deteriorating mobile home, where she had been living with her mother and two daughters. Ortiz enrolled in a financial education program that included classes and financial counseling and was able to lower her debt and obtain a responsible loan. In the winter of 2012, Ortiz purchased a new manufactured home in a south Tucson community. After the family moved in, she said: "Primavera is building another house down the street. Every day I check the progress. I think about how another family will move in and be as happy as we are."

Ortiz's story is just one of many, and going forward Next Step will continue to expand their network and develop new programs to deliver more quality, energy-efficient homes coupled with homebuyer education and fair financing to families nationwide.

ABOUT SHERRY L. FARLEY

Sherry L. Farley is president and CEO of Frontier Housing, Inc., a non-profit housing organization in Morehead, KY that serves eleven rural counties in northeastern Kentucky. Prior to joining Frontier, she spent 25 years in the banking industry as a senior vice president and CFO. During Farley's tenure at Frontier, she has guided the organization to gained loan broker status and achieve the designation as a Community Development Financial Institution, a HUD Certified Counseling Agency and a NeighborWorks Home Ownership Center.

ATTRACTING HOMEBUYERS THROUGH MIXED-INCOME DEVELOPMENTS

Robert A. Goldman, President

Montgomery Housing Partnership

Residents in Montgomery County, MD, were struggling with a shortage of affordable housing, especially first-time homebuyers and county employees. County officials came up with an innovative idea to sell a 32-acre parcel of surplus land in its northern suburb of Olney, and use it for affordable housing development by private industry. But the land sat vacant for more than a decade. Its development for affordable housing initially met with opposition from a small but vocal group of local residents who managed to stall developers' efforts.

Montgomery Housing Partnership (MHP) is a private, nonprofit developer that seeks to preserve and expand affordable housing in Montgomery County for low- and moderate-income residents. We accomplish this mission through housing people, empowering families and strengthening neighborhoods. Olney Springs was the first for-sale community MHP has developed.

Through our first collaboration with Elm Street Development, an experienced private developer, Olney Springs has become a groundbreaking model for new home development in Olney that addressed a need for affordable homeownership opportunities for low- and moderate-income families. The 114 homes built on the 32 acres included 34 affordable, quality townhomes for about half the going market rate. Dozens more homes in the development were priced to be in reach of working families.

CHALLENGE

Like many areas around the country, Montgomery County, MD faced challenges in providing enough affordable housing to its residents, especially first-time homebuyers and county employees. Initial plans to use a 32-acre parcel of surplus land met with opposition, and the lot sat vacant for more than a decade.

The first new homebuyers included, among others, a pizza delivery driver, a high school art teacher, a school bus driver, a deputy sheriff and an administrative assistant at an insurance company.

Olney Springs represents one of the first for-sale, mixed-income communities in the county to feature a combination of affordable and workforce-priced homes, along with market rate homes.

For decades, Montgomery County's inclusionary zoning policy mandated 12.5 percent of units built in developments of 20 units of more qualify as affordable. But our ultimate goal for Olney Springs was to go above and beyond the county's minimum standards, with up to 60 percent of properties available at below market rate to low-income and working-class families.

Olney Springs serves the whole range of the area's income spectrum and is a successful model for sustainable low-income ownership.

After the development team launched Olney Springs in June of 2012, the demand for the affordable homes was fast and furious. Construction started in September of 2012, and sales opened a month later. The first new homebuyers moved in during the fall of 2013, and included, among others, a pizza delivery driver, a high school art teacher, a school bus driver, a deputy sheriff and an administrative assistant who works for an insurance company.

For Alani McDonald and her husband, Melvin, Olney Springs represented an opportunity to become a homeowner in the community where she was raised. McDonald was thrilled to enroll her three children in the same elementary school she attended. She has now become a vocal resident leader.

Residents of Olney Springs enjoy some amenities beyond housing. The community features a wooded conservation area with a stream running through it, two playgrounds with picnic tables, and several common areas with seating where neighbors can sit and chat. We felt that having these community-building opportunities were especially important for the new residents.

The market rate for new home sales (town homes and single-family) is $294,600.

"It's a great feeling of accomplishment for me to own a home. I absolutely love the quiet neighborhood and open spaces where my son can play and meet new friends his own age. It's a terrific place for us to be a family," says Olney Springs resident Carmen Amaya.

Early on in Olney Springs' development, our team worked hard to enlist the support of local civic and neighborhood associations, with a strong communications plan and proactive community outreach to educate residents about how the new mixed-income community would blend in with existing homes. The surrounding area was relatively affluent. Although the county's idea of a mixed-income community was indeed innovative, not all residents were on board with building new developments for families lower on the income spectrum.

Undeterred, MHP and Elm Street Development collaborated with community groups through the duration of Olney Springs' planning process to address outstanding concerns and to ensure the development's eventual construction. Despite some initial opposition, we were able to successfully convince stakeholders with a few design tweaks, that our mixed-income housing plan was the right fit for the neighborhood.

ABOUT ROBERT A. GOLDMAN

Robert A. Goldman has served as president of MHP for the past 15 years. This private, nonprofit real estate developer in Montgomery County, MD, houses people, empowers families and strengthens neighborhoods. MHP has a staff of 30 and a budget of $3.5 million. The organization was formed in 1989 to preserve and expand the supply of affordable housing, and serves more than 1,700 low- and moderate-income residents in transit-oriented neighborhoods around the county.

AFFORDABLE LIVING THROUGH PASSIVE HOUSE ENERGY STANDARDS

Daniel Valliere, Executive Director
Jessica Woodruff, Director of Housing Development

REACH Community Development

Hillsboro is Oregon's fifth largest city and is enjoying a boom of rapidly growing high tech and health care industries that support high wage jobs. Orenco Station is an area of Hillsboro nationally recognized as a model of new urbanism. Over the past 15 years, several thousand housing units have been built in and around Orenco Station, also known as "Silicon Forest."

The growth, however, has focused on market-rate and luxury living. Workers with incomes under $30,000 a year can't afford the new units. The majority of the remaining land in the area is under development for approximately 1,000 additional luxury units with rents that are among the highest in the city.

In 2013, REACH set out to secure an affordable housing site in the Orenco Station neighborhood of Hillsboro. We took a three pronged approach: 1) select a transit-oriented site to lower transportation costs; 2) build affordable units for households making 50 percent of average median income, or less and; 3) use Passive House standard construction to dramatically reduce monthly utility bills. The Passive House standard is an established rating system designed to measure efficiency. It is granted only by third party verification after construction is complete. June 29, 2015, marked the opening of Orchards at Orenco Phase 1, a thriving community, and the largest certified multi-family Passive House building in North Amer-

CHALLENGE

Hillsboro is Oregon's fifth-largest city, home to rapidly growing high tech and health care industries. Over the past 15 years, several thousand housing units around Hillsboro's Orenco Station, also known as "Silicon Forest" have been mostly high-priced luxury homes. Workers with incomes under $30,000 a year can't afford them.

Passive House construction — traditionally available only at middle and upper incomes — can work for lower-income families as well.

ica. The development consists of 40 one-bedroom and 17 two-bedroom units. The building will achieve nearly 90 percent energy reduction for heating, and 60 to 70 percent for overall energy use, compared to a comparable USGBC LEED building. Other benefits include improved indoor air quality provided by the continuous ventilation; better comfort in the units; improved construction quality, reducing the risk of moisture intrusion; and reduction of noise from the adjacent light rail line.

Orchards' super-insulated foundation, walls and roof dramatically reduce heating and cooling loads, and therefore the size and expense of the equipment that provide it. In addition, REACH installed the ImagineEnergy system to track and improve upon residents' energy usage habits. All of this benefits residents, who save an estimated $30 to $45 per month, per unit, a 1 to 2 percent increase in their annual income.

Orchards has earned national acclaim, by showing Passive House construction — traditionally available only at middle and upper incomes — can work for lower income families as well.

"Every day I find a new reason to love it," says Orchards resident Georgye Hamlin. "It's cool, it's quiet, and I don't even hear the train."

Additionally, the transit-oriented location has proven a resounding success. Due to the suburban location, local government was skeptical tenants would choose public transportation. We thought differently, and now have data to advocate for more efficient parking requirements at affordable transit-oriented developments. The local zoning required 1.5 parking spaces per unit. REACH sought a parking reduction variance to 0.8 and the city approved 1.0. Although city regulations required 57 parking spaces, our independent traffic study shows tenants use parking at a ratio of 0.65.

REACH learned several key lessons from this project:

- Get buy-in from all critical team members: the architect, general contractor, structural engineer, construction consultant and Passive House consultant.
- Learn from those who have worked on similar projects, and share with others trying to achieve similar goals.
- Educate staff and tenants early and often about Passive House construction.

As with all innovative endeavors, we initially faced many risks and unknowns. But the success of this project, and the positive response from residents, has spurred us to build another 58-unit Passive House building adjacent to Orchards at Orenco, scheduled to open in June 2016. We believe we are on a path to a cost-effective model for high efficiency affordable apartments to use across our region, and we hope to continue our work.

The Orchards at Orenco building will achieve a nearly 90% energy reduction for heating versus a comparable USGBC LEED building.

ABOUT DANIEL VALLIERE

Dan Valliere serves as the chief executive officer of REACH Community Development, a non-profit community development organization whose mission is to create quality, affordable housing and opportunities for individuals, families, and communities to thrive. REACH serves a primarily disadvantaged population including the formerly homeless, elderly, and physically/mentally disabled, as well as the working poor. REACH houses nearly 3,000 people in Multnomah and Washington counties, in Oregon, and Clark County, Washington. Prior to joining REACH, Dan was executive director with a neighborhood human services organization in Chicago.

RENEWABLE ENERGY: HELPING KEEP AFFORDABLE HOUSING AFFORDABLE

Linda L. Harvey, Executive Director

Laconia Area Community Land Trust

The mission of the Laconia Area Community Land Trust (LACLT) is to assist low- and moderate-income families achieve economic self-sufficiency through the development of permanently affordable housing opportunities and associated support programs. LACLT serves the greater Lakes Region in central New Hampshire, much of which is rural. The area has significant water frontage on New Hampshire's largest lake, Lake Winnipesaukee, and on other smaller lakes. It is a resort area with a large number of expensive second homes. The Lakes Region is a popular tourist destination that hosts a multitude of hotels, inns, restaurants and shops. Most jobs in the tourism industry, which fuels the local economy, are low-wage. Many local residents have only modest economic prospects.

Our region faces a shortage of housing – especially rental housing – that is safe, healthy and affordable for low- and moderate-income people. According to the Joint Center for Housing Studies at Harvard University, housing quality issues are most prevalent in non-metro areas, exactly the kind of communities LACLT serves.

The people here are the working members of the community who take care of our children, tend to our parents in nursing homes and hospitals, serve us meals, service our cars, check us out at the grocery store and perform so many services that we and our local economy depend on. To be able to pay rent, local workers often find themselves making difficult tradeoffs. Making housing payments of-

CHALLENGE

Traditional energy sources for water and electricity meant high utility bills for the residents of the rural Lakes Region, New Hampshire, many of whom work low-wage jobs in the tourism industry. With rent already straining family budgets, the cost of utilities needs to be factored into building any affordable housing developments.

To be able to pay rent, local workers often find themselves making difficult tradeoffs. Making housing payments often comes at the forfeiture of essentials such as food, childcare, transportation and medical care.

ten comes at the forfeiture of other essentials such as food, childcare, transportation and medical care.

For 23 years, LACLT has worked to provide low- and moderate-income people with an affordable place to call home. Our ability to provide safe, healthy and affordable homes requires fiscal discipline and careful stewardship of precious resources. Keeping operating costs down at properties is critical to ensuring they stay affordable. Incorporating green building techniques such as high-efficiency insulation and minimal construction waste among others into new construction and into projects that are rehabilitated helps keep operating costs low. It also helps us achieve our green development and asset management goals. LACLT's Lochmere Meadows I is a great example of how we combine green building with affordable homes for working families in New Hampshire.

Lochmere Meadows I consists of 28 affordable rental units. All units serve very low-income households, earning no more than 50 percent of the area median income. In Tilton, NH where Lochmere is located, the median income is approximately $55,000, so the families living in these homes have household income below $28,000 per year. Its location is ideal for working commuters – just a few miles off New Hampshire's Interstate 93, and near a high concentration of jobs in retail, restaurant and hospitality industries. There is a high demand for Lochmere Meadows units, and a standing waiting list. The importance of Lochmere housing and its 28 affordable rental units cannot be overstated. Like many states across the U.S., waiting lists for public housing in New Hampshire that is affordable for people at 50 percent or below the median income is lengthy, between six and eight years, according to New Hampshire Housing, the state entity responsible for low-income housing programs.

The 28 units in four buildings were built as Energy Star certified homes. Unfortunately, the Lochmere development budget did not allow for the addition of any renewable energy, which would help keep overall utility expenses of the development down, creating more affordability in the long-term. But we wouldn't be fulfilling our mission if we didn't pursue every option available to ensure Lochmere's sustainability and affordability. Because of our relationship with NeighborWorks America, LACLT sought and received capital rehab funding from it to retrofit this property with solar hot water and solar electric. The total cost of the project was $328,733. NeighborWorks awarded grant funding in the amount of $228,733, leaving LACLT a gap to fill of $100,000. LACLT sought and received the remainder of funds needed from the TD Charitable Foundation's Housing for Everyone grant competition.

With financial support from NeighborWorks America, LACLT built solar hot water and electric infrastructure into the Lochmere Meadows development. The solar hot water and electric systems save Lochmere's residents thousands of dollars annually (relative to what they would be paying for propane systems). The clean energy produced by the Lochmere Meadows solar energy installation also offsets over 65,000 pounds of carbon dioxide pollution per year. Ultimately, by investing in renewable energy in an affordable housing development, we have saved energy and lowered operating costs.

The Lochmere Meadows solar energy installation offsets more than 65,000 pounds of carbon dioxide pollution every year.

ABOUT LINDA HARVEY

Linda Harvey is the founding director of LACLT, one of the early affordable housing groups in the state. LACLT specializes in sustained, innovative rental housing production and the compassionate delivery of resident services.

HELPING HOMES GO GREEN IN VERMONT

Ludy Biddle, Executive Director

NeighborWorks of Western Vermont

In western Vermont, many older homes are owned by residents with low- to moderate incomes and are hit with high utility bills due to poor insulation and the lack of energy-efficient appliances. Yet homeowners either don't see the value of retrofitting their houses with energy modifications or they don't have the necessary funds. NeighborWorks of Western Vermont recognized the problem and set an ambitious goal to retrofit 1,000 homes in Rutland County within three years, cutting household energy needs by a minimum of 15 percent, saving $1 million and sharply reducing carbon emissions.

Energy efficiency investments provide tremendous savings for homeowners and create meaningful local jobs. As a nonprofit HomeOwnership Center, NeighborWorks of Western Vermont recognizes this and has always recommended weatherization.

However, despite a robust state financial incentive program for efficiency upgrades – Home Performance with Energy Star – and a pool of certified contractors, the number of retrofits completed prior to 2010 in Rutland County was a paltry 26. At the time, the county represented 10 percent of the state's population, but only five percent of the state's retrofit market.

In 2010, NWWVT received an unprecedented grant from the Department of Energy to create HEAT Squad, a program to help facilitate further energy efficiency upgrades in Rutland County. Our intention was to use our own expertise to leverage the state's incentive program to increase demand for energy efficiency upgrades.

CHALLENGE

Many older homes in western Vermont are owned by residents with low- to moderate incomes and are poorly insulated and lack energy-efficient appliances. Despite their high utility costs, these homeowners either don't see the value of retrofitting their houses with energy modifications – or they simply can't afford to.

"We went from filling our oil tank three or four times a year, to one or two times a year, and reduced pellets by a ton. It's a long-term investment that's returning in the short term."

— Adam and Dalite Sancic of Proctor, VT

In our application for the grant, we argued for a one-stop shop that delivered a low-cost energy audit, recommendations about efficiency improvements, and affordable finance options for installation.

Rather than extravagant incentives for client upgrades, we decided to offer a new model of high-level customer service. To that end, it was essential to get homeowners to run an energy audit – a comprehensive evaluation of a home's energy efficiency. Thus, outreach became a cornerstone of the program.

We established early on that word-of-mouth was our single greatest source of client referrals, and so made it our business to take part in community events such as educational programs, competitions, celebrations, and local forums. This helped stimulate word-of-mouth exchanges and got more people to call and inquire about our services.

The next step was to set a price for home efficiency audits. We learned a lot by using different price points: A homeowner who booked a free audit, generally had no intention of making upgrades, while a homeowner who booked a $50 audit, generally wanted to confirm that their home was already pretty efficient. But, when we priced audits at the market rate of $350, calls stopped. We eventually discovered that $100 was the "sweet spot" for audits. Homeowners found the price affordable, yet felt sufficiently invested to take our recommendations seriously.

Local independent contractors were the next link in the chain. They were critical partners, but presented challenges. For one, doubling the demand for energy upgrades meant a sudden need for more home-efficiency certified contractors. To help, NWWVT offered free building training and certification, heat pump installation training, business training and more. Through these initiatives, HEAT Squad helped create at least 62 jobs as well as three auditing and contracting businesses.

HEAT Squad saved residents more than $1 million annually in energy costs.

Another problem was that many contractors lacked the information and customer service skills needed to promote energy-saving projects. So, we facilitated the Dale Carnegie Weatherization Sales Training Course, and made it mandatory for all contractors in the program. We also established firm timelines for contractors to submit energy audit reports and to contact customers. These requirements netted a marked increase in conversion rates from energy audit to retrofit project.

To help with capacity, we created a temporary labor pool to resolve seasonal workload bottlenecks, and made four equipment loans totaling $139,589. With funding from the Vermont state treasurer, NWWVT also allocated $2 million for energy loans at competitive rates for homeowners.

By the end of 2014, HEAT Squad had completed 1,200 Home Performance with Energy Star retrofits, 1,000 of which were within Rutland County. To date, we have accomplished 1,400 retrofits in an expanded five-county territory, providing homeowners a 32 percent average reduction in energy costs saving the participating residents more than $1 million dollars a year in energy costs. And we finally managed to reach the low- and moderate-income households we set out to help at the beginning of the project. These households are 267 times more likely to install efficiency measures with the help of HEAT Squad than with state incentives alone, according to a study by the independent Cadmus Group. Our very role as a Homeownership Center accustomed to educating and advising has been our greatest asset.

"Ever since I've been here, the house always felt damp and cold. I realized I have to watch my pennies. The improvements are a valuable way to not freeze anymore. It's wonderful," says Angela Combes, a Rutland town resident.

ABOUT LUDY BIDDLE

Ludy Biddle is executive director of NeighborWorks of Western Vermont, managing strategic growth and collaborative efforts in Vermont and nationwide. Biddle is a member of The Development Council at the Federal Reserve Bank of Boston, and worked previously at the National Endowment for the Arts and the Folger Shakespeare Library.

FARM WORKERS BECOME TENANTS IN THE NATION'S FIRST CERTIFIED ZERO NET ENERGY RENTALS

Rachel Iskow, Executive Director

Mutual Housing California

Located in California's north central valley, Yolo County has more than 5,000 year-round jobs in the agricultural sector. The Central Valley is the biggest grower of produce in the state, and provides over half of the nation's vegetables, fruits and nuts. Workers on farms, in packing houses and processing plants have some of the most dangerous and unhealthy jobs in America.

Yet, while farmworkers are the backbone of the agricultural economy, they suffer from a critical shortage of affordable housing in the county, and are often relegated to over-crowded and unsafe housing conditions.

At the same time, the Yolo County town of Woodland is not immune to California's rapidly rising residential rents. Situated a few minutes from the prestigious University of California, Davis, Woodland is home to many university employees and students. A steady flow of new, affluent residents creates pressure on the rental housing supply in Woodland. Agricultural workers are among those least able to compete for scarce, high-quality rental housing.

Seeking to alleviate the housing crisis for agricultural workers, Mutual Housing California sent its multilingual team to interview workers on the farms, in processing plants and in packing houses. Mutual Housing conducted one-on-one interviews, asking workers about their greatest

CHALLENGE

In California, where residential rental costs have significantly outpaced income growth, housing costs for agricultural workers and their families have long been at a crisis point. Farm workers have some of the most dangerous and unhealthy jobs and are most in need of homes that are affordable, safe and healthy.

Low income, high utility bills and expensive rent left little for other necessities or savings.

housing concerns, what type of core amenities were important and how much they paid for housing. What surprised us were their high utility bills. Low income, big utility bills and high rent left little in the way of resources for other necessities or savings.

Mutual Housing selected Housing Development Project Manager Vanessa Guerra to coordinate the development of what would become Mutual Housing at Spring Lake. For Guerra, the work on this housing development was personal. She was raised in a farmworker family in Yolo County. She and her brothers were the first in their family to earn college degrees. Guerra has a bachelor's degree in engineering and construction management and is a certified green building professional.

Having lived in substandard housing in her childhood, she knew the challenges faced by agricultural workers and understood their desire to raise children who would have brighter futures.

Guerra closely studied the goal of lowering utility bills for agricultural workers, the future occupants of the housing she would develop. She became committed to developing Mutual Housing's first zero net energy (ZNE) housing – designed to produce as much energy on site, through solar photo voltaics, as would be consumed by residents and management. Mutual Housing worked with energy consultants, architects and construction firms to create the Spring Lake development.

In May 2015, Mutual Housing at Spring Lake became home to 62 families who earn income from agriculture or who are retired agricultural workers. The families enjoy parks, a walking path, an onsite community room, a computer learning center, a bike-lending library, computer tablets that can be borrowed and free Ivbnternet access.

Marisol Sanabria, a Mutual Housing resident, said that in other places she lived she "was always scared when the bill would come... In total, for the five months we have been living here, [the utility bill] has come out to under $30."

In 2015, the U.S. Department of Energy certified Mutual Housing at Spring Lake as the nation's first rental housing to achieve the Zero Energy Ready Home designation. That means its houses are high-performance homes that are so efficient that a renewable-energy system can offset all or most of their annual consumption. In 2016, the property was awarded LEED Platinum Home status.

The average residential monthly electric bill was $110.21 in 2013.

On the way to this success, we learned a few lessons:
▸ It takes a green team that is flexible during design and construction, willing to try new products and processes, to create a ZNE community.
▸ It also requires the nonprofit developer to have a clear dedication and focus on building ZNE, with a "green builder/cheerleader" on the team to participate in regular meetings during design, development and construction.
▸ A focus on resident education and green resident leadership is critical in order to "live ZNE" after construction.

ABOUT RACHEL ISKOW

Rachel Iskow is executive director of Mutual Housing California, a Sacramento-based nonprofit corporation that develops, operates and advocates for sustainable housing that builds strong communities through resident participation and leadership development. Its Mutual Housing communities are home to over 3,000 low-income residents; the organization has 60 employees and an asset base of $153 million. Iskow is an active advocate on housing access issues and is the board chair of California Coalition for Rural Housing.

Community Building

Tracy Hoover

As the world's largest organization dedicated to volunteer service, we at Points of Light mobilize millions of people to take action and change the world. That change starts every day in communities both large and small.

To the outside world, communities are often defined as neighborhoods – with physical boundaries such as streets, rivers or railroad tracks. Sometimes a community is defined by its location, such as a church community, or a school or hospital. There are communities based on common interests, such as a choral group or a youth sports team. But really what communities are – at least the strong, healthy ones – are collections of people connected by their relationships, no matter what their location is. Robert Putnam, the author of "Bowling Alone," found that the strength of a community depends up on the quality of the relationships among its members.

That's because communities create strong social bonds and a sense of belonging. As social bonds are built, we often see previously disengaged community members come forward – perhaps because they see a need waiting to be filled, or because someone takes the time to ask for their help. The more people who come forward to make a difference in the lives of others, the stronger the community becomes. And the better off everyone in the community is.

People who are active in their communities are a source of strength in times of need, providing meals or carpooling, emergency help or emotional support. Communities also serve as a mechanism for collective action, allowing members to come together to solve some of our toughest problems as a society, whether that means mentoring kids who need a caring adult in their lives or responding to a natural disaster. Communities are the building blocks of strong societies.

With the rise of technology, many people have become increasingly detached from the outside world, including the world right outside their front door, and that can hurt a community. It's the same with suburbanization, hectic lifestyles, and even long commute times that keep families from eating dinner together. At Points of Light we see these challenges every day, but we also see the inspiring power of individuals to create change in their communities.

There isn't a problem in the world that isn't being solved in a community somewhere. In this chapter, you'll find stories about communities of all sizes and shapes, and the good work being done by local organizations to help build engagement. People and organizations who are engaged with their communities are better able to consolidate the talent, resources, and skills needed to solve problems. These are people who have a hammer, so to speak, and go find a nail. The local organizations you'll learn about on these pages operate in urban, suburban, and rural communities and train thousands of local community members each year so that they can spur community development and build strong networks in their neighborhoods. NeighborWorks seeks to provide the opportunity and tools for local community members to improve their own lives and strengthen their own communities. The organizations you'll read about in this chapter have been unusually successful in doing just that. It's an honor to introduce them to you.

Tracy Hoover is the chief executive officer of Points of Light, the largest organization in the world dedicated to volunteer service. Points of Light's mission is to inspire, equip and mobilize people to take action that changes the world toward a future in which everyone has discovered their power to make a difference, creating healthy communities in vibrant, participatory societies. Originally founded in 1990, Points of Light was created as an independent, nonpartisan, nonprofit organization to encourage and empower the spirit of service.

THE SANKOFA INITIATIVE: A MULTICULTURAL APPROACH TO FEEDING AND HOUSING A COMMUNITY

Sharon Conard-Wells, Executive Director
Adeline Newbold
Community Building Manager

West Elmwood Housing Development Corporation

The West End, a mixed industrial and residential neighborhood, in Providence, RI, has been in decline since the 1950s when numerous large industries closed their doors, leaving unemployment and blight in their wake. Today, over 38 percent of residents were born outside the United States, 32 percent fall below the poverty line and 62 percent say they have to choose between paying for housing or buying food. When they moved into the neighborhood, many of these relocated families, mostly from Central America, West Africa and Southeast Asia, began suffering from health problems due to the lack of fresh fruits and vegetables. They couldn't grow their own food and what was available was too expensive or required long treks outside the neighborhood. These newcomers were also concerned about the lack of social services and support they found in their adopted communities.

West Elmwood Housing Development Corporation (WEHDC) was founded in the 1970s by residents seeking to improve housing conditions and homeownership opportunities. Our mission is to develop healthy, sustainable communities through affordable housing and other services to West End residents. In 2011, community leaders, stakeholders, academic partners and nutrition and gardening experts joined us in the search for a response to residents' concerns about access to healthy food.

CHALLENGE

Providence's West End neighborhood, a culturally and economically diverse community, is populated by mostly low-income and moderate-income households, more than 38 percent of whom are immigrants. Access to healthy food, social services and support was limited until West Elmwood Housing Development Corporation and its partners addressed issues in the neighborhood.

What emerged was a multi-faceted plan to transform blighted properties, provide culturally appropriate, fresh, locally-produced food and expand economic opportunities.

The Rhode Island Department of Health awarded us a three-year grant in 2013 to delve deeper in understanding the neighborhood's multicultural food narrative. We used a detailed, grassroots approach to data collection, conducting interviews and focus groups in the subjects' homes or other familiar surroundings such as churches and sporting events. The surveys were often in the subjects' preferred language.

These studies found high levels of obesity, diabetes and other diet-related health problems. Residents wanted better access to healthy fruits and vegetables and land to grow the foods they had back home. Safe, quality affordable housing was also in high demand.

What emerged was a multifaceted plan to transform blighted properties, provide culturally appropriate, fresh locally produced food; expand economic opportunities and strengthen a sense of community among West End residents. The initiative was named Sankofa, which means "to go back and fetch it" in Ghana's Twi language. The expression embraces the importance of learning from the past to make positive changes for the future.

The multiphase Sankofa Initiative includes a community garden and farm where residents can grow their own food and a market where the farmers and local entrepreneurs can sell produce and crafts. A greenhouse allows growers to extend their season and increase the diversity of their produce. The community kitchen provides a facility for food preparation, nutrition and wellness training. The recent closing of the Women, Infants, and Children (WIC) centers left the West End without a federal nutrition supplemental program for mothers and their children. The Sankofa WIC center will reconnect pre and post-natal women and their children to healthy, affordable, local food and provide on-site nutrition education. In addition, 50 housing units built on 10 previously blighted lots throughout the West End will revitalize the neighborhood and provide shelter for low-income residents.

The Sankofa World Market opened in 2014 and had more than 2,400 shoppers in 2015. The public outdoor marketplace brings together residents from the West End and other communities to enjoy affordable, fresh and culturally relevant food. Music, cooking classes and tastings are often held at the market, which also draws craftspeople, artists and other entrepreneurs.

SANKOFA: (v) to learn from the past to make positive changes for the future.

The Sankofa Initiative significantly strengthened our partnership with the city's leader in urban agriculture, Southside Community Land Trust (SCLT), whose grower training program offers an experiential learning opportunity at the market.

For example, Ms. K, a refugee from the Liberian Civil War, brought considerable agricultural skills to her new home. She struggled to support her family and wanted to grow food and develop a farming business that would contribute to the household she shared with her daughter and grandson. Ms. K couldn't find space for growing or selling produce at existing farmers' markets until SCLT provided grower training for Ms. K and other beginning farmers, as well as a table at the market that she shared with two other sellers. The enterprise allows Ms K. to increase her productivity and expand her skills in selling the vegetables most in demand in the African community, such as potato greens and bitter eggplant. She keeps a portion of her crops for her family and her profits go toward her family's financial security.

The Sankofa Initiative's continued development will increase the availability of fresh, healthy, affordable and culturally appropriate food and connect more residents with the opportunity to grow, purchase and share in the community process of cooking and eating. Through this project, we learned: 1) the importance of grassroots data collection in the planning and ongoing development of any community initiative, 2) making the most of a community members' resources, such as farming experience, will produce a more effective outcome and increase community engagement, and 3) working with partners with similar needs and goals yields more holistic benefits.

ABOUT SHARON CONARD-WELLS

Sharon Conard-Wells is the executive director of West Elmwood Housing Development Corporation, where she has promoted community development since 1987. WEHDC offers services ranging from homebuyer education and foreclosure intervention to the creation of an alternative credit home repair loan pool and a workforce development lead abatement program. Conard-Wells has successfully raised more than $100 million in real estate financing for the historic adaptation of Brownfield Mills as well as single-family homes for first-time buyers.

BUILDING ENGAGEMENT IN IMMIGRANT COMMUNITIES THROUGH THE ARTS, CULTURE AND FOOD

Sean I. Robin, Executive Director
Elizabeth Druback-Celaya
Director of Community Development

———

Hudson River Housing, Inc.

The mission of Hudson River Housing is to improve lives and communities through affordable housing development, housing education and services and neighborhood revitalization. Many of our efforts are concentrated in the small city of Poughkeepsie, NY, specifically the Middle Main neighborhood, an ethnically and economically diverse community located in the heart of Poughkeepsie's Main Street corridor.

The Middle Main neighborhood population is over 70 percent non-European American and is home to a diverse immigrant population, a majority from Latin America. Middle Main has more than double the Latino population of any other census tract in Poughkeepsie. The neighborhood has been negatively impacted for decades by multi-lane highways that isolate it from surrounding neighborhoods, long-term structural poverty, crime and decades of limited public and private investment.

At the same time, the immigrant community has stemmed the deterioration of Main Street by filling vacant storefronts, growing new enterprises, filling housing units with families and bringing a vibrancy of culture and heritage, artistic traditions, foods and beverages that are now core assets of the neighborhood.

CHALLENGE

In small cities and neighborhoods across the country, immigrant communities have taken up residence in vacant and blighted downtowns. As we work to revitalize these areas, how do we effectively engage immigrant communities and mitigate challenges such as communication differences, the lack of permanency and scarcity of trust?

"In the end, what we all want is to share our heritage."

— Fel Santos, community leader

Drawn by opportunities for low-cost housing and entrepreneurship and the possibility of living in an immigrant enclave, immigrant communities have taken root in areas that have otherwise been abandoned. Immigrants are by nature risk-takers and they are not daunted by the challenge of building a home or business in a depressed area. The lack of attention from more mainstream public and private entities also forms somewhat of a shield, allowing them to recreate traditions and establish family and community networks with less fear of resistance.

These same dynamics, however, present challenges. As private and nonprofit entities work to bring economic vitality to struggling cities, how can immigrant households and businesses be effectively engaged as participants in revitalization? And how can existing social and economic networks be preserved and strengthened in the process?

In 2009, Hudson River Housing launched the Middle Main Initiative to unite residents, businesses, government and other stakeholders in building a sustainable, inclusive and participatory community. They focused on the creative use of arts, culture and food as a bridge to communication and engagement and placed a priority on celebrating the immigrant community's cultural heritage and traditions. The Dia de los Muertos (Day of the Dead) festival, a celebration of the cycle of life celebrated especially in southern Mexico where many of the residents of Middle Main hail from, is a prime example. Hudson River Housing's efforts showed the immigrant community that they care about their presence and feel it is worth celebrating. The festival builds community pride as immigrant residents see their heritage being showcased. Over five years, the festival has grown from a two-hour event to two weeks of hands-on workshops, informative lectures, art exhibitions and performances. Attendance has multiplied tenfold. Importantly, participants represent a cross-section of cultures and races that learn about the community's history and traditions and gain an appreciation and respect for cultural differences and contributions.

Hudson River Housing has also worked to engage small businesses in neighborhood revitalization efforts. In Middle Main, immigrant-owned businesses are in the majority and many are food establishments offering an array of authentic ethnic fare. In a neighborhood like Middle Main, where most of the housing is rental and the community is fairly fluid, small businesses are a more stable and rooted component. Most small business owners have invested all of their available financial capital in their business and the entire family is involved in operations and have an incentive to see the neighborhood thrive. In addition, businesses are often the best "eyes on the street," providing important information about quality of life and neighborhood dynamics.

Immigrant entrepreneurs launched 28.5% of new businesses in 2014.

Hudson River Housing's business engagement led to the development of the Made in Middle Main campaign, which currently brings 20 neighborhood businesses, half of which are immigrant owned, together to support and promote the neighborhood. Through workshops showcasing the preparation of unique cultural food offerings, "Eat Middle Main" community lunches and language-exchange learning programs, they are both promoting the business community and celebrating the cultural heritage of the business owners as a core asset of the neighborhood.

Hudson River Housing's efforts reveal important lessons learned: 1) go beyond acknowledgement to a commitment to include the immigrant community in organizing efforts and to build trust through cultural competency and a dedication to learning, and 2) build participation through celebrating and showcasing the contributions of immigrant residents and businesses as important to the stability and vibrancy of the neighborhood.

ABOUT SEAN ROBIN

Sean Robin joined Hudson River Housing as executive director in January 2016. Hudson River Housing works to improve lives and communities through the development and management of affordable housing, the provision of housing education and supportive services and neighborhood revitalization. The organization serves over 3,000 people annually throughout the Hudson River Valley of New York State.

BUILDING A CULTURE OF 'FINDING A WAY'

Rick Goodemann, CEO

Southwest Minnesota Housing Partnership

Southwest Minnesota Housing Partnership, based in Slayton, MN, is a small nonprofit dedicated to "creating thriving places to live, grow and work through partnerships with communities." Our organization provides community planning, real estate development, grant administration services and educational programs to communities in 30 rural Minnesota counties.

Growth in healthcare and manufacturing industries helped our communities become more resilient to agricultural cycles, but they are also suffering from their success. We responded to burgeoning housing and community development needs by engaging local leaders and offering community planning and housing development expertise - not as proponents of our own specific projects, but as partners in meeting local needs. In 1992, in our first year of existence, two federally-declared disasters occurred in our region and we quickly offered help. We demonstrated our willingness to jump through hoops for federal funds, focus on community needs, present new ideas and bring allies to the table. As leaders in the disaster area began to talk, communities sought our assistance.

When the agricultural economy rebounded in Worthington, MN (pop. 13,000) and economic diversification efforts took hold, the largest employer, a pork processor now affiliated with JBS, an international meat processing company, had difficulty finding employees and started recruiting from the Twin Cities and elsewhere. Today, over one-quarter of Worthington residents are foreign-born and 56 languages and dialects are spoken at JBS. The ar-

CHALLENGE

After the 1980s farm crisis agricultural communities in Minnesota sought investment of state and local resources to diversify their economy. Now job growth has outstripped the local workforce and available housing. Communities struggle to provide services and homes for new residents from elsewhere in the state and around the world.

Growth in healthcare and manufacturing industries helped our communities become more resilient to agricultural cycles, but they are also suffering from their success.

rival of new residents outstripped the supply of housing. Unemployment remains low and housing vacancy is nonexistent.

In 1995, our organization developed the first new rental project in the community in over 20 years. Our knowledge of housing finance and state program requirements meant that key data was collected on time to meet funding deadlines, critical partners were involved and community listening sessions were held.

After reviewing a requested housing study, we recommended potential new construction and rehabilitation projects, some of which were incorporated into the city's housing plan. Among our recommended projects were the Willow Court Townhomes and several housing and commercial repairs funded by community development block grants. We listened and engaged new partners to deliver results and community leaders responded with their own proposals.

In the early 2000s we sought out more partnerships to meet local needs, identify barriers and increase engagement from diverse households. We developed relationships with Adult Basic Education, churches and employers to reach residents where they are comfortable and where language resources are available. JBS welcomed onsite resources for their employees because it helps them retain workers. Churches wanted their members to have their basic housing needs met in a safe and respectful way. Adult Basic Education needed relevant class topics and beginner-level home maintenance provided a safe space for new American students to ask questions and voice their housing needs. These relationships increased access and participation of new American households in seeking housing and becoming homeowners and business owners.

Some of our dozens of projects and partnerships that maximize health and safety, economic resiliency and community integration include:

▸ Home maintenance classes that introduced new American householders to home maintenance and created relationships with local home improvement businesses.

▸ Innovative multi-family projects that increased energy-efficiency and healthier living for over 200 households through improved ventilation and outdoor space.

▸ A former YMCA that was redeveloped into the Center for Active Living, an indoor-outdoor gathering space.

▸ Corrections work crew projects that enabled dozens of inmates nearing release to build marketable construction skills and work relationships while controlling construction costs for affordable housing.

▸ Housing inspection and rehabilitation programs that improved rental units and engaged landlords in meeting livability standards through rental ordinance and registration.

▸ Youth career and financial literacy programming that boosted engagement with diverse young people and connected youth with community development careers.

▸ Permanent supportive housing for long-term homeless households with services to support stability and success provided by Southwestern Mental Health Center.

▸ Commercial rehabilitation that made downtown a viable location for businesses. We secured microloans through a regional foundation to increase success of new American-owned business ventures.

Today, more than ¼ of Worthington residents are foreign-born.

Twenty years after that first conversation with community leaders, our organization has become a valued partner because we've learned to 1) focus on finding solutions, 2) work together, 3) push forward, and 4) embrace a culture of "finding a way."

ABOUT RICK GOODEMANN

Rick Goodemann is the founding executive officer of the Southwest Minnesota Housing Partnership, which provides community development and technical assistance services in 30 rural counties of southern Minnesota. Accomplishments include the development, preservation, financing or rehabilitation of more than 8,400 housing units with more than $561 million in direct housing development and financing. Goodemann has more than 25 years of experience creating rural development and housing finance programs in public and private settings.

FROM WHEELS TO FOUNDATIONS: STABLE COMMUNITIES CHANGE LIVES

John Fowler, President & CEO

Peoples' Self-Help Housing

Carpinteria Camper Park started out as a cool camper park for vacationing families in the 1960s. However, under management of an absentee slumlord who allowed the site to become overpopulated, the facility developed into permanent housing of last resort for about 80 low-income households, many of them farm laborers in the area. By the time Peoples' Self-Help Housing became involved in 2004, the situation had become desperate. Many trailers were beyond repair and improper sewer connections caused unhealthy living conditions. The single common restroom and shower facility was the only plumbing available for a majority of the households, many with large multigenerational families. Criminal activity, gangs and violence had become commonplace.

The site was a code compliance nightmare for overwhelmed city officials who were at a loss for a solution. As deplorable as it was, it was also the only affordable housing available for the occupants working in nearby agricultural and tourist industries. The City of Carpinteria asked Peoples' Self-Help Housing for help.

Peoples' Self-Help Housing is a community-based nonprofit that facilitates affordable housing and other programs that lead to self-sufficiency for low-income families, seniors and other special needs groups on California's Central Coast.

Our first step at the Carpinteria camper park was to contact community stakeholders, including government offi-

CHALLENGE
To rehabilitate a dilapidated former camper park in the California beach town of Carpinteria, which became housing of last resort for low-income households living under conditions of extreme poverty.

cials, community members, health care providers, law enforcement and local clergy, to learn about the community's needs. Crime and gangs were among the biggest immediate concerns.

We coordinated a system of community policing and installed security fencing with automated entry and exit gates. Not only did this reduce crime, it began to build trust between our organization, the residents and the community. Next, we purchased more than 50 newer trailers to replace a majority of the existing trailers which were in disrepair or too small to accommodate overcrowded living spaces. We helped facilitate communication between residents and property management and started to support families through family counseling, crisis intervention and community en-

gagement with three programs: Supportive Housing, Community Building and Engagement and Youth Education Enhancement.

Supportive Housing is a clinically-based case management and social services program that provides no-cost, voluntary and confidential services to residents with basic, chronic and emergency needs, including anything from food to domestic violence intervention.

As Supportive Housing social workers integrated into the neighborhood, they introduced Community Building and Engagement, which encourages residents to participate in their community. They helped organize cleaning parties, religious celebrations and impromptu potlucks. Yeret, an 8-year-old resident, said, "We didn't like it when it was dirty. We helped people clean up. It was like a big family."

Many residents were concerned about how to help their children with homework, so the Youth Education Enhancement responded with an afterschool program. First, we had to find a location, which was difficult with no common area protected from the elements. We started with an outdoor classroom covered by a tarp and soon replaced it with a large air-conditioned portable classroom filled with books, desks and a credentialed teacher.

The program was so successful that we eventually expanded to nine other properties. Outside of the needed structure and homework help, the children went on summer field trips and learned to paint murals from visiting artists of the local Bellas Artes program. The onsite teacher often accompanied parents to teacher-parent conferences at their schools. In many cases, it was the first time the parent had entered their child's school.

More than ⅓ of all farmworkers in America reside in California and Texas.

"When the trailer – the escuelita [school] – arrived, it showed the children that they could realize their dreams," said Liz, a resident whose son attended the program and now attends Cal State Los Angeles.

Our organization negotiated an adjacent land purchase, a land donation and approximately $12 million in financing to construct 33 units within a mile of the camper site, which were completed in the summer of 2013. We then raised approximately $15 million in financing to construct new affordable apartments on the camper park site. Before construction began, we relocated all remaining tenants to other housing in the community. On April 10, 2014, we broke ground on the long-awaited Casa de Las Flores at the former camper park site. The grand opening was held October 15, 2015. There are 43 spacious apartments and approximately 3,500 square feet of community space including a classroom with a computer room. We replaced the original housing on wheels with high quality affordable apartments on new permanent foundations.

There were mistakes and missteps, but we learned several lessons, including: 1) take a long-term view, 2) plan carefully, 3) make sure you are on the same page as your collaborators, 4) be flexible; things change and it is sometimes necessary to adapt to new circumstances, and 5) plan for the worst. In our case it happened: the historic downturn in the economy and the housing market in 2008.

We are proud of what we have accomplished at Casa de Las Flores and we hope to leverage our success and lessons learned to continue to serve those most in need on California's Central Coast.

ABOUT JOHN FOWLER

John Fowler, president and CEO of People's Self-Help Housing Corporation, has more than 27 years' experience in accounting as well as in corporate and nonprofit management. He is also president of The Duncan Group, an affiliate property management corporation with a large rental housing portfolio for seniors, farmworkers, low-income families and the physically challenged in San Luis Obispo, Santa Barbara and Ventura counties.

BRINGING NEW LIFE TO MOUNTAIN COMMUNITIES: THE ROUTE 123 STORY

Stuart J. Mitchell, President & CEO

PathStone Corporation

The latest U.S. Census survey pegged Puerto Rico's poverty rate at 44.9 percent and the current unemployment rate on the island is 16.5 percent. A lingering recession and out-migration of its people is undermining the island's tax base and leaving an aging population in place. The southwestern part of the island, particularly its many mountain communities, is plagued by some of the highest rates of poverty and unemployment. This area encompasses the Route 123 Heritage Area, which includes five communities along Puerto Rico's Route 123 and its network of roads that reach into more remote parts of the island.

One of Puerto Rico's oldest roads, Route 123 has been the region's main transportation route and commercial artery since the colonial period. It connects the south-central city of Ponce on the Caribbean Sea to the northern city of Arecibo on the Atlantic Ocean.

The Heritage Area's spectacular beauty, rich history and culture and its people's strong sense of entrepreneurship make it ripe for revitalization. But a crumbling infrastructure and an ever-shrinking tax base have crippled the ability of local governments to meet basic needs. PathStone wanted to help by building on the area's existing natural, cultural, historic and economic assets.

We developed a coordinated effort to address the lack of economic opportunity and deteriorating housing conditions with three principles in mind:

CHALLENGE

To rebuild deteriorating housing and employment opportunities in Puerto Rico's Route 123 Heritage Area, amid a crumbling infrastructure and shrinking tax base that have crippled the ability of local governments to meet needs.

The Heritage Area's spectacular beauty, rich history and culture, and its people's strong sense of entrepreneurship make it ripe for revitalization.

1) Create communities with employment opportunities and decent, affordable, housing.

2) Maximize use of the region's natural, cultural and economic assets.

3) Bring innovative approaches to nurturing business and employment opportunities. Central to this strategy is the creation of an eco-tourism and agro-tourism industry centered on the area's coffee culture and the richness of the area's ecology.

Beginning in 2010, we helped complete six housing developments totaling 127 units and created an estimated 244 direct and indirect jobs. We broke new ground with financing from USDA's Farm Labor Housing and Mutual Self-help Housing funds, as well as from the Federal Home Loan Bank System. In the last two-and-a-half years, 227 families have completed homebuyer education and 35 have bought homes. Total new investment from housing activities has been $28 million.

In addition, as the first nonprofit in Puerto Rico to manage the Department of Labor's farmworker training program, PathStone has so far placed 60 adults and nine youths into full-time employment, a daunting task in the current economy.

PathStone has also facilitated 29 small- and micro-business loans in the region since 2013, valued at $805,611. We did so with help from micro-loan programs at the U.S. Small Business Administration, the U.S. Treasury Department and the USDA. In an unprecedented development, the Puerto Rico Planning Board has committed to match PathStone loans to regional businesses on a one-to-one basis. The first two loans have been approved and are being used by two coffee Haciendas to expand their hospitality and visitor facilities.

We also launched the Route 123 Tourism Trail, also referred to as The Coffee Trail, in partnership with Catholic University of Puerto Rico, the Massachusetts Institute of Technology (MIT), The Center for the New Economy, the Puerto Rico Tourism Company and the Puerto Rico Planning Board.

Puerto Rico is America's leading coffee producer.

An aggressive outreach campaign, including a website about the trail (ruta123.com) and a 64-page trail guide, has begun to yield results: over the past two years, PathStone-sponsored bike rallies in the mountain region have brought in approximately a thousand visitors. Hotels, restaurants, museums, ecological attractions and coffee haciendas along The Coffee Trail all report increasing visitors.

We've learned that the investment of attention, care and finance, seems to be paying off and that these communities will rise again.

ABOUT STUART J. MITCHELL

Stuart J. Mitchell is founder, president and CEO of PathStone Corp., a regional nonprofit community development corporation. He has worked for 50 years in the field of social, political and civil rights advocacy.

AN ASSET-BASED, PARTICIPATORY APPROACH TO REDEVELOPMENT

Gregg Warren, President

DHIC, Inc.

In 1974, DHIC was established in Raleigh, NC with the mission to create and support communities that are diverse, economically vibrant and affordable. DHIC develops rental apartments for families, individuals and seniors with limited incomes; offers homeownership counseling, education and down-payment assistance programs; constructs affordable homes for first-time homebuyers, and provides community services that promote healthy neighborhoods, develop resident leadership and encourage resident self-sufficiency and connection to community resources.

In 2014, DHIC purchased Washington Terrace out of foreclosure – an aging 25-acre, 245-unit, low-income housing project in the heart of east Raleigh's historic African-American community. Built in 1950, Washington Terrace is known as the first rental community built for African-American professionals and was the home of many local public figures and leaders. Over the years it has retained a strong sense of community. Today, more than 70 percent of residents at Washington Terrace and in the surrounding neighborhood are African-American, many of them long-time residents who cherish the rich history and culture of the neighborhood.

However, because of chronic disinvestment and its close proximity to the popular downtown area, where rents and housing prices are on the rise, the residents of Washington Terrace and the surrounding neighborhood face the

CHALLENGE

The sale of Washington Terrace, a neglected historic landmark for east Raleigh's African-American community, highlighted concerns about gentrification and displacement. DHIC needed to create a redevelopment plan that would respect the culture of the neighborhood, address displacement fears, and respond to needs of longtime residents and newer, modest-income families.

Washington Terrace offers a rare opportunity to transform a neglected neighborhood, while continuing to honor the important cultural, historic and social elements of this community.

competing pressures of blight and gentrification. The sale of Washington Terrace and the redevelopment goals of Raleigh officials made many residents and neighbors fear that displacement would soon follow. They did not trust that they would have a voice in the redevelopment process.

DHIC recognized that active and authentic community engagement was vital for building residents' and neighbors' trust.

"The people of this community must have a strong voice in this process," said Yvette Holmes, vice president of resource development and partnerships at DHIC. "It's about tapping into the considerable knowledge, insight and needs of individuals and families who are traditionally overlooked, but who stand to gain the most from an authentic process that includes them."

DHIC organized a master planning team of project managers, resident services staff, an experienced urban design firm, city planners and a respected communications consultant who grew up in the neighborhood to develop and implement a highly-engaged community input process for the redevelopment of Washington Terrace. The process included continuous communication and deep relationship-building meetings with the residents of Washington Terrace, neighbors from surrounding communities, an-
chor institutions and community stakeholders such as St. Augustine's University (a historically black university), the YMCA and the Boys and Girls Club. More than 350 residents, civic and non-profit leaders and other stakeholders participated in this process, which included a number of public information meetings, design charrettes, drop-in sessions, one-on-one stakeholder meetings, peer-to-peer meetings and resident-only information sessions. Voices were heard. Concerns were addressed. Suggestions were taken into account.

After a year-long process, the master plan for the new Washington Terrace was presented to the public in December 2015. The Washington Terrace community gave it an enthusiastic nod of approval.

Phase I is now underway and will result in 162 multi-family apartments, a new community center, children's play areas, recreation and green space, a community garden and a child care center. Many residents asked for other amenities such as washer/dryer hook-ups, energy-efficient appliances and better street lighting, which have been included in the master plan. The community-engaged planning process also highlighted the need for services and amenities such as health care, healthy food and family-friendly retail, some of which will be addressed in this or later phases.

Washington Terrace contains 162 apartments, a community center, children's play area and community garden.

Phase II of this development will include 72 units of affordable housing for seniors. Other phases will likely include homes-for-sale. DHIC plans to implement a pilot financial capability workshop series in the neighborhood to build a local pipeline of mortgage-ready families who want to extend their roots in the community.

Proving to be the largest and most significant project in DHIC's history, Washington Terrace offers a rare opportunity to transform a neglected neighborhood while continuing to honor the important cultural, historic and social elements of this community. DHIC's model of community-engaged master planning has set the precedent for future neighborhood redevelopment in other parts of the city. The common goal will be to use an asset-based, participatory approach that aims to maintain affordability and reduce displacement, both of which are concerns of area residents.

This project illustrates the importance of: 1) involving the community and stake-holders at all stages of the redevelopment, 2) building trust with the community through multiple forms of outreach and public engagement, and 3) encouraging community input and incorporating their ideas, needs and suggestions in the development.

ABOUT GREGG WARREN

Since 1985, Gregg Warren has served as president of DHIC. Under his leadership, the organization has constructed, acquired and/or rehabilitated 2,200 affordable rental units in 37 locations in eight counties in North Carolina and created more than 350 new homeownership units in Wake County. Together, these projects leveraged $202 million in direct investment from private and public sectors. In addition, over the past ten years, DHIC's Homeownership Center helped over 1,200 families to achieve their dream of homeownership.

MAKING CENTRAL DOVER STREETS SAFER TO ATTRACT STABLE HOMEOWNERS AND RENTERS

Joe Myer, Executive Director

National Council on Agricultural Life and Labor Research

High crime rates in central Dover have exacerbated problems in Delaware's state capital, where the mostly low-income residents struggle to stem their community's decline. Violent crimes in Dover's downtown hub spiked in 2013, rising nearly 400 percent over the preceding three years. Nearly all forms of crime were three to five times higher than that of the rest of the city. According to a recent survey, 42 percent of central Dover residents said safety was a major concern. Police say that illegal drug trade is driving much of the crime in the downtown area, a low-income neighborhood where run-down homes and vacant properties provide havens for dealers. Drug traffickers prefer to operate in lower income neighborhoods like central Dover, where about 75 percent of the housing properties are rental units, many of them quickly deteriorating.

The National Council on Agricultural Life and Labor Research (NCALL) has been a leader in affordable housing, homeownership and purchasing education and social impact lending for more than 40 years. Recently, the organization expanded its scope to include neighborhood revitalization and targeted central Dover for a multi-year, multi-faceted initiative. Restoring Central Dover, launched in 2015, lays out strategies related to safety, housing, community building and transportation. Steps

CHALLENGE

Crime and safety are the biggest challenges for central Dover, DE and they have a significant impact on other neighborhoods in Delaware's capital city. Central Dover desperately needed to reduce its crime problem with stepped-up policing and by improving homes and investment properties to attract stable homebuyers and renters.

Restoring Central Dover, launched in 2015, lays out strategies related to safety, housing, community building, transportation and more.

taken by the organization and its partners to build a safer community in central Dover include: the deployment of police foot and bike patrols, the expansion of surveillance cameras, improved

lighting in targeted areas and establishing a community policing collaborative with a citizen advisory committee and neighborhood watch groups.

Financing for these efforts came from several sources, including the Neighborhood Building Blocks Fund, the Delaware General Assembly and the Wells Fargo Regional Foundation. These funds are used to deploy new walking police patrols in dangerous areas for 16 hours a day, the hiring of new police cadets and installing surveillance cameras and lighting. At one location, new lights at a public basketball court support an effort underway to revive the Police Athletic League. Twelve new LED light fixtures were installed on a residential block near the main commercial corridor, a crime hotspot where there were 837 police calls in 2015. Officers are assigned to specific areas with the greatest need, generating more contact with residents and establishing trust. This has resulted in making the law enforcement leadership more attentive to the priorities of the affected community.

The launch of two Neighborhood Watch groups in key problem areas is another step towards addressing crime and safety concerns. The Dover Police Department has active community policing officers who meet regularly with the neighborhood watch groups. Additionally, the city's code enforcement department is present to answer questions and document potential code violations that require a follow-up. The Dover Police Department says the watch groups play "a crucial role for the police department, as communication and participation must be a two-way street. These community bonds will help make our communities safer and help break down any barriers." Residents now frequently engage with the police officers and there is mutual respect and friendship at their meetings.

Some residents have demonstrated a commitment to change and leadership by volunteering to run the Neighborhood Watch groups. These leaders plan to meet annually for training and to discuss criminal activity, which often shifts from one hotspot to another. These future leadership programs will be extremely useful in our organization's efforts to equip more residents to make their community more secure.

Restoring Central Dover was instrumental in designating central Dover as the Downtown Development District in 2015, providing access to new revitalization resources. The designation is meant to stabilize communities, stimulate private capital investment and improve job growth and commercial vitality. Following the planning grant, NCALL was awarded $750,000 for a five-year period from the Wells Far-

The Neighborhood Watch program began in 1972.

go Regional Foundation for implementation. Six work groups (Housing, Resident Engagement, Safety, Youth and Adult Services; Economic Development, and Transportation, Green Space and Infrastructure) were formed. Each group has milestones and outputs to be completed by various target dates.

Throughout the Restoring Central Dover we've learned several lessons, including: 1) the need to include law enforcement agencies in the strategic planning process. The Dover Police Department was an engaged stakeholder in the initial stages of our effort. Now we have them at the table to respond quickly and productively to issues that fall under their authority; 2) Leadership is critical, but without sufficient human resources to support it, progress stalls. Locating funds to hire additional police officers has been key to achieving NCALL's goals over a sustained period; and 3) Safety must be a priority for attracting potential residents and businesses. The homeownership rate in central Dover is notably low and commercial vacancies are high. Efforts are underway to build affordable housing units, attract new investments, address unemployment and underemployment and attract new businesses that can create jobs. Making these new stakeholders feel safe is essential.

ABOUT JOE MYER

Joe Myer, executive director of the National Council on Agricultural Life and Labor Research, is responsible for the overall management and administration of the organization's housing programs, which include technical assistance, direct housing services and lending for the Mid-Atlantic and Northeast regions. Under his leadership, NCALL has helped 8,000 families become homeowners.

AFTER A DISASTER, TRANSFORMING NEIGHBORHOODS INTO MORE RESILIENT COMMUNITIES

Cynthia W. Burton, Executive Director
Jacqueline Standridge
Director, Planning and Development

Community Service Programs of West Alabama

On April 27, 2011, the Tuscaloosa metro area was hit by multiple tornados. The result was one of the most devastating natural disasters in the nation's history, yet it all took place in just six minutes. The tornado cut a path of destruction six miles long and a half-mile wide through the middle of the City of Tuscaloosa. In the following weeks the community received distressing reports: 53 dead, 1,200 injured, 12.5 percent of the city's buildings and infrastructure destroyed and 5,362 homes damaged or demolished. Seven thousand people were left homeless and thousands of jobs were lost.

A large section of buildings that were destroyed were a mix of low-income and public rental housing and University of Alabama off-campus apartments. The students were eventually able to find other housing, leaving only the need to rebuild units for displaced low-income residents.

The city mourned the loss of family and friends and began the task of trying to make sense out of the rubble. At the time, it was quite difficult to fully comprehend the total effects of the damage caused by the tornados. But one thing was certain – rebuilding homes needed to be an intense focus for the agency over the next 12 to 36 months.

CHALLENGE

In 2011, tornados struck Tuscaloosa, AL, completely leveling businesses and residential communities. A large section of low-income and public rental housing was destroyed. The city began the difficult task of finding housing for its most vulnerable residents.

If there is any silver lining in the darkness of a natural disaster, it's the opportunity to transform neighborhoods into more resilient communities that can better withstand future disasters.

As a community action agency and community housing development organization, Community Service Programs of West Alabama (CSP) realized that low-income families and elderly individuals were particularly hard hit and vulnerable. CSP's goal was to mitigate the risks to these families by addressing their housing needs as quickly as possible yet also taking the time needed to produce durable and affordable housing. NeighborWorks America quickly partnered with CSP to mobilize resources to address the immediate and long-term housing needs of this population.

CSP identified a parcel of land that a previous developer had begun preparing for construction in 2009 but abandoned due to the economic downturn. The infrastructure was partially complete, most of the grading was complete and more than half of the sanitary sewer pipes and gutters had been installed. But no residential construction had begun.

The property is located in Hurricane Creek, in the eastern part of Tuscaloosa County, which is known for its natural beauty. Hurricane Creek spreads into the westernmost point of the Southern Appalachians and is the southernmost free-flowing stream in Appalachia. Residents of the community were concerned about the proposed project and the impact of the development. CSP worked closely with the residents of the area to ensure that the new construction would fit with the environment.

CSP proposed developing the property with 50 single-family homes for senior housing. The agency turned to NeighborWorks and recruited other partners, including the City of Tuscaloosa and the Alabama Housing Finance Authority, to help finance the project.

If there is any silver lining in the darkness of a natural disaster, it's the opportunity to transform neighborhoods into more resilient communities that can better withstand future disasters. The agency's response to the natural disaster was ultimately twofold. It first addressed the immediate needs of families harmed by the event. With NeighborWorks as its partner, CSP channeled resources to provide basic housing for the families displaced by the tornado. In doing so, they built trust with the families and residents in the area that helped in the long-term recovery goal of creating an affordable housing development.

Secondly, our agency was able to take the time needed to listen to the community. The result was housing that improved the quality of life for a vulnerable population and also satisfied the need to fit in with the cultural characteristics of the long-established Hurricane Creek residential neighborhoods. The result is a stronger social cohesion between the "old" neighborhoods of Hurricane Creek and the new development.

12.5% of the city was destroyed. 7,000 people were left homeless and thousands of jobs were lost—all in a matter of 6 minutes.

In addition to forging this new social collaboration and providing needed housing, our agency learned several lessons:

1) While it can be helpful for generating funds and attention, being designated as a presidentially declared disaster area can also overwhelm local capacity and necessitate a need to bring in a myriad of resources. Each resource will have its unique set of documenting and reporting requirements that can be cumbersome. Time must be taken to examine the financial resources and the subsequent requirements that may need to be addressed.

2) Communication with the community is key. CSP had to address concerns of residents in the neighborhood of the proposed development while also working with elderly individuals and their families who had been displaced by the disaster.

3) Be part of the solution. The City of Tuscaloosa delayed immediate rebuilding efforts so they could first conduct a series of community planning meetings and develop a master plan that would guide the recovery efforts. CSP participated in the meetings and worked closely with city officials to ensure the needs of the agency's constituency were represented.

Our organization was able to turn the destruction of the tornado into a positive outcome for seniors in our area through careful planning, communication and collaboration with government and nonprofit partners.

ABOUT CYNTHIA W. BURTON

Community Service Programs of West Alabama Executive Director Cynthia W. Burton has experience overseeing many successful housing and social service programs, including the construction of 95 single-family houses in Tuscaloosa and Eutaw, AL. Under her administration, the agency has conducted major renovation to multiple residential and commercial properties. Burton has more than 30 years' experience in effective management practices including as chairman of the board of a multi-site regional health-care facility and has also served as deputy district director for Alabama's 7th Congressional District.

TURNING OBSTACLES INTO OPPORTUNITY

Suzanne M. Walsh, CEO

Kennebec Valley Community Action Program

It's tough trying to fit a square peg into a round hole, yet that is the metaphorical challenge many people with limited income face when trying to access social-assistance programs. Some examples: A single mother faces eviction because she is unable to afford the required garbage bags and bucket. A single father without a car can't run errands because he lacks a stroller to transport his growing son. An elderly couple with serious medical conditions cannot leave a homeless shelter due to inability to put down a security deposit. A young woman has insurance to cover her eye appointment, but no funds to actually purchase the glasses she needs to see effectively.

There are no public-assistance programs that will pay for garbage bags, the stroller, the security deposit or glasses. So who helps these people overcome their challenges?

In Waterville, Maine, and the surrounding community, it's the Community Investor Initiative, a program of the local Poverty Action Coalition – a group of concerned individuals and organizations who came together to address barriers to prosperity. Each and every one of the above situations was resolved with the support of a community willing to help neighbors in need.

In January 2014, the first meeting of the coalition was convened by the mayor of Waterville. The Kennebec Valley Community Action Program (KVCAP), whose mission is to eliminate poverty and the conditions of poverty, joined with other community stakeholders to fight a staggering blight. In Waterville, the poverty rate is nearly 22 percent, compared with 13.4 percent for the county

CHALLENGE
There are many families in need of services who don't fit the criteria necessary for government assistance. While not technically under the poverty line, many families still struggle with insecurity and scarcity, but have no safety net to fall back on in times of difficulty.

While the individual outcomes may seem small, a pair of glasses here, a security deposit there, even a kitchen sink – the collective contributions of Community Investors make a world of difference.

and 13.6 percent for the state. Nearly 70 percent of Waterville's children under the age of five live in poverty. According to the Maine Department of Education, more than two thirds of students in the Waterville school district qualify for free or reduced lunch.

The Poverty Action Coalition, spearheaded by KVCAP, is by definition a collaborative endeavor. Its 85 members include Waterville city officials, representatives from the local college, public library staff, social service providers and dozens of other stakeholders. Anyone who is interested in working on poverty issues in the Waterville area is welcome at the table.

Established in 2015, the Community Investors Initiative (CII) is the first program developed by the coalition. It exists to make small grants or assist with other interventions when emergency assistance is needed to overcome an immediate problem and prevent a long-term catastrophe. To avoid duplication of services, an application process ensures that every other avenue of assistance is pursued before a request is brought to the CII.

CII investors, currently made up of more than 200 members, are asked to develop solutions to resident issues, whether it is sharing an unknown resource or donating money/items. If no solution is offered by the Community Investors members, then the Poverty Action Coalition may choose to fulfill the request through the Hope Fund, which was specifically set up to meet these types of needs.

In 2015, 61 individuals were helped with assistance that included a bus ticket back to go home to a more stable support network, a security deposit, a microwave and a storage-unit fee.

Because we were not sure in the beginning what types of assistance would be needed, it was not possible to set rules ahead of time. Understanding the necessary logistics of the program and how to best meet the clients' needs has evolved with the types of requests received. We found that meeting once a week for the first three months significantly helped. We were able to keep each other updated on areas we were finding too difficult to administer. For example, we tried to collect and deliver furniture for our clients but discovered, as a group, that this was extremely challenging to manage and sustain. Instead, we set up a relationship with a furniture store and Habitat for Humanity Restore to address this need.

The most unique aspect of the program is how many people are helped without having to involve the community investors. More importantly, we found new ways to approach clients and their challenges.

The poverty rate is nearly 22% in Waterville.

While the individual outcomes may seem small – a pair of glasses here, a security deposit there, even a kitchen sink for one family – the collective contributions of the Community Investors make a world of difference. Moreover, the initiative has enhanced relationships between partner agencies over our shared clients. The interest generated by the success of the CII has encouraged other communities to look at implementing a similar model in their regions.

ABOUT SUZANNE M. WALSH

Suzanne M. Walsh serves as CEO of Kennebec Valley Community Action Program (KVCAP), a nonprofit community action agency that serves more than 30,000 people in over 90 primarily rural communities in central Maine. KVCAP's mission is to partner with area residents, organizations and government entities creating solutions to end poverty in order to strengthen individuals, families and communities.

BUILDING A LEADERSHIP PIPELINE AS HIGH AS APPALACHIA

Colin Kelley, CEO

NeighborWorks Western Pennsylvania

In the space of just a few decades, two adjacent Pittsburgh neighborhoods – the Hill District and Uptown – have gone from thriving to struggling. Their story of disinvestment and decay is all too common in the areas served by our network.

Steep hillsides and streets in the area act as tremendous physical boundaries that sometimes prevent these communities from uniting to address shared problems. This has been exacerbated by the need for new community development leadership, something noted in the report from the Uptown Community Vision (2009), a local initiative which aimed to build local "capacity to organize and advance this shared community vision." This idea was further developed in The Greater Hill District Master Plan (2011), which aimed to develop leaders within the Greater Hill District.

NeighborWorks Western Pennsylvania addresses these challenges through the NeighborWorks Leadership Collaboratory Program. The purpose of the program is to empower neighborhood leaders by forming a supportive learning group or cohort made up of six to eight people carefully selected from the community. Over a 24-month period, each cohort takes part in local and national workshops and training in community development. Participants build leadership and professional skills as the cohort works together on community issues. At the end of the period, each person earns a professional certificate in

CHALLENGE

To revitalize two struggling Pittsburgh neighborhoods by investing in people and leadership within those communities.

This program is about community building and empowerment — because change that starts from inside a community is far more effective than when it is imposed from the outside.

either Community Engagement or Community and Neighborhood Revitalization through NeighborWorks America's National Training Institutes.

In the summer of 2015, we received critical funding from a local foundation, McCauley Ministries, to bring the program to Pittsburgh's Hill District and Uptown neighborhoods. Just a few months later, the first cohort was convened. NeighborWorks Western Pennsylvania partnered with local leaders to recruit and select participants in a competitive application process. We cast a broad net that covered board members and known local leaders as well as lesser-known residents and volunteers who wanted to develop their community and leadership skills. Another eight-person cohort launched in fall 2016.

The process has already taught us a great deal about the importance of leaders embracing a positive attitude. Neighborhood revitalization can seem daunting; problems are often systemic and deeply entrenched, and community members aren't always quick to embrace change. That's why our program aims to keep a constructive, hopeful and fun vibe.

For example, during the cohort's first session, members spent some time talking about what they liked best about their community. The discussion made the cohort proud and excited and set them off in an optimistic direction. These attributes are priceless for residents trying to address difficult issues in their communities.

A single cohort of eight people is unlikely to be able to completely resolve all of this community's issues. But they certainly can have an effect. Take the issue of bringing more healthy food choices to the area. The cohort by itself may not be able to completely remake the food culture and business of the neighborhood. But it can set the groundwork for a fresh-food truck, fundraise for a local food bank, plan a vegetable garden or organize healthy food drop-offs from local businesses.

Maybe that campaign could lead to further resources or policy reform that addresses food scarcity in struggling neighborhoods.

More than any specific issue, this program is about community building and empowerment – we are equipping residents with the skills and training to revitalize their neighborhoods in ways they best see fit – because change that starts from inside a community is far more effective than when it is imposed from the outside.

Over the next decade, nonprofits will need to attract and develop some 640,000 new senior managers.

Together with the cohort, NWWPA learned to be patient and realistic about our goals. We also have a renewed conviction about our own resiliency as a neighborhood. Our hope is that while being mindful of the area's rich history we can continue to repair the fabric of our community and create a better future for our children.

ABOUT COLIN KELLEY

Colin Kelley is CEO of NeighborWorks Western Pennsylvania, a charter member of NeighborWorks America, a nonprofit organization that promotes homeownership and stable communities in western Pennsylvania. He has over 15 years of experience in the community development field, including program development, management, applied research, community organizing and leadership development.

BUILDING HISPANIC LEADERSHIP IN SOUTHWEST WISCONSIN

Bill Reinke, *Executive Director*
Rebecca Gomez, *Homeownership Center Assistant*

Neighborhood Housing Services of Southwest Wisconsin

Neighborhood Housing Services of Southwest Wisconsin (NHSSW) works to expand its services to Hispanic people through a multi-pronged engagement strategy. While there are several ways to increase connections with the Hispanic community, the approach that we believe is most effective begins with building strong in-house capacity via our Hispanic Leadership Initiative. We also partner with organizations that share our mission, such as the one established with the MultiCultural Outreach Program (MCOP), an organization that provides needed support to our neighbors who are enriching the community. In addition to these formal steps, we think success is driven by program-specific connections and alliances with other community groups in the region.

The ultimate objective of these inter-related efforts is to develop Hispanic leaders and to implement strategies that spur greater participation by the Hispanic community in the area's community and economic life. Purposeful participation by the residents of the community is the foundation of long-lasting success.

To lead its Hispanic Leadership Initiative, NHSSW brought on a Spanish-speaking staff member, who is better able to engage and encourage residents in the language with which they're most comfortable. Through the initiative, NHSSW has formed partnerships with business and civic leaders in the Hispanic community,

CHALLENGE

Southwest Wisconsin has a growing population of Hispanic residents, drawn by jobs in the dairy and meat packing industries. There is thus an increasing need to expand the Hispanic community's access to employment, housing, economic and civic leadership opportunities in the area.

The ultimate objective is to develop Hispanic leaders and to implement strategies that spur greater participation by the Hispanic community in the area's community and economic life.

including the dairy industry, a sector with deep and connections and importance to the southwest Wisconsin region. We built ties with a veteran leader from the dairy industry who holds a strong rapport with Hispanic workers in the area. Hispanic workers have become increasingly important to the economic health of the Wisconsin dairy industry, with as many as 40 percent of farm workers identifying as Hispanic, according to a University of Wisconsin survey.

NHSSW staff has also traveled to surrounding regions with more established Hispanic populations to learn from Hispanic government workers about effective strategies for better serving and engaging Hispanic communities. Going forward, NHSSW plans to bring these government officials to the local area for networking with other government leaders and community stakeholders regarding inclusive strategies to better involve Hispanic residents in government-related, economic and community activities and service. These three forces – government, economic and community – when working together are like a three-legged stool, sturdy and able to support broad-based progress for everyone.

Partnership with the right organization propels success. NHSSW's partnership with the MCOP, also representing southwest Wisconsin, has been a springboard for our agency's efforts to reach out to and build leadership among the Hispanic population. Key NHSWW staff created a tenant/homebuyer education course. Many people are unaware of their tenant rights and the home buying process is very complicated. By creating this course, we've equipped members of the community with the information they need to maintain stable and quality housing, while laying the foundation for wealth creation via homeownership.

Another important tool involves helping to ensure that existing and emerging Hispanic leaders are connected to the community. To that end, NHSWW regularly invites local Hispanic leaders to participate in and promote multicultural events that allow them to hear directly from the residents how policy is affecting lives. And while the value of one-on-one connections can't be overstated, it's also important to have an accessible resource of information for people to use when seeking services. To that end, NHSSW tasked a homeownership center staff member to translate an existing resource directory of Richland County into the latest Spanish version. We helped it get distributed and now more members of the Hispanic community know where to go for the services that they need.

6% of Wisconsin's population is Latino.

More generally, NHSSW staff members have had meetings with key civic and educational leaders to discuss their experiences working with Hispanic families and how ours and other organizations can partner to create multicultural interaction in Richland County.

An essential partnership has been built with the public school's English as a second language teacher, who invited NHSSW staff to have an information table at a Spanish language presentation for parents during parent/teacher conferences. For the Hispanic community to thrive, its children must thrive, too, and engagement like this pays enormous dividends in the future.

The NHSSW staff member who attended was able to talk with Spanish-speaking parents in the community and to give out NHSSW and MCOP materials, thus creating relationships, building trust and promoting these important programs. Now, others counties involved with the MultiCultural Outreach Program are brainstorming ways they can use our local model to build partnerships with school districts for planning special multicultural activities.

ABOUT BILL REINKE

Bill Reinke serves as executive director of Neighborhood Housing Services of Southwest Wisconsin, founded in 1983, the country's first rural program in the NeighborWorks America Network. NHSSW has been providing housing services for over three decades, serving over 4,000 households and generating a $60 million community reinvestment. The agency's programs include a homeownership center, community housing lending, real estate development and community building. Reinke has 20 years of program, development and managerial experience with nonprofit housing and community development organizations. He has developed and administered several housing programs and developed affordable housing projects totaling over 500 units, including those serving low-income families, persons with disabilities and the homeless.

THE WESTSIDE LEADERSHIP INSTITUTE: EMPOWERING A NEIGHBORHOOD BY FOSTERING SELF-RELIANCE

Maria Garciaz, Executive Director

NeighborWorks Salt Lake

Salt Lake City's Westside communities are rapidly changing as new immigrants, mostly from Latin America, Somalia, Iraq and Burma, settle in the area. The Westside is home to 80 percent of the city's immigrant population, 40 percent of whom are Hispanic. The majority of the neighborhood's children qualify for free or reduced price lunches at their schools, which struggle to address the cultural and linguistic differences of the students and their families. High school graduation and postsecondary education rates are significantly lower than those of the city's nearby Eastside neighborhoods. Participation is low in public decision-making meetings such as local community councils, parent teacher associations or city government. However, this underserved community needs a voice in the public forum to effect essential change.

NeighborWorks Salt Lake (NWSL) was created in 1977 to reverse the decline of blighted neighborhoods in Salt Lake City through partnerships with residents, businesses and government agencies. In 2004, NWSL developed the Westside Leadership Institute (WLI) to cultivate and develop leadership in target neighborhoods and engage their diverse residents.

The Institute offers leadership workshops taught by the University of Utah and community leaders to equip citizens to take civic action and to provide learning opportu-

CHALLENGE

More than 500 refugees settle in Salt Lake City, UT annually, many in the Westside neighborhood where schools struggle with cultural barriers and more than 100 different languages are spoken. This underserved population rarely attends local government or parent teacher association meetings and lacks a voice in effecting urgently needed change.

nities for university faculty and students. The training connects residents to local decision-making bodies, funding sources and other resources. The program expands participants' leadership experience by having them share what they have learned with their families, friends and co-workers.

One Institute graduate, Lourdes Rangel, a single mother of three autistic children, struggled to help her family because of her language barrier and limited knowledge of services for autistic children. She attended a three-hour class once per week for 12 weeks because she wanted to seize the opportunity to learn about accessing resources for her children and others in similar situations.

"I was very scared coming to the WLI because I was going out of my comfort zone and I didn't speak English very well," says Rangel. "I felt overwhelmed and vulnerable, but I needed to face this fear for my kids. I needed to acquire leadership skills to advocate for my kids and other autistic kids."

Rangel learned how to frame and understand a community issue and practice management strategies along with new skills such as leading meetings, resolving conflicts, communicating ideas and using social media. She was particularly motivated to learn about grant writing and how to educate government agencies about her concerns.

Rangel earned three college credits, qualified for a WLI grant and was awarded a leadership certificate. She then established key partnerships and founded Proyecto Autismo (Autism Project), a nonprofit that provides services for Spanish speaking families with autistic children. Rangel, who was mentored by a University of Utah Spanish instructor, now serves as the primary instructor for the Institute's Spanish sessions.

"I wish every community had this type of leadership development because it really does change people's lives. It lets people know that they are not alone and ultimately it lets people know that their voice and opinion matters," says Rangel.

More than 400 students have graduated from the Institute, which hosts two 12-week sessions annually in English and Spanish. The graduates receive official non-credit transcripts from the University of Utah and certificates of completion. Several graduates have taken on roles as legislators and as members of the city council and school district board. Others have gone on to create nonprofits and many have accessed resources far beyond NWSL's capacity.

More than 3 million refugees have arrived in the U.S. since 1975.

WLI graduates include:
- Sandra Hollins, who participated in the first class in 2004, made history in 2014 as the first black female elected to the Utah State Legislature.
- Rosie Peralta took the WLI English class because she wanted to join the Parent Teacher Association to get help communicating with her two teenagers. After graduating, she attended PTA meetings and later became the organization's president, a co-instructor for a leadership class at an elementary school and served on several community boards.
- Charlotte Fife-Jepperson established West View Media, a nonprofit news organization that focuses on the diverse communities in West Salt Lake City and is the only news outlet to cover an area of Salt Lake City that has traditionally been undervalued and misrepresented by the mainstream media.

One element of the Institute's success stems from our organization's understanding that change doesn't happen overnight and requires a long-term commitment. A community is best served by teaching it how to become self-reliant through neighborhood engagement and leadership. We learned that a thorough understanding of a neighborhood's needs and abilities is also key to effecting positive change. We conducted studies to determine demographics, renter/homeowner ratios and the area's economic base, followed by door-to-door surveys to measure the residents' interest in supporting NWSL and the types of programs that will best serve their needs.

ABOUT MARIA GARCIAZ

Maria Garciaz, executive director of NeighborWorks Salt Lake, was born and raised in Salt Lake City. NeighborWorks Salt Lake, a nonprofit housing organization created in 1977 to reverse the decline of neighborhoods experiencing blight, has an operating budget of $5.4 million and assets of $32 million. The organization, which has a 19-member staff with a 17-member volunteer board of directors, provides services including lending, real estate development, economic development and community engagement.

RESIDENT LEADERSHIP IN BLOOM: CULTIVATING COMMUNITY IN THE IVY STREET GARDEN

James A. Paley, Executive Director

Neighborhood Housing Services of New Haven

Newhallville, a six-by-eight block neighborhood of New Haven, CT with a population of nearly 8,500, was once known as a bedroom community for employees of the Winchester Repeating Arms Company from 1866 until the manufacturer's decline in the 1980s. When the company reduced production, many employees lost their jobs and either left New Haven or remained and experienced economic distress.

A drastic drop in population left houses abandoned and prone to blight, forced businesses to close and created an environment that fostered crime and gang violence. Neighborhood Housing Services of New Haven (NHSNH) committed to restoring Newhallville to its former vibrancy. The organization acquires and rehabilitates blighted properties, offers pre- and post-purchase homebuyer education and works with residents to help them take charge of their neighborhood.

The Community Building and Organizing (CB&O) team at the agency distributes Success Measures surveys periodically to gauge residents' feelings about issues in the community. In the 2012 survey, residents expressed their dissatisfaction with the quality and safety of outdoor community spaces. For instance, 45 percent of respondents ranked the quality of parks, playgrounds and out-

CHALLENGE

A 2012 survey by Neighborhood Housing Services of New Haven (NHSNH) found that many residents in the Newhallville neighborhood of New Haven, CT felt disconnected from their community and unsafe. Many respondents wanted to become more involved in their community but were unsure how to help most effectively.

> # "This community garden is a blessing to this neighborhood. I had worried about the whole Newhallville neighborhood going into the ground, but today is the day I see it's going up."
>
> — Ida Felder, gardener

door recreation centers as "poor" or "very poor," while 35 percent of respondents perceived the safety of children playing outside as "not that safe" or "not safe at all."

While these results did not come as a surprise, they did allow the CB&O staff at NHS to better direct their efforts in working with resident leaders to address the most important issues. The CB&O team and resident leaders who participated in the Community Leadership Institute (CLI) in Orlando, FL identified improving outdoor community spaces as a top priority and envisioned a community greenhouse in the Ivy Street Community Garden.

The Ivy Street Community Garden was only used by 10 resident gardeners, but its size and location made it a perfect place for a community greenhouse. Neighbors imagined this community green space not only as an educational area to be used by local schools and families, but also as a source of fresh produce for neighbors year-round.

Resident leaders and agency staff members reached out to their networks to promote the garden and greenhouse as a community space. Local groups including the Ivy Street Gardeners, City Seed and the New Haven Land Trust became involved in the project. Young people began using the garden when the neighboring Lincoln-Basset Elementary School and Solar Youth, a nonprofit that supports youth in low-income neighborhoods, began offering outdoor education. As partnerships developed, more people became involved with the care and maintenance of the garden and excitement began to build among participants.

Resident leaders worked alongside various partners to secure funding for the project. They produced detailed site drawings, advocated for the project during Newhallville Community Management Team meetings and made a formal request to the City of New Haven (the landowner) for specific changes to the site. Once the appropriate approvals were in place, construction of a 15-by-

30-foot greenhouse was completed with help from the United Way of Greater New Haven and PCL Walsh Company Venture II.

Today, the Ivy Street Community Garden greenhouse stands on the corner of Ivy Street and Shelton Avenue in Newhallville. The structure's success has not been without setbacks, however. During the winter of 2014, the greenhouse collapsed under record snowfall. Gardeners were frustrated, but bonds were strengthened as gardeners and community partners came together to repair the greenhouse and rebuild it into an educational and environmental oasis for all.

From 2008-2013, community gardening households increased 200%—to about 3 million.

While the site is collectively maintained, resident gardeners continue to take a leadership role in programming for the greenhouse. A number of organizations continue to use the greenhouse including Lincoln-Basset School, Solar Youth, Squash Haven, Sound School, Common Ground High School and Yale University's Dwight Hall student groups. Resident gardeners take the initiative to engage with young people and share their knowledge.

The garden also serves as a place of remembrance for Al, Robert and Leroy, three resident gardeners who passed away since the inception of the project in 2012. Through this emotionally difficult time, the garden provided space to pay tribute to those who revitalized the garden.

Through the Ivy Street Community Garden project, NHSNH learned two lessons, including: 1) the project's success can be credited to the fact that residents were given a chance to have their voices heard and truly lead a project at their own pace from conception to completion, through the various trials and tribulations of its execution, and 2) the role of the organization is to support residents in their efforts using its network to secure funding and government approvals and to garner community involvement.

ABOUT JAMES A. PALEY

James A. Paley has been executive director of Neighborhood Housing Services of New Haven for the past 36 years and executive director of the New Haven HomeOwnership Center since its inception in March 2001. Paley has presided over a program that has grown from a small housing rehabilitation organization to a housing development corporation that concentrates on neighborhood stabilization, affordable housing production and homebuyer education programs. Paley is currently chair of the board of directors of Community Housing Capital, a Community Development Financial Institution that provides financing to organizations comprising the national NeighborWorks network.

DEVELOPING COMMUNITY LEADERSHIP TO MEET LOCAL CHALLENGES

Gary Pollio, Executive Director

Interfaith Community Housing of Delaware

All too often, neighborhood revitalization is governed by those outside the community. But research and practical experience demonstrates that successful and sustainable revitalization must be rooted in support from community members, residents and stakeholders. Transformative community revitalization efforts must include the engagement of local residents to be truly successful and avoid gentrification-triggered displacement.

Wilmington, DE, has its share of challenges in need of a transformative approach. In the last census, nearly a third of the population and a quarter of families were below the poverty line. About half of residents under the age of 18 and 17 percent of those 65 and older were living below the poverty line.

Meanwhile, the city's at-risk neighborhoods are populated with resident leaders whose enthusiasm is untapped. Many self-identified community leaders are frustrated by bureaucratic hurdles and lack of resources, organizational skills and training. Many also have reasons to not trust "the establishment." Moreover, in transient/rental-heavy communities, such as Wilmington's West Center City, it often is difficult to sustain lasting working relationships.

Thus, with funding from NeighborWorks America and the Laffey-McHugh Foundation, Interfaith Community Housing of Delaware implemented a pilot Resident Leadership Development Academy in 2015. The goal

CHALLENGE

In struggling parts of Wilmington, DE, neighborhood engagement was low and emerging community leaders were under-resourced. The city's most impoverished areas were represented by those who wished to take on the challenges, but needed training to help them overcome bureaucratic hurdles and gain access to vital resources.

Many self-identified community leaders are frustrated by bureaucratic hurdles and lack of resources, organizational skills and training.

was (and is) to encourage resident engagement and develop leadership skills in those living in Wilmington's at-risk/in-need communities.

Using the NeighborWorks "Building Leaders, Building Communities: A Resident Leadership Development Curriculum," we introduced the academy with the goal of empowering graduates to implement local improvement projects, thereby encouraging enthusiasm from neighbors and fellow community members. Upon graduation from the academy, community leaders applied for and were offered grants of up to $1,500 each to implement a project, and each leader was encouraged to recruit five neighbors to assist in implementation.

Here are some highlights from the results:

- Twelve residents from four of Wilmington's most at-risk communities enrolled.
- Ten of the 12 participants (83 percent) graduated.
- Nine of the 10 graduates (90 percent) completed and submitted grant applications for community-based improvement projects. All grants were approved and awarded.
- Additional funding was granted to a young resident videographer to create a short film that will document the implementation of the community-based projects.
- Four neighborhoods benefitted from graduate projects: West Center City, Quaker Hill, East Lawn and North East.
- To date, seven projects have been completed. Three are still in progress as of this writing.
- Feedback from academy graduates was nearly 100 percent positive.

Among the projects, two are art-based (mural and film), two involve beautification, two focus on youth voices, and one each related to disability awareness, public safety (lighting), community signage and overall community engagement.

One of the ripple effects was increased resident engagement in four of Wilmington's most at-risk communities, due to the mandate that each of the graduates engage a minimum of five neighbors.

The goals of engaging 12-15 residents and implementing10 community-based projects both were met. However, project staff members all agreed we underestimated the time and attention graduates would need to implement their projects. While the majority of the graduates implemented their projects with little assistance from ICHDE, a few needed a little more "hand-holding."

NeighborWorks trained more than 7,000 resident leaders in FY15.

A related lesson learned was that computer and technology skills did not parallel the enthusiasm and dedication of some of our graduates. To remedy this gap, in the future we will deploy an intern to assist graduates of the next academy when needed.

Another improvement in the future will be more rigorous evaluation of successful leadership development. NeighborWorks America has developed a tool as part of its Success Measures Data System to assess changes experienced by resident leaders involved in leadership-development activities. This tool is now available to all NeighborWorks America affiliates (such as ICHDE) and will be used for the next academy.

ABOUT GARY POLLIO

Gary Pollio, executive director of Interfaith Community Housing of Delaware, Inc. (ICHDE), has held his current position for 16 years. ICHDE is a nonprofit community development organization which serves as a catalyst for revitalizing and strengthening neighborhoods by providing sustainable housing and homeownership services that support low- and moderate-income households, empowering residents for leadership, and promoting individual and community asset building. With a staff of only 14, ICHDE has had the consistent, sustainable and meaningful outcomes of similar agencies, which are larger in both budget and staff. During Pollio's tenure, ICHDE has developed/redeveloped more than 650 units of affordable housing, counseled and created over 1,500 new first time homeowners and amassed a rental portfolio of 350 affordable rental housing units.

CLIMATECARE: ENGAGING A VULNERABLE COMMUNITY TO FACE CLIMATE CHANGE THREATS

Phil Giffee, Executive Director
Hannah Dorfman, AmeriCorps VISTA Member

Neighborhood of Affordable Housing

East Boston is perhaps best known as home to Logan International Airport, but it also has six subway stops, three tunnels, two bridges, a major highway and is bordered by Masschusetts' second-most contaminated waterway, Chelsea Creek. Overall, it is the fifth-most environmentally-burdened community in the state. A collection of five islands joined by a 19th century landfill project, the neighborhood is surrounded on three sides by water and has no land connection with the rest of the city of Boston. This makes it particularly vulnerable to rising sea levels and coastal flooding, when residents can become isolated from work and family with no access to public safety providers, such as fire, police or hospitals. Many of the residents are poor, non-native English speakers and people of color who had little awareness of these climate change threats and lacked the means to influence policies to address these issues. After multiple local conversations and meetings with informed experts, Neighborhood of Affordable Housing (NOAH) found key concerns included the need for information about transportation disruption and evacuation routes in the event of a dangerous storm, revised flood maps residents could understand and translated materials for non-English speakers.

NOAH worked with neighbors on environmental justice issues for decades but to address these emerging problems,

CHALLENGE

Pollution, rising sea levels and climate change threaten East Boston. The majority of the 40,000 residents in the neighborhood are immigrants and people of color who faced social, economic and linguistic barriers to understand and address these issues until the Neighborhood of Affordable Housing's inclusive community engagement process began.

"Having an opportunity to give our input as community residents and have a voice as a community has had a really positive impact, because we don't always get a seat at the planning table."

— Heather Rents, East Boston resident and ClimateCARE resident representative

the East Boston-based organization launched a campaign in 2015 called Community Action for Resilience through Engagement or EB ClimateCARE. Backed by significant multiyear resiliency grant funds from the Kresge Foundation and support from NeighborWorks America, the program has three key elements: boosting community engagement, working with the city on climate change actions and partnering local residents with city and state agencies to forge preparedness and response plans.

Raising awareness about the potentially devastating effects of global warming has been critical in this environmentally challenged, overburdened community. An initial survey, performed by NOAH's environmental youth program, found that fewer than ten percent of East Boston residents had any idea of the dangers posed by global warming. NOAH recruited university climate experts to hold technical briefings in the residents' native languages, offering education on areas such as climate change impact science and ways to gain influence in policymaking. Community members participated in a series of supported community planning process workshops to collaborate with key agencies and departments on prioritized action plans for Boston's climate change resiliency efforts. To boost attendance, NOAH provided free food, childcare and translation services to residents, many of whom work two or three jobs at or below minimum wage. Community insights proved crucial to the preparation phase of the three-year ClimateCARE resiliency plan. Thirty residents participated in the workshop series and six have been selected as delegates to a working group tasked with deepening inter-agency plans, holding officials accountable on climate change issues and helping inform more residents of the coming changes and challenges. The City of Boston has proven to be a strong and supportive partner, as have Logan Airport and other agencies.

Resident delegate Heather Rents said ClimateCARE has been particularly effective in giving the community influence in policymaking. "We don't always get a seat at the planning table and our voice is not always included," she said. "This program has helped us effectively engage in meaningful conversation with stakeholders from transportation, infrastructure and government agencies."

Founded in 1987, NOAH is a leader in community development and environmental justice advocacy and ClimateCARE serves as another example of engagement with a range of stakeholders. A youth survey following ClimateCARE's initial phase found a sharp increase in storm surge awareness in East Boston. In 2015, NOAH engaged over 2,000 community members in its many environmental campaigns. A waterfront access program provided a safe boating and kayaking clinic with 1,800 local participants. NOAH hopes to build a national model from its supported community planning process to engage communities on climate change awareness and resident-led actions.

Massachusetts–area waters could rise 16 inches by 2050.

Through our experience with ClimateCARE we learned about three effective elements that will be implemented in NOAH's future projects: 1) promoting awareness and understanding residents' concerns through surveys and community meetings to discover what is most relevant to them, 2) facilitating participation by providing services such as translation and childcare, and 3) partnering with city and state agencies to collaborate on effective and feasible action plans.

ABOUT PHIL GIFFEE

Phil Giffee has served as Neighborhood of Affordable Housing's executive director since its founding in 1987. Located in East Boston, NOAH is a regional bilingual nonprofit community development corporation supporting residents in areas such as affordable housing, environmental justice, community planning, leadership and economic development. NOAH serves over 2,000 clients annually, providing assistance on issues including first-time home buying, foreclosure prevention and mitigation counseling, rental housing, financial capability, youth programs, English as a Second Language, senior home safety repairs and environmental action, as well as developing and maintaining affordable housing units.

BUILDING BETTER COMMUNITY IN ONE DAY AT THE FAIR

Deborah White, Executive Director

Mid Central Community Action

Mid Central Community Action (MCCA) serves as the lead agency for the West Bloomington Housing Collaborative (WBHC). The formation of the WBHC in January 2012 brought residents, nonprofit agencies, academic institutions, city government, small businesses and a large corporation together to pursue coordinated strategies and advance revitalization in West Bloomington.

WBHC is guided by the following core values and philosophies:
▸ Communities are based on strengths that can be leveraged.
▸ Residents must be empowered to take ownership of change and revitalization at the individual and systemic levels.
▸ Neighborhoods are lifted up by a safety net woven together by people and organizations working together.
▸ Effective stewardship of shared resources and community trust is vital to our success.
▸ Social change takes steady leadership, passion and time.

The collaborative's overall goal is for every family to live in safe and affordable housing, be financially stable and be engaged in the community. The collaborative launched a Community Innovation Fair, with help from a Neighbor-Works Community Impact Grant, to promote resident engagement in planning West Bloomington's future.

The Community Innovation Fair provided an unusual opportunity for residents and nonprofit organizations to present ideas for West Bloomington at booths at a street fair. Residents and community groups applied to reserve

CHALLENGE
West Bloomington lags economically in the city of Bloomington, IL. After years of disinvestment, the area suffers from complications related to housing, education, unemployment, crime and overall neighborhood quality.

MCAA set out to host a one-time event to help foster innovative ideas for neighborhood revitalization and provide a voice for local residents. But we quickly learned we had created much more.

a booth to highlight entrepreneurial ideas and visions for neighborhood vitality. Applicants were paired with mentors to assist in creation of both their booth and the story of their idea. Ideas focused around neighborhood improvement, community engagement, youth activities, social innovation and small entrepreneurship. The fair booths represented ideas in all stages of development: brainstorming, early development or early implementation.

In our first year, 11 residents and 10 nonprofits hosted booths to showcase their ideas for the neighborhood. Individuals highlighted a catering business; an adopt-a-pot plan to care for street planters; a laundry detergent business that donates one bag of detergent to low-income individuals for every purchase and a "Humans of the Westside" photo project. Fair attendees browsed resident booths, shared feedback and suggestions and voted for the top idea. The first-place resident received $2,500 to jumpstart their idea and the second-place resident received $1,500. The top nonprofit idea also received $2,500.

The fair attracted a large crowd and included a financial fitness game led by State Farm Bank, live musicians and food trucks.

The first Community Innovation Fair successfully turned good ideas into reality.

First place winner, Sisters By Experience, provides guidance and teaches young women the importance of self-love, dedication and determination. The group will use its winning funds to obtain 501(c)(3) status and create marketing materials to highlight their work. Currently, the group hosts monthly meetings, focusing on the strengths of young women in the neighborhood and addressing goals and barriers. Many participating young women will be first generation college students; the group's goal is to provide young women in West Bloomington with the skills they need to succeed in college and beyond.

The Community Innovation Fair's nonprofit winner, the Tool Library, is a free tool lending program designed to empower residents to handle repair and maintenance tasks. The library provides the opportunity for residents to make modifications to their property or complete their projects, allowing them to maintain a feeling of independence and dignity. The nonprofit used their winning funds from the fair to offer workshops for children in local schools and for residents of all ages at the Tool Library.

Street fairs play a significant role in creative branding of a shopping district, main street or business community.

Our organization planned to host a one-time event to help foster innovative ideas for neighborhood revitalization and to provide a voice for local residents. We quickly learned we had started something more valuable than one event. Residents of the neighborhood came together to talk about ideas, enjoy a meal together and celebrate the award winners. West Bloomington is a neighborhood where residents value creative ideas, learn from each other and are committed to neighborhood change.

Planning is underway for this year's Community Innovation Fair, now an annual event. We look forward to celebrating another group of neighborhood innovators who are making a positive difference in West Bloomington.

ABOUT DEBORAH WHITE

Deborah White serves as the executive director of Mid Central Community Action, a non-profit organization whose mission is to educate, equip and empower individuals and families toward financially secure, violence-free lives. MCCA helps people improve their quality of life and living conditions through services related to healthy relationships, healthy finances, healthy homes and healthy neighborhoods. In a typical year, MCCA serves more than 5,000 families.

COMMUNITY BUILDING AND ENGAGEMENT EFFORTS LEAD TO PARK RECLAMATION

Rebecca Reynolds, Executive Director

Little Dixie Community Action Agency

In 2012, Little Dixie Community Action Agency was awarded a grant from the Substance and Mental Health Services Administration to implement a Drug-Free Communities (DFC) program in Choctaw County. Our service area ranked among the highest in the state for drug and alcohol abuse by young people (grades 6 through 12). The primary goal of the DFC program is to raise awareness about the prevalence and dangers of alcohol and drug abuse and to implement strategies to fight it.

Our DFC program director, Michele Frazier, engages area youth in activities that educate them, their peers, parents, teachers and the community as a whole in a fun, interesting and engaging way. She works to redirect youth to more productive activities, which in a very rural area such as Hugo is a challenge. Other than school sports and summer leagues, there is little in terms of recreation for area youth – no skating rinks, movie theaters or rec centers.

Many of the participants also are members of one or more local youth groups. Michele spearheaded an effort to bring them together into a coalition, recognizing they could be more effective if they worked together. Thus, "YouCo!" – the first youth-led coalition in Choctaw County – was founded. The participants visited city council meetings, civic luncheons and community-based organizations to learn how a community operates and identify the various "players". They discovered they loved the discipline of

CHALLENGE
In its prime, Ansley Park offered a place for residents and visitors in Hugo, OK, to gather and enjoy recreation. But the public park fell into disrepair and attracted crime that drove away many families.

"People from every community sector and every background came together and barriers ceased to exist."

— Michele Frazier, park renovation leader

---

community engagement and realized the community they lived in was theirs as well.

To introduce their newly formed coalition to other residents, the members decided to take on a project that was sure to get noticed and positively impact the overall community. That project was named "Take Back Ansley Park". It is the only park available, situated just at the edge of town and featured tennis courts, playground equipment (although old) and a skateboard area. In its heyday, Ansley Park offered recreation and enjoyment for residents and visitors and was frequently used for community-wide events. On any given weekend, one would find families enjoying a picnic or birthday party, and children playing on the merry-go-round or climbing the bigger-than-life, spider-shaped monkey bars. Unfortunately, over time, a slow but steady transformation occurred and the park became more associated with anti-social activity. Other than being mowed by city officials, it was not maintained. A visit to the park would most likely reveal a tableau of empty alcohol containers, crack cocaine vials, needles, cigarette butts, broken glass and trash.

Members of YouCo put together a detailed plan of action, which they presented to the city council. Their presentation was quite elaborate and included visual aids, such as a collage of photos of the park showing beer cans strewn about, graffiti on the benches and picnic shelters, broken playground equipment and even used syringes on the grounds. They informed the council of their plans to repair, renovate and reclaim the park and requested its approval to move forward. The proposal was approved unanimously.

The 25-member youth coalition then launched a marketing campaign to secure resources to carry out its plans. A $15,000 community building and engagement grant from NeighborWorks America was a significant help. Seventy-five volunteers – including youth, Little Dixie employees, city and county officials, state representatives and business leaders – came together and completed the project during the June 2015 NeighborWorks Week.

Over the course of just three days, they transformed the park back into a community amenity. On July 4th, we celebrated the refurbishment of Ansley Park, including the dedication of the future site of the Choctaw County Veterans Monument. Since the project's completion, there have been no reported crimes in the area, the park remains clean, and children and families use it daily.

More than 14,000 volunteers participated in NeighborWorks Week 2016.

ABOUT REBECCA REYNOLDS

Rebecca Reynolds is the executive director of the Little Dixie Community Action Agency, where she has served since 1994. Founded in 1968, LDCAA is a nonprofit organization that provides economic and tourism development and educational services. The organization also manages parks, marina and resorts. In addition, LDCAA offers home loans and homeownership training assistance services. The organization has more than 200 employees and is a member of the NeighborWorks America Network.

BUILDING A COMMUNITY FROM THE GROUND UP

Robert Tourigny, Executive Director

NeighborWorks Southern New Hampshire

The neighborhood of West Granite in Manchester, NH was already troubled in 2006 when the property tax rate for multifamily homes skyrocketed. The following year oil prices tripled and in 2008 the housing crisis and recession hit, causing many landlords to abandon their properties. Diane Bourque, a resident of West Granite, says the neighborhood went from bad to worse beginning in the spring of 2006.

"That was when someone threatened to shoot my daughter," she says. "That was the height of the trouble in the neighborhood. People were selling drugs and there were fights in the street."

That summer the Manchester Police Department asked Bourque to start a neighborhood watch group. And that fall, she joined the Community Services Committee of NeighborWorks Southern New Hampshire along with other concerned neighbors and property owners recruited by our organization to address quality-of-life issues. They soon identified West Granite as one of Manchester's most troubled areas and started to lay groundwork for greater investment in the area. They addressed everything from trash and graffiti to negligent property owners and helped organize neighborhood cleanups and block parties.

The challenges were acute: In 2008, 77 percent of residents rented and two-thirds of their landlords lived outside the neighborhood, according to a committee survey. The vacancy rate was around 25 percent, compared to eight percent for Manchester as a whole. Only nine percent of those surveyed felt the condition of their neighbor's homes added value to their own.

CHALLENGE

The West Granite neighborhood of Manchester, NH was full of abandoned properties and even occupied properties were in serious disrepair in 2008. In addition, a neighborhood survey revealed that residents felt unsafe. The neighborhood needed reinvestment to clean up the buildings and instill a sense of neighborhood pride.

"When you take properties which are full of crime and absolute filth and turn them into some of the nicest around, you change the feel of the entire neighborhood"

— Pastor Rich Clegg, Grace Haven Baptist Church

The lack of investment was exacerbated by the 2008 housing crisis. Outside of a few dedicated residents fighting against the decay, the neighborhood was characterized by vacant buildings, rising crime rates and declining property values.

NeighborWorks Southern New Hampshire supported Bourque's neighborhood watch and helped a local pastor organize a community center for kids and other residents.

"Pastor Rich Clegg and Assistant Pastor Matt Hasty, who led Grace Haven Baptist Church, a small storefront church on the corner of Granite and West streets, made our efforts to organize in that community much easier," said Will Stewart, a former community building specialist for NeighborWorks Southern New Hampshire. "Their relationships with residents were critical in helping us establish trust and credibility in the neighborhood. Additionally, Rich and Matt were very generous with their space, allowing the church to be used as a staging ground for everything from neighborhood block parties to nonpartisan voter registration efforts."

Both Bourque and Clegg served extended terms as committee members and moved to the organization's Board of Directors.

In addition to these grassroots efforts, NeighborWorks Southern New Hampshire targeted several properties on the West Side for reclamation and revitalization. One property in particular, 414 Granite Street, was a real problem. "At some hours of the day the place right across from the church was like a McDonald's drive thru with the amount of people coming in and out buying drugs," Clegg recalls. "When you take properties which are full of crime and absolute filth and turn them into some of the nicest around, you change the feel of the entire neighborhood. These were once scary, unwelcoming places, and now when you drive by you might see the property owner out working on the yard or his kids out playing in the snow. That is how you change attitudes and begin to turn things around."

Over the next seven years, NeighborWorks Southern New Hampshire pooled more than $5 million from federal, municipal and corporate sources to revitalize the neighborhood and increase the homeowner occupancy rate. The deeds require owners to live in the properties, ensuring the purchasers and all future owners are committed to investing in their new community.

NeighborWorks Southern New Hampshire acquired 11 of the most blighted properties in the area, containing 32 of the city's worst rental units. Addressing the concerns of residents, we managed to reduce the density and increase off-street parking and open space in the neighborhood, leaving nine properties with a total of 21 units. In addition, by eliminating one of these problem properties, we were able to create much needed additional parking at a nearby senior center. The reclamation of these neglected properties from havens for crime supported other neighborhood quality of life changes.

In 2014, a property crime occurred every 3.8 seconds in the U.S.

In 2013, the Community Services Committee conducted another survey of the neighborhood: Two-thirds of respondents said they would recommend the neighborhood to others and 75 percent said they had some satisfaction in their community.

The West Granite success occurred over time – the result of dedicated volunteers, funders and residents who care about their community, like Bourque and Clegg.

"It may seem like an easy thing to say now, but the fact is everything we have accomplished on the west side is due entirely to the input we received from these passionate city residents," said Jennifer Vadney, neighborhood development manager for NeighborWorks Southern New Hampshire. "This kind of grassroots organization really guided us and it provides us with a great template as we look to continue our work in other neighborhoods."

We learned that engaging residents to improve their own community is essential to success.

ABOUT ROBERT TOURIGNY

Robert Tourigny, executive director of NeighborWorks Southern New Hampshire, joined the organization in May 2005, bringing more than 20 years of experience in urban and rural housing development that covers homeownership, multi-family and single-family development, home repair and weatherization and rental management.

A NEW PARK PAVILION BRINGS COMMUNITY TOGETHER

Mark Dahlquist, Executive Director

NeighborWorks Pocatello

Since 1993, NeighborWorks Pocatello (NWP) has built more than 150 new homes and completed over 300 home improvement projects. The progressive alliance in southeast Idaho between residents, business, and government revitalizes targeted areas by promoting affordable housing and community pride by establishing vital, healthy neighborhoods.

NeighborWorks Pocatello recognizes that truly revitalizing a neighborhood means doing much more than building and renovating homes. It means paying attention to things like enhancing curb appeal and bringing more balance in housing values throughout the community. Perhaps most important of all is community building - organizing and supporting grassroots efforts by residents to make the quality of life in their neighborhoods the best it can be.

As NPW neared its 20th anniversary, the organization wanted a significant, visible and permanent way to mark the milestone; one that would raise awareness about its accomplishments and promote its services. A committee formed to consider options and recognized the need for a covered structure in Caldwell Park, a 2.5-acre city green space without any shelter. Initially discussion focused on replicating a gazebo from another city park, but after much discussion it was decided that what was really needed was a more impressive structure that blended well with the historic neighborhood surrounding Caldwell Park. This would be in keeping with the organization's mission to preserve an area's character while building new homes in established neighborhoods.

CHALLENGE

For more than 20 years, NeighborWorks Pocatello (NWP) in southeast Idaho successfully revitalized communities, but without support from local residents it could never fulfill its goals. NWP sought a way to demonstrate its commitment to the community and raise awareness about the organization as it marked a significant milestone.

An architect offered options for an imposing yet complementary pavilion. Ultimately, two building architects and a landscape architect joined the effort at no cost, offering their services because they saw the project would add value to the community. The new pavilion completed in 2014 features 1,500 square feet of covered space and includes power hook-ups, lighting and full accessibility for people with disabilities. New landscaping surrounds the structure and a grassy slope offer spectators a place to gather for performances or community events.

The NeighborWorks Pocatello pavilion is triangular with three supporting pillars representing the three sectors that make up the organization: residents, business and government. The color scheme was carefully selected to complement the surrounding neighborhood. The copper-colored roof even corresponds to the roof of another nearby historic building.

Now more visitors come to Caldwell Park thanks to the new pavilion, which frequently hosts concerts, family re-unions and weddings. An inscription in the pavilion's granite reads: "Providing shelter to all, the NeighborWorks Pavilion stands as evidence that being a good neighbor works – for the individual, the neighborhood and the community."

With much help from neighborhood leaders and multiple generous funders, the organization completed the project in less than two years. To cover the pavilion's $127,000 cost, NWP first had to secure a lead donor. Fortunately, the private Ifft Foundation, which supports community beautification efforts in southeast Idaho, stepped forward with a $10,000 seed grant and later awarded more grants totaling $40,000. NeighborWorks Pocatello committed $10,000 of its own funds in the initial phase and this combined early funding facilitated efforts to secure other donors. Potential funders were now able to see the project as viable. In an effort to encourage and recognize smaller donors, those in the $100 range, two large granite plaques with donors' names were placed on the pavilion columns. This method secured a total of 125 smaller donors. Many of these new donors had never contributed to housing programs, but the pavilion motivated them to support NeighborWorks Pocatello.

Many valuable lessons were learned through this process. First and foremost, devising and completing a public project creates excitement and collaboration in the community and promotes goodwill toward your organization. Many prospective donors who would not initially contribute to bread-and-butter programs like housing will start to do so as they come to understand the organization's broader mission. Including residents affected by the project also generates significant support and resources. Finally, set standards high and never lose enthusiasm for telling the community why you are here and how you make a difference.

> **Since 1993, NeighborWorks Pocatello has built more than 150 new homes and completed more than 300 home improvement projects.**

ABOUT MARK DAHLQUIST

Mark Dahlquist has been the NeighborWorks Pocatello executive director since 2007. Previously, he worked in various capacities at Farmers Insurance, including underwriting, marketing and management. Dahlquist served as president of the Homeless and Housing Coalition of Southeast Idaho, a board member for the National NeighborWorks Association, president of Portneuf Valley Pride and is the chair of the Pocatello/Chubbuck Beautification Council.

PHOTO VOICE: NURTURING COMMUNITY ENGAGEMENT THROUGH THE CREATIVE PROCESS

Ludy Biddle, Executive Director

NeighborWorks of Western Vermont

In 2012, a shocking drug-related car accident took the life a young woman just exiting her place of work in Rutland, VT. The incident became a call to action – a symbol of the unprecedented toll the drug epidemic had taken on the city. In response, the community took an all-hands-on-deck approach to bettering the city, with innovative programs in mental health, education, law enforcement and other areas. It was collectively known as Project Vision.

NeighborWorks of Western Vermont focuses on rehabilitating blighted properties and creating parks in an area of northwest Rutland struggling with drugs, crime and poverty. We organized cookouts and block parties and helped build community gardens in an effort to involve the community in the process of change. But our efforts did not engage residents to the degree we had hoped.

The Photo Voice Project was conceived as a way to change this dynamic. The concept was to provide a group of locals with the tools necessary to communicate resident experiences through photography – to show others the neighborhood through their eyes.

We identified nine residents interested in the project, armed each of them with a digital camera and technical training, and asked them to tell the story of their neigh-

CHALLENGE

Can community engagement, pride and cohesiveness be achieved through an artistic project that puts digital cameras and training in the hands of residents in a Rutland, Vermont neighborhood struggling with drugs, crime and poverty?

Photo Voice participants were not censored in any way. They were, in fact, encouraged to tell the truth as they saw it: the good, the bad and the ugly.

borhood. We sought all ages, all backgrounds and varied perspectives. The final nine included a high school teacher, a mediator, two sisters in middle school, a city alderwoman, a retired artisan stonecutter, a resident of a home for transitioning former prisoners and a high school student.

We asked that each participant select several of their most meaningful images and exhibit them along with a written artist statement.

We enlisted local artist Donna Goodhale as a photographer to train and support the participants. Though we asked Goodhale to donate an hour every week, she ended up contributing many more hours. Not only did she provide technical instruction, she also guided and supported the participants' creative process.

Goodhale helped facilitate regular group forums, which fostered creative growth and helped participants appreciate different perspectives. Remarks such as, "I never looked at it that way before" were common in these meetings. She became both mentor and art teacher.

Participants were not censored in any way. They were, in fact, encouraged to tell the truth as they saw it: the good, the bad and the ugly. This meant that there were some difficult and emotional conversations regarding different experiences – and perceptions – of the community. Yet there was a catharsis to this conflict: Participants built strong bonds with each other and felt an investment in each other's success.

It wasn't just the bonds between the participants that nurtured new community engagement, it was the very exercise of paying attention to the details of the community. The daily grind of family responsibilities, school and work can disconnect anyone from their immediate surroundings - the most disturbing elements, as well as the most beautiful. The participants soon discovered that, among other things, a camera can be a powerful tool for making people pay attention.

Photographers engaged with people when they took photographs. They had to get signed waivers from people they photographed, which often forced them to interact with new people.

The most gratifying part of the project is seeing the continued positive change in the lives of those involved and in providing community uplift and inspiration. It is a source of pride for the community. The exhibitions garnered interest from major publications and the photos have been shown at the Chafee Gallery, The Vermont Folk Life Center, Rutland Regional Medical Center and the Vermont State Capitol.

Pictures from the Photo Voice project have been shown at the Chafee Gallery, Vermont Folk Life Center and the Vermont State Capitol.

All the participants have attended at least one of the public events about their work and they are always excited to connect with other photographers from the group. The resident of Dismas House, transitioning back into society from prison, has thrived since participating in the project, finding full-time work and encouraging his peers to give back to the community. He attended a recent groundbreaking in the neighborhood along with other participants.

We learned that impact of Photo Voice could be larger than anticipated. The project was the first collaborative effort of Project Vision and its success was a powerful validation of its mission. Photo Voice inspired a similar project in another section of Rutland and has garnered interest from Middlebury College, which sponsored a recent public discussion in the Sociology Department.

ABOUT LUDY BIDDLE

Ludy Biddle is executive director of NeighborWorks of Western Vermont, managing strategic growth and collaborative efforts in Vermont and nationwide. Biddle is a member of The Development Council at the Federal Reserve Bank of Boston and previously held positions at the National Endowment for the Arts and the Folger Shakespeare Library.

MOBILIZING THE COMMUNITY TOWARD A PLAN FOR ACTION

Michael Renken, CEO
Patricia Anderson-Sifuentez, Community Builder

NeighborWorks Lincoln

Lincoln, NE has many beautiful old homes, some dating back 100 years or more. But as people moved from the city center, their homes were converted to rental properties, stripping them of their historic character and filling the neighborhoods with poorly maintained buildings. The change brought a severe increase in density, poor maintenance, crumbling infrastructure and a decline in the community's quality of life. Some stalwart residents loved the old homes in the urban center, as well as the close proximity to the city, the walkability and history. In the 1970s and 80s, residents started organizing to revitalize the neighborhoods. Unfortunately, those efforts proved an uphill battle.

NeighborWorks Lincoln (NWL) was founded 30 years ago, with a mission "to keep Lincoln safe and prosperous by revitalizing neighborhoods and promoting homeownership." The organization operates throughout the city but focuses primarily in high poverty areas. These areas are the most diverse in the city, with significant refugee populations and high rental housing ratios ranging from 60-96 percent of the total housing stock.

As resident organizations fought to be recognized and have a voice in decisions about their neighborhoods, their frustration grew. Our staff members were frustrated when efforts to address health and building code violations had short-term effects or were ignored. They soon realized that neighborhood organizations were concerned with the same issues but lacked a unified voice to influ-

CHALLENGE

Many homes in the oldest neighborhoods in Lincoln, NE were converted to poorly maintained apartments. Some residents wanted to preserve the old homes and crumbling neighborhoods, but building an effective coalition to effect change in the highly diverse community, where 90 percent of the properties were rentals, proved daunting.

A broad spectrum of residents, business owners, landlords, stakeholders and city staff provided input into a unified Neighborhood Plan for Action.

ence policy changes and have a broad, long-term impact. In 2008, NWL and the neighborhood groups joined to form the Lincoln Policy Network (LPN).

The network brought together representatives from nearly 30 independent neighborhood associations to develop a unified neighborhood plan for action. Neighborhood leaders identified priorities to demand action from city staff and elected officials to stabilize and improve Lincoln communities.

A broad spectrum of residents, business owners, landlords, stakeholders and city staff provided input in the plan's drafts, which the neighborhood associations took to their boards. In the end, 27 neighborhood associations supported the final version, which garnered local media attention. Copies of the plan have been sent to the mayor and to city council meetings, elected officials are frequently invited to the network's monthly meetings and city staff are available to assist in problem solving.

Mayoral aide Jon D. Carson says the plan backed by so many wide-ranging neighborhood groups is fundamental to understanding the community's priorities. "There's no doubt that it has helped shape policy, programming and budgetary discussions within city hall and beyond," he said.

The network often educates the public through creative means. For example, while seeking to address abandoned, dilapidated properties, NWL hosted "problem property potlucks" at the blighted sites. This led to the city's first Neglected Property Ordinance, which registers relevant properties and imposes fines on the owners. To raise awareness about the campaign, NWL held a Halloween "Blight Fright Open House" at a dilapidated property slated for demolition. It was in such poor condition that only five people at a time were allowed to tour the house for safety. A few questioned the need for demolition, but once inside the crooked house, no one disagreed. Other successes include a six-inch weed height ordinance, support for increased code violation fines, an anti-graffiti ordinance, performance-based code inspections, mandatory garbage pick-up and a ban on couches stored outside.

The Lincoln Policy Network learned the importance of bringing together a broad coalition to realize significant change. Crafting a detailed plan for executing that change was also key – as was patience. It took nearly a year to write the plan and present it to the community businesses, stakeholders, city officials and neighborhood associations. It took more hard work to build the essential consensus among stakeholders, who can make or break a project.

NeighborWorks Lincoln hosted "problem property potlucks" to address abandoned, dilapidated properties.

ABOUT MICHAEL RENKEN

Michael Renken is CEO of NeighborWorks New Lincoln, a nonprofit organization dedicated to community revitalization through an active partnership of resident leaders, private businesses and public officials. Continually opening doors for people to achieve their dreams of home ownership and for others who desire a safe and attractive neighborhood, under Renken's leadership, New Lincoln is poised for more history making success.

A COMMUNITY ENGAGEMENT MODEL THAT IS TRANSFORMING THE OPERATING CULTURE OF A COMMUNITY

J. Michael Pitchford, President & CEO
Luann Tia Blount, Vice President of External Relations
Khyati Desai-Seltzer, Director of Resident Engagement

———

Community Preservation and Development Corp.

In 1995, Community Preservation and Development Corporation (CPDC) acquired Edgewood Terrace in NE Washington, D.C., an apartment community with nearly 800 homes and more than 1,000 residents. In the early 90s, Edgewood Terrace was nicknamed "Little Beirut" because of the level of violence and disinvestment. Although CPDC specializes in tackling complex development projects, Edgewood proved to be one of our greatest challenges. Extensive renovations were required across the massive 11-building campus. But more difficult to address was a resident population that struggled with low literacy rates, unemployment, substance abuse and other issues.

Following the acquisition of the campus, CPDC completely revitalized property, partnered with residents and police to address safety concerns and brought in a range of programs, services and amenities. These transformations, among others, caused Edgewood Terrace to become CPDC's flagship community, earning national recognition as the first affordable housing community in D.C. to offer free Internet access to residents – an effort made possible in partnership with Microsoft Corporation. Edgewood was also widely recognized for its early investments in programs geared toward technology, youth development, adult literacy, workforce development and senior care.

CHALLENGE

Deep-rooted social ills including poverty, crime, substandard housing and inadequate economic resources are often intertwined and can significantly impact how members of a community interact and behave. Sometimes making physical renovations to a property and providing resident services can begin to shift the culture of a community, but sometimes it's not enough.

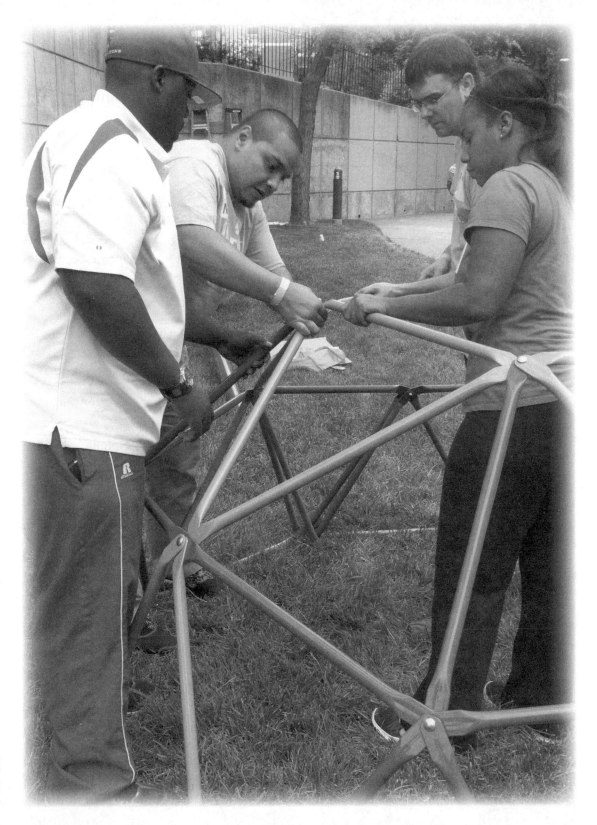

Edgewood Terrace became CPDC's flagship community, earning national recognition as the first affordable housing community in DC to offer free Internet access to residents.

Despite these early successes, social issues and division persisted at Edgewood. A walk across the property revealed a campus separated by fences left over from an earlier renovation; residents avoiding eye contact with one another and being reluctant to use playgrounds and other outdoor amenities; and little to no interaction between residents and the staff charged with keeping the community clean, safe and in compliance.

In 2013, the 20-year housing assistance payment contract at Edgewood Terrace was up for renewal. There were also market forces in the broader Edgewood-Brookland neighborhood pushing for the

conversion of affordable units to be available at market rate. Likewise, the entire Edgewood campus – four separately financed deals – was in need of its next revitalization.

CPDC began planning a $50 million reinvestment to upgrade units, renovate the buildings' interiors and exteriors, remove physical barriers on the property, and add new features such as a fitness trail, a community garden, and water features designed to bring residents and community members together. The community was rebranded as "Edgewood Commons" with the goal to create an economically diverse community and, most importantly, address the operating culture through trust-building and collaborative action.

To help shift the pattern of social beliefs, behaviors, norms and habits of those living and working at Edgewood, CPDC collaborated with Trusted Space Partners, a company focused on creating positive change at the community level, to develop the ONE Edgewood Network. This innovative community engagement model connects resident to resident, resident to neighbor, and resident to CPDC staff and property management. Through the Network, CPDC removes barriers, builds trust, and enhances residents' quality of life, creating a greater and deeper sense of community.

CPDC has been successful at beginning to change the environment and culture at Edgewood Commons as a result of the Network. Residents now take consistent self-directed actions to improve the physical and social environment. Examples include: an active community network with over

150 active resident members; 40 residents consistently participate in monthly community meetings; the introduction of 40 resident-led initiatives; residents applied for (and won) a $2,000 NeighborWorks Community Building Grant to increase the involvement of 16-24 year olds at Edgewood and one resident was appointed Advisory Neighborhood Commissioner for the local Ward in D.C.

17% of all Americans lack access to adequate broadband service.

CPDC's strategy involved a four-step process and reflects the lessons learned through developing and implementing this model:

1) Understand the importance of an interdependent vs. an altruistic framework: Shifting away from the notion that "poor people need professionals to provide them with housing and social programs to pursue a quality life" and embracing the belief that to create high quality places to live and work, it is important to recognize that everyone in a given eco-system (residents, staff, partners) has something to contribute and is interdependent on one another to achieve high-quality living.

2) Seek to change the operating culture instead of starting a new program: Focusing our efforts on listening, developing relationships, building trust and understanding the underlying issues behind how we operate as opposed to prescribing 'interventions.'

3) Introduce new spaces and practices with quality, zest and consistency: Creating highly intentional and efficient spaces in which to practice new behaviors and to spark individual and collective action. We also make room for small groups and "in-between" relationship building, follow up, and consistent opportunities to invite others into the space.

4) Form a network (which includes everyone) and not a resident organization: Cultivating a diverse network involving residents, staff, partners and neighbors to increase synergy and greater outcomes.

In short, when these actions work together, a community is stronger and Edgewood Commons is proof.

ABOUT J. MICHAEL PITCHFORD

J. Michael Pitchford is president and CEO of Community Preservation and Development Corp., a not-for-profit developer that acquires, redevelops, constructs and operates affordable housing communities across Washington, D.C., Maryland and Virginia. For more than 25 years, CPDC has increased the stock of affordable housing in the Mid-Atlantic region and today owns and operates more than 5,000 residential apartments serving nearly 10,000 residents. The organization's portfolio has a total development value approaching $500 million. Its site-based programs, services and partnerships in local communities help residents thrive and spur development and opportunity.

THE POWER OF A STICKY NOTE

Margarita de Escontrias, CEO

—

Cabrillo Economic Development Corp.

Cabrillo Economic Development Corporation (CEDC) provides comprehensive housing services and community economic development activities through a holistic community-centered approach that encourages self-sufficiency for individuals and families who are most lacking in opportunity in Ventura and Santa Barbara Counties, as well in adjacent areas in Los Angeles County.

In the spring of 2015 our Community Building and Neighborhood Revitalization (CBNR) team assessed service obligations and social trends at our twenty-four affordable housing developments throughout Ventura County. Our team met with our diverse community members including seniors, farm workers, low-income and special needs households and developed a strategy to prioritize fundamental programs and services and enhance communication throughout the entire portfolio. We wanted to understand what programs and services had the greatest impact to our residents and why. We thought using resident surveys would be the most efficient and direct means of getting resident input.

The surveys we used to assess future program and service development were surprisingly unsuccessful. This was the first time our staff developed a plan of action with our residents and, as we later discovered, it was the first time our residents were asked to share an opinion regarding their ideas, interests or goals. This was especially true in our farm worker communities. Residents often felt they would negatively impact their housing if they answered a question incorrectly or shared too much information with the staff. When a staff member asked "What types of programs or services would you like to see at your property?" - the room was silent. Without a previously estab-

CHALLENGE

Cabrillo Economic Development Corp.'s challenge was to become a one-stop shop for resident services that would require changes in our organizational culture and input from residents about their needs and preferences. We needed to strengthen our partnerships and work harder to know our residents.

The sticky note provided an opportunity for our residents to be heard without actually speaking and to interact, to share, to participate, to vote, to request— all while not being ridiculed or belittled.

lished relationship or connection to our communities, our team did not have the necessary sense of trust developed to pose these questions. The goal of this forum was to create a sense of trust between CEDC and our residents and indirectly increase the opportunity to create stronger connections to available opportunities, resources and social networks.

While we continually use informal feedback from residents to shape our programs, we decided to take a more formal and quantifiable approach. In order to make the most of these forums, our

CBNR team distributed identical sticky notes to every resident in the room. Our team re-asked the initial question, "What types of programs or services would you like to see at your property?" But now we said, "Write down your answer on your sticky note. When you are finished, raise your hand and we will collect them." We went from zero responses to 19 responses.

Thus the sticky note provided an opportunity for our residents to be heard without actually speaking and to interact, to share, to participate, to vote, to request – all while not being ridiculed or belittled. The sticky note created a safe space where all ideas and suggestions were welcome. Through this process, we learned that our residents were interested in educational programs such as children's programs, health programs and English as a Second Language. Our residents all shared the same desire: to learn. By working collaboratively with residents, we identified assets and strengths of the community itself and we were able to implement changes to engage residents.

This reciprocal approach to community building provided an opportunity for our residents to develop recommendations that reflected the character and values of their communities. These interactions allowed communities to improve the quality of life and character of their neighborhoods by incorporating their diverse cultural backgrounds. The result was a three-part phased implementation strategy with a progression of activities that starts by identifying our core service audience – CEDC residents – and ends with inclusive, data-driven strategic and resource planning based on the input from residents gathered in the sticky notes.

How can your organization engage residents in a creative way?

In phase one, we developed Service Planning Areas around each property in our portfolio throughout Ventura County, focusing first on most commonly underserved communities. We used Google mapping technology to identify pre-existing assets in the community, such as schools, libraries, community organizations and places of worship within one-fourth of a mile of a CEDC property. We were able to leverage existing contributions to the community and establish a stronger relationship with potential partners. We now prioritize children's programs and health-related classes programs and work more closely with local universities and health care providers to ensure we can offer programs on a regular basis.

Throughout this process we learned two lessons: 1) we needed to know more about our residents and 2) we needed a more strategic approach to our partnerships. The sticky note proved to be the key to creating and adopting a new strategy: after having our discussion forums with our residents, we had a better idea of what was actually happening in each of our communities. Therefore, every strategic planning meeting with partners was much more intentional; we had a stronger understanding of our expectations, shared responsibilities, goals and outcomes.

ABOUT MARGARITA DE ESCONTRIAS

Margarita de Escontrias, CEO of Cabrillo Economic Development Corporation (CEDC), a nonprofit community housing development organization in Ventura, CA, has worked in the public sector for 30 years specializing in underserved urban and rural communities. She has worked on issues related to poverty, housing and homeless services and has community development experience, particularly specializing in affordable housing, urban infill and transit-oriented development projects. CEDC developed 24 communities totaling over 1,100 units and serves over 3,000 residents.

PRESERVING AFFORDABILITY IN A GENTRIFYING NEIGHBORHOOD THROUGH COMMUNITY BUILDING AND ENGAGEMENT

Mary Lawler, Executive Director
Jenifer Wagley, Deputy Director

Avenue Community Development Corp.

Avenue provides affordable housing and homebuyer education for low and moderate-income families in the Near Northside of Houston, where the predominantly Hispanic population of 25,000 struggles with cycles of generational poverty: one-third of residents live below the poverty line. Quality affordable housing is scarce, disparities in health and educational outcomes are pronounced and the area lacks vibrant commercial hubs which can offer reliable employment opportunities. However, Near Northside also has great potential for revitalization due to Houston's population growth, the extension of light rail into the neighborhood and the area's proximity to downtown. Redevelopment is accelerating.

New construction and rising housing costs put increasing pressure on low-income families to move to distant suburbs, farther from employment centers and their supportive social networks, leaving the benefits of redevelopment to newcomers. Low-income communities need a comprehensive revitalization strategy to address these issues.

In 2009, Avenue launched an intensive community building and engagement initiative, implemented as part

CHALLENGE

Blighted low-income areas in Houston offer attractive opportunities for developers, but luxury townhomes change the character of historic neighborhoods and threaten to displace residents. Avenue Community Development Corp.'s challenge is to help low-income families remain in their neighborhoods and enable them to participate in the community's revitalization.

"With time and results, I realized that people really do have the power to make a difference so long as they are willing to exercise that power and fight for change."

– Gwen Guidy, resident of 28 years

of GO Neighborhoods, Houston Local Initiatives Support Corp.'s Building Sustainable Communities program. Avenue engaged residents in identifying changes they wanted to see in their neighborhood, provided them with tools to advocate for resources and supported them in revitalizing the community according to their vision. Avenue provides guidance and staff support to resident-led teams. With the help of NeighborWorks America and other partners, over 14,000 volunteers have implemented more than 200 community-led projects which have leveraged over $64 million of investment. Seven teams attended the annual NeighborWorks Community Leadership Institute and those teams created numerous programs benefitting the community.

Two initiatives illustrate the community's success in preserving affordability:

1) Minimum lot size protections: Over the past three years, residents organized numerous campaigns to advocate for minimum lot size designations in single-family residential areas, preventing the subdivision of lots for townhouse development. The designations protect over 1,200 properties in Near Northside, a great success in preserving the neighborhood's historic character and keeping housing affordable.

2) Volunteer home repair program: In 2014, Avenue partnered with residents and the nonprofit Rebuilding Together Houston to start a volunteer home repair program for very low-income senior, veteran and disabled homeowners. "Rebuilding Northside Together" has preserved existing housing stock by rehabilitating 35 homes so far with the help of hundreds of community volunteers.

The initial listening and planning phase of the community building and engagement initiative created the foundation for success. This phase brought residents together in thoughtful discussion, revealed common concerns and helped them find their voice to address those concerns.

Once residents participated in – and succeeded at – just one initiative of importance to them, they were better prepared for future civic participation. Over time, residents broadened their vision and turned their collective talents from smaller-scale projects to wider efforts.

Avenue learned that two elements are essential to their success: a shared leadership model and ongoing development of resident leadership skills. With shared leadership, all community members participating in the group have equal standing; meeting leadership rotates between members, and project responsibilities are shared. Community actions are taken only after consensus is built, rather than as a result of voting, where the majority decides for the group and the minority has to go along.

Since 2009, more than 14,000 volunteers have implemented more than 200 community-led projects— leveraging more than $64 million in investment.

Extensive staff time is required to nurture the skills and processes of shared leadership, but ongoing mentorship helps community leaders manage this sometimes challenging process to produce collaborative, resilient plans that are backed by the community and have greater potential to succeed.

To create a pipeline of residents engaged in Near Northside, Avenue is building on the train-the-trainers 'each one teach one' concept in its leadership training, so that each resident who gets involved learns to lead and to pass these skills on to others.

To share leadership in the larger community, Avenue has trained other nonprofits to be conveners for GO Teams within their programmatic focus, such as family income and wealth, education and health. These organizations offer critical expertise and resources to residents and are engaged at a new level with the communities they serve.

Through robust community engagement and community-led programming, Avenue seeks to provide a replicable model for creating healthy, vibrant and economically diverse neighborhoods in other areas of Houston.

ABOUT MARY LAWLER

Mary Lawler, executive director of Avenue CDC since 1996, serves on the Executive Advisory Board for Bauer College of Business Graduate Real Estate Program at University of Houston, the Advisory Council for Nonprofit Management Program at University of Houston Downtown, the Board of the Greater Northside Management District and the Real Estate Advisory Committee for NeighborWorks America. She is a delegate to Super Neighborhood Council 51 and is a member of the International Women's Forum.

PUTTING RACE AND SOCIAL EQUITY AT THE CENTER

Tony To, Executive Director

HomeSight

To promote equitable growth in the greater Seattle region, HomeSight organized a collaborative in 2010 that advocated for a race and social equity focus in the region's Sustainable Communities Planning grant from the U.S. Department of Housing and Urban Development. Known as the Growing Transit Communities (GTC) program, the grant supported a regional process to plan development around the area's light rail system, which had just opened with one central line in 2009 and other rapid transit. HomeSight secured 15 percent or $750,000 of the $5 million award to create, organize and staff the Puget Sound Regional Equity Network (REN) to engage a broad range of community members and drive community-led, equitable strategies for transit-oriented development.

Puget Sound Regional Equity Network and the influence it had on the transit planning program became a national model for resourcing and structuring equitable growth efforts. Putting equity at the center of the process meant that, instead of the usual planning processes where community members are relegated to one committee, we shifted the structure so that every committee had community representation. REN members were also placed in leadership positions. Tony To, REN co-chair and HomeSight's executive director, served as vice chair of the program and network members served on committees that developed equitable transit-oriented development strategies. Through this structure, race and social equity perspectives were threaded throughout all conversations instead of being relegated to one space outside of the major discussions.

CHALLENGE

Low-income communities and those populated with people of color are often excluded from government planning and when growth comes to these neighborhoods it benefits wealthier new residents and harms long-term residents and businesses. Rising costs and the loss of culturally relevant services often drive these residents from their own neighborhoods.

Through this structure, race and social equity perspectives were threaded throughout all conversations instead of being relegated to one space, often outside of the major discussions.

The Puget Sound Regional Equity Network grew into a cross-sector coalition of 40 community-based organizations in three counties engaged in health, housing, community development, youth organizing and small business organizing. The network developed a vision statement and set of principles that provided a foundation for many of the transit-oriented development strategies adopted by the GTC program partners to guide equitable development around light rail.

Broad community engagement and organizing were key strategies used by the network to identify community assets, equity concerns and community-driven solutions. In addition to securing community representation in all aspects of the planning program, the network developed an innovative Equity Grant Program and organized the first Puget Sound Equity Summit to support broad community conversation and engagement in the GTC program.

The REN Equity Grant Program didn't simply bring new voices to the planning table, it changed the entire concept of what constitutes the planning table; especially when contrasted with typical planning processes that seek engagement solely through formal public meetings which are often one-way communications. Instead, the network built relationships with community-based organizations and, through small grants, supported the work these organizations were already doing to advance race and social equity in their communities. REN invested $450,000 through small grants of $5,000 to $15,000 to 29 community-based organizations working along the transit corridors in King, Pierce and Snohomish counties on a range of organizing, research and outreach projects. By building these relationships with community-based organizations, supporting the work they were already doing and connecting them with a broader network, we fostered deeper conversations about the real issues communities face, highlighted community-led approaches and identified needed resources and strategies. The grant investments leveraged an additional $574,500 in community resources.

Puget Sound Regional Equity Network organized the first Puget Sound Equity Summit in November 2013, which brought together more than 400 community members, policymakers, public agency staff, philanthropists and other stakeholders to share strategies and connect with other organizing efforts. It identified cross-sector equity issues and efforts throughout the region including education, jobs, housing, health, transportation, environment, safety, youth concerns and preventing displacement.

Puget Sound Equality Summit brought together more than 400 cross-sector stakeholders in 2013.

By shifting the structure of the planning process, redefining the planning table and providing community grants and spaces for connecting, REN met low-income and people of color communities where they were and effectively opened the planning process to their perspectives. As a result of this holistic and inclusive framework, race and social equity is central to a set of 200 strategies that were adopted to guide equitable development along transit corridors.

In addition, the network's work with GTC partners and jurisdictions has resulted in: 1) a new Regional Equitable Development Initiative Fund that will provide financing for land acquisition around light rail to preserve or develop affordable housing and community anchors, 2) a new requirement passed by the state legislature requiring development of affordable housing on transit agency properties at light rail stations and 3) the development of an equity analysis in the City of Seattle's Comprehensive Plan update.

Puget Sound Regional Equity Network's experience illustrates the following lessons learned: 1) planning processes can fully include of people of color and low-income communities by providing resources and creating a structure that supports community engagement and 2) full inclusion changes outcomes. Instead of typical planning recommendations focused solely on physical infrastructure needs, the REN process put people at the center and resulted in strategies that will create opportunities in communities.

ABOUT TONY TO

Tony To worked at HomeSight beginning in1990 as a project manager and became the executive director in 2004. He served as the vice chair of the Regional Growing Transit Communities Partnership and also as co-chair of the Regional Equity Network (REN) Steering Committee and now serves as REN's representative to the Puget Sound Regional Council's Regional Transit Oriented Development Advisory Committee. He served on the Washington State Affordable Housing Advisory Board as the nonprofit developer representative for the past nine years and for two terms on the Seattle Planning Commission, where he was elected the chair in 2009.

OPERATION RENOVATION: HELPING VETERANS SAVE THEIR HOMES

Ronald E. Miller, *Executive Director*
Kelley Coates, *Director of Neighborhood Building*

Neighborhood Housing Services of Greater Berks, Inc.

An estimated 21 million veterans live in the United States, many in their 60s and 70s and living on fixed incomes. While homelessness is a critical problem for many former service members, a large majority do own homes thanks to loans and services from the Veterans' Administration. But that assistance can fall short for some veterans who cannot afford to maintain their homes or make them accessible for those with disabilities. Roughly one million veterans who own their own homes are critically burdened by the cost. Greater Berks County in Southeastern Pennsylvania, home to 29,000 veterans, has many communities that are financially distressed and battle problems such as poverty, inadequate housing and blight. Many veterans in these communities live in dilapidated homes or face homelessness.

Neighborhood Housing Services of Greater Berks, Inc. (NHS) is a nonprofit providing Berks County families with affordable housing programs, education and loans for buying, improving and maintaining homes. In 2015, NHS brought together a coalition of nonprofits, government agencies and volunteers to provide help for veteran homeowners in need. The week-long Operation Renovation: A Veterans Affair (ORVA) event deployed armies of volunteers to complete a range of projects for senior, disabled and/or low-income veteran homeowners. Volunteers painted interiors and exteriors, performed home

CHALLENGE

Nearly 30,000 veterans live in Greater Berks County in southeastern Pennsylvania, many of whom face housing challenges ranging from homelessness to difficulty repairing or remodeling their homes. Some veterans with disabilities are unable to adapt their homes to meet their needs.

> # "Operation Renovation is no small event in an urban environment where there is so much poverty. It is a game-changer for many veterans who are considered financially at-risk, with so many living in decrepit homes to avoid becoming homeless."
>
> — Dale G. Derr, Berks County VA director

weatherization projects and constructed or repaired wheelchair ramps. In all, 262 volunteers completed 29 projects at a total value of $73,638 in labor and materials.

"Operation Renovation is no small event in an urban environment where there is so much poverty," said Dale G. Derr, director of the Berks County Department of Veterans Affairs. "It is a

game-changer for many veterans who are considered financially at-risk, with so many living in decrepit homes to avoid becoming homeless."

Operation Renovation: A Veterans Affair was modeled after another program, Operation Facelift which was launched in 1989 by NHS and Boyertown National Bank (now BB&T).

Operation Facelift provided local and community volunteers an opportunity to get their hands dirty by painting and repairing homes in a two-to-three block radius. Once we retired Operation Facelift, we decided to focus on veterans' homes and extend the single day of work to an entire week.

In addition to the home improvement event, we collaborated with Save-A-Warrior (SAW), which supports those with Post-Traumatic Stress Disorder (PTSD). Each day 20 veterans in this country commit suicide. SAW works with veterans and first-responders suffering from PTSD, with 100 percent success rates. Proceeds from fundraising during our Operation Renovation: A Veterans Affair netted $8,000 for SAW to continue their work.

Propelled by the success of our first event, Operation Renovation: A Veterans Affair 2016 more than doubles the number of projects to 72. The expansion is thanks in part to our recent collaboration with Group Cares, a Christian ministry that provides youth volunteers and other resources for humanitarian projects. The 450 volunteers are divided into teams of six people, with one or two adult supervisors. The work includes interior and exterior painting, completing home weatherization projects and constructing or repairing porches and wheelchair ramps.

During ORVA, 262 volunteers completed 29 projects—valued at more than $73,000 in labor and material.

Operation Renovation continues to work toward our goal of making our neighborhoods safer places to live, work and play while contributing to the revitalization of our neighborhoods and greater community. We are collaborating with the City of Reading, Berks County Veterans Affairs Department, Group Cares, Wells Fargo, BB&T and the Little Acts of Love nonprofit. We learned that by bringing together the many talents, resources and skills of these volunteers, organizations and agencies we can make a greater impact in the community.

ABOUT RONALD E. MILLER

Ronald Miller is executive director of Neighborhood Housing Services of Greater Berks, a nonprofit that facilitates and provides affordable housing programs and initiatives that will expand home ownership opportunities for all people of Berks County, especially low to moderate income families.

QUIXOTE VILLAGE: TINY HOMES AS PERMANENT SUPPORTIVE HOUSING

Linda Hugo, President and CEO
Ginger Segel, Senior Housing and Community Developer

Community Frameworks

Working throughout the Pacific Northwest, with offices in Bremerton and Spokane, WA, Community Frameworks develops affordable multifamily and supportive housing, creates homeownership opportunities and provides budgeting, credit and homeownership counseling. The organization provides technical assistance, financing and affordable housing development for other nonprofits.

In 2013, Community Frameworks' senior developer, Ginger Segel, led a team in the development of Quixote Village in Olympia, WA, which grew out of Camp Quixote, a homeless tent city hosted by a group of churches. Panza, an organization formed by the churches, supported the self-governed camp by raising funds for a resident advocate, utilities and other expenses and functioned as a backstop for the camp's self-governance, monitoring its decisions for consistency and legal compliance. The two-acre Quixote Village, one of the first publicly subsidized permanent supportive tiny house communities in the country, includes 30 tiny rental cottages with half-baths for homeless adults, a community garden and building with a large kitchen, bathing rooms and two multi-purpose common spaces.

The cottages are large enough for a standard-size bed, chair, table and some storage; are heated, insulated and have electricity and a standard ceiling height, and are sustainably built for long-term use.

CHALLENGE
The tiny house concept, implemented to respond to homelessness in many communities, faces challenges including accessing both capital and operating financing; designing for community building and resident privacy, and overcoming land use, zoning, building and housing code barriers.

Tiny houses provide a promising model for permanent supportive housing for single homeless adults, reducing the per-unit cost while providing individual private space and shared community space.

Tiny houses provide a promising model for permanent supportive housing for single homeless adults by reducing the per-unit cost by more than half and by balancing individual private space with shared community space to foster positive community engagement.

In spite of this cost-effective solution, compiling capital and operating financing poses some challenges. Residents are extremely low-income and many have no income. Generally, the capital funding must be in the form of grants, not loans, since the project will not generate enough rental income to support debt service. Project leaders need to understand the unique aspects of available financing and to adapt via waivers or variances when possible. Economies of scale could potentially be achieved by a statewide or regional approach.

Organizations operating this kind of housing need to assess their management capacity and possibly look for partnerships with local housing authorities, nonprofit housing developers or other experienced agencies. A clear management plan that details how the project will be operated, ensuring compliance with laws and contracts and having well-reasoned substance abuse, rule enforcement and eviction policies, is critical.

For long-term success, communities using tiny houses as permanent supportive housing also need a strong and committed community organization, with broad support; development expertise in financing, design and land use issues; a site located near public transportation and services; zoning approval and building and housing code compliance, which may require code changes; a design that meets funder requirements and sufficient operating funding.

Quixote Village's excellent team included community organizations and government support. Panza's board, comprised of very capable people, used their connections and savvy to work with residents to develop the permanent supportive housing project to replace the camp in 2010. Government contributions included a county land donation, zoning amendments by the city and $1.5 million from a set aside in the Washington State Housing Trust Fund.

The board and residents were essential drivers to persuade private and public funders and the community. Community Frameworks operated in the background to pull the technical pieces together, bring the project to fruition and prepare it for operations and compliance.

The average cost to build a tiny house is $23,000, if built by the owner.

Success stories at this community include one college graduation, two residents attending college, two residents fully employed, one operating a freelance business and others working as day laborers. Two staff members help residents with onsite mental health care, enrolling in health insurance and recovery programs and other services, including providing haircuts and organizing a running group. According to Panza's 2014 annual letter, "Village residents have created a community that supports people in recovery from addiction and encourages collaboration in the kitchen, vegetable garden and planning and organizing events. The Village is a place where everyone can contribute to their community."

The lesson we learned through the development of Quixote Village is that a team approach, including partnerships with funders, service providers, community members and experienced managers, is essential to long-term success.

ABOUT LINDA HUGO

Linda Hugo, president and CEO of Community Frameworks, has extensive experience in public and private financing, program design, collaborations and partnerships, strategic planning, marketing and evaluating and improving program performance. Hugo has been with the organization since 1984. Her prior experience includes private commercial construction and small business management.

EXPANDING THE REACH OF HOUSING SERVICES VIA THE INTERNET

Jim Grenfell, Executive Director

Wyoming Housing Network

Wyoming, known for its vast plains and Rocky Mountain range, has just 5.8 people per square mile. Rural residents often have to travel far to obtain healthcare and social services, such as housing education and assistance. For those with limited incomes, the need to travel could mean forgoing the dream of homeownership.

The Wyoming Housing Network (WHN), tasked with serving the entire 97,818-mile state of Wyoming with one office and a small staff, has been a top producer of new homeowners in the NeighborWorks network since 2009. In the 2014-2015 fiscal year alone, we enrolled 1,160 clients in our homebuyer education program, reaching them through a system we launched in 2010.

We discovered that though Wyoming's communities may be far flung, the Internet can bridge those gaps. Wyoming ranks 13th in the nation in connectivity, with more than 74 percent of residents connected to the Internet in their homes. This high connectivity provides us with a vehicle for overcoming the challenge of serving clients across the wide open spaces.

Our system allows clients to complete an online course that can be accessed via personal computer or mobile device. The course is available 24 hours a day at the client's convenience wherever Internet access is available. The online component is followed by one-on-one consultations with one of our counselors. These most often take

CHALLENGE

Access to services that require traveling long distances can be daunting for people living in rural communities, particularly low-income residents. Homebuyer education, an essential service to help people become homeowners, is often required for financial assistance. Providing this education to residents in Wyoming, the nation's least populated state, is challenging.

Our staff works hard to make sure that though we may never meet face-to-face, our clients feel that the experience is high-quality and personal.

place over the telephone because our clients generally live in communities' hours from our office. At every step, we are in contact with clients through email and over the telephone, thus providing them with a personal connection and support as they navigate the homebuyer process.

"My homeownership counselor was very personable and relatable," said Genny Rose, a homebuyer. "She answered all my questions and gave real-life examples."

We are committed to serving all our Wyoming clients, so our educators may forgo the online element and offer one-on-one education sessions in person or over the telephone for those who are uncomfortable with the Internet. All the sessions use the Realizing the American Dream curriculum, which includes teaching tools, activities, worksheets and visual aids.

In addition to the Internet's vital role, we would not be able to reach so many prospective homeowners without strong partnerships. Community lenders, real estate agents and social service providers are eager to support our education programs. Being responsive and accessible to those partners across the state is an ongoing commitment of our education programs team.

Our closest partner has been the Wyoming Community Development Authority (WCDA), the state housing finance agency. WCDA requires homebuyer education for all its loans, which include interest-free down payment assistance to make homeownership possible for many families. The agency includes information about our education program in its marketing materials, outreach efforts and lender education. It also provides payments to us for every WCDA client who completes our education program. This has contributed significantly to the homebuyer education program's sustainability and to our ability to provide additional services, such as financial capability coaching. Grants and contributions from banks and other institutions have increased our reach and sustainability as well.

Our homebuyer education model allows us to take advantage of technology and community partnerships as we serve close to 1,000 clients annually through a financially sustainable business line. We are most proud of the quality and valuable service we bring to our clients. Our staff works hard to make sure that though we may never meet them face-to-face, our clients feel that the experience is high-quality, responsive and personal. In fiscal year 2015, 99 percent of our clients said the education they received from us will make them stronger homeowners and 97 percent said they would refer a family member or friend to us.

74% of Wyoming residents are connected to internet in their homes.

This process has been as instructive as it has been productive. We learned that technology can vastly broaden our reach and that developing a model for harnessing that power increases the number of people we can serve. Understanding individual needs and abilities allows us to tailor our delivery system appropriately by offering the choice of consultations via the Internet, email, telephone or in person. Finally, a partner can provide more than financial support, it can help us get our message out by including our programs and materials in its own enterprise.

ABOUT JIM GRENFELL

Jim Grenfell has been the executive director of Wyoming Housing Network since 2014. WHN's mission is to strengthen Wyoming communities by providing quality resources and opportunities for people to reach their housing goals. WHN has a staff of eight and an annual revenue budget of $1.3 million. The organization serves approximately 1,200 people through our education programs annually and about 600 residents in affordable housing apartments.

CHANGING CULTURE: CREATING COLLEGE-READY COMMUNITIES

Joe Garlick, *Executive Director*
Margaux Morisseau
Director of Community Engagement

NeighborWorks Blackstone River Valley

While high school graduation rates have slowly increased in Rhode Island, Woonsocket has the state's highest dropout rate and the number of dropouts has risen in recent years. Teen pregnancy rates are among the state's highest. Seventy-six percent of third grade students in Woonsocket do not meet English language arts standards. Increasing numbers of students are non-native English speakers and must enroll in special education programs. Only 68 percent of high school students graduate. The economic and social costs of poor student performance weigh heavily on the northern Rhode Island town, where one in five children lives in poverty and a third of the population depends on food stamps. These conditions exacerbate problems for the students, making them more likely to suffer behavioral and physical problems, become teen parents and earn less as adults.

For over 18 years, NeighborWorks Blackstone River Valley (NWBRV) has offered youth programs as a cornerstone of our mission to strengthen the communities in our region. The program has grown from offering field trips to youths living in our housing to a structured academic program that ensures all the students in our residences are college and career ready.

Our Mary A. Longtin C3 (Community, College and Career) Center caters to middle and high school students. Enrollment is free and it is open year-round with after

CHALLENGE

More than a quarter of the students fail to graduate from high school in Woonsocket, RI, both a symptom and a cause of the city's overall decline. How do we get these poorly performing students to graduate, go to college and break the cycle of poverty?

school hours and daylong sessions during winter and summer breaks. The facility is considered a cool place to hang out thanks to its computer lab, kitchen, community center, environmental lab and classrooms.

But it's the teachers or Community Builders-In-Residence (CBIR) as they're called, who make the center so special. We offer highly-qualified entrepreneurs, artists, educators and other professionals a deeply discounted apartment in exchange for 16 hours per week of community service. Residents are expected to live and work at the C3 Center for a year-to-year renewable rental agreement.

Shanikqua Dandy said she had been a "spiraling" kid who made trouble for the great-grandparents raising her. She got involved in our youth programs in 2005 with a zero grade point average. She boosted her GPA, graduated high school, went on to college and is one of our teachers.

"Now I am part of the staff that changes the lives of kids," she says. "I provide supportive communication with youth who were once in my predicament. Having grown up in this community myself increases the students' connectivity with me."

Having teachers work for free onsite keeps the program sustainable in an inconsistent grant world and provides round-the-clock role models for the students. Many of these young enthusiastic teachers grew up in the neighborhood and went to the same schools. They constantly talk about their college experiences at schools such as Rhode Island College, Brown, Harvard and Boston College. Their conversations with students often begin "When you go to college…"

The students commit to a disciplined schedule and high expectations. They may start by playing basketball, talking with their teachers or working on projects, but when 4:00 p.m. rolls around, they settle into their mandatory two hours of homework and study time.

The program targets K-12 youths living in our 345 affordable housing units. It provides academic, social, emotional and college preparatory support through before- and after-school programs, vacation week sessions and summer learning opportunities. The College Ready Community program is an inclusive education program offering tutoring, health and exercise classes and entrepreneurship activities. It also offers instruction in science, technology, engineering, arts and math (STEAM) education, leadership, environmental citizenship, gardening and neighborhood beautification. The activities prepare youths for college and focus on building their leadership skills and self-esteem while creating stronger connections with their community at-large.

In Woonsocket, 68% of high school students graduate, compared to the 2014 national rate of 82%.

The Sure Track to College program, led by a staff member who works collaboratively with the school department prepares youths for college entrance exams, helps them choose the right schools and guides them through the application and financial aid processes. We partnered with Navigant Credit Union to create S.A.F.E. (Savings Advantage for Future Education) deposit-only college savings accounts for students beginning in middle school and to provide financial literacy classes. Recently, NWBRV partnered with the Woonsocket Education Department to increase academic achievement in the Woonsocket's Constitution Hill and Fairmount neighborhoods through the College Ready Community program. We share data such as grades and attendance with the education department, schools, teachers, parents, students and our staff. Increased communication ensures that students are getting the help they need and engages the whole community in the students' success.

The results of our program have been remarkable: 99 percent of our youths now graduate from high school, 94 percent go to on to college and there have been no teen pregnancies. Many graduate and return to live and work in the community as social workers, pharmacists and teachers.

Through this initiative we've learned that this formula works: set high expectations, seek proper support from many partners, track progress as well as setbacks and give a voice to those you seek to serve – and listen to them.

ABOUT JOE GARLICK

Joe Garlick is the executive director of NeighborWorks Blackstone River Valley, a nonprofit community development corporation that works with residents, businesses, neighborhood institutions, partners, and communities to enrich neighborhood life and make affordable housing opportunities available throughout northern Rhode Island.

A CREATIVE RESPONSE TO BUILDING OUR YOUTH COMMUNITY

Robert E. Ansley, President

Orlando Neighborhood Improvement Corp.

In 1998, the Orlando Neighborhood Improvement Corp. (ONIC) recognized a need in the community: Many of the after-school programs simply didn't meet the needs of the city's at-risk youth. They provided little more than a babysitting service for young people – basically, just "roofs and walls." As a result, some of these young people – many of whom lived in ONIC's multi-family rental communities – engaged in destructive behaviors such as petty crime.

Propelled by a belief that zip codes should not limit opportunity, the ONIC Resident Services Program sought partners to help develop alternate after-school options. These partnerships led to innovative youth programs that have created a haven for local youths, along with meaningful personal development.

Among these programs are Prodigy Cultural Arts Program, Sista2Sista, Sister Circles, tutoring workshops and anti-bullying initiatives. These programs were specifically designed to nurture life skills, leadership strengths and self-esteem and to prevent destructive behaviors.

Prodigy Cultural Arts is a free, research-based, after-school program for at-risk youth ages 7-17 that uses visual and performing arts to teach life skills such as effective communication, problem solving and anger management. First established in 2000 by the University Area Community Development Corp to serve seven counties

CHALLENGE

To truly engage Orlando's at-risk youth in community building through after-school programs that provide more than just "roofs and walls."

Propelled by a belief that zip codes should not limit opportunity, the ONIC Resident Services Program sought partners to help develop alternate after-school options.

in west central Florida, Prodigy has achieved a non-recidivism rate of 85-93 percent among youths diverted from the juvenile justice system, with an overall average of 89 percent.

Research has shown that Prodigy graduates show improved ability to control their behavior and a significant decrease in anger, depression, anxiety, suicidal thoughts and related physical symptoms.

In terms of cost, Prodigy has proven to be among the lowest-cost prevention and diversion programs, at an average of $1,577 per youth.

ONIC became a host site for Prodigy in 2007, serving about 400 local young people on an annual basis. Emerging leaders from the ONIC program and others attend Florida's Children's Week, an annual celebration for child advocacy agencies, where the youths meet with legislative officials at the state capital and tour local colleges. It is a testament to the program's continued success that after aging out of the program, many young people remain involved through volunteering and community events.

Meanwhile, two other programs specifically target girls and young women: Sista2Sista provides a safe space for young women, with a goal of building confidence and self-esteem. It's also a pipeline for formal leadership development programs such as NeighborWorks America's Community Leadership Institute and The Venture Philanthropists of Orlando. ONIC's Sister Circles has a different focus; the 12-week, intensive support group is designed to reduce the major risk factors of poor nutrition, inactivity and unmanaged stress in African-American women.

We have witnessed remarkable positive changes in our youth community through these proactive approaches and others. Some youths have even become involved in community development work with ONIC as well as with organizations such as VISTA and AmeriCorps.

Youth programming has taught ONIC a great deal about how to best approach and engage residents in our area. Here are a few of these lessons:

Product vs. process: When implementing arts-related programs, it is easy to be concerned solely about the end result, the art itself. Inevitably, the production is not flawless and the pieces of art are not masterpieces. But no one is any less proud. The lesson is not in the product, but in the process it took to create it.

132 NeighborWorks organizations offered education or extracurricular activities in FY15.

The value of life skills: We've learned that the incorporation of life skills coaching into other programming such as the arts is a valuable strategy for engaging parents and helping youth overcome destructive behaviors. Life skills include coping with aggression and bullying, using a non-judgmental approach.

Benefit of partnerships: The provision of affordable housing can be leveraged gainfully to create leadership development opportunities. As an affordable housing developer, ONIC was able to help Prodigy reach a more diverse audience of youth.

ABOUT BOB ANSLEY
Bob Ansley is president of the Orlando Neighborhood Improvement Corp., a nonprofit company that develops affordable housing in central Florida. He is a member of the College of Fellows of the American Institute of Certified Planners and serves on the board of the Florida Housing Coalition. He served on the Florida Governor's Commission on Affordable Housing from 1993 to 1994.

NOTHING ABOUT ME, WITHOUT ME

Patrick McNamara, CEO
Jaime Joshi, Communications Coordinator

Housing Partnership, Inc.

Housing Partnership Inc. (HPI) helps families living in areas of concentrated poverty and risk. They believe that every family in their community should have the tools to overcome adversity and live a healthy, stable and rewarding life.

Through a strategic planning process, HPI recognized that their programmatic silos were impeding their work. They needed to find a better way to change the odds for the people they serve. Enter the "pocket strategy."

HPI formed cross-program "Pocket Teams" and a "Design Team" to focus on two neighborhoods ripe for change. The teams used a "design-and-do" approach experimenting, collecting data, learning and taking action. They met monthly to reflect on success and failures, highlight lessons learned and plan next steps.

One of the teams focused on Stonybrook Apartments, a property with many young families using Section 8 housing vouchers. The apartments are located in Riviera Beach, FL, which has a Neighborhood Scout crime rate of four on a scale where 100 represents the safest area. With a history of violent and drug-related crimes, Stonybrook earned a tough reputation in the community.

For years, nonprofits and churches offered prefabricated solutions, none of which yielded lasting positive results. HPI's interactions with the complex were mostly via social services responding to child welfare calls for abuse or neglect.

CHALLENGE
Community development practitioners often wrestle with complexity and look for solutions rooted in their practice habits and noble intentions. Sometimes this can lead to programmatic silos which actually impede their work. How can organizations break through these silos to make a lasting impact in their communities?

"People have tried this before and it didn't work, so they gave up. We didn't give up. We won't give up."

— Cleveland Wester, director of targeted case management

The pocket team's initial goal was to reduce child abuse rates by engaging residents, providing financial and parenting workshops and increasing access to services. Cleveland Wester, director of Targeted Case Management and Jibby Ciric, director of Client Outreach Services, led the team in a "boots on the ground" approach, starting with a resident survey conducted by knocking on every door. The residents got to know the staff and began opening up.

However, the next step was more of a stumble. Workshops and meetings were poorly attended and frustration started to mount internally and between residents and HPI's team. Continuing the conversation, they realized that reducing child abuse rates was the organization's primary objective, not the residents'. HPI's prefabricated solutions weren't working.

Residents said that safety was their top concern, which is what Patrick McNamara, HPI's CEO, heard a decade earlier when he was providing services at Stoneybrook.

"We need to honor their voice and make this our top concern too," said McNamara. "Treat this like you're untying a knot. What has contributed to the 'knot' of unsafe conditions? How has it been tied? What's the relationship between stakeholders - property management, police, the city, and residents? Can we find a way to help residents 'pull the string'?"

The police were a regular presence within Stonybrook and property management had been taken to task on several occasions, both by police and HUD. HPI realized that every stakeholder was involved except the residents. To create a safer environment, HPI needed to harness and amplify the residents' voices.

As a public subsidy property, residents have the right to form an association. HPI helped them create one, enabling them to come to the table alongside property management and the police to voice their concerns.

The first meeting had five residents; the next had 12. At the last meeting in February 2016, almost 15 percent of all the residents showed up, resulting in positive feedback from police and management about the level of resident engagement.

In 2015, the NeighborWorks Community Leadership Institute had 900 participants.

Through resident participation, HPI created a rich learning experience for their staff, transforming them from therapists, case managers and housing specialists to community builders. Cross-program, indeed.

After several months, police calls from the complex had dropped by a staggering 80 percent. Residents began signing up for parenting, family counseling and financial coaching services. Five more residents found jobs. Child welfare calls started slowly decreasing. One resident just became a new homeowner.

HPI continues to assist residents in building their capacity to run the association, brokering relations with property management and police. The association's new goal is to be autonomous by the end of 2016.

HPI learned that Stonybrook wasn't a problem to be solved; instead, they joined with residents as problem solvers.

From this project HPI also learned that inclusive resident participation is the crux of building safe and sustainable communities and that stepping outside of their preconceived solutions and habits enabled them to see the problem from a different angle. HPI understands that they need to engage in situational social work even as they have a game plan and focus on results. They've added the capacity to engage, reflect and adapt, while remaining determined to promote family resilience and decrease child abuse in the area.

ABOUT PATRICK MCNAMARA

Patrick McNamara, CEO of Housing Partnership since 2007, joined the organization in 1999 as director of supportive housing. A licensed clinical social worker and mortgage originator with 12 years of management experience, McNamara is also a board member of the National NeighborWorks Association and the Florida Community Loan Fund. An alumnus of Leadership Palm Beach County, Pat was also awarded the illustrious Leadership Excellence Award in 2013.

MY FRONT PORCH: FROM VACANT TO VIBRANT

Ray Ocasio, Executive Director
Felix Moulier, Community Organizing Manager

La Casa de Don Pedro

First, here's a little background on the Lower Broadway neighborhood of Newark, NJ: Lower Broadway is a 1.2-square-mile neighborhood located on the northern fringe of Newark's central business district. With more than 14,000 residents, Lower Broadway is one of the most diverse neighborhoods in the city. It remains a largely Hispanic community (51 percent vs 32 percent in Newark overall); however it now also has a wide mix of residents from Puerto Rico, Ecuador, the Dominican Republic and Mexico. The black population has also increased steadily and includes African-Americans as well as a growing number of West Africans.

One quarter of the residents are under the age of 18, and one out of every five households is headed by a female with children under the age of 18. The unemployment rate hovers around 14 percent.

Lower Broadway clearly has some challenges, but it is a neighborhood in the midst of transformation, with a lot of success stories. This one began during the Neighbor-Works America's 2013 Community Leadership Institute, when Yolanda Vann, a member of the Lower Broadway Neighborhood Association, had lunch in a unique "common space" in Sacramento, CA. The space was located in a formerly "useless" lot between three restaurants, but had been transformed into a comfortable area where people could congregate, socialize and enjoy a meal. Vann immediately decided that the Lower Broadway neighborhood in Newark would benefit from a similar public

CHALLENGE
The Lower Broadway neighborhood of Newark, NJ has limited open space for outdoor recreation and socializing. Nearly 20 percent of the community resides in apartment buildings with no outdoor space, yet there are a number of vacant lots that could be transformed into active, usable space.

My Front Porch transformed the neighborhood. Residents of Lower Broadway who had rarely participated in community-driven activities were suddenly dancing, singing and eating together.

space. Community leaders supported Vann's vision, and she and others set to work finding a lot that could be converted into a vibrant outdoor community space in Lower Broadway.

Organizers encountered many challenges during the planning process, including some doubt about the feasibility and value of the vision, logistical hurdles, budget constraints and volunteer burnout. Nonetheless, Krystyna Soljan and Kevin Alonzo from La Casa de Don Pedro, with collaboration from the Lower Broadway Neighborhood Association, persevered and found creative ways to engage the community and motivate residents to dare to think big.

The result was a plan for a space that would host outdoor performances and other social activities in a format called My Front Porch. One of the first major steps was to acquire a permanent site. Eventually organizers identified a spot in the perfect location: 57 Crane St., a long-neglected, unsightly parcel of land – home to an old industrial building that had burned down 20 years earlier. The property was marred by large chunks of concrete, refuse, tall weeds and decades of accumulated debris, but it had lots of potential.

"Reclaiming" the lot was physically demanding. Some volunteers suffered burnout, but most persisted and came back after they'd had some time off.

The next step was to transform the lot into My Front Porch. With a limited budget, community involvement was essential. Nearby Barringer High School's wood shop students created seating for the venue, along with tables, a stage and raised plant beds. A variety of local organizations donated furniture and other supplies.

To build anticipation, a local band called Lot on 7th, which describes its music as "alternative hip-hop/neo-soul," began hosting open mic nights for musicians in Lower Broadway. Residents came out to listen; others brought instruments to perform. The concerts brought residents together.

When My Front Porch finally debuted, it transformed the neighborhood. Residents of Lower Broadway who'd rarely participated in community-driven activities were suddenly dancing, singing and eating together. Activities range from an open-mic stage, to movie showings, to kids' activities. The space is a safe haven for Newark residents. Seeing the smiles of the children and the glow in their eyes has been one of the most rewarding benefits of My Front Porch.

95% of people think a strong community includes access to parks and public spaces.

"I saw that lot for 15 years look like a mess, with weeds and debris and everything in there. When we got in there and cleaned it up, it became a really nice space," says Pamela Mclean, a Lower Broadway resident. "It was good to see everybody pitch in."

We've learned a few lessons along the way to this success:
- Plan ahead and conduct as much outreach as possible to recruit volunteers; this type of project needs many dedicated volunteers (otherwise your organizers get burned out!).
- When residents see volunteers working or playing in the space, they will generally join for a spell. In other words, "perform and they will come!" We met so many residents simply by spending hours in the space.
- Ask lots of questions; you may learn the most important lessons through informal interactions.

ABOUT RAY OCASIO

Ray Ocasio is the executive director of La Casa de Don Pedro, a 44-year-old, community-based service and development agency in Newark, NJ. The organization provides social services, affordable housing and financial planning assistance to its service community.

BRINGING NEIGHBORS TOGETHER WITH PAINT BRUSHES AND POWER WASHERS

Michael Tubbs, CEO

Holly T. Hicks, Communications and Marketing Specialist

Community Action Partnership of North Alabama

For the Community Action Partnership of North Alabama, a block makeover during NeighborWorks Week was the perfect challenge for its Community Impact Measurement area. By involving residents in the restoration of both the aesthetic appeal and the pride of the neighborhood, long-term measurable change would be possible.

The residents of East Decatur are more often than not weary and wary of outsiders parachuting in with unsolicited aid as a temporary fix to a permanent problem, so the notion of inspiring this neighborhood of strangers to join a local nonprofit in a week-long project gave many pause, including those who held the reins from the idea's initial spark. But over the course of five days of intense focus and hard labor by hundreds of volunteers and local partners, an East Decatur block was transformed in appearance and in spirit. More than 35 corporate partners provided materials and labor alongside some 200 volunteers to restore multiple homes. Neighbors became re-acquainted with one another, teamed up and helped the enthusiasm spread beyond the defined limits of the block makeover.

Palpable excitement marked the first day of the East Decatur block makeover as a silver utility trailer bearing the red and blue brand of the Partnership arrived at the stag-

CHALLENGE

Creating sustainable change in a neighborhood requires an understanding of residents' needs beginning with housing and running the gamut of services that may be taken for granted by those outside the realm of poverty. Addressing these needs can make change a reality for individual residents and an entire community.

Through the block makeover we learned how important it is to engage neighbors in a communal improvement effort.

ing area and a week of hands-on sweat and toil got underway. Every home improvement tool imaginable emerged from the trailer, was methodically categorized by Partnership staff and assigned to volunteers. Each of the 18 houses due for transformation on Seventh Street, SE was tagged with a black and white branded yard sign, the collection of them peppering the edges of the weedy lawns of those who elected to participate in the makeover. Volunteers signed in, grabbed a pair of work gloves and began to bring some order to the organized chaos that unfolded.

Partnership CEO Michael Tubbs assumed temporary ownership of a power washer and began removing years of dirt, grime and a substandard paint job from the first house of many to undergo a facelift. Through the roar of the washer's engine others could be heard dictating specific needs: "These limbs need to come down. I need help pulling this fence up. Does someone have some clippers I can borrow?"

Through the chatter could be heard the thud of the delivery of the large City of Decatur dumpster that would become the final resting place of worn-out vines and overgrown brush from years of neglect. Hundreds of volunteers from middle schoolers to retirees and groups from around the city showed up to make a difference. Pockets of motivated workers evolved into a dynamic force of evolutionary change that quickly had the neighborhood in its grasp.

Each day the block makeover made strides toward the ultimate goal: to build a true community through resident involvement and improve the aesthetic appeal of the area. Connections with residents were made through door-to-door greetings by Partnership employees, engagement with volunteers and neighborhood participation. The spirit of the community evolved before our eyes as neighbors emerged from their porches to help. Some painted others' porches while others spread mulch or trimmed branches. Residents became actively engaged in their own property makeovers by pruning shrubs and mowing lawns.

Through the block makeover we learned how important it is to engage neighbors in a communal improvement effort. As a result of the collective efforts of neighbors helping neighbors, the East Decatur Community Association was formed to create opportunities for residents to improve their neighborhood and build a strong community. What started as a suggestion in a team planning meeting quickly grew to be the single greatest community service project in the Partnership's 50-year history as a Community Action Agency.

NeighborWorks organizations helped more than 7,700 homeowners rehab their homes in FY15.

ABOUT MICHAEL TUBBS

Michael Tubbs serves as the CEO of Community Action Partnership of North Alabama. The Partnership is a comprehensive community action agency with over 50 years of delivering results in the Tennessee Valley region of Alabama. The Partnership's mission is to reduce or eliminate the causes and consequences of poverty for families and communities. The Partnership's 600 staff serve through a variety of federal, state and local programs that address the needs of young children to senior adults, energy conservation, basic family needs, housing rehabilitation and homeownership preparation. As the premiere Head Start grantee in Alabama, the Partnership manages over 150 classrooms for young children and their families. The agency is also the largest non-profit developer of affordable housing in Alabama, has over 1,500 apartment units and is involved in community building in its service area.

PAINT YOUR HEART OUT: GIVING A HOME AND A LIFE A LIFT

Sharlene Wilde, Executive Director
Diane Heslington, Housing Coordinator and Counselor

NeighborWorks Provo

Roylene Lunt met her husband in college and raised four children with him. They had always wanted to paint and fix up their home in Provo, Utah, but the demands of work and family always put the project on the back burner. The project was sidetracked further when Lunt was diagnosed with cancer. After treatment, she went into remission, but then was later found to have stage four cancer.

Roylene and her husband decided that it was a good time to cross a few things off of her bucket list. She and some of her childhood friends from Idaho decided to take a trip to see the Grand Canyon. They saw the sights and thoroughly enjoyed the trip. One afternoon, Roylene called her husband from her hotel. He said he was tired and had to run because he was late for a meeting. When she got home the next day she found he had died in their bedroom that night. After 38 years of marriage, Roylene was suddenly and unexpectedly alone. She continued with her medical therapy, but she had all but given up on her wish to see her home of 30 years painted while she still lived to enjoy it. By this time, the home was in dire need of a face lift.

Roylene's situation is particularly heart-wrenching, but not unique in many other ways. Inflation, low-wage jobs, health problems, improper planning, the recent financial crisis and dozens of other challenges mean too many seniors just scratch by rather than savor this time of their

CHALLENGE

Homeowners with financial problems often neglect their homes when they lack the funds or the time to maintain their property. Neglected homes can be a blight psychologically as well as physically. A yearly beautification day can boost neighborhood values, homeowners' spirits and community connections.

Roylene Lunt was brimming with gratitude for the outpouring of support from NWP, neighbors and city officials. The volunteers, for their part, said they received much more than they gave.

lives. Nine out of 10 Americans 65 and older rely on Social Security, and the average monthly benefit is $1,262. Many receive much less than that.

According to the Social Security Administration, 53 percent of married couples and 74 percent of those who are unmarried receive 50 percent or more of their income from Social Security. The median income for seniors 65-74 is $36,320; if you're older than 74, it drops to $25,417 according to the U.S. Census Bureau. Twelve percent of those 65 and older are living at the poverty level. Provo is no exception. A third of our residents live in poverty.

NeighborWorks Provo (NWP) has provided vital community services to the residents of downtown Provo neighborhoods since 1992. One of the many ways we help them enjoy their later years is through home maintenance. Every year for 19 years, we have organized a Paint Your Heart Out event to beautify a resident's home at no cost to the owner. NWP does the planning, coordinates permits and orders supplies. NWP works closely with a neighborhood association leader, who plays a key role in recommending potential projects and coordinating volunteers to do the work. Roylene was chosen for our 2015 home makeover.

The exterior of the house was in pretty rough shape. The paint was faded and peeling and the rafters needed repairs. Bird and wasp nests and an overgrown tree were causing additional damage to the home. We had more than 20 volunteers join NWP staff and board members to accomplish the task. As everyone showed up for the day's work, it looked like we might be in for a downpour, but the clouds moved on and we had clear skies for the rest of the day.

The end result was a beautifully restored home; even the deck and backyard swing set were painted. Roylene was brimming with gratitude for the outpouring of support from NWP, neighbors and city officials. For their part, the volunteers said they received much more than they gave. One father whose wife also was struggling with cancer managed to take the time to help a neighbor in need and was grateful for the opportunity. And it wasn't only adults who volunteered; some brought their children as well to teach them the value of community service.

Nationally, the average cost to paint a house is $2,581.

As always, NWP was proud to have been key in orchestrating the event. It is but one of our many services, which include foreclosure avoidance and remediation counseling, homebuyer education classes, credit restoration counseling, rental services, homeownership opportunities and community event planning. But Paint Your Heart Out is vital to supporting and broadcasting our mission. Our employees are dedicated to serving the community and our neighborhood partners are willing to spend their time and energy to improve their neighborhoods.

ABOUT SHARLENE WILDE

Sharlene Wilde serves as the executive director of NeighborWorks Provo in Provo, UT and Sun County Home Solutions in St. George, UT. These nonprofit organizations provide education on the pathways to homeownership, providing affordable housing solutions, improving housing quality, upgrading and maintaining high quality rentals and promoting neighborhood pride and unity.

Cross-Sector Collaboration

David J. Erickson

Individuals and organizations that aspire to improve the lives of people living in poverty may share goals but have vastly different approaches to the myriad challenges of low-income households. Public, private and philanthropic groups each have a role to play in community development. An essential element of successfully creating economic opportunity for underserved individuals is the ability of these groups to recognize the inherent value of cooperation and collaboration. The successful exploration and execution of cross-sector collaboration is the focus of this section.

Cross-sector collaboration wasn't in the lexicon of Dorothy Mae Richardson when she stood up in her Central Northside community in Pittsburgh against the long-term trajectory of disinvestment and the threat of urban renewal bulldozers. "The solution was not to tear down the whole neighborhood," she said. "The solution was to fix the houses." Richardson's cross-sector efforts ultimately brought local government and banks together with residents to begin to restore her neighborhood.

Dorothy Richardson represents a wonderful example of a great person standing up to improve the future of her community, but more than that, she triggered a revolution that helped remake systems in finance and public policy. Banks and all levels of government agencies began to reorient their activity to be more respectful and more encouraging of local revitalization efforts, changing the way urban revitalization was done in this country. The organization Richardson helped create, now known as NeighborWorks America, continues to honor her principles and helps community groups across the country execute on her ideals.

Today's leaders, many of whom are represented in the following chapters, know that system-wide change is dependent on cross-sector partnerships leveraging community capacity to develop local and sustainable solutions. While housing is the framework of our communities, it is also a platform from which together we can improve the life opportunities of low- and moderate-income people. NeighborWorks organizations understand that solving an affordable housing problem also requires helping someone with health issues, job skills and financial literacy. These leaders know that education is more than just building a local school, it also depends on encouraging parents to get involved and further their own education. These leaders understand that healthy living requires a lifestyle change and access to nurturing food, not just a health clinic. It is the nexus between housing and education, healthcare, workforce development, financial literacy and other areas that we seek to explore and develop.

The organizations you'll hear from in this section write about the importance of winning the trust of local residents; how shared leadership requires taking the time to listen to each other's goals and plan together for cooperation and how this leadership demands finding and fostering the right partnerships. Today's challenges, whether they are siloed budgets, issues of turf associated with multiple organizations or policies that frustrate cooperation, are being overcome by the leaders writing in the following pages. You'll hear from groups like Chicanos Por La Causa in Phoenix who partnered with United Healthcare Community and State to create a center where local residents could get help with health and social issues and financial literacy. You'll learn about how the Cambridge Neighborhood Apartment Housing Services in Cambridge, MA partnered with Cambridge Elder Services to go beyond providing affordable housing for seniors to add social and healthy amenities like a garden and exercise classes to their facilities.

Like Richardson, these organizations are exercising their leadership to develop an environment that promotes better cross-sector interventions and more equitable and viable places to live. I am honored to introduce this section of stories about leaders and organizations around the country coming together for the greater good.

———

David J. Erickson *is director of community development at the Federal Reserve Bank of San Francisco and serves as community development officer for the Federal Reserve's twelfth District. In this role, he leads the community development team toward its mission to advance economic opportunity for lower-income Americans.*

Erickson launched and now advises the Federal Reserve journal and previously served as research manager for the Center for Community Development Investments, where he fostered initiatives exploring innovative community development financing models and greater intersections with the health, arts, and environmental sectors to identify new investible opportunities that benefit lower-income communities.

CREATING OPPORTUNITY: LIFTING HOME VALUES IN SLOW RECOVERY NEIGHBORHOODS

John O'Callaghan, President & CEO

Atlanta Neighborhood Development Partnership, Inc.

The housing crisis diminished the largest source of family wealth and destabilized neighborhoods in the metro Atlanta area. To assess the lingering impact of the crisis, the Atlanta Neighborhood Development Partnership (ANDP) examined the 113 zip codes in metro Atlanta. Fifty-four zip codes had a median negative equity rate of nearly 50 percent, compared to the other 59 zip codes with only 20 percent.

The low-equity communities represent more than one-third of the region and include 92,127 homes that lost $5.2 billion in home equity. Loss of equity traps owners in their homes and limits their ability to pay for college or participate in economic opportunities. These struggling neighborhoods need systemic change and catalytic intervention to stem plummeting home values and strengthen economic opportunity.

In 2010, ANDP created Piece by Piece (PBP), a regional foreclosure response initiative with 155 partner organizations. The leadership team includes Atlanta Regional Commission, ClearPoint, Enterprise Community Partners, Federal Reserve Bank of Atlanta, Greater Atlanta Home Builders Association, the Home Depot Foundation, the National Housing Conference and Neighbor-Works America.

PBP focuses on expanding access to loan modifications and consumer counseling resources, lowering vacancy

CHALLENGE

While economic opportunity has returned to some Atlanta neighborhoods, more than 90,000 homeowners still encounter blight and vacant homes in their communities. Those conditions call urgently for a scaled response to stabilize neighborhoods and recover lost wealth.

With underwriting from NeighborWorks America, we are working with community leaders to address neighborhood stabilization and help residents understand how to increase demand for homes to raise values.

rates and addressing underwater homeowners. In 2015, more than 200 representatives attended our "Underwater Atlanta" event, connecting private and public organizations, neighborhood leaders, concerned citizens, federal and state program leaders and policymakers to discuss reduction of negative equity. The symposium resulted in a county-based negative equity initiative, local and national media coverage of the issue and the inclusion of Atlanta in FHFA's Neighborhood Stabilization Initiative.

Recognizing that housing recovery funds were diminishing, ANDP forged partnerships to increase its foreclosure redevelopment capacity, provide affordable homeownership opportunities and lift values in foreclosure-impacted communities. First, we piloted innovative partnerships with pri-

vate equity developers to rehab homes at scale without utilizing government subsidies. Next, our loan fund partnered with the nation's leading Community Development Financial Institution, Reinvestment Fund, to increase community development capital in the region. Lastly, we are deploying federal HOME funds with three local governments to further single-family redevelopment and create economic opportunity for homeowners.

Our pilot private-sector partnership has proven successful, with 26 homes redeveloped and additional acquisitions underway. Key successes of the program include: streamlining the development timeline while ensuring a quality rehab, and reducing days on market and connecting buyers to local and state down payment assistance. With new partners added, we are now on a path toward 50 homes in this program.

"My neighbors and I were worried about vandalism and squatting and how that could impact our home values, which were already falling because of the foreclosure crisis," says Tracey Powell, an Atlanta homeowner in a development that was foreclosed on before the community was complete. "But then ANDP bought the available homes and helped homebuyers with down payment assistance. It really changed our neighborhood outlook."

With underwriting from NeighborWorks America, we are working with community leaders to address neighborhood stabilization and help residents understand how to increase demand for homes to raise values. Focusing on code enforcement, mortgage modification programs and neighborhood branding ultimately attracts new homeowners and commercial development.

Of the top 10 hardest-hit zip codes in the country for negative equity, 9 are located in metro Atlanta.

In 2015, we trained 100 neighborhood leaders on these topics and shared materials with hundreds more electronically. Several neighborhood leaders who attended our training participated in NeighborWorks' Community Leadership Initiative and subsequently provided valuable input for a June 2016 training event for 100 additional neighborhood leaders.

We partnered with Douglas County and Epic Intentions, an interdisciplinary society at Georgia Tech, to review local sales and tax data. We discovered that a $2.3 million rehab investment in 53 of our homes lifted the value of surrounding homes by $14.6 million. As of late 2015, the negative equity rate in the targeted zip codes has fallen to 34.9 percent, compared to 11 percent in healthier metro Atlanta neighborhoods, 17.4 percent in Georgia and 13.1 percent in the United States.

The lesson learned through this ongoing initiative is that forging partnerships across business, government and nonprofit sectors and engaging neighborhood stakeholders is essential. Working with partners who share a mission commitment and willingness to tweak models, we've learned that good partners focus on the success of each other's mission and financial sustainability.

ABOUT JOHN O'CALLAGHAN

Since 2006, John O'Callaghan has served as the president and CEO of ANDP, a mixed-income housing-focused nonprofit organization addressing the lingering impact of the region's foreclosure crisis. One of the nation's largest nonprofit redevelopers of vacant foreclosed homes, ANDP is engaged in a multi-year initiative to stabilize metro Atlanta neighborhoods by rehabbing vacant, deteriorating homes for new owners and lease purchase tenants. O'Callaghan relaunched the organization's Community Development Financial Institution lending arm, providing affordable housing developers with access to capital. The organization has acquired, redeveloped and repopulated more than 525 previously foreclosed homes.

UNLIKELY PARTNERS, COLLECTIVE IMPACT

David Adame, President and CEO

Chicanos Por La Causa

Chicanos Por La Causa (CPLC) recognizes that affordable housing is rarely the only need of a low-income family. The families we serve in the southwestern United States are often faced with impossible decisions like whether to forgo medical treatment to pay for rent or forgo rent to pay for food. Issues with health, housing and basic needs may stand between a client and steady employment. Families must often connect with different service providers to meet each need, which can be a major barrier when transportation and time are already scarce. A family may be provided with numerous referrals and never make their first appointment.

CPLC is a community development corporation committed to building stronger, healthier communities as a lead advocate, coalition builder and direct service provider. CPLC serves more than 200,000 individuals annually each year through housing, economic development, education, and health and human services programs designed to empower families to become financially stable, healthy and self-sufficient.

After nearly 50 years of service, CPLC recognizes that family issues are complex. Unstable income, unsafe housing or food insecurity can all negatively affect health. According to findings from County Health Rankings, only 20 percent of an individual's modifiable health outcomes are attributed to access to or quality of clinical care, while 80 percent is determined outside of the healthcare setting:

▸ 40 percent is a result of factors such as education, employment, income and community safety.

CHALLENGE

Affordable housing is rarely the only thing low-income families need. Often they are faced with impossible decisions like whether to forgo medical treatment to pay for rent or forgo rent to pay for food. Issues with health, housing and basic needs may stand between a client and steady employment.

As grant funds remain volatile and communities' needs increase, we can seek partnerships in unlikely places to remain financially sustainable, leverage knowledge and resources, and truly achieve collective impact.

- ▶ 30 percent is a result of health behaviors such as nutrition, exercise, substance use and sexual activity.
- ▶ 10 percent is a result of the physical environment such as housing, air and water quality.

Clearly, a family may require a wide range of services to make sustainable improvements in their lives but may not have the time to meet with numerous providers. In response, CPLC established a cross-sector partnership with UnitedHealthcare Community and State (UHC) to meet the needs of the families we serve. Although CPLC provides services that address many of the social determinants of health, coordination and collaboration with other agencies was needed to ensure families consistently received the support necessary to move from instability to self-sufficiency.

Though it is a for-profit entity, UHC, like CPLC, has a significant interest in improving the health of vulnerable families. UHC Community and State provides health insurance coverage to individuals eligible for Medicare, Medicaid and the Children's Health Insurance Program. The company has found that approximately 20 percent of its client base is using 80 percent of the healthcare resources, representing a significant cost to the company and the community. By targeting these high-need individuals through investments in preventive care and social services, UHC can substantially reduce healthcare system utilization and consequently reduce costs.

The UHC-CPLC partnership created the myCommunity Connect Center, located in a 30,000-square foot CPLC facility in a low-income neighborhood of Phoenix. The Center houses a broad range of health and social services provided by nonprofit and government agencies under one roof to achieve collective impact. Each service is sustained by its own grants and funding mechanisms.

Services include:
- Primary, dental and behavioral health care
- Workforce development
- Affordable housing
- Financial literacy
- Healthy food and nutrition education
- Medical transportation services

40% of an individual's modifiable health outcomes are attributed to education, employment, income and community safety.

When clients arrive at the center, they meet with a community health worker to complete a comprehensive needs assessment and develop an individualized service plan. Clients are then directly connected to onsite services and receive help navigating funding streams to cover service costs. A single software program tracks client progress, providing shared data to ensure all partners are working toward the same goal.

Researchers are evaluating the effects of the program on individual health outcomes and healthcare costs. This knowledge will help improve service delivery and attract additional investment.
In its earliest stages, the partnership has provided nearly 3,000 meals from its diabetic food pantry, placed 250 people in jobs, provided 200 bus passes to facilitate transportation to work, and offered housing support services to 200 individuals.

Additionally, UnitedHealthcare Community and State provided capital for CPLC to acquire and rehabilitate apartments in the low-income neighborhoods surrounding the facility. A portion of the units will provide affordable housing for clients at the Center, while market-rate units will provide a sustainable funding source to support the cost of Center operations. Upon full implementation, the project will be financially self-sustaining.

Evidence shows that health and housing are inextricably linked. We learned that as grant funds remain volatile and communities' needs increase, we can seek partnerships in unlikely places to remain financially sustainable, leverage knowledge and resources and truly achieve collective impact.

ABOUT DAVID ADAME
David Adame has served as president and CEO of Chicanos Por La Causa since October 2015. He is a third-generation Arizonan with more than 20 years of experience in the banking industry. Since coming to CPLC, Adame has generated more than $250 million in resources for the organization through grants, strategic partnerships and for-profit subsidiaries. He specializes in diversifying revenue sources for the organization, especially through the launch of mission-driven, for-profit social ventures to contribute toward the cost of nonprofit operations.

THE TROPICAL FOODS PROJECT: MAKING ACCESS TO HEALTHY FOOD A REALITY

Jeanne Pinado, CEO

Madison Park Development Corporation

For years, it was impossible to find fresh affordable food in Boston's Roxbury neighborhood, where 54 percent of its 56,000 residents live at or below the poverty line. The community has some of the city's highest rates of heart disease, diabetes and cancer. Until 2015, this historic center of Boston's African-American community had no supermarket, only expensive convenience stores and bodegas carrying little fresh produce, meats and dairy. Venturing beyond this food desert was a cost of time and money, a significant hurdle for Roxbury residents with limited resources.

The seeds of the neighborhood's success story were planted a half-century ago. In 1966, community activists challenged the city's urban renewal plans that called for razing homes and businesses in the low-income neighborhood. They formed Madison Park Development Corporation (MPDC), one of the nation's first resident-led community development organizations. Today, MPDC provides affordable homes to more than 3,000 families and continues to work to revitalize Roxbury's Dudley Square commercial district. At the same time that MPDC was established in the 1960s, Cuban immigrant Pastor Medina arrived and opened Tropical Foods in Dudley Square. The grocery store catered mostly to shoppers seeking Caribbean and South American foods, but Medina's grandsons, Ronn and Randy Garry, eventually wanted to expand the store beyond its tight quarters and limited selection.

CHALLENGE

Historically, access to healthy food has been a challenge in Boston's Roxbury neighborhood. The community has some of the city's highest rates of heart disease, diabetes and cancer, but the mostly African-American neighborhood had no supermarket, only high-priced convenience stores and bodegas carrying little fresh produce, meats and dairy.

The project expands local business opportunities and employment, revitalizes a commercial district formerly in decline and serves as a key remedy for the community's food insecurity.

MPDC saw the Garrys' intentions as an opportunity to collaborate on a redevelopment project that would prove highly important for Dudley Square, and in 2012 the two joined forces to secure funding and approval to develop a city-owned lot for multiple purposes.

As the lead developer of the venture, MPDC worked with the Boston Redevelopment Authority on the design for the new store, which boasts large windows overlooking a tree-lined boulevard and a strikingly modern exterior. Now triple its former size, Tropical Foods has expanded to include a deli, fish market and bakery.

The project has made an important impact on the local economy. The rebuilt Tropical Foods created 30 new permanent jobs, buys many of its products from local vendors and supports local charities and other nonprofits.

Opened in 2015, the new supermarket is the centerpiece for MPDC's three-acre redevelopment plan for the Roxbury site. The renovation of the former Tropical Foods store to provide mixed-income housing and retail space is under construction and will open in 2017. Construction of a 59,000-square foot commercial building is the third and final phase.

This first privately-led development of city land in the neighborhood is a striking example of effective cross-sector collaboration. The project expands local business opportunities and employment, it revitalizes a commercial district formerly in decline and, it serves as a key part of the remedy for the community's food insecurity.

Meanwhile, the venture has prompted improvements within the MPDC organization as well. Early in the construction, protesters picketed the site over concerns that some workers were not paid a fair wage. Though those wages were paid by a subcontractor, MPDC stepped in and forged a policy ensuring a $15-per-hour minimum wage for all workers for all of its projects. The intense scrutiny played a role in spurring MPDC and Tropical Foods to increase the number of local residents and people of color in its construction workforce. Eventually, the project's workforce included 41 percent Boston residents and 55 percent people of color.

The Tropical Foods partnership enhances MPDC's community building and engagement activities, in particular its Health Equity and Wellness initiative, which works to address health disparities in the neighborhood. An MPDC food-access project now includes nutrition workshops and cooking classes that offer participants tours of the supermarket. People learn how to read nutrition labels and bring home ingredients for trying new recipes provided by MPDC's health and wellness partner, Cooking Matters.

In 2014, the food insecurity rate in Suffolk County was 15.9%.

The store's co-owner Ronn Garry hosts the tours and says: "Our customers shop here because we not only offer a complete, modern supermarket shopping experience but also have special product offerings catering to Hispanic, Caribbean and other ethnic consumers."

Today the "Gateway to Dudley Square," once a blighted vacant lot at the intersection of two busy roadways in a dense residential neighborhood, is a welcoming entryway to the neighborhood, offering its residents affordable access to healthy food. Financing for the $15.5 million project was provided by Bank of America, a MassWorks grant, the U.S. Department of Health and Human Services' Healthy Food Initiative and the Commonwealth of Massachusetts Executive Office of Housing and Economic Development.

The project imparts three important lessons: 1) local business can benefit greatly by partnering with a committed CDC to achieve mutual objectives; 2) partnerships require compromise and attention to trust-building and, 3) when intense scrutiny is met by transparently addressing community concerns, everyone benefits.

ABOUT JEANNE PINADO

Jeanne Pinado is the chief executive officer of Madison Park Development Corporation, a nonprofit community development organization with a full-time staff of 33 and a $5.5 million budget. MPDC serves 12,500 people annually from Roxbury and greater Boston. In addition to the construction and preservation of 1,252 affordable housing units, MPDC has robust community engagement programs, which include the Hibernian Hall performing arts center and MPDC's community action initiatives. Pinado has guided MPDC since 1998 as it has expanded to build the power of the Roxbury community through partnerships, cross-sector collaboration and advocacy. Pinado's affiliations include Zoo New England, Foley Hoag Foundation, Citizens Housing and Planning Association, Massachusetts Association of Community Development Corporations, Boston Private Bank Advisory Board and NeighborWorks Capital.

HEALTH AND HOUSING: A VITAL COLLABORATION

Gloria Ortiz-Fisher, Executive Director

Westside Housing Organization

Studies continue to demonstrate that an unhealthy home environment can lead to illness and injury, particularly in demographic groups that spend a majority of their time indoors, such as seniors and children. Common environmental hazards include exposure to lead, which can result in developmental delays, speech delays, kidney problems and even death. Indoor exposure to radon, mold, pests, tobacco smoke, water leaks, drafts and asbestos can result in respiratory illness, allergies, poisoning or immunocompromised conditions. A 2011 study that looked at the impact to low-income children with asthma of home-based environmental intervention and education found significant caregiver-reported reductions in pediatric asthma severity.

The negative effects of unhealthy housing are disproportionately felt by low-income people and people of color who often live in aging homes and in neighborhoods in need of investment. The demographic groups most at risk of illness are children below the age of six and pregnant women, those living below the poverty line or in older housing and children of color. While healthy home interventions, such as minor home repairs, can reduce and prevent illness, low-income people often lack the means to pay for repairs and may experience a financial crisis when home maintenance is required for larger home systems such as heating/cooling, windows or plumbing.

Though Westside Housing's core competency includes quality home repairs, the organization lacked the know-how and funding to pursue a healthy homes strategy

CHALLENGE

Illness and injury are often the result of household hazards that can be addressed through basic repairs. Though Westside Housing had the skills and resources necessary to complete quality home repairs, it lacked the know-how and funding to pursue a healthy homes strategy.

The connection between housing and healthcare is essential to restoring equity in the neighborhoods we serve and to meeting the mandate of our mission to build robust, sustainable communities.

without collaboration from healthcare organizations. Recognizing that Westside's mission and strength is in affordable and healthy homes, we were confident that, with the guidance and financial support of a healthcare practitioner, Westside Housing could play an essential part in improving health for low-income people.

Westside Housing pursued strategic partnerships with local healthcare organizations that are also committed to holistic and equitable approaches to home-based health interventions. Westside Housing has collaborated with the Kansas City Health Department around such initiatives as lead safe homes, smoke-free homes and healthier communities through urban gardening. Through Westside Housing's relationship with Children's Mercy Hospital, our staff received training on conducting healthy home assessments aimed at identifying household hazards that impact children. Once hazards are identified home repairs can be made that prevent or reduce environmentally triggered illness. We have subsequently repaired dozens of homes for low-income families with children ages six and under in the greater Kansas City area.

In addition, Westside transitioned its multi-family rental homes to smoke-free environments and with supportive funding from the Kansas City Health Department, continues to maintain and grow its urban gardens, which contribute to the sense of community and health of the residents on the Westside.

"Words cannot express how thankful I am for all of the work you helped coordinate for my home. The repairs done were things I couldn't afford and they have made a huge difference. Thank you so much for all your hard work, especially when things were tough," said a participant in Westside Housing's health homes program.

Though this work is fairly new to the organization, we are confident that healthy housing sits at the fore-front of our mission. The connection between hous-ing and healthcare is essential to restoring equity in the neighborhoods we serve and to meeting the man-date of our mission to build robust, sustainable com-munities. Healthy homes work is not incidental to our mission; it is our mission. We are confident that

In Boston, 27% of young children live below the poverty line.

healthy housing will be a focus for affordable housing, healthcare and governmental organizations over the long-term.

Westside Housing's experience demonstrates that partnerships with healthcare organizations can significantly expand the knowledge and resources available to affordable housing practitioners. Westside Housing's staff received healthy homes assessment training at no cost from Children's Mercy Hospital, and uses Kansas City Department of Health funding for lead abatement work and other healthy homes repairs.

We are confident that this work will continue to be a focus for governments and healthcare orga-nizations for the long-term. Partnerships with those addressing healthy home environments are critical to intervening in environmentally triggered illness. Identifying funding for the expense of home repairs is a challenge. While the city of Kansas City continues to be interested in funding this work, Mercy Children's Hospital has only limited funding beyond what it provides in staff training. Like Westside, Mercy Children's Hospital is pursuing funding from corporations and foundations interested in solutions to the problem of unhealthy home environments. Fortunately, our relationship with them means that when they are funded, Westside will be a partner in that funding.

Healthy housing work also opens up new venues for philanthropic support. Instead of seeking support from funders whose singular interest is in affordable housing, Westside Housing is now pursuing support from healthcare sources, which may prove to be a significant opportunity over the long run.

ABOUT GLORIA ORTIZ-FISHER

Gloria Ortiz-Fisher brings over 30 years of business and financial management experience. She has a bachelor's degree in accounting from Park College and a master's of business administration degree from Keller Graduate School. Previously, Ortiz-Fisher served as the director of finance and purchasing for Jackson County, Missouri from 2003-2007. Throughout her career, Ortiz-Fisher has been an effective advocate for healthy, energy-efficient and affordable housing.

THE FARMORY: INDOOR FARM GIVES A DOWNTOWN NEIGHBORHOOD A HEALTHY BOOST

Noel S. Halvorsen, Executive Director

NeighborWorks Green Bay

Despite revitalization in the Navarino neighborhood in downtown Green Bay, WI, the low-income area still suffered from lingering poverty. One major symptom was the lack of access to healthy affordable food. Meanwhile, a big historic building that once housed a military armory had sat shuttered in the heart of the neighborhood for nearly half a century. Attempts over the years to convert the dilapidated armory into something constructive for the community were thwarted by the massive renovation costs.

About a decade ago, NeighborWorks Green Bay (NWGB) acquired the unique property that operated as a military armory up until the early 1970s. NWGB had led much-needed renovation projects in the low-income Navarino neighborhood surrounding the armory, but the residents still suffered from some problems stemming from poverty. One of the biggest is that the area was still a food desert, where residents had no access to healthy, affordable fresh food.

Throughout the past few years, several attempts were made to bring the 20,000-square-foot historic armory back to life and give the neighborhood an economic boost. However, a 14-inch thick concrete floor separating the first and second stories and other structural challenges made renovations too costly and limited what could be

CHALLENGE

The Navarino neighborhood in downtown Green Bay, WI has seen some revitalization in recent years, but the low-income area still showed signs of lingering poverty. One of the biggest problems is the lack of access to healthy, affordable food.

Ultimately this urban farm community center is seen as a self-sustaining social enterprise that addresses both financial and food issues for the community.

altered in the original structure. NWGB had to think innovatively about the project, which was unlike anything it had previously undertaken.

In 2013, a local business approached NWGB and asked about converting the vacant building into an indoor farm. They wanted to create a not-for-profit business that would grow food and provide work for military veterans. They didn't have much more than the concept, but were eager to explore it. That same year, NWGB was participating in a social innovation leadership program sponsored by regional community and family foundations. As part of the program, the group

toured Growing Power, an industry leading urban farm using aquaponics in Milwaukee, Wisconsin. That experience inspired new ideas for NWGB and the local business.

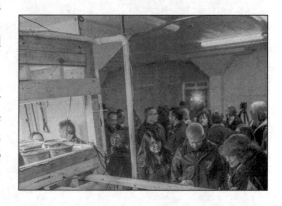

NWGB came up with a plan to turn the armory into The Farmory, an indoor farm to provide the neighborhood with foods like fresh vegetables, herbs and fish. The Farmory, which is slated to open in October 2017, also brings jobs and educational opportunities to the community.

Volunteer workers who complete The Farmory program will earn materials to build backyard "hoop houses." This way, residents are not only learning how to grow food indoors by volunteering, they are able to take this knowledge and hands-on experience home to provide for their families. A hoop house acts as a greenhouse and extends the outdoor growing season by several months. The Farmory aims to increase the self-sufficiency of area residents by providing educational programming as well as a variety of volunteer program pathways to earn rewards. It also offers scholarships for further education or entrepreneurial training, links to area employment programs, materials to start their own growing operations and fresh Farmory produce.

In 2015, NWGB and its subsidiary, the Urban Partnership for Community Development Corporation (CDC), secured funding for architectural services, engineering and hazard control and hired a design-build firm to draw up the plans. NWGB also purchased an adjacent property for The

Farmory's future expansion. A total of $550,000 was raised from multiple sources, including the Green Bay Housing Authority, NeighborWorks America, the Basic Needs Giving Partnership, the U.S. Conference of Mayors and Wells Fargo. The most talked about result that was initially achieved is a test aquaculture grow system. Fully operational since February of 2016, this system operates to pilot farming techniques for The Farmory's full-scale operation, which is 50 times larger.

In 2013, 6-9% of U.S. households were without access to healthy food choices.

The Farmory will include two acres of grow systems in vertical stacks that will produce plants fed by water flowing from the fish tanks. Community residents, particularly those unemployed or underemployed, will be hired to assist in the food-growing operations. Produce sales will fund job skills development programs, entrepreneurial training and college scholarships. Ultimately, this urban farm community center is seen as a self-sustaining social enterprise that addresses both financial and food issues for the community.

In 2016, a Farmory's open house marked the project's public launch. Over 400 people attended the event, which was publicized through social media and day-of local media interviews alone. That year, we also launched a campaign to raise $3 million for the ongoing renovations.

The project is unprecedented for NWGB and Green Bay, and there have been plenty of lessons learned along the way. Our team found that developing a project timeline and setting achievable, detailed goals is essential to driving a large project forward. Receiving money too early in the process can be a challenge if it comes with expectations of success that can't be realized until after many more dollars are raised. A project like this requires a team with varied expertise and oversight and coordination are essential when bringing together alternative farmers, builders, bankers, academics and community residents.

ABOUT NOEL S. HALVORSEN

Noel S. Halvorsen has been serving as executive director of NeighborWorks Green Bay since 2000. Halvorsen has led the acquisition, renovation or development of 180 units of housing and 29,000 square feet of commercial space. During his tenure, NeighborWorks Green Bay has counseled more than 8,000 area households and helped more than 2,000 families to purchase homes. Halvorsen is active in other organizations including the Green Bay Neighborhood Leadership Council, the NeighborWorks Alliance of Wisconsin and the National NeighborWorks Association.

HOUSING AND HEALTH CARE NONPROFITS WORK TOGETHER TO ACHIEVE AFFORDABLE HOME-BASED HEALTHCARE

Tim Bolding, Executive Director

United Housing

All too often, seniors and people with disabilities find themselves forced into nursing homes because they don't have access to long-term care and other support in their homes. In many cases, they may not require the costly skilled care from an institution, just nursing care or therapy and help with medication, transportation and grocery shopping. But long-term insurance, including Medicaid, may not cover such residential services, and while some states do offer financial assistance for home- and community-based care, financial hurdles still exist across the country.

In Tennessee, more than 20,000 Medicaid recipients live in skilled nursing facilities, according to the latest figures from TennCare, Tennessee's Medicaid program. Over 8,000 recipients are cared for through residential and community-based services, an option provided for the elderly and people with disabilities who prefer to remain in their homes. Extending such residential services to more patients rather than institutionalizing them would significantly cut costs, but traditional approaches fail to incorporate more cost-effective systems.

United Housing Inc.'s (UHI) mission is to provide quality housing opportunities to Mid-South residents through financial education, mortgage lending, home building and renovation, and creative partnerships with public, private

CHALLENGE

Many Medicaid patients are prematurely placed in institutions because they can't afford to receive care in their own homes or make them safe and accessible. In Tennessee, more than 8,000 Medicaid recipients do get residential or community based services, but another 20,000 live in facilities which cost far more than home-care would.

and nonprofit entities. UHI serves residents that are underserved by the traditional homeownership and banking industry, as well as individuals with disabilities who need accessible homes to live comfortable, stable lives.

The success of our endeavors is in large part due to the establishment of regional networks and to investments from many national and federal programs and sources. These relationships positioned UHI to play a leading role in helping stabilize western Tennessee's most threatened residents and neighborhoods.

Recently, UHI partnered with TennCare and others to help Tennessee residents stay in their homes. The initiative is aimed at providing the elderly and people with intellectual, developmental and physical disabilities with quality home care and accessibility modifications to their residences. This includes not only supporting those who want to stay in their homes, but those able to move back home from institutions.

TennCare has long provided medical care for the state's sick and elderly residents by covering their nursing home costs. But the work of UHI and our partners, Shelby Residential and Vocational Services (SRVS) and Meritan, demonstrates that it is possible to cut TennCare's costs significantly by providing care in the home.

Key to this initiative is expanding housing options and services. TennCare has an affordable housing program for developing, purchasing and rehabilitating single-family homes, duplexes and/or small groupings of tiny homes or apartments. These homes can be used to house recipients of one or many of TennCare's healthcare programs.

SRVS, a nonprofit offering assistance and services to people with disabilities in Shelby County, has a unique model in which three individuals live together in a single-family home that has been retrofitted to be accessible in accordance with the Americans with Disabilities Act.

Meritan, a nonprofit home health care service provider, has a similar program. Meritan's clients have a wide range of disabilities. In addition to the primary diagnosis of a developmental disability, many of their clients also have mobility issues and limited vision, hearing and speech. Medical residential services (MRS) are provided in a home where all residents require direct skilled nursing as well as habilitative support that enables an individual to acquire, retain or improve skills necessary to reside in a community-based setting. MRS patients require direct skilled nursing care on a daily basis and at a level that cannot be provided through two or fewer daily skilled nursing visits. Licensed nurses can provide all of these services in the home.

About 4.2% of the 65+ population are in nursing homes at any given time.

Each one of the TennCare's affordable units will follow state accessibility guidelines. Those include step-free entry with features such as wheelchair ramps, lowered cabinets and accessible restrooms. This allows people with cognitive or physical disabilities to maintain some independence while receiving top-quality care. It also means large-scale savings for TennCare, which can now employ less costly care in homes and communities instead of footing nursing home bills. TennCare also saves on construction by deploying the expertise of nonprofit housing developers.

But UHI's partnership with Meritan and SRVS benefits not just these health care organizations, the residents and TennCare. Generating income through our developed area of expertise means that UHI earns revenue and expands our capacity to do more while maintaining a healthy organization.

As UHI begins strategic planning for the next five years, our vision is to provide the necessary housing for a diverse population. While traditionally UHI has focused on homeownership, the organization understands how health intersects with housing and neighborhood environments. UHI stands ready to provide healthy homes through creative partnerships while maintaining our traditional homeownership work.

We have learned that while complex partnerships such as these are beneficial to all, they are not always easy to achieve. We needed the support of the NeighborWorks network to help us expand through capacity building. This in turn encouraged each organization to develop strategies that pull the best from the public and private sectors.

ABOUT TIM BOLDING

Tim Bolding is the founder and executive director of United Housing, a nonprofit housing agency serving West Tennessee. UHI's mission is to provide quality housing opportunities through financial education, foreclosure mitigation, home construction and mortgage lending. UHI has a staff of ten full-time employees and a budget of $2.8 million. The organization serves 600 people annually through a variety of programs.

HEALTH, HOUSING AND EDUCATION – THE NEXUS

Frank Shea, Executive Director

Urban Edge

Children from poor neighborhoods are more likely to live in substandard homes, and studies have linked quality, stable housing with positive health and education outcomes. Student performance varies dramatically among rich and poor neighborhoods, with wide proficiency gaps in reading and math. Meanwhile, many of the health problems and costs associated with poor housing opportunities could be prevented or reversed through education that can modify behaviors and lifestyles. Those changes are simple, novel, evidence-based approaches, which include exercise, proper nutrition and anti-stress activities.

Unfortunately, schools in poor neighborhoods lack the financial resources needed to provide even these simple remedies to improve the performance and health of their students. In Boston's Hyde Park neighborhood, budget cuts forced the closing of two schools in 2015; the following year Boston schools' proposed budget threatened to fall short by $50 million. Addressing the gap opened by shrinking school funding is thus critical to improving the health and academic performance in Boston's neighborhoods.

For over 40 years, Urban Edge has been building and preserving quality affordable homes and promoting housing stability through programs such as eviction prevention and economic resiliency programs. Roughly 3,000 people live in Urban Edge's housing, and 85 percent of those households have school-age children. Over the years, we have seen fewer evictions and other signs of increased housing stability in the 1,400 units we own in Boston.

CHALLENGE

Budget cuts in a Boston neighborhood forced the closing of two schools. Shortly thereafter, Boston schools' proposed budget threatened to fall short by $50 million. What was needed was a way to fill in the funding gap to provide Boston's neighborhoods with the resources to overcome both health and educational challenges.

This innovative, multi-faceted, dual-generation approach holds great promise for enhancing the educational and health/wellness opportunities for the families served by Urban Edge.

However, rising costs for student services in our communities cannot keep up with current revenue sources.

To fill this critical gap for students in need, Urban Edge joined forces with several partners to improve health and education opportunities in the Egleston and Jackson Square neighborhoods. Our 2015-2020 strategic plan provides an integrated approach to community development with holistic programs that supplement our housing work with new initiatives in early education, financial resiliency, youth engagement and public health and wellness.

Urban Edge teamed up with Union Capital Boston (UCB), Families First Parenting programs, Jumpstart and local health organizations to create a pre-K readiness program that incorporates comprehensive wellness benefits through healthy habits. The goal of the program is to increase children's developmental gains, as well as provide caregivers with the knowledge and skills necessary to prepare children for kindergarten. This pre-K readiness program assists the entire family. It provides an opportunity for parents to help improve their children's literacy, expose them to school settings, increase parenting skills and knowledge about child development. It also builds stronger families and their connection to the community.

The Families First Parenting programs provide parents with the tools they need to become effective advocates for their children's education. Research shows that when parents take an active role in a child's development, they can promote their mental, emotional and physical health, thus breaking the cycle of poverty for their families.

The program, which is specifically designed for young parents and their children, offers exercise classes and education on healthy diets. Nutritional instruction, grocery shopping tips and zumba classes are just some of the resources offered. Fitness, nutrition, and social support services are the pillars of the program, which promotes healthy life skills and helps put parents on the path to self-sufficiency.

One woman said the program made a tremendous difference in her child's progress. "My daughter was diagnosed with autism at age 2. She had no language. Since this September when school started [she] started saying words. We are so excited for her!"

In a classroom of 30 children, about 3 are likely to have asthma.

UCB offers a financial perk for joining the program. Its mobile-based loyalty program for low-income families gives social and financial service rewards in exchange for community involvement in schools, health centers and civic programs. Every time a parent attends a pre-K readiness class, they check in via the UCB app. Residents accumulate points for each check-in, which can be redeemed for gift cards and other prizes at the end of the program.

This innovative, multi-faceted, dual-generation approach holds great promise for enhancing the academic and life opportunities for the families we serve. The participating parents have emerged as leaders in the community, recruiting other participants and planning and implementing future programming in paid, part-time positions.

We are in the early stages of this plan, but we've gained many insights in the process. First, lack of funding to further our goals doesn't need to be a deal-breaker. Innovative approaches and partnerships can fill those gaps. And sometimes the most effective remedies to a problem are the simplest, like promoting positive change by providing basic information on wellness and parenting skills. Finally, those you seek to serve in your endeavors can turn out to be the best promoters – like our program's participating parents who have taken the reins into their own hands.

ABOUT FRANK SHEA

Frank Shea was appointed as CEO of Urban Edge in 2015. Previously, he served as the executive director for Olneyville Housing Corporation in Rhode Island for 15 years. He led the growth in that organization from two staff members and an annual budget of $100,000, to a staff of 14, with an annual operating budget of $1.6 million, and more than $35 million invested in the neighborhood. Shea has more than 20 years of experience with federal and state affordable housing and community development programs and extensive experience implementing strategic partnerships.

HEALTHY HOMES – HEALTHY RESIDENTS

Rick Goodemann, CEO

Southwest Minnesota Housing Partnership

Housing-based health hazards such as pests, mold and moisture, radon and lead erode residents' quality of life, increase the likelihood of injury and illness and complicate housing affordability with excess medical expenses. In most communities, the oldest housing in the poorest condition is overwhelmingly occupied by households with the least ability to address the problem. These households may not have the knowledge, the physical ability or the financial resources to fix the problems or secure other housing.

Southwest Minnesota Housing Partnership (SWMHP), based in Slayton, MN, is a small nonprofit dedicated to creating thriving places to live, grow, and work through partnerships with communities. SWMHP provides community planning, real estate development, grant administration services and educational programs to communities in about thirty rural Minnesota counties.

Since 1992, our organization has inspected thousands of owner- and renter-occupied homes in Minnesota as part of housing rehabilitation programs. In Pipestone, Worthington, Mankato and other communities, low-income families with children, refugee and immigrant households, seniors and persons with disabilities had to choose between unaffordable housing and unhealthy housing. For families and communities to thrive, housing rehabilitation and design had to do more than meet minimum requirements.

We employ a health first approach in rehabilitation, new construction and community engagement programs,

CHALLENGE

Household hazards such as pests, mold, radon and lead erode residents' quality of life, increase health risks and complicate housing affordability with high medical bills. Most of the oldest homes in the poorest condition are overwhelmingly occupied by residents with the least ability to address the problem.

We employ a health first approach in rehabilitation, new construction and community engagement programs, even when it isn't the stated goal.

even when it isn't the stated goal. In owner-occupied rehabilitation programs, which operate with a first-come first-served model, we met with public health nurses, community education providers and refugee programs to target resources to households with high risk of childhood lead poisoning, asthma and other health concerns.

Our health first response blossomed in 2004 with the rehabilitation of Viking Terrace Apartments, which had water damage, pests, ventilation issues and a disconnect from community. Through our involvement with Enterprise Green Communities, National Center for Healthy Housing, Blue

Cross Blue Shield of Minnesota Foundation and the Center for Sustainable Building Research (University of Minnesota), Viking Terrace became a test case for green and healthy improvements in affordable housing.

We conducted meetings with residents and project partners to plan the redevelopment through a green and healthy lens and prioritize materials, design, and construction practices with likely health benefits. We focused on ventilation, pest management, moisture control, radon reduction and enhanced exterior space to encourage active recreation and community building. Two impact studies were conducted: the University of Minnesota measured water and energy conservation performance, and an NCHH study measured the health of residents compared to a pre-rehabilitation baseline. Researchers documented improvements in respiratory issues for children and adults and about one-third reported better overall health.

"Underhoused or unsheltered households have two to three times the healthcare costs of adequately housed households," said Scott Johnson, executive director of Southwestern Mental Health Center. "We see health improvements for long-term homeless individuals who enter our supportive housing programs."

We improved four other properties, evaluating the lessons from previous projects to select high-impact investments for resident health. At Orness Plaza, a public housing building in Mankato in need of repair, we provided health-focused development services to another property owner. The renovation focused on ventilation, moisture and mold reduction, seamless integration of indoor/outdoor connections and onsite services. As part of the Green Rehabilitation of Elder Apartment Treatments Study, researchers documented that our rehabilitation choices resulted in improved mental and general physical health, prevented falls and reduced exposure to tobacco smoke. (Research partners included the National Center for Healthy Housing, Mankato EDA and the Center for Sustainable Building Research. The research project was funded by U.S. Department of Housing and Urban Development, Blue Cross Blue Shield Foundation of Minnesota and The McKnight Foundation). The project also reduced management expenses through system upgrades and energy and water efficiency improvements.

4.6 million cases of asthma in the U.S. are attributed to dampness and mold exposure in the home.

Through our healthy housing initiatives, we've learned that 1) owners, renters and property managers need to be engaged to take advantage of the health benefits of better buildings; 2) establishing green and healthy property management standards in our more than 1,600 housing units empowers residents and encourages managers to suggest effective green and healthy cleaning products and support healthy resident behaviors regarding waste and recycling; 3) our home maintenance courses, when paired with Adult Basic Education and English Language Learner courses, have been especially effective in targeting households most vulnerable to poor housing conditions; 4) healthy housing assessments, which reach high-need households identified through school nurses, social workers and church leaders engage public health and housing inspectors to provide balanced perspective on physical condition of housing as well as behaviors that affect a family's health; and 5) partnerships with local public health agencies and city housing inspectors generate interest from new funders, enabling us to better target housing rehabilitation funds and assessments with support from state, federal and private resources.

ABOUT RICK GOODEMANN

Rick Goodemann is the founding CEO of the Southwest Minnesota Housing Partnership, which provides community development and technical assistance services in 30 rural counties of southern Minnesota. Accomplishments include the development, preservation, financing or rehabilitation of more than 8,400 housing units with over $561 million in direct housing development and financing. Goodemann has over twenty-five years' experience creating and delivering rural development and housing finance products and programs in public and private settings.

IMPROVING HOUSING AND HEALTH FOR UNDERSERVED RESIDENTS

Walter Moreau, Executive Director

Foundation Communities

Foundation Communities, a nonprofit affordable housing provider based in Austin, TX, noticed a disturbing pattern. Almost every day, medical emergencies brought ambulances to their supportive housing communities for formerly homeless single adults. At their family communities, many residents were struggling with chronic diseases and obesity. Faced with similar and increasing health needs of both client groups, Foundation Communities began a systematic effort to improve the health of its residents.

Foundation Communities owns and operates 19 affordable housing communities in Austin and North Texas, providing homes to over 5,000 residents. In 2008, Foundation Communities' supportive housing properties, home to 345 formerly homeless men and women, accounted for 338 emergency calls in Austin. That year, 65 percent of formerly homeless move-outs were because of behavior-related issues, often the result of substance abuse and ineffectively managed mental health conditions. While staff worked to connect residents with health and medical services, barriers existed. Formerly homeless, non-suicidal and non-homicidal resident patients reported having to wait three months to see a psychiatrist.

Residents at Foundation Communities' supportive housing properties were not the only ones facing significant health challenges. At our family communities, chronic

CHALLENGE

Almost every day, medical emergencies brought ambulances to housing communities for formerly homeless single adults and families. Many residents were struggling with chronic diseases, obesity and substance abuse. A fundamental disconnect between health and housing needed to be addressed.

Foundation Communities concluded that a fundamental disconnect between the health and housing sectors was undermining its mission.

conditions such as hypertension, diabetes and obesity were preeminent health concerns, a common problem across Texas, which has the 10th highest obesity rate and the seventh highest adolescent obesity rate in the nation. In Austin, approximately 35 percent of students in grades 3 to 12 are overweight or obese. In Travis County, where Austin is located, 37 percent of adults are overweight. Chronic disease is another concern in Travis County, where three out of four deaths are attributed to chronic diseases such as cancer, heart disease, stroke, lung disease and diabetes.

Foundation Communities concluded that a fundamental disconnect between the health and housing sectors was undermining its mission and preventing some of its residents from thriving.

Over the next seven years, we developed a holistic strategy to incorporate health into our onsite support services. Today, a corps of 18 resident "Health Champions," similar to the "community health worker" model common in health settings, organizes health and wellness classes for more than 2,000 residents and community members per year. Community gardens, walking paths and new fitness "caminos" at our communities make healthy choices easier. We also tested, implemented and refined new strategies to increase physical activity in our after-school program. At our communities serving formerly homeless adults, integration of behavioral and physical health services improved health, reduced housing insecurity and reduced ambulance visits. Ultimately, we were able to support a culture of health through key partnerships, financial resources and resident leadership.

In 2010, Bianca Enriquez, one of our success stories, lost her home and needed a job. As a mother of two young boys, the stress of finding a sense of stability weighed on her health. To her surprise, Foundation Communities had more to offer than simply a place to live.

"I'm so thankful for all of the programs they offer. There is no other apartment complex that is going to offer health classes, free childcare and financial classes," says Enriquez. "My kids are at the point in their life that they are really active. I want to be able to be active with them."

A year after moving in, Enriquez landed a part-time job as a pre-literacy teacher at one of Foundation Communities' Learning Centers, a springboard to a full-time position at the City of Austin Health and Human Services Department as a neighborhood services unit administrator.

18 resident "Health Champions" organize health and wellness classes for more than 200 community members per year.

Enriquez took the newly introduced Zumba classes at her apartment complex to get active and relieve stress and was asked to become a Health Champion, a resident leader to coordinate health activities for their community. Enriquez's experience working at Foundation Communities, her interest in health and wellness and her motivation to be an example for her two young boys made her a perfect candidate.

Enriquez organizes weekly exercise and nutrition classes for her community, plans a yearly health fair and organizes special health programming every three months such as a diabetes awareness course. To engage her neighbors effectively, she delivers fliers, goes door-to-door to ask if people are interested in attending a health class, invites people to classes whenever she sees them and frequently asks her neighbors what they want to get out of each class to make sure the classes are meeting their needs. Enriquez loves being able to exercise at her property and to learn new things.

Foundation Communities learned that healthy living is intricately involved with housing and affordable housing communities can succeed by developing onsite wellness programs.

ABOUT WALTER MOREAU

For 18 years, Walter Moreau has been the executive director of Foundation Communities, a local nonprofit providing affordable homes and free onsite support services for thousands of families, veterans, seniors and people with disabilities. Under Moreau's leadership, Foundation Communities was the first in Austin to combine housing with support services, realizing that both are essential to truly transforming people's lives.

RESTORING NEIGHBORHOOD VITALITY AND IMPROVING RESIDENT HEALTH

Peter Gagliardi, CEO

HAPHousing

In 2004, abandoned houses and vacant lots plagued the Old Hill neighborhood of Springfield, MA. Property values had dropped to the point that lenders and the city were unwilling to foreclose and take responsibility for these derelict properties. The neighborhood was also beset by an active drug market and local gang activity. In addition, Old Hill residents experienced a disproportionately high rate of chronic disease and struggled with limited access to healthy foods with no full-line grocery store nearby. Residents were discouraged and doubted anything would change.

HAPHousing, serving western Massachusetts for over 40 years, develops housing throughout the region. We also provide property management, rental assistance, education and counseling for homeownership, and programs that shelter and rehouse as well as prevent families from becoming homeless. Based in Springfield, the organization is committed to revitalizing urban neighborhoods through collaboration, community planning, housing development, resident leadership and engagement.

Old Hill, historically an African-American neighborhood, is now 44 percent black, 42 percent Hispanic and 11 percent Caucasian. The neighborhood has many assets and high profile neighbors including MassMutual (a Fortune 100 company), a technology park and three colleges. In 2004, after the completion of the Old Hill Master Plan, HAPHousing, Springfield Neighborhood Housing Services and Greater Springfield Habitat for Humanity formed a limited liabili-

CHALLENGE

The Old Hill neighborhood of Springfield, MA, was plagued with abandoned houses and vacant lots. Property values had plunged and an active drug market and gang activity imperiled the neighborhood. The residents were also prone to chronic diseases and had limited access to healthy foods.

"Residents are excited to be developing strategies to improve the health of their neighbors while continuing to revitalize the neighborhood."

— Awilda Sanchez, Old Hill Neighborhood Council vice president

ty company in collaboration with the Old Hill Neighborhood Council and Springfield College. We aimed to not only stabilize but transform Old Hill by improving the physical environment, increasing resident confidence and wellbeing and catalyzing the private market to reinvest in the neighborhood.

HAPHousing also created a land-banking fund to acquire and assemble distressed properties for the development of new one- and two-family homes for sale to eligible buyers. On the policy front, we convinced the city to move from a tax title auction process to a far more effective request for proposal process, which contributed key parcels to their assembly of clusters for redevelopment. Their house designs mirrored the architecture and streetscape of the neighborhood. Ultimately, we developed 68 new or rehabbed homes.

Rebuilding Together – now Revitalize Community Development Corporation – joined the effort and worked with Springfield Neighborhood Housing Services to improve curb appeal, undertake critical repairs and refurbish 82 homes. Since 2004, the efforts of HAPHousing and our collaborators have cut the number of vacant and abandoned properties in half. Together we have developed or refurbished 150 homes, creating a palpable difference in the neighborhood.

HAPHousing was also part of a larger coalition that renovated the gym and schoolyard of a neighborhood elementary school through a private/public partnership. We also attracted funding for the redevelopment of three parks in Old Hill and many roads and sidewalks. An early childhood education center was completely renovated and public safety was improved through a Weed and Seed Initiative that invested in youth programs and an enhanced police presence.

Building on these successes, HAPHousing hired consultants to come up with a new plan for the neighborhood. The Old Hill Action Plan 2015-2020 includes 12 primary goals covering capacity building, physical improvements, culture and community building and public safety. Plans also include addressing the remaining vacant lots, creating a community gathering space and enhancing community spirit through a neighborhood garden and more celebrations.

HAPHousing has achieved dramatic improvements, but there is still more to be done. As the Action Plan was being completed, we were awarded a planning grant from a national awards program, the BUILD Health Challenge, to launch the Healthy Hill Initiative. This new multi-sector collaboration includes Partners for a Healthier Community, the City Departments of Health and Human Services, Police and Housing, the Old Neighborhood Council and five other community-based organizations. Springfield's two hospital systems are also playing key roles. Baystate Health is providing data to analyze health conditions by census tract. Mercy Medical Center recently received a multi-year grant to launch a Transforming Communities Initiative in several Springfield neighborhoods.

HAPHousing's neighborhood transformation celebration has grown from 80 to 800 participants since 2004.

The Healthy Hill Initiative addresses health inequities through improving public safety, housing, parks and access to physical activity and fresh food. A centerpiece of the initiative is a plan to develop a full-service grocery store. Even though health was not their specific target, several collaborative efforts over the last 12 years have addressed many social determinants of health. With an enriched perspective, several of the most troubling health issues can be addressed with a focus on increasing physical activity for residents of all ages in order to reduce obesity, diabetes and other chronic diseases. With support from many funding partners, HAPHousing will help Old Hill residents adopt healthier lifestyles and improve their health and wellbeing. As the Old Hill neighborhood transforms, residents' lives continue to improve, fostering positive changes that will create a more vibrant neighborhood.

This project illustrates several important lessons: 1) Through multi-sector collaboration, we were able to accomplish many improvements in housing, infrastructure, education, public safety, and community spirit; 2) despite many successes in neighborhood revitalization, the residents still have a disproportionately high rate of chronic disease; and 3) the Healthy Hill Initiative must take a comprehensive approach to address multiple social determinants of health in order to achieve transformative change.

ABOUT PETER GAGLIARDI

Peter Gagliardi has served as CEO of HAPHousing since 1991. A nonprofit housing organization founded in 1972, HAPHousing is the largest developer of affordable housing in the region, often working collaboratively to bring affordable housing to suburban communities and to revitalize inner-city neighborhoods. It offers leadership training engaging urban residents in neighborhood planning and improvement efforts. Providing rental assistance to over 5,000 households in three counties, HAPHousing also manages a portfolio of 670 rental units in 19 properties. HAPHousing also leads the Western Massachusetts Homeownership Collaborative, which offers a wide range of housing counseling, foreclosure prevention and homebuyer education services throughout the four counties of western Massachusetts.

HEALTHY HOMES FOR ELDERS IN CAMBRIDGE

Peter Daly, Executive Director

Cambridge Neighborhood Apartment Housing Services

Cambridge Neighborhood Apartment Housing Services (CNAHS) purchased an elderly facility that risked losing its affordability requirements. However, the residents needed more than just a stable home. With rising healthcare costs and limited income, many of the senior residents felt stuck and unable to live well. They yearned for independent living, but required better healthcare access. So CNAHS developed innovative ways for residents to age in place.

Ninety three percent of residents at Putnam Square Apartments, a 94-unit senior living facility in Cambridge, MA, are over the age of 65. Some 86 percent have at least one disability, which means three times as many residents have diminished abilities per capita compared with the general population in the city. Disabilities range from hearing and vision loss to numerous ambulatory and cognitive issues. Due to the impending expiring affordability restrictions, the preservation of Putnam Square Apartments was the first step in ensuring the senior residents would remain safe from dislocation.

CNAHS understands the importance of providing age-appropriate services to allow residents to age in place. We met with residents who expressed concern about rising costs of health services at assisted living and nursing home facilities, and who worried that their fixed income would not match the costs of medical services. Residents wanted to live independently as long as possible. Many relied on family or friends to help with basic needs such as grocery shopping and attending medical appointments, but others lacked this option. A high number of the el-

CHALLENGE

Cambridge Neighborhood Apartment Housing Services purchased an elderly facility to ensure that the apartments would continue to be affordable. However, with rising healthcare costs and limited income, many of the senior residents felt they needed more than simply housing stability.

Putnam Square Apartments presented an opportunity to meet the needs of senior residents while creating a lasting partnership with a dependable local health provider.

derly tenants had physical disabilities and needed better living accommodations to fit their health needs. CNAHS met with residents to understand the best approach to take for the property's rehab.

CNAHS's rehab including a new boiler, new elevator, windows and envelope repairs that contribute to a higher level of temperature control throughout the building to increase the comfort level and quality of life for residents. Improvements to make the property more accessible included walk-in showers, hand rails and alarms for medical emergencies.

Along with physical improvements, social amenities were added to reduce isolation among residents. Those include weekly exercise programs, a garden club, a peace garden, additional space for social activities, a computer lab and training center and a redesigned community room with a patio and deck. Recent events in the community room include a workshop on wills and estate planning by the Massachusetts Women's Bar Association, live owls brought in by Eyes on Owls and a restaurant-themed night where youth volunteers prepared and served a three-course dinner.

Events and workshops foster a greater sense of community within the building and bring people out of their apartments to get them talking to their neighbors. The exercise classes attract 25-30 residents and include senior chi gong, senior yoga and light cardio equipment available for independent use. The garden club offers a way for residents to harvest flowers and vegetables in the outdoor area of the property and engage with other residents. Residents also congregate in the peace garden. Putnam Square residents joined with the Art Connection, a local nonprofit, to select artwork from the collaborative to display at the property alongside original artwork donated by residents.

CNAHS partnered with Somerville Cambridge Elder Services (SCES), a local health service provider, to offer free health services to tenants. Putnam Square residents have access to in-home care when needed. Services include: housekeeping, personal care, transportation to medical appointments, grocery delivery, companion services and lifeline equipment. Currently, 76 of the building's 94 units are receiving some form of in-home care from SCES. These efforts have improved the quality of life for all residents while ensuring permanent affordability for the property.

In 2010, healthcare spending amounted to more than $18,000 per person for people over 65.

Putnam Square Apartments presented an opportunity to meet the needs of senior residents while creating a lasting partnership with a dependable local health provider. Ultimately, CNAHS delivers a variety of services catered to the needs of the residents while ensuring the permanent affordability of the project. The residents played a key role in expressing their needs and concerns and are happy to continue living independently.

Lessons learned through the Putnam Square project include: 1) listening to resident concerns is the first step to addressing needs, 2) senior and disabled residents need physical and social support including health and daily needs assistance, and 3) partnering with a local health service provider enabled us to ensure livability and comfort for residents.

ABOUT PETER DALY

Peter Daly is the executive director of Cambridge Neighborhood Apartment Housing Services, a nonprofit housing developer in Cambridge since 1983. He works with 11 staff to promote housing affordability and inclusion. Programs include developing affordable housing, lending for privately owned multifamily rental properties, individual development accounts, a scholarship program and a foreclosure prevention initiative. Daly increased the organization's rental portfolio from 17 units to 1,257 rental units plus 60,000 square feet of commercial space.

PROVIDING HOUSING AND SERVICES TO PROMOTE INDEPENDENT LIVING FOR SENIORS

Jackie Mayo, President & CEO

HomeSource east tennessee

While many affordable housing developers provide inexpensive, safe housing, their senior residents often lack vital services to assist them with healthcare, food and transportation. Unfortunately, the developers and their staff are just not equipped to address these complex health and aging-related issues.

In 2010, John was wandering aimlessly around Knoxville, TN. Suffering from the early onset of dementia, he had forgotten where he parked his car and where he lived. Local law enforcement eventually picked him up, scared and alone, and brought him to a local church. While he was unable to tell them his name or where he lived, he remembered the name of the property manager at his home. After some investigating, the church was able to contact the HomeSource east tennessee property manager. John was so excited about seeing a familiar face that he immediately gave her a hug and let her drive him home.

John's story was not unique to the residents at Home-Source's senior properties. Like many affordable housing developers, HomeSource provided safe affordable housing, assuming that their residents would have access to other vital services, such as healthcare, food and transportation, through other social service providers. But they came to realize that many of their residents were not receiving the medical, home health or mental health services they need-

CHALLENGE

Many affordable housing developers provide inexpensive, safe and healthy housing, but many of their senior residents do not receive the medical services, home health or mental health services that they need. Developers and their staff are rarely equipped to address these complex health and aging-related issues.

HomeSource came to realize that many of its residents were not receiving the medical, home health or mental health services they needed to age with dignity.

ed to age with dignity. In addition, many suffered from hunger and financial stress.

HomeSource's mission is to strengthen communities by providing sustainable housing. But the board and staff realized that the traditional model did not go far enough to fulfill their mission of providing sustainability. They realized that they needed to expand the scope of their services to address the mental, physical and emotional well-being of their tenants.

HomeSource hired a senior care coordinator to help manage services, provide workshops and training, and promote healthy living for their residents. After just eight months, the care coordinator had signed up over half of the residents to participate in the program. Working with two students from the University of Tennessee College of Social Work, the coordinator helped many of their customers access transportation, in-home care and other critical services. In addition, their onsite workshops helped educate the customers on nutrition, the importance of physical activity and mindfulness techniques. The students, while not serving as counselors, were able to dedicate a significant amount of time to provide the customers with a "listening ear," a practice that validates and empowers the residents.

Ellie is a resident at HomeSource's Riverbirch Village Apartments and was one of the first to sign up for our program. "I think it is so good to have someone encouraging us to get out," she says. "The exercise classes are especially good. We have a lot of great people who live here and it is great to be out with them."

Perhaps equally important, the care coordinator helped the residents access the in-home services that they needed to live independently. Many of them have difficulties with one or more daily living activities. The common reaction of adult children when their parents have difficulty living on their own is to put them into a nursing home. This is rarely the desire of the seniors and is an expensive drain on the taxpayer-funded healthcare system. A more appropriate solution is to identify in-home care resources that can help the customer with daily living, often with just one or two home visits a week.

In addition, HomeSource researched senior services outside the housing sphere and discovered that the network of services is inefficient, underfunded and disjunctive. There are simply not enough services available and many services, such as those provided by the healthcare system, are ineffective. Therefore, they also began to focus on promoting smart policies that would address the full range of their residents' needs.

On the regional level, HomeSource partnered with Fahe, a member-led non-profit that consists of 50+ housing developers in six central Appalachian states. Working with Fahe, along with groups in West Virginia and Kentucky, HomeSource is promoting policies that improve service delivery. In the last 12 months, Fahe has convened regional and state meetings around senior housing and services throughout the Appalachian region. They are working on turning these coalitions into instruments to promote more effective senior housing policies.

In 2015, the average daily cost for nursing home care was $220, versus $160 for at-home care.

HomeSource is also part of a state-wide group looking at policies around affordable senior housing and services. On the national level, HomeSource was invited to participate in a focus group discussing rural senior housing.

On all levels, existing stakeholders have been surprised to find housing organizations coming to the table. Traditionally left out of the conversation, housing organizations are now recognized as an important contributor to the conversation. Stakeholders now realize that housing organizations can play a big role in the well-being of their residents by providing safe housing, being aware of their residents' conditions and managing services and programs for them.

This project illustrates three important lessons: 1) housing developers cannot assume that their residents are getting all the services they need, 2) hiring an onsite care coordinator can help to promote healthy living, 3) there needs to be change on the state and national policies, and 4) working with partners is key to making a difference.

ABOUT JACKIE MAYO

Jackie Mayo serves as the president and CEO of HomeSource east tennessee. HomeSource provides affordable housing opportunities, counseling, financial capability coaching and building performance guidance in Knox County and several surrounding east Tennessee counties. HomeSource excels at providing homes with increased energy efficiency and verifiable durability and healthy living benefits. HomeSource has been part of collaborative efforts to bridge the gap between housing providers, social service organizations, government agencies and the health field to broaden the housing options for very low-income seniors and those with special needs.

FROM FLOOD TO FRAMEWORK: BUILDING ACROSS STATE LINES

Don Patrick, President & CEO

North East Community Action Corporation

The Great Flood of 1993 along the Mississippi River left $15 billion in damages across 30,000 square miles, including a 35-county region known as the tri-state area of northeast Missouri, southeast Iowa and west-central Illinois. The flooding river hit a record height of 32.13 feet in Quincy, Il. Fifty people died in the flood and at least ten thousand homes were destroyed.

North East Community Action Corporation (NECAC) has offered housing and other programs in the 12-county Missouri portion since 1965. When the 1993 inundation cut off vital transportation links in the tri-state area, government agencies, businesses and residents collaborated to solve the problem. NECAC was there.

A Tri-state Development Summit set recovery goals in areas affected by the Great Flood. Drawing on our housing expertise, NECAC helped organize the group's Housing Task Force, which still holds quarterly meetings more than 20 years later. In 2005, NECAC hosted (along with planning partners in Iowa and Illinois) the first Tri-state Housing Summit.

Many years later, the collaborations brought on by the Great Flood still promote progress in the tri-state region, especially related to the development of new housing and investments that encourage broad-based economic growth.

"The Housing Task Force has played an important part in achieving the Tri-state Development Summit goals,"

CHALLENGE

The North East Community Action Corporation (NECAC) is committed to creating affordable housing opportunities in rural areas of Missouri. When a flood hit NECAC's service region, as well as neighboring areas in Illinois and Iowa, the nonprofit agency was forced to coordinate housing strategies with multiple government agencies across state lines.

> ## "We looked beyond what separated us as a region and toward what unites us. Working together, we have watched as our barriers collapse and have seen the foundation build for amazing opportunities."
>
> — Carla Potts, NECAC deputy director for Housing Development Programs

said Patrick Poepping, a member of the group's steering committee and a civil engineer with offices in all three states.

Poepping credits NECAC and the Housing Task Force for helping to bring the U.S. Department of Agriculture's Great Regions designation to the tri-state area in November 2013. Great Regions creates opportunities for training, technical support, actions to foster intra-regional collaboration, infrastructure project funding and housing development. The overarching goal is to create an environment for economic growth that benefits everyone in the region.

NECAC's housing summits are cost-effective ways of encouraging substantive dialogue and sharing incremental successes. How to apply new financing tools to encourage affordable homeownership, discussion of ways to repurpose existing building for new uses, and how to preserve older homes, are frequent topics at the housing summit.

The story of Hilly Jacklin is an example of what can follow one of these housing summits. Jacklin, who lives in Hannibal, Missouri, was facing serious budget pressure because of the cost of heating and cooling her home. She lives in the kind of house that helped Hannibal live up to its moniker, "America's Hometown." But her home, built in the 1890s, is the type of two-story structure that needed a modern facelift.

Built like many houses were at the turn of the 20th century, Jacklin's home was structurally sound, but it needed to be made more energy efficient. NECAC stepped in with weatherization and other system upgrades, improvements that are often needed for homes in the region. New windows and a new furnace were installed, substantially reducing air loss. Thanks to weatherization and energy efficiency programs that are often discussed at the housing summit, NECAC was able to tap into funds to pay for the rehab and cut Jacklin's utility bills in half.

By placing our attention on this type of housing rehab and community preservation that is at the heart of the Tri-state Development agenda, NECAC is able to measurably improve lives in the region.

The average flood insurance policy costs $700 per year.

"You guys are awesome," Jacklin said.

During one 18-month period in 2014 and 2015, NECAC leveraged more than $11.3 million of direct investment dollars for housing efforts.

In 2015, our organization's success and the broader efforts of the Housing Task Force drew the attention of Nathalie Janson, an Edward M. Gramlich Fellow in Community and Economic Development at the Joint Center for Housing Studies of Harvard University. She visited with the Housing Task Force and published a report on her findings. Janson noted the group's "ability to make connections with organizations whose purview has traditionally been outside the housing field as a benefit of working as part of the Tri-state Development Summit."

Cooperation and outreach efforts have inspired new programs and opportunities among the three states.

"We can accomplish more working as a region than by working independently," said Elaine Davis of the Two Rivers Regional Council of Public Officials in Quincy, Illinois.

Carla Potts, NECAC Deputy Director for Housing Development Programs and founder of the Tri-state Housing Summit, agrees. "Our Housing Task Force has looked beyond what separates us as a region and toward what unites us as a region," Potts said. "Working together, we have watched as our barriers collapse and have seen the foundation built for amazing opportunities."

ABOUT DON PATRICK
Don Patrick has led the North East Community Action Corporation (NECAC) for 30 years, first as executive director and then as president and CEO. NECAC offers social services and housing assistance to low-income, elderly, youth, disabled and disadvantaged populations in 12 eastern Missouri counties. The agency has 100 full-time and more than 200 part-time employees.

DISASTER RESPONSE: HELPING HOMEOWNERS RECOVER AFTER DEVASTATING TORNADO

Roland Chupik, Executive Director

Neighborhood Housing Services of Oklahoma City

Tornados are common across the Oklahoma landscape with dozens touching down throughout the state each year. But the 2013 tornado season was different. In Moore, OK, that year a category E5 tornado – the most powerful measure – hit with winds exceeding 200 miles per hour and led to the loss of more than 20 lives. The some $2 billion in residential and commercial devastation was unprecedented.

The town of Moore is within our service area and Neighborhood Housing Services of Oklahoma City (NHSOKC) knew that we had to do what we could to help the thousands of families who had lost everything, including their homes. As we were planning our next steps, we realized that we didn't have the financial resources to do all that we wanted to do. That's where having a relationship with NeighborWorks America was essential.

Preliminary damage estimates were coming in as we stayed in touch with NeighborWorks and together we concluded that the best course of action for us was to focus on immediate housing issues. Housing is our business, so that's where we would place our attention.

A major part of our energy in this first phase of post-disaster activity was directed at helping residents work with the Federal Emergency Management Agency, insurance companies, mortgage lenders and others that were providing financial assistance. Each of these organizations

CHALLENGE
Two tornadoes struck Oklahoma in 2013, flattening entire blocks and neighborhoods. Suddenly, thousands of Oklahomans found themselves homeless. There was an urgent need for immediate, temporary housing for the victims.

We learned that the emotional impact of losing your home is almost impossible to imagine. Most homeowners are overwhelmed with that loss, which can make it difficult to shift gears to start the recovery process.

had its own forms, processes and guidelines. A dizzying array of information was required from each homeowner. Because of housing counseling experience at the NHSOKC, we were able to help people navigate the process a bit easier. NHSOKC staff immediately jumped into action and offered our help to homeowners applying for assistance and completing insurance claims.

The going was slow and tough, but progress could be measured.

The reality of the situation crystalized in conversations with residents. We learned that the emotional impact of losing your home is almost impossible to imagine. Most homeowners are overwhelmed with that loss, which can make it difficult to shift gears to start the recovery process. But applying for assistance is only part of the challenge. Where were the more than 12,000 people whose homes were damaged and the more than 1,400 whose houses were completely destroyed going to live?

In the second phase of response, we worked to secure temporary and permanent housing. Using a $100,000 grant from NeighborWorks America and donations of 15 foreclosed properties by J.P. Morgan Chase and Bank of America, we were able to offer real, tangible housing help quickly.

In addition to the grant helping NHSOKC to immediately start fixing up homes and give victims a place to live, the cash helped the organization pursue funds from other funding sources, so that we could rehab all 15 donated homes as quickly as possible.

With needs in the immediate aftermath of the tornado being addressed from a variety of angles and with a plethora of different resources, NHSOKC began to strategize about preparing for the next disaster.

There would be another tornado in the region; Oklahoma ranks third in the number of tornados that touch down. Thankfully, many of these storms are not in places as populated as Moore, but it takes only one massive event to ruin thousands of lives. We took it on as our job to help mitigate future disaster.

Only 3.5% of homes in the greater Oklahoma City metropolitan area have a storm shelter.

The third phase of the recovery effort is focused on a critical, long-term need: storm shelters. Again, here is where a nonprofit like NHHOKC was fortunate to have a partner who is aligned with our goals. NeighborWorks America also is affiliated with two other nonprofits in Oklahoma – the Community Action Project of Tulsa and the Little Dixie Community Action Agency in Hugo. Together we worked to develop strategies for building storm shelters in existing single-family homes and multi-family projects, and for incorporating storm shelters into future developments.

It's not enough to rebuild; it's important that all of us rebuild better.

The collaborative and multi-pronged approach to dealing with post-tornado housing in Oklahoma is a model for disaster response everywhere. Assessment of community needs by multiple local stakeholders that is supported by a national organization is a solid way forward, one that is working for us and we believe would work elsewhere, too.

ABOUT ROLAND CHUPIK

Roland Chupik is the executive director of Neighborhood Housing Services of Oklahoma City. The nonprofit organization was created to provide affordable housing options for Oklahomans with low to moderate incomes. Founded in 1982, NHSOKC is a chartered member of NeighborWorks America, a national nonprofit created and funded by Congress for the purpose of revitalizing neighborhoods across the country.

THE SUPERBLOCK MODEL: RECLAIMING NEIGHBORHOODS FROM THE INSIDE OUT

Kristin Faust, President

Neighborhood Housing Services of Chicago

During the housing crisis, the 500 block of North Central Park in West Humboldt Park experienced a rapid increase in foreclosure, abandonment and marginalization. "There were eight vacant properties on this block, and only a faint pulse," says John Groene, neighborhood director of the West Humboldt Park Neighborhood Housing Services (NHS) office. In response, Groene and his team championed the "superblock" approach to development, with the goal of reviving the block by working collaboratively, and pouring multiple resources into a concentrated hub of the community.

When this block became a target area for the City of Chicago's Micro Market Recovery Program (MMRP), NHS created a strategy for visible improvements on the block that would reverberate throughout the neighborhood. MMRP provides structure that NHS and cross-sector partner organizations use to focus housing and community development resources (e.g., foreclosure court receivership or forgivable loan purchase assistance grants) on a geographically defined set of blocks. One of the main MMRP goals is aimed at reoccupying vacant residential buildings and helping existing residents remain in their homes.

NHS focused on the 500 block of Central Park because it is the southern gateway into the community. "Perception is reality. When residents entered West Humboldt Park they were greeted with a morose image," says Groene.

CHALLENGE

In Chicago's West Humboldt Park, the 500 block of North Central Park was considered one of the severest areas of blight in the neighborhood. This block had historically high vacancies, lack of private investment and a high crime rate, making it difficult to attract potential homeowners.

Planning for the physical appearance of a neighborhood is important, but equally important is tapping into the heart and soul of a community that raises up voices, values and visions.

To support its work, NHS used its strengths of established resident relationships and a neighborhood office. The organization held hundreds of meetings at local NHS office, with a focus on collaboratively reclaiming vacant buildings on the block.

NHS partnered with Mercy Housing to acquire several of the buildings, featuring one to four residential units. Community Investment Corporation and Bickerdike Redevelopment Corporation worked to bring in multi-family building owners. NHS also partnered with The Neighborhood Foundation, which installed decorative board-ups over windows and doors of vacant buildings to discourage vandalism and beautify the neighborhood.

NHS further acquired, rehabbed and repurposed four properties on the superblock that were in danger of being demolished. The buildings now serve as affordable rental housing for veterans with children (managed by nonprofit partner Childserv), and as commercial property. A single remaining vacant building on the block is currently under renovation and under contract with a pre-approved NHS buyer.

"Raise the resident commitment and there will be a ripple effect of investment back into the community," says Groene. Indeed, that's just what happened in West Humboldt Park.

A community resident created the Ujima Garden at the northeast corner of the North Central Park block. This led to the creation of the West Humboldt Park farmer's market, located in the parking lot of the NHS office. "Ujima Garden is ADA-accessible and utilized by neighbors, local schools, churches and community groups," says the founder, Nita Hailey-Gamble.

West Humboldt Park's positive transformation extends to the Chicago Avenue main commercial corridor. Along with infrastructure improvements, new businesses have opened, including Brother-In-Law Ribs and Turkey Chop Gourmet Grill. New educational institutions include Rowe Clark Math and Science Academy and the Richard M. Daley Library. The five-acre Salvation Army Freedom Center campus and Children's Place Association opened their new three-story, 19,000-square-foot facility at the corner of Chicago Avenue and Drake.

"Our next superblocks will be the 900 block of North Drake and then the 700 block of North Central Park," says Groene. "NHS now owns two properties on Drake, and soon will own three more. We'll go through the same process as with the 500 block of North Central Park, but hopefully reduce the time it takes to turn around a block."

In 2013, Cook County, which includes Chicago, was home to 200 high-vacancy neighborhoods.

Lessons learned from the superblock project in West Humboldt Park include: 1) Promotion of neighborhood change has to be organic; 2) Developing a pipeline of pre-approved, first-time homebuyers is essential; 3) Developing marketing materials showing the stages of the building rehabbing process helps resident visualize and 4) Working on several buildings at once creates economies of scale.

The West Humboldt Park superblock model is a great example of reclaiming vacant properties from the inside out. If residents take the lead, identify outcomes and create an environment for action, resulting leadership will trump any unwanted and external redevelopment plans created. NHS attributes its success to being present in the community and listening to resident needs. Planning for the physical appearance of a neighborhood is important, but equally important is tapping into the heart and soul of a community that raises up voices, values and visions.

ABOUT KRISTIN FAUST
Kristin Faust joined NHS of Chicago as president in October of 2014. Faust is responsible for providing visionary and creative leadership to address the changing needs of the communities and populations that are served by the organization. She is charged with ensuring financial management of the organization, as well as diversifying NHS' lines of business, programs and funding sources. Before joining NHS, Faust was the chief credit officer at Partners for the Common Good in Washington, D.C. Faust received an undergraduate degree from Brown University and a master's degree in planning from Harvard University.

WORKING TOGETHER TO CREATE A DIFFERENCE

Dawn Lee, Executive Director & CEO
Melanie Seawright Steele, Manager of
Community Strategies, Advising & Education

Neighborhood Housing Services of the Inland Empire

In California, people often work in one county and live in another, and these "blended boundary lines" can lead to challenging situations for funding and resources. San Bernardino County is the largest county in the nation spanning over 20,000 square miles and is the 12th most populous with over two million residents. It is the most inland county in Southern California, sharing its borders with Los Angeles, Orange, Riverside, Kern and Inyo counties. Of these counties, San Bernardino is the most affordable. It also has the highest need.

In 2011, San Bernardino's per capita contributions, grants and gifts were $4.48 as compared to $195.31 in Los Angeles County and $96.17 in Orange County. The lack of investment forced local agencies to compete for limited funds. There was little support or encouragement for them to collaborate or leverage their resources and capacities.

At the heart of the county, the City of San Bernardino with a population of 215,000 has its share of challenges: 31 percent of its residents live in poverty, it lacks affordable housing stock and has one of the highest crime rates in the state. The 2012 dissolution of the city's Redevelopment Agency, a large source of funding for urban renewal projects, coupled with the city's bankruptcy filing, forced it to make deep cuts in services further straining the community and leaving little money available for revitalization.

Since its inception 35 years ago, Neighborhood Housing Services of the Inland Empire (NHSIE) has been locat-

CHALLENGE

Community revitalization is most effective when partners from all levels work together. Yet, due to years of minimal funding and competition among agencies, there were few examples of that in the city of San Bernardino, CA, which filed for bankruptcy in 2012.

HOMEBUYER EDUCATION
FINANCING
REAL ESTATE SERVICES
www.nhsie.org
909.884.6891

All have come to understand that broad-based collaboration between the public and private sectors is required to overcome the huge challenges that poverty, low educational attainment, unemployment and crime place on a neighborhood.

ed in one particular neighborhood of San Bernardino. Initially, the agency focused on assisting low-income families attain homeownership within the city, but over time it expanded its services to the broader Inland Empire region which includes both Riverside and San Bernardino counties. As the housing boom and the foreclosure crisis gained momentum, NHSIE's work centered on helping families purchase, repair and prevent foreclosure of their homes. Little attention was directed to what was happening in the surrounding three-mile area where there is less wealth, equity and opportunity than in the rest of the city. Given the city's bankruptcy and the decline in its capacity to help its residents, NHSIE decided it was time to invest in their own backyard.

At the time, NHSIE had just been awarded NeighborWorks America's Stable Communities Catalytic Grant, a place-based initiative intended to transform communities struggling with the effects of foreclosure and disinvestment. Knowing that community revitalization does not happen in a vacuum, NHSIE looked for other organizations with investment and place-making strategies underway in the same neighborhood.

NHSIE partnered with the Institute for Public Strategies (IPS). IPS had recently received a Byrne Criminal Justice Innovation Grant to address crime in a subsection of the area covered by NHSIE's grant. NHSIE and IPS worked together with city police and code enforcement to identify and address commercial and residential hot spots by demolishing structures, clearing lots, installing murals, rehabilitating abandoned homes and employing Crime Prevention through Environmental Design practices to improve neighborhood safety. NHSIE and IPS also joined forces with National Community Renaissance (National CORE), a nonprofit affordable housing builder redeveloping the public housing in the neighborhood.

In 2015, NHSIE, IPS and National CORE brought together over 50 community and faith-based groups focused on health, education, job development, youth services, housing and safety. From this meeting, 20 organizations joined together to create the Neighborhood Transformation Collaborative (NTC). NHSIE and their partners took on the leadership role while NTC's members committed to provide data to demonstrate the impact of their programs, partner with other members to seek funding, collaborate on service delivery and actively participate in monthly meetings. NHSIE created a website and a video highlighting

San Bernardino County is the largest county in the nation, spanning more than 20,000 square miles.

the NTC's goals, neighborhood baseline data, membership and services offered and progress on achieving planned goals. The website brings the community's needs, achievement and resources to light and holds the membership accountable for bringing about positive change.

Just 12 months since inception, NTC members have played a key role in the submission of a comprehensive HUD Promise Zone application, organized two collaborative events, implemented a Community Leadership Institute incubated CPTED project to improve residential street lighting and commissioned a commercial corridor market analysis and action plan. They also convened city and county staff and elected officials to discuss collaborative strategies and investment in this "transformative place." Local city officials recognize the NTC as an asset to the community and have begun to offer their support and resources. All have come to understand that broad-based collaboration between the public and private sectors is required to overcome the huge challenges that poverty, low educational attainment, unemployment, and crime place on a neighborhood.

This project illustrates three important lessons: 1) an organization, by stepping forward and partnering with others, can help foster a spirit of collaboration; 2) focusing on the needs of a particular place can help to bring organizations together to coordinate their efforts; and 3) aligning resources, building capacity and telling the story strengthens the individual and collective impact in a community.

ABOUT DAWN LEE

Dawn Lee has served as the chief executive officer of NHSIE since 2010. NHSIE is a nonprofit community housing stabilization organization dedicated to creating homeownership opportunities. It has a staff of 18 and annually assists over 1,000 people in the Inland Empire through its homeownership promotion efforts, recognizing that homeownership builds community stability by increasing personal and familial wealth, breaking the cycle of poverty, and enhancing civic involvement. Lee's commitment to and experience with the social issues related to homelessness, housing affordability and access to housing has propelled NHSIE into collaborative partnerships with various organizations throughout the service area.

COLLABORATING TO BUILD OPPORTUNITY AT HOME

Mike Mullin, President & Founder

Nevada HAND

Founded in 1993 to address a lack of affordable homes in Las Vegas, Nevada Housing and Neighborhood Development (HAND) improves the lives of low-income residents by providing housing solutions and supportive services.

There is no shortage of need among families and communities in Las Vegas, but in light of research that demonstrates how crucial safe, stable homes are for children's long-term outlooks, HAND is making education, enrichment and safety for kids a priority. Families in our communities need places and programs for kids to learn and grow, including at home.

Throughout Las Vegas, many young people are left behind by the school system with few opportunities to catch up. Troublingly, there are not enough constructive ways for kids to spend time after school. Quality after-school programming can help, but in low-income communities like those HAND serves, its availability is sorely missing. Creating positive environments where kids can reach their full potential is a major undertaking, but we were determined to find a solution.

To help us develop youth-centered programming, HAND reached out to local experts, the Boys and Girls Clubs of southern Nevada. The Boys and Girls Clubs specializes in creating after-school programs where activities encourage kids to build skills in five diverse areas: character and leadership development, education and career development, the arts, sports fitness and recreation, and health

CHALLENGE

Some Las Vegas neighborhoods lack after-school programs that help youths learn, develop life skills and stay safe. But Nevada HAND's organizational expertise has primarily been in affordable housing. How could we collaborate to create an environment where homes, and the services offered there, become the foundation for successful lives?

"Without the club, I don't know where I would be. The club is like my second home."

— Sydney Wilson, clubhouse member, age 17

and life skills. Their strong history in the community and demonstrated success left us certain that this was a great solution for us, so we teamed up.

The Boys and Girls Club is a well-known resource for improving the educational and emotional development of underserved kids, ages five to 18. The Boys and Girls Club's mission to enable all young people to reach their full potential as productive, caring, responsible citizens was precisely the kind of opportunity we wanted to provide to young residents in Las Vegas. In initial meetings between HAND and the Boys and Girls Club, the organizations' leaders explored the philosophies powering their respective missions and a shared vision of creating stronger communities for every-

one. The activities center at Apache Pines, the 274-unit community where HAND and the Boys and Girls Club launched the partnership, provided physical space for collaborative youth programs.

This collaboration led us to create Boys and Girls Clubhouses on-site at both our Apache Pines and Desert Pines communities. These clubhouses provided great access for residents as they are located just outside their front doors. And these sites are bustling with the nearly 400 registered families who participate in various Clubhouse activities. Within months of launching our first clubhouse with the Boys and Girls Club, HAND learned some important lessons. First, on-site solutions are key to boosting resident engagement. Club members' parents were able to work longer, uninterrupted hours thanks to the club's convenient on-site location, and because the club was doing pickups from the local elementary school and walking kids back to the clubhouse.

"This club makes me feel safe in every way. It's a place you can come and be yourself," says 17-year-old Sydney Wilson, an Apache Pines Clubhouse member. "Without the club, I don't know where I would be. The club is like my second home."

Despite these encouraging reviews, and high demand for clubhouse services, we quickly discovered that programming beyond the clubhouse's scope remained as essential as ever. To most effectively serve our community, HAND concurrently offered a range of enriching services through our resident services programming.

Nearly 1 in 4 families currently has a child enrolled in an afterschool program.

With the lessons of Apache Pines in mind, HAND opened our second clubhouse two years later, in 2015. The Desert Pines clubhouse, located within a 700-unit apartment complex, proudly offers a computer lab, art studio, learning center, game room and teen center. This clubhouse has become a valuable community asset, serving nearly 340 neighborhood families. As HAND continues to develop our innovative Boulder Highway campus, we're focused on expanding community impact. This site will incorporate affordable homes, a health clinic, a community resource center, a school and a state-of-the-art, 10,000-square-foot Boys and Girls clubhouse, three-times larger than our other clubhouses.

We also learned that resident engagement requires holistic solutions. We initially thought that our first clubhouse could replace regular resident services in the community, but we quickly discovered that residents needed access to services and programs that were well beyond the clubhouse's scope. Another lesson we learned is that collaboration is an on-going relationship that will evolve.

For nearly 25 years, HAND has remained committed to creating safe and stable communities for Southern Nevada. Through collaboration, we seek to embody a "housing-plus-services" model, where home and opportunity go hand-in-hand.

ABOUT MIKE MULLIN

Mike Mullin is founder and president of Nevada HAND. Previously, Mullin spent 14 years as a residential and commercial real estate broker with the largest real estate company in Nevada.

CREATIVE COLLABORATION BRINGS ACCESS TO FINANCIAL, HOUSING RESOURCES IN RURAL COUNTIES

David A. Geer III, Executive Director

Origin SC

Since 1888, Family Services (now doing business as Origin SC) has provided financial and housing advocacy, counseling and education to individuals in South Carolina and beyond. Most of its financial education and homeownership services are targeted to three counties in greater Charleston also known as the Tri-county area: Berkeley, Charleston and Dorchester.

However, the need remained great, especially in rural, hard-to-reach areas. South Carolina ranks third-worst in the nation for household financial security and nearly half of South Carolina residents are living on the edge of financial disaster, according to a January 2013 report produced by the Corporation for Enterprise Development. To step up our response to that need, collaboration is necessary. As the Stanford Social Innovation Review concludes: "Large-scale social change requires broad, cross-sector coordination, not the isolated intervention of individual organizations."

Origin SC reached out to Trident United Way and Goodwill Industries of Lower South Carolina to collaborate on bringing multiple in-person services to the more rural sections of the Tri-county area. As a result, the three organizations opened two Prosperity Centers, one in Moncks Corner (Berkeley County) in 2013 and one in Summerville (Dorchester County) in 2014. The centers

CHALLENGE

The rural counties of Dorchester and Berkeley faced the greatest number of foreclosures in South Carolina. Remote and underserved, they also struggled with multiple issues, including parenting, literacy and GED preparation. How could organizations based in Charleston work together to provide services to these remote counties?

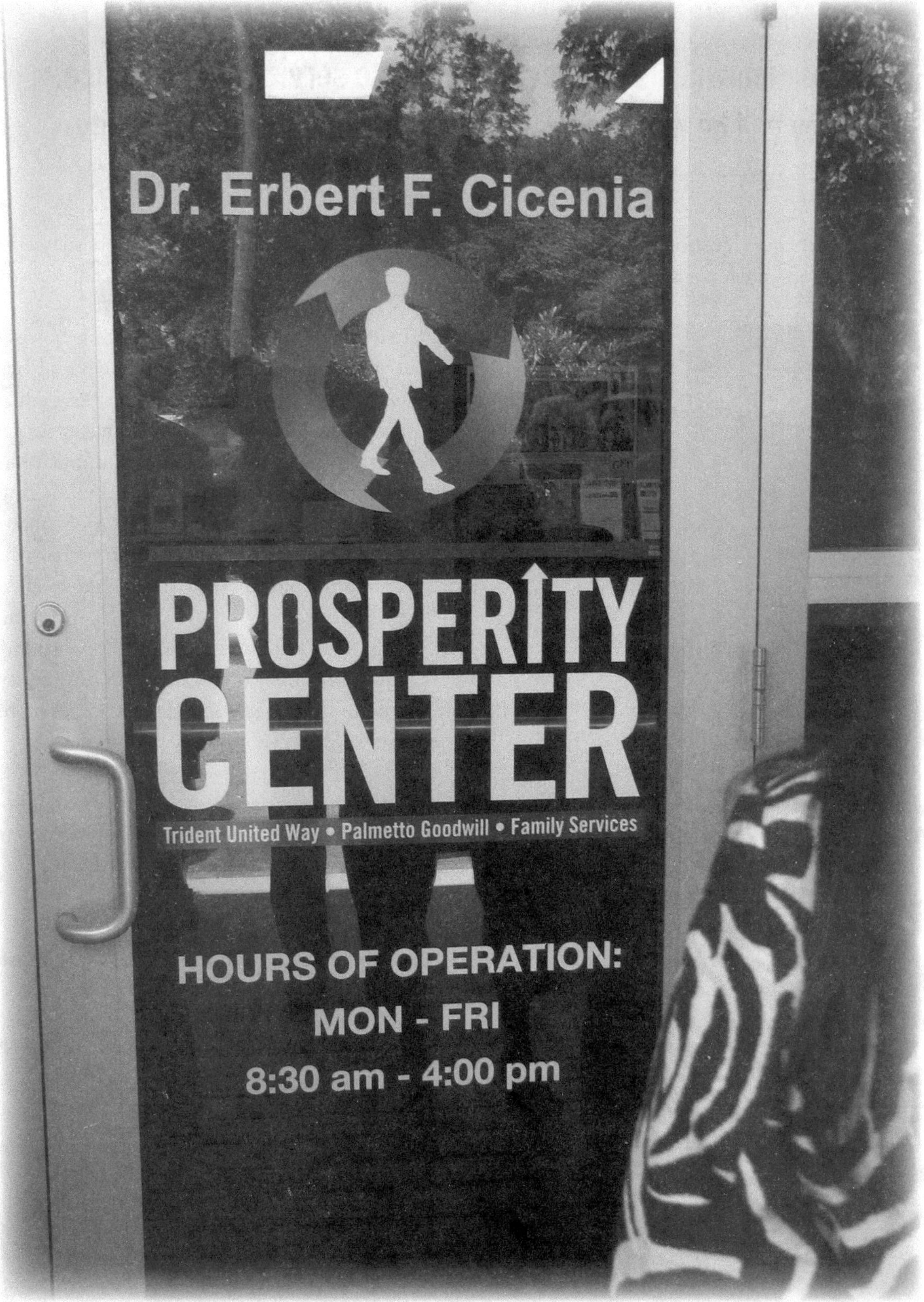
Dr. Erbert F. Cicenia
PROSPERITY
CENTER
Trident United Way • Palmetto Goodwill • Family Services
HOURS OF OPERATION:
MON - FRI
8:30 am - 4:00 pm

When individuals can receive multiple services in one place, they will be more successful in attaining financial stability.

provide financial education and housing counseling, job-search help and basic needs assistance in one place at no charge.

The work was slow to get started, however, as the partners worked through logistics such as technology needs, staffing and office space. The marketing teams from each organization stayed in constant communication and strategized a new brand and marketing plan for the Prosperity Centers. Once a manager was hired to do outreach, an increase in community interest was immediately seen and workshop offerings, such as "Making Ends Meet" and "Foreclosure Prevention," grew along with it. In 2014, the Prosperity Centers served nearly 500 people. By the end of 2015, more than 2,300 individuals access more than 6,100 different services.

Early on, the partners discovered that more services were needed in areas such as parenting, literacy, GED prep, expungement of criminal records and benefits. They invited other nonprofit organizations to provide their services at the centers and eventually, the Alston Wilkes Society, Family Corps, Trident Literacy Association and SC Thrive joined them.

Most individuals who visit the centers need more than one service or resource. Such was the case for Anne, who was unemployed and behind on her mortgage when she first went to one of the Prosperity Centers in December 2013. After the center's foreclosure counselor helped her avoid losing her home, Anne caught up on her mortgage and received monthly assistance – that is, until she exhausted the $36,000 in aid. At that point, Anne only had a part-time job teaching a fitness class and wasn't able to keep up with her payments. Origin SC completed a loan-modification application and referred her to Goodwill's staff counselor to help her improve her resume and look for better work. Anne went to the Berkeley Prosperity Center a few times a week to search for a job while also receiving guidance from her Origin SC financial coach. By the end of 2014, Anne was employed full-time and was on her way to financial and housing stability.

After going barely avoiding foreclosure on three separate occasions, Gloria and her husband reached out to the center in desperation. The couple entered Origin SC's Housing Stability program, and its counselors now manage their money. Within three months, they were current on all of their monthly expenses. "Without [Origin SC and the Prosperity Centers], I would be completely lost – six feet underground," Gloria says. "Sometimes you just have to take a chance, a leap of faith. Don't hold the burden alone and don't be afraid to talk to someone and to take a chance."

In 3 years, the Prosperity Centers went from serving 9 individuals to 2,300 individuals.

Throughout the collaboration process, Origin SC learned two critical lessons: 1) it takes time to see sustainable results from a new business line, product or service; and 2) offering multiple services in one location is not only efficient, it achieves greater financial stability. There is no reason to "reinvent the wheel" when there are organizations already in place that are experts in providing those services. Clients do not just receive referrals to make appointments with other organizations; they can receive those services on the spot. When services are combined to reach a similar goal, everyone wins.

It requires great effort to make a new product or service successful. The first year did not provide the results that Origin SC expected or projected. But Origin and its partners saw the need and believed the centers could be a success. Instead of closing the doors early on, Prosperity Center persevered with a three-point strategy: hiring a motivated center manager, expanding the services menu and collaborating creatively.

ABOUT DAVID A. GEER, III

David A. Geer, III is the executive director of Origin SC in North Charleston, SC. For the last 12 years, Geer has led the 128-year-old organization, building the multi-million dollar programs to reach more than 10,000 clients every year in areas of housing stability, homeownership and financial literacy promotion, and home preservation.

THE DIFFICULT ROAD TO 'COMMUNITIES OF OPPORTUNITY'

Stuart J. Mitchell, President & CEO

PathStone Corporation

Nearly a third of Rochester, NY, citizens live in poverty, and it has the highest extreme poverty rate and childhood poverty rate among comparable U.S. cities. The public city and suburban school systems are segregated by race and class. The education gap between upper- and lower-income students is a sad tale of two, largely disconnected communities, literally minutes from each other by car. The city school district graduates less than 50 percent of its students, while several suburban schools are rated nationally as best in class.

In early 2015, the City of Rochester and Monroe County launched a plan to reduce poverty in the region by 50 percent over the next 15 years. The initial investment was $500 million.

The Rochester Monroe Anti-Poverty Initiative has embraced the concept that large-scale social change will require broad cross-sector coordination in order to be successful. A 2015 report made 33 recommendations through eight different community-based workgroups: education, health and nutrition, housing, jobs, justice system, safe neighborhoods, child care and transportation.

There were three common themes:
- Address structural racism
- Address poverty-induced trauma
- Build and support the community

CHALLENGE

Rochester, NY, has the highest rates of extreme and childhood poverty among comparable U.S. cities. The public schools are segregated by race and class, and fewer than half of the students graduate. In 2015, the city's plight triggered a plan to reduce poverty in the region by 50 percent over 15 years.

Our hope is to create 'communities of opportunity' that integrate low-income households and provide quality housing, safe streets, affordable child care, good schools, health care and public transportation.

PathStone, a regional nonprofit community development corporation, co-chaired the Housing Workgroup, a diverse partnership of affordable housing advocates, community representatives and government officials. They made four bold recommendations designed to increase access to safe, affordable housing:

▸ Develop a cross-cultural plan reaching across socio-economic lines to dismantle the thoughts, attitudes and behaviors that exclude people who live in poverty from access to quality, safe,

equitable, affordable housing in a location and type of their choice

▸ Protect long-term residents of neighborhoods from displacement caused by gentrification

▸ Create a solid foundation of life skills, which will greatly increase the potential for households to move to self-sufficiency and thrive

▸ Create a countywide affordable housing policy to serve the needs of households living in poverty.

Conflicting perspectives and different areas of expertise in the workgroup complicated efforts to reach consensus on these issues. To foster effective access to affordable housing, the local government needed to commit to a robust, multi-year initiative comprising both city and suburban communities.

The vast majority of affordable housing projects developed in the Rochester region are located in high poverty inner-city areas. In this, developers of affordable housing, including PathStone, have often taken the path of least resistance, which has perpetuated racial segregation in the city as well as in the suburbs. The hope going forward is to create "communities of opportunity" across the region that integrate low-income households and provide quality housing, safe streets, affordable child care, good schools, health care and public transportation.

The Rochester Monroe Anti-Poverty Initiative will succeed only when leaders commit to integrating both the city and the suburbs. In addition, because racism is often baked into our institutions, it is a major determinant in confronting the root causes of poverty. Before we can execute the housing task force recommendations, a legion of community and political leaders must become sophisticated and organized champions of racial and economic integration. PathStone will continue to do everything in its power to work toward that day.

Rochester's city school district graduates fewer than 50% of its students, while several nearby schools are rated nationally as best in class.

ABOUT STUART J. MITCHELL

Stuart J. Mitchell is a founder, president and CEO of PathStone Corporation, a regional nonprofit community development corporation. He has worked for 50 years in the field of social, political, and civil rights advocacy.

NEWCITY: SHARED VISION LAYS THE FOUNDATION FOR A VIBRANT COMMUNITY

Terri B. North, President & CEO

Providence Community Housing

Simply helping families return to New Orleans following Hurricane Katrina wasn't enough. New Orleanians needed safe and affordable housing, a familiar network of family and friends and supportive services to connect residents to opportunities toward stability and self-sufficiency.

Since 2006, Providence Community Housing developed more than 1,200 units of housing and helped over 450 individuals and families become homeowners in the Greater New Orleans area. Providence fosters healthy, diverse and vibrant communities with a belief that strong communities can address the needs of low-income individuals and families. We primarily focus on the neighborhoods of Tremé/Lafitte, Tulane/Gravier, and Seventh Ward, including Faubourg Lafitte, a redeveloped community of mixed-income families on the site of the former Lafitte public housing development. Since 2005, more than $5.5 billion has been invested in projects in this area to create or improve housing, infrastructure, arts and culture, education, healthcare and neighborhood amenities. Recognizing this unprecedented opportunity for neighborhood revitalization, Providence established the NEWCITY Neighborhood Partnership with 15 community leaders in 2007.

NEWCITY was created to maximize the benefits of one of the largest urban renewal projects in our nation's history by providing a space to share information, discuss

CHALLENGE

Following the devastation of Hurricane Katrina in 2005, neighborhoods in New Orleans were targeted for one of the largest urban renewal projects in U.S. history. This unprecedented opportunity for revitalization could only succeed by bringing together a diverse group of stakeholders invested in the future of these culturally significant neighborhoods.

NEWCITY is an intersection where everyone can see common ground.

issues and build partnerships. Since its inception, NEWCITY has attracted a diverse coalition of residents, businesses, developers, funders, service providers, faith-based groups, schools and universities and government agencies who have a long-term interest in the viability of these historic neighborhoods.

"By bringing people together, we knew much more could be accomplished than going at it alone," said Jim Kelly, a founding member of NEWCITY and a board member at Providence. "NEWCITY members have a shared vision and are genuinely interested in the hopes, dreams and successes of the neighborhood. It is a truly catholic vision."

Today, NEWCITY includes 80 participating organizations that meet monthly at the Sojourner Truth Neighborhood Center. NEWCITY serves as an engine for educational, economic and housing development by sharing resources and information about neighborhood projects, programs and policies. The initiative sparks discussion among members with multiple perspectives and creates a forum for partners to present work, seek support, build partnerships and collaborate for change. Ultimately NEWCITY is committed to building upon the existing strengths and historical significance of the neighborhoods to foster a more vibrant community for residents and businesses.

NEWCITY focuses on helping members with data-driven projects and has created reports for three residential surveys in 2012, 2013 and 2015, as well as four parcel surveys of approximately 5,700 parcels from 2008, 2011, 2013 and 2015.

Through NEWCITY, Providence collects, analyzes and shares extensive Community Impact Measurement survey data to establish benchmarks, inform planning and assess the needs of residents, businesses and industry in our area. We collect new and existing data related to specific areas that members have highlighted as being of vital importance, namely public health, children, planning and development, water management and crime.

"NEWCITY was put together very purposely with an up-from-the-bottom structure that was not imposed by anybody," said Lisa Amoss, a founding member of NEWCITY. "NEWCITY grew out of the meetings of its early participants. As we got bigger, I am proud that NEWCITY has retained its organic structure."

What keeps NEWCITY relevant is consistency in its meeting format and continued outreach as the neighborhood evolves. By rotating the meeting facilitator role among members, no single group or individual has too much influence.

"People come to NEWCITY meetings because it's important to them, they always learn things that they didn't know before and they make connections they didn't have before," said Amoss. "That to me is the biggest success."

Providence Community Housing created NEWCITY Neighborhood Partnership in 2007 with 15 community leaders.

During the development of NEWCITY, we learned: 1) collaboration requires leadership to maintain momentum and, 2) there are few opportunities to successfully bring together groups and individuals with many different goals. NEWCITY is the intersection where everyone can see the common ground.

ABOUT TERRI NORTH

Terri North is president and CEO of Providence Community Housing, a New Orleans- based nonprofit established in 2006 to address the need for affordable housing and bring former residents home following Hurricane Katrina. Providence develops, operates and advocates for affordable, mixed-income rental and homeownership housing and provides resources for supportive services and employment opportunities for individuals, families, seniors and people with special needs to build self-sufficiency, mitigate crisis and maximize potential. As chief financial officer, North led the financing and development of more than 700 affordable homes and provided oversight of over $80 million. Under her direction as CEO since 2011, Providence has helped more than 461 families become homeowners.

BUILDING TRUSTING RELATIONSHIPS AND A COMMUNITY

Arden Shank, President & CEO

Neighborhood Housing Services of South Florida

In September 2013, Neighborhood Housing Services of South Florida (NHSSF) was one of 14 organizations awarded a grant from the Low Income Investment Fund and Citi Foundation to address widespread problems in an area known as the 79th Street Corridor in Miami-Dade County. The 79th Street Corridor is an area ripe for revitalization, one that has been long overlooked and suffers from blight and neglect. The organization worked with Ron Butler, executive director of the 79th Street Corridor Neighborhood Initiative, to reach out to residents, local government, small businesses and other organizations to identify community needs and intervention strategies.

The first year after the grant was approved was devoted to developing a multi-disciplinary collaborative, building trust and commissioning a market study to evaluate the demographics and economic and social needs of the area. With the resources from the Low Income Investment Fund and Citi Foundation grant in place, along with other funding, we were able to serve as a community quarterback for initiatives that are driven by residents and stakeholders themselves.

Organizations, agencies and businesses inside and outside the community have offered things to fix the neighborhood in the past and then those things just didn't happen. Naturally, residents heard about our organization's plans and thought, 'here we go again.' It took a lot of work to get stakeholders to understand that something would actually come of our plans.

CHALLENGE
The housing crisis and ensuing recession touched nearly every household in the United States, but the far-reaching effects were felt even more deeply in low-income neighborhoods already suffering from blight and neglect.

> ## While funders often want quantifiable results, NHSSF has been able to help funders recognize the importance of collaboration and coalition-building and redefine their perspective on measurable outcomes.

After getting over the hurdles to get organizations and people to pay attention to the issues in the area and to secure trust, the 79th Street Coalition for Change (79StCFC) was created. The past participation of NHSSF in the community was instrumental in the formation of the 79StCFC.

For the first time in Miami-Dade County, residents and stakeholders joined together in support of a unified vision and shared goals. After a year of meetings, a Community Action Plan was written and began implementation in 2015.

The comprehensive Community Action Plan outlined specific goals and outcomes and assigned partners to implement various activities in the following areas:
- Housing and supportive services
- Built environment and economic opportunity
- Health, safety and quality of life
- Education and community engagement

Within those areas, numerous projects have already begun and more are planned, such as housing and financial workshops; securing government funds for improving infrastructure in the community and compiling lists of code violations; partnering with schools and the tech industry to create more opportunities; supporting walking and biking events, community gardens and rehabilitating small grocery stores; and ongoing meetings with community leaders to strengthen collaboration within the neighborhood.

The 100-page Community Action Plan is a multi-year endeavor with deliverables on a macro level. It employs people- and place- based intervention strategies to affect meaningful change in the lives of the community members. As plans progressed for the 79StCFC, NHSSF faced another challenge: the need for more funding. While funders often want quantifiable results, NHSSF has been able to help funders recognize the importance of collaboration and coalition-building and redefine their perspective on measurable outcomes.

The lessons NHSSF learned through this ongoing project include: 1) strengthening partnerships and building trust in the community take time but are essential for long-term success; 2) addressing numerous issues in one location can have a greater impact on residents than focusing on individual issues in a broader geographic area; and 3) cross-sector collaboration requires organizations to give up some of their independence in favor of achieving shared goals. This can be accomplished in a setting in which every stakeholder is heard and no one group dominates.

Almost ⅓ of the households in Miami–Dade county earned less than $25,000 in 2013.

While the goals for the 79StCFC are broad, robust and all-encompassing, NHSSF is committed to continuing its role as community quarterback and seeing the 79th Street Corridor become a vibrant and prosperous community of choice.

ABOUT ARDEN SHANK

Arden Shank, president and CEO of Neighborhood Housing Services of South Florida, used his 30 years of diverse nonprofit housing and community development experience to expand the organization from a three-person agency to a professional organization with a 14-member board and an expanded territory including Miami-Dade and Broward counties. Under Shank, NHSSF assisted over 8,000 low- and middle-income families with their housing needs; created 700 new homeowners; developed, preserved or repaired 105 housing units and counseled homeowners facing foreclosure, saving more than 1,000 homes. Shank is former board chair and president of the South Florida Community Development Coalition, founder and board chair of the Community Reinvestment Alliance of South Florida and a member of the Federal Reserve Board Community Advisory Council.

HELPING COMMUNITIES BECOME A BETTER PLACE TO LIVE

Chris Krehmeyer, President & CEO

Beyond Housing

Beyond Housing works to provide the support and services low-income families need to achieve their long-term goals, with a mission of helping every community in the Normandy school district become a better place to live. When the organization started in 1975, we focused solely on housing, but our leadership realized that while housing assistance helped, it was just one of the many issues to be addressed if we were going to achieve real impact. The situation required a strategic, comprehensive plan to address core issues faced by residents every day and cause systemic change.

In 2010, Beyond Housing secured a $3 million funding commitment and began a five-year odyssey to turn the vision of building a thriving community into reality with a network of passionate leaders and volunteers focused on the mantra "Ask, Align, Act." We began by listening, hosting 450 community meetings in one year featuring residents weighing in with their experiences, needs and ideas for an entirely new community.

The result was the 24:1 initiative, which represents 24 municipalities with one vision for strong communities, engaged families and successful children. Education is key to giving individuals the tools to live a successful life, so we partnered with the Normandy school district. We learned that kindergarten students arrived unprepared for the structure and learning requirements, setting them up for failure before their school careers even began. This discovery led to the creation of 5ByAge5, a Pre-K program to prepare children starting at age 2½ for success in kindergarten and beyond.

CHALLENGE

The 24 communities in the Normandy school district are typical of many other struggling urban areas. The median household income is about half of the national average. One-fourth of the households are led by a single mother and almost one-fourth of the population lives under the poverty line.

Instead of getting overwhelmed by the weight of what needs to be done, little wins inspire us. Beyond Housing tackles a heavy load of deep systemic problems but we are inspired by the ability of the residents to thrive with even a little assistance.

Most children living in the 24:1 area grow up believing they will never be able to afford college. To instill hope for a better future, we began teaching financial literacy and offered both a $3-to-$1 matched college savings program and 529 college savings accounts with a starting gift of $500 for every student entering kindergarten. Over 1,400 accounts have been opened with a waiting list based upon need and resources.

Other initiatives were smaller but impactful. For example, after learning that many kids didn't want to come to school because their clothes were dirty and there was no way to wash them at home, we provided schools with washers and dryers so students can wear clean school clothes with pride. Similar holistic investments remove roadblocks so children have a clearer path to high school graduation, college and beyond.

One of the biggest challenges we face is moving at the speed of trust. We came to the 24:1 communities with knowledge about housing and a passionate desire to provide helpful resources, but we first had to gain the trust of people who had been promised much but experienced little help for decades. We started with infrastructure construction so that residents would see physical signs of improvement and (literally) concrete examples that we were listening to their requests, were passionate about helping and had the resources to turn our good intentions into real, lasting, practical support.

Sheena, an assistant manager at a 24:1 cinema, says she would be on the streets if not for 24:1. Beyond Housing helped her find her job, a home for her family and the services of the Early Childhood Center for her child.

Eboni, who bounced from one homeless shelter to another as a child, recently graduated with a journalism degree from Columbia University after four years on a full scholarship. With help from the college savings program and other Beyond Housing programs, Eboni saw a path through high school not just to college, but an Ivy League school.

Ask.

Align.

Inform.

Sheena, Eboni and others have found the path to success, but there is still a long road ahead. Our next challenge is to scale up services, reach many more than the 10 to 15 percent of residents and students currently served and continue building infrastructure so that students, families and residents of all ages can find their personal path to success.

Beyond Housing has learned, sometimes painfully, that communication and transparency are key to growing trust. If a new program doesn't go the way we hoped, we go to the community, find out what went wrong and regroup. Instead of getting overwhelmed by the weight of what needs to be done, little wins inspire us. It's hearing someone who was helped to get into a home and obtain a job say, "You have no idea the difference you've made in my family's life." Beyond Housing tackles a heavy load of deep systemic problems, but we are inspired by the ability of the residents to thrive with even a little assistance.

There still is no quick fix for all the problems that exist in these communities even with the $75 million dollars we have invested over the past four years. Beyond Housing has created a model for success that we can and will successfully replicate, improving family life and building strong, healthy communities for generations to come.

ABOUT CHRIS KREHMEYER

Chris Krehmeyer, president and CEO of Beyond Housing, a NeighborWorks America organization in St. Louis, leads a staff of more than 126 with a budget of almost $14 million and assets worth nearly $110 million. The organization focuses on improving all of the areas in the North St. Louis' Normandy Schools Collaborative that make up a thriving community: education, housing, health, employment readiness and access and economic development. Among the initiatives completed under Krehmeyer's leadership are the construction of a grocery store, a senior housing and retail complex with a full service bank, the formation of a community land trust and the building or remodeling of 29 homes, new health services, retail and a four-screen movie theater.

BUILDING COMMUNITY ON ROOFTOPS

Dana Totman, President & CEO

Avesta Housing

In 2013, Avesta Housing built 409 Cumberland, an affordable multifamily complex in the Bayside Redevelopment Area of downtown Portland, ME, as part of the "Vision for Bayside" revitalization plan unanimously adopted by the Portland City Council. The Bayside Plan states that it "will fill in, extend and enhance the existing residential fabric with a substantial amount of new housing units" and that "a diversity of dwelling types will enable citizens from a wide range of economic levels, age groups and life circumstances to live in Bayside." Affordable housing was critically needed in the neighborhood, where 38 percent of the population is below the poverty rate and 83 percent live in low-and-moderate income households.

Among the 57 apartments at 409 Cumberland, 46 are affordable to households earning less than 60 percent of the area median income. The mixed-income development has attracted a diverse resident population, including formerly homeless people, immigrants, retirees, young professionals and graduates from a local program that provides post-secondary education and training to young adults with developmental disabilities. Residents can walk or bike to shops, restaurants and services in downtown Portland. The building has sustainable features such as a super-insulated building envelope, a high-efficiency heating system, a low-impact storm water management system, energy-efficient appliances and lighting and environmentally-friendly paints, materials and plumbing fixtures.

CHALLENGE

More than 40 years of developing and managing affordable housing has taught Avesta Housing that building a large room, putting in some tables and chairs and labeling it "community room" is not enough. But what does it take to build and sustain community in affordable housing?

"Avesta develops innovative housing that integrates with and adds value to the community it serves."

— Cordelia Pitman, Director of preconstruction services for Wright-Ryan Construction

City planners requested that the first floor create a sense of life that incorporates outside activity, so this level is surrounded by floor-to-ceiling windows that blur the line between indoors and outdoors. Residents can relax, work or socialize in comfortable couches or at high-top tables. Community groups use the first floor for free for health-related events and classes, most of which are open to the residents. The building hosts yoga, cooking and meditation classes and is becoming the neighborhood's hub for healthy food and healthy living.

Avesta's vision for 409 Cumberland included the creation of a community that reflected the priorities of Portland as a whole, such as the city's focus on health and food systems. The building combines healthy living and an urban location to create an exceptional community. The rooftop features garden beds and a greenhouse where residents can grow their own vegetables year-round and the Healthy Living Center on the ground floor includes a demonstration kitchen where residents can learn how to make the most of their harvest, thanks to special programming by local nonprofit Cultivating Community.

A Cultivating Community Urban Agricultural Specialist works with residents to plant, maintain and harvest their garden plots. Following their experiences with food from seed to harvest, residents bring food they grow to the demonstration kitchen to learn, practice and share healthy cooking techniques and recipes. Residents bond as they help each other learn and succeed in the gardens and kitchen and share their history and culture through food.

In a resident survey, respondents indicated vast improvement in their living conditions. Some residents were previously homeless, while others experienced a significant rent decrease upon moving to the building. In addition to affordability, residents cited location, quality of apartments, gardens and the healthy-living focus as key improvements to their lives.

Affordable-housing developers and property managers face the challenge of designing a building that will create community and bring residents together for meaningful and positive shared experiences that develop their interest in supporting one another. Avesta learned several lessons through the 409 Cumberland experience, including:

83% of Bayside residents live in low- and moderate-income households.

▸ The vision for community starts in the building design. Community spaces must be thoughtful and intentional. The rooftop urban agriculture, teaching kitchen and community rooms were all part of the original design. These spaces are critical to the programming and activity so essential to this community.

▸ It takes more than a good design to create and support community. "If you build it, they will come" does not work. It takes services and programs to create a community room that residents use. Avesta increasingly invests resources into engaging residents in meaningful ways that become more about building community and less about building rooms.

▸ Know what you don't know. Although Avesta had a clear vision that healthy-living and urban agriculture would be the core values at 409 Cumberland, we also recognized that those topics are not our strengths. By partnering with Cultivating Community, we benefit from expert urban agriculture guidance.

ABOUT DANA TOTMAN

Dana Totman, president and CEO of Avesta Housing, has devoted his career to nonprofit and government management and leadership, specializing in leading organizations through significant change. For the past 16 years, he has championed affordable housing in Maine and New Hampshire, and is a founding member of the Maine Affordable Housing Coalition. Since joining Avesta in 2000, Totman has guided the nonprofit through significant growth – increasing assets from $40,000,000 to $260,000,000. Avesta currently provides homes to over 3,500 people.

PAINT THE TOWN: TAKING THE LEAD ON LEAD PAINT

Bud Compher, CEO
Lesley Krone, Community Engagement Consultant

NeighborWorks Boise

NeighborWorks Boise has organized the community building event Paint the Town for 34 years. The program coordinates teams of volunteers who paint homes for elderly and disabled residents who do not have the financial or physical means to do it themselves. This program also revitalizes the neighborhoods by increasing property values, improving distressed properties and building pride among neighbors. It has been a highly-visible tradition helping thousands of homeowners, one that garners great support and awareness within the community.

But when new EPA lead paint regulations went into effect, we were blocked from painting any homes built before 1978 due to the potential presence of lead paint and the risks involved in prepping the houses for repainting. Boise has a large stock of pre-1978 homes, and we were forced to turn away many Paint the Town applicants, some in urgent need of our help.

So in 2015, NeighborWorks Boise partnered with a local environmental company, Torf Environmental Management, which conducts training for lead-certified renovators. They were eager and willing to help us with this problem and to spread awareness about lead safety.
"Paint the Town volunteers are helping maintain our neediest homes and protecting our friends and neighbors from exposure to poisonous lead," said Torf Environmental Management CEO Mark Torf.

CHALLENGE

For more than three decades, NeighborWorks Boise has painted thousands of houses owned by low-income, senior or disabled residents. But new EPA lead paint regulations limited our ability to safely prep homes that were built prior to 1978, and we were forced to turn away many homeowners.

> ## "Paint the Town volunteers are helping maintain our neediest homes and protecting our friends and neighbors from exposure to poisonous lead."
>
> — Mark Torf, Torf Environmental Management

We conducted thorough lead testing of the homes; the company donated its time to train volunteers in proper lead paint stabilization and provided on-site support as volunteers conducted the work. The training included information about safety, EPA regulations, how to prepare for the work, containing the dust during the work and cleaning up and disposal of materials. We were able to recruit some amazing teams to suit up and prep these homes so that everything was safe for the volunteer teams to begin painting. We also received cooperation from the paint industry, which provided supplies needed to do the work, such as masks, suits, paint scrapers and plastic sheeting to line the house.

In the first year of our partnership in 2015, approximately 20 volunteers received lead paint training and prepped five homes with lead-safe practices. These homes would have been turned away from our program if we had not partnered with this company, even though they were the homes with the most need for repainting.

For our 2016 event, we simplified the training process with a shorter training session prior to the work and additional on-site training at each project location. We also improved scheduling the work to have a morning crew and afternoon crew at the same location to reduce the time needed for setup and cleanup if we could complete a project in one day. This also limits the time each volunteer spends working, since it can become tiring to conduct the work for long stretches.

In order to consider potential projects, we have an extensive selection process for Paint the Town. The first step is a homeowner application, where residents must indicate whether their home was built before 1978. Once finalists are chosen by the selection committee, homes are evaluated by a professional painter and residents are interviewed by a member of the committee. The evaluator will test the paint on the home with an instant lead test kit, which is donated by a corporate sponsor. If a home is confirmed to have lead paint, we then use a professional lead testing agency to indicate the locations of the lead. The agency provides pictures with instructions on exactly where the lead paint is and their recommendations on how to proceed. We also have this company test some homes that initially tested negative with the kits to confirm the home is lead-free and safe for volunteers. Based on all the information gathered, the selection committee makes its final decision on the recipients for the year.

In 2014, nearly 24 million housing units had deteriorated lead paint.

By the second year of this partnership we had learned a lot. One main lesson is that anything is possible when you reach out to community members and find people who are passionate about your cause. Finding the right kind of volunteer is also key. Some volunteers were concerned about the risks, but once they were given lead paint safety training, they were more aware of actual risk level and were able to see how they could provide an incredibly valuable service for the homeowners.

We also discovered that professional lead paint testing was vital – and expensive. But by explaining this to our partners we were able to get significant discounts. Working with a community partner is key to many elements of the project, especially when it comes to delivering efficient and comprehensive volunteer training.

This hasn't been easy work, but our community is caring and willing to support its neighbors if they are given the tools and training to do so. Boise's stock of pre-1978 homes is vast, but if we continue to stabilize five homes every year, we can eventually eliminate this dangerous problem.

ABOUT BUD COMPHER

Bud Compher is the CEO of NeighborWorks Boise. He joined NeighborWorks Boise as the director of real estate development in early 2015 and was appointed to CEO in the midst of transition in October 2015. He has 23 years of experience including 13 years managing a nonprofit housing program, as well as developing single-family housing throughout Idaho in conjunction with state and federal programs.

PRIORITIZING CRIME REDUCTION IN COMMUNITY DEVELOPMENT

Ann Houston, Executive Director

The Neighborhood Developers

Chelsea is the smallest and most densely populated city in Massachusetts, with 36,000 residents occupying 1.8 square miles. Forty-seven percent of residents are foreign born, poverty rates are high, and the crime rates make it one of the most dangerous cities in the state. Reducing crime is key to revitalizing Chelsea, and the nonprofit The Neighborhood Developers (TND) set an ambitious goal for cutting the crime rate by 30 percent over 10 years.

In 1991, rampant corruption and near fiscal collapse led the state to step in and place Chelsea into receivership. The state-led intervention led to a new city charter that adopted a city manager and city council system. Many in Chelsea point to the city's emergence from receivership in 1995 as the time when things began to turn around.

And yet as the years passed, it became clear that there were still difficult times ahead. Even with more efficient and accountable governance, the city faced a long road back to fiscal strength, especially as it was handicapped by low bond ratings, a weak housing market and declining industry.

In 2009, TND and the City of Chelsea – with funding from NeighborWorks America – co-sponsored a community planning process to develop a plan. For six months, over 100 residents worked with us to craft an action plan for a three-block area hit hard by foreclosures. The three-

CHALLENGE
Chelsea is the smallest city in Massachusetts, and the second most densely populated. Poverty rates are high, and the crime rates make it one of the state's most dangerous places to live. Reducing those rates was essential to revitalizing the city.

For The Neighborhood Developers, the launch of Chelsea Thrives has deepened our capacity to manage a broad and complex initiative with many partners.

year plan allocated resources to help with traffic, garbage, parking, forecloses, public parks and policing.

In 2013, after success with the small project, the city and TND led a second planning process centered on downtown Chelsea, this time with 18 stakeholders. It was called Chelsea Thrives.

Initially, Chelsea Thrives had a broad scope that sought to engage residents, businesses, nonprofits and municipal leaders on a number of issues. A year in, we determined the scope was too broad, diffusing impact and partner participation. We tightened our group of partners and zeroed in on one main priority: crime.

Chelsea Thrives seeks to empower 400 residents and 45 institutions to manage and deploy resources that address the following drivers of crime:
▸ High incidence of substance abuse and trauma
▸ An isolated and disengaged population that under-reports crime
▸ Poor physical environments, such as downtown Chelsea
▸ Insufficient youth programming

The city has provided new resources where the community says it needs it. For example, it now funds two "community navigators" to provide mental health and substance abuse services to individuals on the streets. This frees police for other work. The city has also provided resources for drug abuse treatment.

One of the most exciting results of Chelsea Thrives is called The Hub. Chelsea is the first U.S. city to replicate this successful Canadian crime-prevention model. It's a weekly roundtable of 34 public and private sector agencies that identifies families in crisis, and tries to arrange the resources those families need to navigate their difficult situations. Within 48 hours, outreach is made to the family with an offer of coordinated services.

Maria Godoy with the state's Department of Children and Families describes her experience with The Hub as "absolutely incredible." She reports that: "Interventions happen quicker and access to services is faster." Since its launch in mid-2015, just under 100 cases have come before The Hub. TND now analyzes and presents Hub data on a quarterly basis in support of shared learning.

16,000 communities participated in National Night Out in 2016.

Resident leaders are also deeply integrated into our program. Some attend monthly meetings to point out crime hotspots to the city. Some take part in crime watches and cleanups. And some are members of a task force that will soon make policy recommendations to the city about youth programming.

For TND, the launch of Chelsea Thrives has increased our capacity to manage a broad and complex initiative with many partners, something we hope to build on as we continue to nurture community development in Chelsea and the surrounding area.

ABOUT ANN HOUSTON

Since 2004, Ann Houston has served as executive director of The Neighborhood Developers, which builds vibrant and sustainable communities using integrated investment strategies. Over the past decade, TND completed over $85 million of real estate development, and it engages over 2,500 neighbors annually and, through CONNECT, a partnership of six non-profits, provides financial education and workforce development services to 4,000 clients annually.

SAN FRANCISCO'S KELLY CULLEN COMMUNITY THE LINK BETWEEN HEALTH AND HOMELESSNESS

Donald S. Falk, CEO

Tenderloin Neighborhood Development Corporation

Our goal was lofty: to provide housing to serve homeless people in the country's most expensive housing market during the recession that followed the 2008 housing market crash. We also sought to restore a seismically vulnerable, vacated structure that had long served as a focal point for the Tenderloin community. The plan was to renovate the city's historic former Central YMCA, a nine-story structure built in the classical style in 1910.

The project required coordination with an array of stakeholders, including the city and county of San Francisco, in the largest affordable housing renovation in the city's history. In addition to the significant financing challenges, the adaptive reuse project demanded complex architectural and construction planning to update 100-year old building systems in order to both meet our space needs and comply with stringent historic preservation rules.

While Tenderloin Neighborhood Development Corporation (TNDC) had a strong record in real estate development, this project represented the largest and most complex in our 35-year history. Needing to generate $95 million from a dozen sources, capital and operating funding was a monumental challenge. Each funding source presented its own, often-conflicting requirements and spending caps, and equity investors – both for the low income and historic tax credits – were unwilling to risk

CHALLENGE

To address problems associated with the homeless population in San Francisco – the most expensive housing market in the country – during the Great Recession that followed the 2008 housing market crash.

> ## "This is the first time I've had a place of my own. I tell everybody here: 'I got a big 'ol mansion.' From the bottom to the top to my neighbors, they're my family."
>
> — Sean Williams, Kelly Cullen resident

supporting such a large-scale project during a perilous economic period. Ultimately, the American Recovery and Reinvestment Act made the project possible, providing over $50 million in tax credit financing in the face of the investor community's unwillingness to finance the project.

After seven years and more than $90 million, the result was Kelly Cullen Community, named after the TNDC's late, iconic executive director. It provides 127,000 square feet of residential space (172 units), an 11,700 square-foot health center, and a team of nearly a dozen social workers and nurses that operate on site. In keeping with the historic uses of space, dating back to its 1910 design, the project also resulted in the restoration of every element of the architecturally meaningful building, including the auditorium, gym, atrium lobby, meeting spaces and grand staircase. More than 30 percent of the building's square footage is devoted to community space.

"Being homeless since 1999, going through all the things I was going through, it [Kelly Cullen Community] is very important," says Sean Williams, a resident since 2012. "It's giving you a sense of responsibility because this is the first time I've had a place of my own. I tell everybody here: 'I got a big 'ol mansion.'"

The Tom Waddell Urban Health Clinic, occupying part of the ground floor, makes explicit the project's connection between housing and health. Built by TNDC for, and operated by, the San Francisco Department of Public Health, it provides medical, psychological and social services for residents of Kelly Cullen as well as an annually anticipated 25,000 patients from the community.

Kelly Cullen Community represents a national model for its integration of housing and supportive services in a building dedicated 100 percent to formerly homeless residents with chronic health problems. A multi-agency team of social workers and nurses, with TNDC as the lead coordinator, provides health and property management services to tenants of Kelly Cullen, including medical, mental health, money management and substance-abuse treatment.

A coordinated model to reduce the public costs of high hospitalization use for homeless individuals, the $1 million annual subsidy to fund services and subsidize the rents of the formerly tenants represents a lower cost to the city than if its residents were to remain in shelters and on the street. The Department of Public Health directs to the building 50 people who are among the highest cost users enrolled in the San Francisco Health Plan.

More than 7,500 people in San Francisco were homeless in 2015.

Kelly Cullen Community makes explicit the critical connections between health and homelessness. New York University researchers, with the support of the Corporation for Supportive Housing, which selected the project for one of its Social Innovation Fund grants, are undertaking a formal evaluation of the effectiveness of Kelly Cullen and three similar programs. The evaluation may build the evidence base to support further the cost effectiveness of housing-first models that link community health and housing systems.

The success of the supportive housing model is the principal lesson learned from Kelly Cullen Community: Providing a stable housing platform with integrated supportive services for homeless individuals is more effective and less costly than allowing them to remain homeless. Supportive housing reduces costs otherwise borne by the public by reducing hospitalizations and other costs associated with caring for vulnerable populations.

Kelly Cullen Community has restored a treasured historical asset for community use, while providing a platform for homeless residents to stabilize their lives. Marcia Sims, a Kelly Cullen resident since January 2013, echoes this transformation. "I like being independent and that's what it gives me here," she says. "It's a community, it's beautiful. This is my home; this has given me a great sense of direction again."

ABOUT DONALD S. FALK

Donald S. Falk is CEO of Tenderloin Neighborhood Development Corporation, a nonprofit housing development and social services agency in San Francisco. He chairs the Enterprise Community Leadership Council and is on the boards of directors for Enterprise Community Partners and CSH, the Corporation for Supportive Housing.

BUILDING STRONG COLLABORATIONS TO TACKLE HOMELESSNESS

Brenda Torpy, Executive Director
Chris Donnelly, Director of Community Relations

Champlain Housing Trust

Between 2008 and 2015, the number of homelessness in Vermont rose by 60 percent, the third highest increase in the nation. The state provided emergency vouchers for motel rooms after several homeless people died in the cold, and spending doubled to over $4 million. Meanwhile, Vermont's hospitals had dozens of patients they could not discharge for lack of a safe landing spot. The costs of caring for preventable health needs of homeless people grew.

The Champlain Housing Trust (CHT), founded in 1984, serves communities in three counties in northwest Vermont. CHT manages 2,200 affordable apartments, stewards 575 owner-occupied homes in a shared-equity program and provides homebuyer education, financial fitness counseling, services to six housing cooperatives and affordable energy efficiency and rehab loans. In 2012, in the midst of significant increases in homelessness in Vermont, CHT decided to increase support for this most vulnerable population.

When fraud and abuse were discovered in the motel voucher program, lawmakers determined it was ineffective and inefficient. Our organization proposed a non-profit motel with onsite social services.

Financing for the 59-room Harbor Place motel was primarily provided by the Vermont Community Loan Fund,

CHALLENGE

Homelessness rose by 60 percent in Vermont between 2008 and 2015, the nation's third highest increase. After several homeless people died in the cold, the state introduced emergency vouchers for motel rooms. Meanwhile, Vermont's hospitals had dozens of patients they could not discharge for lack of a safe landing spot.

> ## "I felt like I was going to freeze to death in my car, but now I am alive and have a home of my own."
>
> ### — Robert, Harbor Place resident

a Community Development Financial Institution. The state's Department of Children and Families (DCF), the administrator of the motel voucher program, contracted 30 of the 59 rooms for approximately half the cost the state paid for private motels. Other financing included a $200,000 reserve fund with contributions from DCF, the University of Vermont Medical Center and our local United Way chapter, as well as a grant from the Vermont Housing and Conservation Board of $265,000. Harbor Place produced about $700,000 worth of savings on the reduced room rate alone in the first two years and has served approximately 650 households per year. The motel has been consistently full in every season.

Case management services are provided onsite by a community action program, a health center and a domestic violence agency. Other partners provide mental health and addiction services and support new parents. The Medical Center committed to using our rooms for homeless patients who were ready for discharge.

Having case management service on site means guests are five times more likely to be engaged with their managers, according to the agencies that serve them. Case managers report that people with easier access to these services at Harbor Place were also five times as likely to find permanent housing as those scattered at private motels. The Medical Center's evaluation of 95 people renting rooms at Harbor Place after hospital discharge found that the number of encounters with hospital services was reduced by 42 percent and saved nearly $1 million in health costs.

Our collaboration at Harbor Place with the Community Health Center of Burlington's Safe Harbor Homeless Health Care Program and the Medical Center led to an initiative to house 63 chronically homeless and medically vulnerable adults. Some were housed in our existing rental portfolio, but low vacancy rates limited our ability to help more of them.

CHT found a small hotel to convert to 19 efficiency and one-bedroom apartments, which cost approximately $100,000 per unit – less than half the typical cost for new construction. The State's Housing and Conservation Board provided a $500,000 grant for redevelopment. Safe Harbor supplied a full-time case manager with $100,000 funded by the Medical Center and the local housing authority provided non-elderly disabled and Shelter Plus Care portable vouchers for tenants that offered flexibility after one year.

The Harbor Place residence has reduced needs for hospital services, saving nearly $1 million in health costs.

"I felt like I was going to freeze to death in my car, but now I am alive and have a home of my own," says Robert, who stayed at Harbor Place. "Last winter I was in the hospital ER many times, but no trips this winter."

Neighbors near the apartments donated kitchen utensils and other household goods, and CHT staff have put in a community garden for the residents. Staff members are securing health information waivers from residents to document health system changes to identify savings on Medicaid expenses and unreimbursed health costs. CHT and the UVM Medical Center are collaborating on a public education campaign on the connection between health and housing, and the Medical Center committed a $3 million investment into additional health-related housing and community development initiatives led by CHT.

Through these two initiatives we learned the importance of leveraging the financial resources and services available through public and private organizations and to find the synergies between CHT's mission and the goals of other organizations to house and support the most vulnerable members of our communities.

ABOUT BRENDA TORPY

Brenda Torpy has 34 years of experience in the affordable housing field, starting with rural community development and affordable housing advocacy in northern Vermont. As the Community and Economic Development Office's first housing director for the City of Burlington, Brenda led the development of the Burlington Community Land Trust, now Champlain Housing Trust, and served as the founding board president. In 1991, she joined the staff as executive director.

Champlain Housing Trust is the nation's largest community land trust with over 6,000 members, 90 employees and 2,600 affordable homes in northwest Vermont, including 566 in their shared appreciation homeownership portfolio along with multiple nonprofit facilities, retail and commercial tenants. Under Brenda's leadership, CHT was selected as the 2008 winner of the UN World Habitat Award and Brenda has travelled extensively as a speaker and to assist start-ups of CLTs both nationally and internationally.

CROSS-SECTOR COLLABORATION HELPS SENIORS AGE IN PLACE

Daniel Ellis, Executive Director
Susan Tifft, Chairman of the Board of Directors

Neighborhood Housing Services of Baltimore

The National Association of Homebuilders now estimates that more than 70 percent of homeowners doing remodeling projects are planning for their own future needs or those of their parent. With approximately 10,000 people turning 65 everyday, 45 percent of all homeowners will be over 55 by the year 2020.

Yet, in many cities and towns, programs designed to help residents with home improvements operate independently with little coordination of services.

Launched in September 2015, Housing Upgrades to Benefit Seniors (HUBS) is Baltimore's response to the challenge of allowing older residents to safely stay in their homes. HUBS is a broad collaboration of community development, social and health service providers. It was funded in 2015 for three years by the Leonard and Helen R. Stulman Charitable and Hoffberger foundations, two Baltimore-based philanthropies that focus on providing low-income elderly people with access to health care and other services that enable them to remain safely in their homes.

The HUBS collaborative consists of a central leadership team that provides resources to five providers on the ground. The leadership team – Neighborhood Housing Services of Baltimore (NHSB), CivicWorks, Rebuilding

CHALLENGE

Aging residents are often isolated in their homes and invisible to the various government and nonprofit programs designed to help them. These seniors want to stay in their homes as long as possible and need access to the resources critical to their health and safety.

After working with a HUBS social worker, Mr. Harris resolved an outstanding water bill and is in the process of repairing his house's structural deficits.

Together Baltimore and Green and Healthy Homes (formerly the Coalition to End Childhood Lead Poisoning) – establishes policies, provides executive oversight and works to ensure there are sustainable resources available for housing upgrades. All leadership team members offer property rehabilitation services in Baltimore City.

The local providers are Banner Neighborhoods, Action in Maturity (AIM), Meals on Wheels of Central Maryland, Sinai Hospital of Baltimore/Comprehensive Housing Assistance, Inc. (CHAI) and Strong City Baltimore. Each operates in a different catchment area, working collaboratively to provide services for older adults throughout the entire city. This diversity in providers allows us to see the results of different models and determine the strengths of each. Of particular interest is the collaboration between traditional community development groups and health care providers.

Each of the five provider sites received a portion of the Stulman-Hoffberger grant to fund a social worker dedicated to coordinating housing and related services for Baltimore adults aged 65 and older who earn 80 percent or less of the area median income. The goal for each is to assist 75 seniors annually for three years – HUBS social workers conduct outreach in Baltimore's communities, meeting one-on-one with clients, assessing their home-modification needs and determining what resources are available. Services include minor improvements, such as the installation of grab bars and better lighting, major repairs like the installation of exterior access ramps, general repair help, tax assistance and guidance related to foreclosure prevention.

Although housing is a central focus of services aimed at helping people to age in place, there are many more factors beyond the house that are critical to residents. Research has shown that being greeted by people on the street provides a daily experience of belonging. A sense of security is derived from familiarity with the wider community, both in terms of people (such as neighbors in one's smaller community) and places (the local supermarket or health service provider). The friendships, clubs, access to resources and familiar environments help seniors feel attached to their communities as comfortable "insiders."

38% of Baltimore senior households have an annual income of less than $20,000.

One of HUBS' clients is Mr. Harris, a Vietnam veteran and long-time resident of Baltimore City. At 68 years old, Harris is an amputee and has lost most of his sight. Despite his age and multiple disabilities, he wanted to remain in his home, a house that was structurally unsafe and desperately in need of weatherization and other repairs. After working with a HUBS social worker, Harris resolved an outstanding water bill (and avoided a forced house sale), and is in the process of repairing his house's structural deficits.

HUBS has provided Harris, and other seniors much like him, access to opportunities for a better home and a stable neighborhood life.

ABOUT DANIEL ELLIS

Daniel Ellis became executive director of Neighborhood Housing Services of Baltimore in September 2011. Ellis speaks on urban housing issues nationwide and has received numerous awards for his professional work. Ellis was named the 2015 National NeighborWorks Association Emerging Leader for his advocacy at the local, state and federal levels. He is a 2014 graduate of the Greater Baltimore Committee LEADERship Program.

MAKING MORTGAGES AFFORDABLE AND ACCESSIBLE FOR FIRST-TIME HOME BUYERS

Dennis Oshiro, Executive Director

Hawaii HomeOwnership Center

Condominiums are often the primary option for homeownership for low-income families. But most low-income buyers cannot afford a 20 percent down payment and need to secure their loans with mortgage insurance. However, many condominiums in Hawaii do not have the 50 percent owner-occupancy rates required for mortgage insurance.

While FHA loans, with low 3.5 percent minimum down payments, seem like a viable alternative, many condominiums are not FHA approved. Also, FHA's insurance cost is 1.75 percent of the loan amount, paid in cash at closing or added to the principal loan amount, which amounts to $5,250 for a $300,000 mortgage. Add to that the cost of FHA's monthly insurance, 0.85 percent or $212.50 per month on a $300,000 loan, and these loans are out of reach for many prospective homeowners. The size of the down payments, monthly fees and requirements often prevent otherwise well-qualified borrowers from purchasing a home.

In 2003, the Hawaii HomeOwnership Center (HHOC) was created to provide support to first-time buyers through education and individual coaching. After a few years, seeing the challenges that homebuyers face, HHOC created the Down Payment Assistance Loan (DPAL), a second

CHALLENGE

Due to the high cost of homes, condominiums can be an affordable alternative for low-income families. But with costly down payments, pricey mortgage insurance and strict FHA requirements, it can be difficult for first-time homebuyers to secure loans for these purchases.

"It only took me one month to find a condo with this program; previously, my realtor was hunting for nine months with no success."

— Joanne Lui, DPAL borrower

mortgage program that eliminated the need for mortgage insurance and created more affordable and flexible financing options for prospective homeowners.

In designing DPAL, HHOC noted that government programs provided attractive incentives but were often only available for a short period. When funding ran out, the product was no longer available. They knew that they needed to ensure that DPAL would be available on a consistent basis, but they did not have the resources to do this on their own. They needed to find a partner that would accept their limited monies as a reserve fund to cover potential loan losses in exchange for making funding available for DPALs.

HHOC identified University of Hawaii Federal Credit Union (UHFCU), as a potential partner and began to cultivate a relationship with them. Working with UHFCU, they carefully crafted conservative approval standards to make home-ownership possible while avoiding potential losses due to borrowers not being able to sustain their mortgage payments. To ensure that they were offering loans with a high probability of repayment, they added a minimum FICO credit score of 700, homebuyer education and savings reserves for the borrower as part of the loan approval requirements.

After arriving at the initial agreement, HHOC and UHFCU needed to work out the challenges of implementing the project. They met frequently during the initial stages of the partnership to establish procedures, roles and responsibilities and address challenges that arose during the processing of the first DPALs. The solid track record HHOC established with UHFCU since has provided the foundation for a second agreement to further increase their funding limit with HawaiiUSA Federal Credit Union.

Since the inception of DPAL five years ago, HHOC has assisted 83 families into homeownership. There have been no 30-day delinquencies in their loan portfolio or in those with their partner credit unions. All the borrowers are paying their loans on time. In addition, eight of their loans were paid off early or refinanced, making additional loan capital available and reinforcing the notion that educated borrowers can plan ahead to address and repay their DPALs.

As of 2016, the median price for a single family home in Hawaii was $720,000.

"It only took me one month to find a condo with this program, whereas with the FHA loan program, my realtor was hunting for nine months with no success," says Joanne Lui, one of the first DPAL borrowers.

The combination of educating the borrower to prepare them for sustaining their home and mortgage payments, establishing strict qualification criteria and building partnerships to leverage our funds have made DPAL possible and still available to this day.

Through this project, HHOC learned: 1) trusted relationships and collaborations are needed to partner on an untested project, 2) conservative approval criteria are important to establish the partner relationship and ensure the financial success of the project, 3) financial programs need to be available and offered on a consistent basis, and 4) continued investment in the relationship with the partner is critical to the project's success and continuation and expansion of the project.

ABOUT DENNIS OSHIRO

Dennis Oshiro has been the executive director of the Hawaii HomeOwnership Center (HHOC) for the past 8 years. Oshiro came to HHOC with 38 years of experience in mortgage lending and related businesses and was the founding president of the Hawaii Association of Mortgage Brokers (HAMB). He continues to serve as a board member of HAMB. With this deep history in the lending business, Oshiro has successfully connected the work of HHOC with partners in the real estate and lending industries and continues to strive to develop creative collaborations for the benefit of low/moderate income homebuyers.

STRENGTHENING COMMUNITIES BY CREATING LASTING AND RESPONSIBLE HOMEOWNERSHIP

Jessica Padilla-Gonzalez, Executive Director

Housing Partnership for Morris County, Inc.

The Housing Partnership for Morris County in Dover, NJ, strengthens communities by creating lasting and responsible home ownership through education and financial coaching. Based on their typical client's income and the local housing market prices, it was imperative that the Housing Partnership find affordable mortgage products for which the residents could easily qualify. With the average income of their clients between $40,000 and $60,000 and average home sales prices over $300,000, they needed to explore creative ways to make homeownership a realistic long-term affordable option.

They developed and implemented a system allowing banks to become members of the Housing Partnership, known as Banking Partnership Opportunities. This enables banks to showcase their specially designed first-time homebuyer mortgages to their desired target market. In return, Housing Partnership's clients gain direct access to these loan products, which streamlines the process and reduces the burden of buying. This banking partnership provides direct funding to the organization that is based not on the number of loans the lenders receive but on the quality and benefits that consumers gain from the educational services. Each level comes with different benefits to the lenders, which include speaking opportunities and varying levels of engagement with the organization.

CHALLENGE

Dover, NJ faces a limited inventory of affordable houses. While new construction is vital, preparing new homeowners to be financially stable is also essential. Yet many organizations lose sight of the people they serve and the services they need, focusing only on the construction of the new homes.

A cross-sector partnership works in everyone's favor and reduces duplication of efforts.

As members of the Banking Partnership Opportunities, banks can market their Community Reinvestment Act (CRA) loans. In return, the clients who have already completed homebuyer education and are mortgage ready at the time of their loan application can choose to work with one of the enrolled bank members. The products offered also provide clients with affordable financing options that are designed to make homeownership a real possibility. The mortgage products

help streamline the buying process for clients by having very clear and defined requirements. Offering benefits such as reduced down payments, no private mortgage insurance and grants to help with closing costs reduces the mortgage payments. The products all require the completion of homebuyer education. As a result, the homeowners have a better understanding of the financial responsibilities of owning a home.

In 2015, the Housing Partnership was proud to assist 100 new homebuyers into their first homes. This was, in part, a result of the banking member offering products meeting their client's needs, the collaboration between the organizations and what the banks require for success in awarding CRA credits. The ultimate goal of meeting the client's needs comes full circle with the partnership opportunity.

The three most critical lessons learned from this effort are:
1) Lenders have a system in place for funding (CRA credits) but creating a partnership and collaboration between the organization, the banking industry and the community provides a better match for clients. In the end, the clients win by being given options otherwise unavailable.

2) A cross-sector partnership works in everyone's favor and reduces the duplication of efforts. It allows for the nonprofit to focus on education for the clients and for mortgage companies to im

prove the services offered to the clients and community. It also creates a healthy competition among the financial members who want to serve the homebuyers.

3) You must be an advocate for your organization's mission and the clients you serve. Corporations understand that we are the voices for those in the underserved populations and should never underestimate the scope of our ability to make positive change for them.

The average home price in Morristown is $300,000, which is unaffordable for the average income of $50,000.

ABOUT JESSICA PADILLA-GONZALEZ

Jessica Padilla-Gonzalez serves as the executive director of the Housing Partnership for Morris County, whose mission is strengthening communities by creating lasting and responsible home ownership through education and financial coaching. The Partnership has five fulltime staff offering pre- and post-purchase counseling, foreclosure intervention and educational classes in English and Spanish. It also serves as the administrating agency of affordable housing for six municipalities.

PROVIDING LOW-COST SOLAR ELECTRICITY TO UNDERSERVED COMMUNITIES

Katie Bowman, Executive Director

Housing Resources of Western Colorado

Grand Junction has some of the highest unemployment and poverty rates in Colorado. It also has a tremendous need for affordable housing and housing services. Low-income families and individuals would greatly benefit from having access to inexpensive, clean renewable energy sources. Unfortunately, the high cost of purchasing and installing solar systems puts this resource out of reach.

For over 35 years, the Housing Resources of Western Colorado (HRWC) has provided affordable housing and quality housing services to low-income families in Grand Junction, also known as the Grand Valley. Part of HRWC's mission is to promote the wise and sustainable use of resources in western Colorado. HRWC also serves 12 other counties in western Colorado through their weatherization, self-help housing, the housing rehabilitation loan program and property rentals programs.

According to the February 2016 City of Grand Junction's Housing Needs Assessment, unemployment in Grand Junction has fallen over the past few years, but it remains higher than the state average. By June 2015, the unemployment rate in Grand Junction was 7.8 percent, while the state's rate was 4.5 percent. The 2014 American Community Survey data showed the poverty in the Grand Valley increased to 16.6 percent.

Housing costs are particularly troublesome for low-income households in Grand Junction. Some 35.8 percent

CHALLENGE
Grand Junction, CO, has some of the highest unemployment and poverty rates, and affordable housing and housing services are urgently needed. Low-income residents would greatly benefit from having access to renewable energy sources, but the cost of solar systems puts this resource out of reach.

Families subscribing to the community solar garden will experience saving benefits whether they rent or own their home.

of Grand Valley residents were cost burdened, spending more than 30 percent of their income on housing. In addition, some 50.2 percent of renters were cost burdened.

HWRC, Grand Valley Power (GVP), an electric cooperative utility based in Grand Junction, and GRID Alternatives, the nation's largest non-profit solar installer, developed the solar garden partnership to assist low-income individuals and families in the Grand Valley. GVP, GRID, and volunteers from the community constructed a solar array, consisting of solar panels lined up in rows, much like a garden. The solar panels collect sunlight, which is converted into electricity and transferred to the electric grid.

Eight families in Mesa County are participating in the first community solar garden project in the nation. Each family will continue to pay a utility bill as well as contribute $.02 per kilowatt hour generated by the solar garden and 16 hours of sweat equity to support the project's development. Families subscribing to the community solar garden will experience savings whether they rent or own their home. Families are re-qualified every four years for the program. If they have moved outside the GVP service area or their income increases, this will open another spot for a qualifying family. The 29-kilowatt array will generate over $100,000 in electricity bill savings over the next 20 years.

GRID provided the materials, design and program development expertise to build the solar garden. GVP provided the site, interconnection facilities and administrative support for the project. Additional partners, including local banks, the National Renewal Energy Laboratory, solar companies and other regional companies pitched in. There was also financial help from some of the national solar equipment manufacturers, including SunEdison, Enphase Energy and Iron Ridge.

Replication has already begun locally. In February of 2016, GRID began developing a low-income community shared demonstration project in partnership with Delta-Montrose Electric Association (DMeA) and the Colorado Energy Office (CEO). This project will be similar to the Grand Junction solar garden, which should have the capacity to serve approximately 43 low-income households that are DMEA members. CEO is in the process of conducting outreach to solicit subscribers to the system, targeting homes that received weatherization services from 2010 to 2015. A primary goal of the solar garden project is to complement the work CEO is doing to address home heating costs with a program that helps households further reduce their energy bills by addressing electric costs.

The solar garden project will generate more than $100,000 in electricity bill savings over the next 20 years.

One of the eight families participating in the solar garden became interested in applying for the solar garden project from past experience with CEO's Weatherization Program administered by HRWC. Ms. Riley, a widow on a fixed income, saw significant savings on her energy bills after weatherization was performed on her home three years ago. "I am always looking for ways to save money, and being part of the solar garden has significantly helped me do that. I didn't pay anything!"

Through this project, HRWC learned that education was key for helping the community, staff, other nonprofits, businesses and the media to understand what a solar array garden was. And because many were skeptical about the program, it was important to have a coordinated response and continuous communication.

ABOUT ANNA KATHERINE (KATIE) BOWMAN

Katie Bowman is the executive director of Housing Resources of Western Colorado. For over 35 years, the nonprofit has provided affordable housing and quality housing services to low-income families. HRWC serves 13 counties in western Colorado through their weatherization, self-help housing, the housing rehabilitation loan program and property rentals programs.

STUDENTS BUILD HOMES FOR BLIGHTED BLOCKS

Ken Lyons, President & CEO

NeighborWorks Home Solutions

The city of Council Bluffs, IA, has a large inventory of vacant lots and abandoned homes that cost the city in lost tax revenue. The dilapidated houses and blighted properties plague neighborhoods across the city. Building new homes on those lots would not only provide much needed revenue for the city, it could give first-time home-buyers and moderate- and low-income residents access to quality affordable housing.

NeighborWorks Home Solutions (NWHS), a nonprofit promoting quality affordable housing and neighborhood revitalization, responded to these challenges by establishing a program with the City Planning Department and Iowa Western Community College (IWCC). Both NWHS and IWCC have had their own individual programs for years, but the collaboration was enhanced and made more fruitful for all three partners. The partnership formed in 2011 gives the school's construction technology students the chance to build two houses each academic year, equipping them with hands-on skills and broadening their employment options. The homes go to moderate and low-income residents, with NWHS often helping families by augmenting down payment assistance when needed to buy their first home. The city provides the building sites from its inventory of vacant lots and down payment assistance to the homebuyers. In return, it gets stable homeowners who will maintain the homes and revitalize the neighborhoods, putting money into the city's coffers.

CHALLENGE

Vacant lots and dilapidated homes blight neighborhoods across Council Bluffs, IA, where moderate- and low-income residents are in need of quality affordable housing. The unsightly lots cost the city tax revenue and contribute to the neighborhoods' economic and social decline.

"I cannot believe the quality of the craftmanship that was put into our home."

— Vernon Dye, resident and homeowner

And the homebuyers get affordable, quality homes with new technology and energy efficient systems. They also experience the pride in changing from renter to homeowner.

Joseph and Victoria Pfaff love their beautifully constructed home built by the students of IWCC. "It is unbelievable that we are able to own such a gorgeous home. We hope the [program] lasts forever and allows other first-time buyers such an opportunity."

Vernon Dye also welcomed the opportunity to own his home, and he's impressed with its construction. "I cannot believe the quality of craftsmanship that was put into our home," he said. "I am so happy and proud of my new home."

NWHS coordinates the other agencies' work, funds the construction, provides management over-

sight, markets the property, obtains qualified buyers and handles the sale. Every year, without exception, each property has paid for itself and thus ensures the program's sustainability. The quality of work and innovative technology and products that go into the homes make them charming and highly marketable. Buyers benefit by providing their families a desirable home along with financial and personal stability. Local businesses, subcontractors, realtors and lenders all benefit from the additional business and income.

The partnership allows IWCC to focus on what it does best- teach and prepare students for the job market. Previously, IWCC had to develop the site and handle the financing and sale of the property. By taking over these functions, NWHS allows IWCC to focus on their primary responsibility- teaching.

The students are perhaps the partnership's biggest beneficiaries. They learn that there is more to constructing a home than simply pounding a nail into a board. While building a real house they are involved in all aspects of the construction process while working in realworld elements and uncertain conditions. They are taught the value of planning and cooperation when dealing with material suppliers and a plethora of trade specialists. And knowing that the home is the buyer's first instills a sense of genuine pride and sense of community.

This program has also successfully met the students' academic goals. Over the last five years, the IWCC program has matriculated 30 to 60 students per year and graduated over 80 percent of the students. Ninety percent of the graduates either go into the workforce, adding to the number of local construction workers, or they have gone on for higher degrees. All residual revenues from the project helps fund scholarships.

90% of IWCC graduates enter the workforce or go on to attain higher degrees.

The benefits to NWHS have been numerous; with the construction of two new homes every year we are turning more renters into buyers. We have also increased the number of our partnerships and beneficiaries exponentially. The Iowa West Foundation provides initial funding for construction. American National Bank offers follow-up construction loans to sustain the program's cash-flow needs. NP Dodge Realtors donates the cost of listing and brokerage fees and commissions for the sale of the homes, which are, in turn, earmarked for additional construction technology scholarship awards.

The collaboration has also provided our organization with an invaluable and very informative experience. We've learned new internal communication practices to meet the daily functional needs of the program and how to forge an annual reporting and evaluation schedule based on agreed upon measurable metrics. The most essential elements for our success include influential partnerships, down payment assistance, a practical hands-on teaching environment and the city's unwavering support in securing properties.

ABOUT KEN LYONS

Ken Lyons is president and CEO of NeighborWorks Home Solutions. The nonprofit based in Council Bluffs, IA, provides affordable housing choices that spur investments in Council Bluffs and Omaha, NE. Our community development and revitalization efforts are supported by active engagement with residents and efficacious partnerships with the local government, educational institutions philanthropic organizations and other nonprofits. Lyons has over 30 years of business experience, including employment with Northern Petro Chemical and Mobil Oil's Polymer Division. He has managed, established, and rebuilt offices in New York and Chicago. He serves on the board of National NeighborWorks Association as board secretary and chairman of the External Policy Committee.

THE HIGH SCHOOL HOUSE: TEENS BUILD HOMES – AND CAREERS

Sheila Rice, Executive Director

NeighborWorks Great Falls

Great Falls, MT, is rich in history. The magnificent falls on the Missouri River proved one of the most challenging stretches for the Lewis and Clark expedition. The arrival of the railway in the 1880s brought a boom to the town and the beginnings of an architecturally rich era. Today homes from the city's storied past include styles such as Colonial, Revival, Queen Anne, Victorian, Second Empire and Craftsman. But these beautiful houses often sit alongside vacant lots and blighted buildings, discouraging new homebuyers from settling in the neighborhoods. NeighborWorks Great Falls (NWGF) was founded in 1980 with a mission to revitalize the city's historic neighborhoods, provide affordable housing and help residents become first-time homebuyers. A primary strategy in our work is collaboration with local partners, and one of the most significant examples of this is our High School House program.

NWGF joined forces with Great Falls public schools and the city to create the program, which provides new homes for residents with low or moderate incomes and gives high school students valuable employment skills. In the past 18 years, students from the Great Falls and C. M. Russell high schools have built 37 homes on vacant lots in historic neighborhoods. The students provide the labor while the city contributes community development block grant funding. NWGF supplies the lot, arranges subcontractors and finances the construction. We also work with potential homebuyers to get them mortgage-ready with

CHALLENGE

Great Falls, MT, boasts many beautiful old homes, some dating back more than a century. But the aging houses are interspersed with vacant lots and blighted buildings and the aging neighborhoods urgently needed revitalization. Meanwhile, working families and low-income earners needed affordable housing to break the cycle of poverty.

homebuyer education, individual homeownership planning and down payment assistance through a matched savings program. The buyers must be first-time homeowners, and many have become first generation homeowners.

This fruitful partnership has produced multiple advantages on all sides. The students get to work in an outdoor worksite two hours a day all school year long, escaping from the confines of the classrooms. Some who were at high risk for dropping out of school stay to work on the High School House Program and graduate with their class. The off-campus classroom settings provide real-world work environments – snow, wind and high temperatures – everything a construction worker must endure. The program also equips the students for future career path decisions and use-

ful training they can put into practice right away. Frequently, local builders and subcontractors visit High School House teachers at the end of the school year and ask: "Which of these kids are ready to come to work?" Some students realize that the labor side of the construction trade is not for them, so they continue their education, often in engineering or architecture. Still, that one year in construction offers them skills that last a lifetime.

Landon Stubbs came from a construction family and figured he did not need a high school diploma to make a living. But when he had the opportunity to work with the High School House program his senior year, he decided to finish school and graduate. Building a house made Stubbs realize how much he loved the program and loved teaching other students how to build, so he went to college to get his degree in industrial arts education. In less than three years, Landon landed what he calls his dream job as a High School House Program teacher. "I am one lucky guy," he says.

The program is a plus for the city since the tax base increases when a new home replaces a vacant lot or blighted building. The school district benefits from higher graduation rates and the positive visibility of its contribution to the community. And, of course, the homebuyers come away with a brand new, quality-built home that they can afford thanks to the students' free labor and the deferred mortgage program. "Homeownership changed my family's future. In one day, we went from poverty to middle class," says High School House homebuyer Erika Graves

The neighbors around the High School Houses love the idea that their community is improving and new homebuyers are moving in. The construction projects also bring people to the neighborhoods they would not ordinarily visit, as they drop by to see their children and grandchildren working or to attend ground breaking and completion open houses.

NWGF has reaped considerable rewards from the High School House program. It allows us to build two new homes every year and promotes our mission to provide affordable housing. The program's high visibility builds awareness of all of our lines of work, such as homebuyer education and neighborhood engagement. The High School House Program involves non-construction students in interior design, landscaping, welding and food services (to cater the open house celebration). NWGF has also come away with valuable lessons: seeking partnerships can provide support from untapped or unrecognized resources, and engaging the community in our work promotes our mission and raises awareness of our services.

In the past 18 years, students from Great Falls and C.M. Russell high schools have built 37 homes on vacant lots in historic neighborhoods.

ABOUT SHEILA RICE

Sheila Rice is the executive director of NeighborWorks Great Falls, where she signed on 13 years ago following a successful career as a gas utility executive. She has served on the National NeighborWorks Association board of directors and received the organization's Emerging Leader Award. Rice completed the Achieving Excellence program at Harvard Kennedy School of Government. Because she grew up in a stable home, Rice knows how much that means to children and she is dedicated to the mission of building strong neighborhoods, creating successful homeownership opportunities and promoting the development of quality, affordable rental apartments.

Financial Stability

Rodney A. Brooks

Today, people talk about financial literacy like it's a new concept. It's easy to forget that we realized it was important years ago. But then it was dropped by the wayside, just like those mandatory physical education classes to which we were once subjected.

At my elementary school in Newark, New Jersey, we would bring our savings passbook to class every week. The teacher would collect them from the class, with our $1 or $2 deposits, which somehow found their way to the local bank. We were all so proud when we got them back showing our account balances. (Of course, that was in the days when you could get 5 percent interest on your savings account.)

That passbook account introduced me to savings and also resulted in my first trips to a big bank.

The point is, we used to have at least some focus on financial education in schools – at least the importance of saving. And then we didn't. And look at where we are today as a nation. The housing "bubble" burst, the Great Recession descended, and millions of people still find themselves living from paycheck to paycheck.

Identifying scams, planning ahead and making the dollars you have last are survival skills critical to anyone of any age who eventually wants to pay for school, buy a home, start a business or retire comfortably. A NeighborWorks America survey in spring 2016 found that 28 percent of adult Americans have no emergency savings in place. The most vulnerable are those with lower incomes, people of color, and relatively speaking, women and young adults. Sixty-one percent of adults do not follow a follow a formal budget plan.

Today, there is a broader focus on "financial capability." Just what is that and how is it different? It's an approach that combines financial education (to share basic skills and knowledge), counseling (to resolve specific issues and challenges in the short term) and coaching (to encourage behavior change and achieve positive and sustainable long-term outcomes). In short, it's the ability to navigate life's events.

The case studies in this section provide several examples of innovation on the ground – Neighbor-Works organizations finding ways to help their residents achieve fiscal stability and even growth in an uncertain environment.

For example, NeighborWorks member Portland Housing Center in Oregon was concerned by a 50 percent decrease in the number of African-Americans purchasing a home. That led to a series of focus groups with African-Americans to better understand their challenges. In response, it started Getting Your House in Order, a culturally specific financial literacy class created by and for African-Americans. The program also offers one-on-one counseling, homebuyer education and down-payment assistance for qualified households.

Another example close to my heart is a program of the Ariel Community Academy on Chicago's South Side, where – starting in kindergarten – students learn how to manage an actual $20,000 stock portfolio and learn all of the financial terms that go with it. By the time they get to the sixth grade, the students are actively managing the portfolio.

When they graduate, they have to give the $20,000 back to the school for the incoming kindergarten class, but they get to keep half the profits. And with that, they start a college fund.

There's no doubt that financial education makes a difference. Consider a study by EverFi and Higher One a few years ago. It found that first-year college students who were required to take a financial literacy course in high school were "significantly" more likely than their peers who didn't take the class to be financially responsible.

"It's never too late," former Education Secretary Arne Duncan once said in an interview. "It's so much better to start early. I don't want to say it's too late. But if we want to give people a better chance at life, to get into the middle class, buy homes and support a family, you have to start with our babies."

Rodney A. Brooks *is a columnist for The Washington Post. His "On Retirement" column appears in the Sunday Post as well as The Washington Post personal finance website, Get There. He has also written on retirement for Black Enterprise magazine and TheStreet.com. He was formerly Deputy Managing Editor/Personal Finance and retirement columnist for USA TODAY. Brooks is author of "Is One Million Dollars Enough: A Guide to Planning for and Living through a Successful Retirement."*

COMMUNITY LOAN CENTER: SMALL DOLLAR LOAN PROGRAM

Nick Mitchell-Bennett, Executive Director
Jeremy Stremler
Resource Development and Strategic Planning

Community Development Corp. of Brownsville

The Rio Grande Valley MultiBank (RGVMB) was created in 1994 by six financial institutions interested in an alternative financing vehicle to support affordable housing and small business development in Cameron County, with eventual expansion into Hidalgo, Starr and Willacy Counties. The Community Development Corp. of Brownsville (CDCB) manages and operates the bank.

In 2011, CDCB and RGVMB created the Community Loan Center (CLC), an alternative for their many clients who were burdened by predatory auto title and payday loans. The CLC, an employer-based, short-term, small dollar loan program allows employees of participating companies to receive fairly priced small-dollar loans and free financial counseling through CDCB's La Puerta program.

To give context to the issue of predatory lending in the Rio Grande Valley, there are more than 20 predatory lending businesses within a two-block radius of the CLC and over 56 in the Brownsville metropolitan area. Weak industry oversight in Texas combined with a large working poor population has made the state a profit center for many of the highest-cost loan providers. Some payday lenders charge their mostly lower income borrowers the equivalent of an effective 1,000 percent annual interest rate in fees. The majority of these borrowers are not able

CHALLENGE

The need for quick cash can lead to rash decisions such as accepting a predatory loan. In 2014, Texas payday and auto-title lenders collected $1.5 billion in fees, with an effective annual interest rate of 660 percent. Alternatives to predatory loans are needed.

We hope to put payday lenders out of business and allow low-income Americans the financial freedom they deserve.

to repay these loans on time and incur high refinance fees. According to Pew Charitable Trusts, only 14 percent of borrowers are able to pay off their loan during the standard two-week period. Pew says the average payday loan borrower is indebted for five months, spending a total of $895 for a $375 loan. On average, auto title loan borrowers had to refinance their loans twice in 2014 incurring roughly $600 in fees on loans averaging $960. In 2015 over 15 cars a week were repossessed in the Brownsville area.

Our organization changed this model by offering employees of participating employers small loans. Employees may borrow up to $1,000 at 18 percent interest with a $20 administrative fee and have up to 12 months to repay with no prepayment penalty.

The RGVMB franchised this model to other organizations that are committed to combating predatory lending. Currently, there are eight local CLC lenders in Texas serving the markets of the Rio Grande Valley, Brazos Valley, Dallas, Waco, Laredo, Austin, Houston, as well as a franchise that lends in areas between markets and two franchises in Indiana. The program anticipates having a franchise in all 50 states in the near future. Currently the franchises have a combined potential borrower pool of over 47,000 employees.

The CLC's success is rooted in offering a quality product and service that is easy to access and improves the financial stability of consumers that use it. Since its launch in 2011, the CLC has originated over 12,600 loans, totaling over $10.4 million. The lack of other affordable small-dollar credit options makes this program an important piece of the consumer financing puzzle.

One of the main reasons for the program's success is the model of working with employers to provide access to CLC loans as part of their benefits package. Consumers must verify they are employed by a participating employer, allowing the franchises to use direct deposit to receive payment from loan holders. This process has helped to keep delinquency low with a loss rate of under five percent, well below industry average.

By franchising out the model and maintaining control of loan processing and servicing through our own online proprietary lending and servicing software, RGVMB created sustainable growth that allows the CLC to expand nationwide and continue to serve consumers in need of small dollar loans. We hope to put predatory lenders out of business and allow low-income Americans the financial freedom they deserve.

Some payday lenders charge up to a 1,000% annual interest rate in fees.

ABOUT NICK MITCHELL-BENNETT

Nick Mitchell-Bennett serves as the executive director of the Community Development Corp. of Brownsville, a community housing development organization that serves the Rio Grande Valley in south Texas. CDCB, one of the largest affordable housing providers in Texas, helps an average of 150 clients a year attain affordable housing. Mitchell-Bennett also serves as the administrator of the Rio Grande Valley MultiBank of which CDCB is the managing partner. Nick has been a community development leader in south Texas for more than two decades as director of the Mennonite Partnership Building Initiative and development director at the United Way of Southern Cameron County.

"CENTSIBLE FAMILIES": A COMPREHENSIVE APPROACH TO FINANCIAL LITERACY AND ASSET BUILDING

Michael Claflin, CEO
Matthew Manning, HomeOwnership Center Director

AHEAD, Inc.

As community leaders in northern New Hampshire, AHEAD has a responsibility to help build an infrastructure that supports financial literacy programs, economic inclusion, college aspirations and asset building in order to face the challenges of generational poverty and the trend of young families leaving the area in search of opportunity.

In November 2015, after years of research and developing and testing curriculum, AHEAD and our partners successfully launched the Centsible Families initiative in two elementary schools in Coös County, the state's most financially stressed area. This initiative takes a comprehensive approach to financial stability to ensure the next generation is equipped to enter an increasingly complex economic environment and is empowered to achieve their educational goals after graduation.

The first phase of the Centsible Families collaboration with The New Hampshire Charitable Foundation and Passumpsic Savings Bank, brings financial education to Coös County students in grades one through three. AHEAD staff works with classroom teachers to deliver a six-week schedule of once-a-week, 45-minute lessons. The modules covered include recognizing and counting money; earning and value of money; wants vs. needs;

CHALLENGE

Coös County, the most northern and rural county in New Hampshire, leads the state in financial stress indicators such as liquid asset poverty, asset poverty and it has the state's second highest rate of underbanked citizens. These conditions undermine family relationships and financial stability and ultimately lead to diminished financial independence.

> ## "Studies suggest that children who use long-term, asset-building accounts to finance higher education demonstrate consistent savings behaviors and increased college attendance."
>
> ### — Anthony Poore, Federal Reserve Bank of Boston

checkbook, debit cards and bills; setting goals and charitable giving; savings vs. spending and asset building. To date, 260 students have received 5.5 hours of financial education.

Phase two is an evening workshop for parents and children titled "Centsible Families." The goal of the workshop is to bring children and their parents together to discuss what the children have learned and to play games based on the covered material. We provide dinner for the families and, to add to the fun, we give out prizes throughout the night. We want parents to feel confident in their ability to continue the conversation at home and also, if they see fit, to contact AHEAD to discuss building their own financial success plan.

The third phase of Centsible Families includes a partnership with Passumpsic Savings Bank to provide Coös County students, grades one through three, a custodial savings account with the hope that it will be used for post-secondary education. Passumpsic Savings Bank provides the initial $25 deposit into the account and if the student receives free or reduced lunch, an additional $10. A third deposit of $25 is provided if the children and their family attend the multi-generational workshop. AHEAD provides ongoing "Savings Deposit Days" each month that school is in session for children to make deposits to their accounts. Each time students make a deposit they get to pick a prize from the "One Time" prize bucket. When students make their fifth deposit, they can pick a prize from the "Five Time" prize bucket and start the count back at one, or they can hold off and make five more deposits and at that time select a prize from the coveted "Ten Time" bucket. This helps students understand the concept of delayed gratification and goal setting. Additionally, all students who make regular deposits over the course of two months will have their name placed in a raffle. The winner receives a sweatshirt from a local public university.

At the first four participating schools, 62 families have returned the required paperwork to have their children's savings account opened, 37 students are saving on a regular basis and a total of $2,300 has been deposited into accounts.

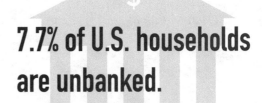

7.7% of U.S. households are unbanked.

Parental engagement is challenging. The lure of "seed" money or free food is not enough to get parents to return required paperwork to open an account for their child. It may be that the parents do not have a traditional relationship with a bank, or that they are concerned about "strings" that may accompany the account. It could also be that they feel it could potentially impact means testing for other services or aid the family receives. Our presence at open house nights as well as the creation of a Frequently Asked Questions document was helpful.

We are still in the early days of the program and are continuing to develop it. We have quickly learned that collaboration is powerful. We have built a successful program through partnership with public education, a private foundation and a private banking partner. This collaborative effort is committed to providing significant resources to fund the children's savings accounts and with AHEAD providing the coordination and financial education in the classroom; we hope to continue this program long into the future.

Low- and moderate-income children with college savings between $1 - $499 are three times more likely to attend college and four times more likely to graduate. Kids love to learn about money. The lessons are the same whether we are using calculators and spreadsheets with adults or play dough with children.

ABOUT MICHAEL CLAFLIN

Michael Claflin is AHEAD's CEO and is responsible for overseeing the organization's development and outreach. AHEAD owns and operates 330 units of affordable housing for families', seniors and people with disabilities in nine northern New Hampshire communities. Additionally, AHEAD's HomeOwnership Center has provided pre-purchase homebuyer education classes to more than 1,600 families that have resulted in 510 families becoming first-time homebuyers. Claflin takes on leadership roles in community organizations that improve and build collaborative partnerships to sustain AHEAD's role as one of the premier community development organizations in the state.

FINANCIAL EDUCATION BEGINS BY KNOWING THE AUDIENCE

Dean Matsubayashi, Executive Director

Little Tokyo Service Center

In 1979, representatives from various Japanese-American organizations came together to address the lack of linguistically and culturally appropriate services for residents of the historic downtown Los Angeles neighborhood known as Little Tokyo, as well for the broader Japanese American community. Little Tokyo Service Center (LTSC) was formed to fill this gap, and has since evolved into a multilingual community development agency.

A significant number of Asian-American seniors in and around Los Angeles struggle economically and face barriers to accessing helpful resources. For example, Korean Americans have the highest poverty rate of seniors from any racial group with roughly one in five living below the poverty line.

Clients come to LTSC in a variety of financial situations, like when collections agencies come after them unduly, or when a parent suddenly becomes a dependent. While LTSC provides individual case management, we wanted to avoid draining staff time and resources, so we looked for ways to step up education and prevention efforts to address financial issues.

LTSC reached out to local banks and financial planners and started a direct dialogue. We discussed financial issues of particular concern to seniors in Asian-American communities. Together, we've helped each other better offer our clients culturally-appropriate financial counseling.

CHALLENGE

Asian-Americans constitute the fastest growing racial group in the United States, but many face barriers as they age. The health insurance system often overwhelms those used to national health care abroad. The legal system can feel intimidating. And anything beyond basic saving and checking accounts can befuddle even the college-educated.

At some workshops, we coordinate multiple languages, including syncing three screens to project slides in English, Japanese and Korean.

LTSC began focusing on financial workshops to our target communities. We invited expert speakers and provided simultaneous interpretation so that those with limited English proficiency could learn and ask question.

Early feedback from workshop attendees was overwhelmingly positive, and this pushed us to do more. We found that attendees wanted translated materials in addition to simultaneous inter-

pretation. Although it requires planning far in advance, we work with speakers to translate and test the materials not only for accuracy, but also readability. This is particularly important because literal translations may be technically correct, but not make much sense to a target audience. At some workshops, we coordinate multiple languages, including syncing three screens to project slides in English, Japanese and Korean.

Our biggest impact occurred among participants with limited English proficiency. Planning for long-term care (LTC) such as caregiving and extended nursing homes stays is one example. Many people do not realize that Medicare does not cover LTC. Immigrant families may be particularly underprepared for the cost if the health care system in their country of origin includes LTC because they tend to assume it is offered in the United States also. When we invited an expert to talk about LTC insurance, more than 50 people attended. Most of the immigrant families attending heard about LTC insurance for the first time.

While events are important, education starts with outreach. Our staff have expanded the number of presentations they make, in several Asian languages, to residents of senior housing buildings and social groups. We also cultivate relationships with ethnic media in order to continue to reach a broader audience.

When we heard about tax scammers targeting people with foreign-sounding names, for example, we submitted articles to our bilingual community newspaper. We received many calls from people, particularly from monolingual Japanese speakers, who said they had gotten threatening calls and were scared until they saw the article. One woman even called months later to tell us she had taped the article to the wall by her phone to be prepared. When she eventually got a scammer's call, she proudly told them off.

Culturally-appropriate information and targeted outreach take time and resources to develop, but they help to start important conversations to prepare for the future.

Korean–Americans have the highest poverty rate of seniors from any racial group with roughly ⅕ living below the poverty line.

ABOUT DEAN MATSUBAYASHI

Dean Matsubayashi is executive director at Little Tokyo Service Center (LTSC), located in Los Angeles, CA. LTSC is a community development corporation and has been an important resource for the residents of a diverse community. LTSC is a nonprofit charitable organization serving Asian and Pacific Islanders throughout Los Angeles County who are in need, especially those facing language or cultural gaps, financial need, or physical disabilities. LTSC collaborates with other nonprofit, community-based organizations to help them build multifamily affordable housing projects that serve their communities, and increase the capacity of the organizations.

BUILDING BRIDGES TO SUCCESS FOR IMMIGRANTS

Joe Myer, *Executive Director*
Denise Freeman, *Housing Counseling Director*

*National Council on Agricultural Life and
Labor Research Fund*

In Delaware, a household must earn $21.09 an hour to afford the median $1,096 rent on a market rate two-bedroom apartment. The average renter earns $5.73 per hour. That equation becomes even more challenging for the state's many non-English speaking citizens. Many of the state's foreign-born people live below the poverty line. Children in immigrant families are more likely to live in crowded conditions than children in native families.

The National Council on Agricultural Life and Labor Research Fund (NCALL) is a Delaware-based nonprofit working to promote affordable housing, community improvement and sustainable development, primarily in rural areas. We recognized that small groups of our population with limited English were struggling to access some of the most basic services. We wanted to find a way to create a bridge for these underserved residents and provide them with opportunities for homeownership, community engagement and economic stability.

Immigrants are often hidden within their communities and their linguistic and cultural differences can silence them. Difficulties in accessing services and seeking medical care means some families go months without assistance or could be misdiagnosed due to language barriers. Unfamiliarity with U.S. banking systems can encourage families to keep money under the mattress or in the informal "savings circles" prevalent in other countries. Whether they are documented or not, many immigrants

CHALLENGE

Securing an affordable home is challenging for low-income people, particularly for immigrants, who can be exploited by unscrupulous landlords. Lack of English proficiency and information are barriers to accessing assistance. Unfamiliarity with the U.S. banking system hinders immigrants' ability to obtain loans and can prevent them from prospering.

Unscrupulous landlords may threaten immigrant tenants with deportation, increasing their hurdles to obtaining safe, affordable housing.

find it extremely difficult to obtain driving permits and in rural Delaware public transportation is often not an option. Immigrant status, cultural barriers and a tendency to isolate within family boundaries can prevent engagement in the broader community, limiting economic opportunities. Undocumented immigrants often assume they have no rights and those who cannot speak English are easy targets for discrimination. Unscrupulous landlords may threaten immigrant tenants with deportation, increasing their hurdles to obtaining safe, affordable housing.

When NCALL's financial coaches and pre-purchase housing counselors began looking for ways to increase community outreach, they narrowed down the possibilities to a group not often readily identified: the emerging immigrant population. Two financial coaches were assigned to provide

financial literacy to a few small English as a Second Language (ESL) workshops in the area, primarily held in local schools, churches and poultry plants. Later, the coaches met one-on-one with the participants who expressed interest in receiving financial coaching services.

Among the challenges we face are that some immigrants have difficulty speaking and learning English, especially if they are not literate in their native languages. Fortunately, our financial coaches can provide services that other ESL instructors cannot: communication in the immigrant's native Spanish or Haitian Creole language, free one-on-one coaching and access to housing services and banking programs. Families seeking to buy homes are offered tools and coaching for preparation and then transferred to a certified housing counselor to become mortgage ready.

After we launched this effort in 2015, word spread to other organizations about our services. Our coaches have held dozens of financial literacy classes with hundreds of immigrant participants at 10 sites. One of our coaches also coordinates a number of savings circles (an alternative financial system practiced worldwide) which is linked to a local credit union, jump-starting their access to establishing credit.

When assessing populations not well served by NCALL's housing services, we've learned that if another program is reaching that group, such as ESL classes, it is best to partner with that service. Together, we can better serve that population and expand our ability to meet the needs of our community.

One of the most valuable things our coaches offer is an ability to understand the struggles of those they seek to serve. We learned early on that this was key. Our American values and goals are not necessarily the same as our immigrant clients. Once this is acknowledged and respected, these families feel safe and confident in sharing their challenges and achievements. Our dedicated financial coaches tailor the financial literacy courses to meet the needs of the families they serve. They travel to sites throughout the southern half of the state to hold workshops and meet with families, sometimes after normal business hours to facilitate those with jobs. Our site coordinators have witnessed the real connections between the coaches and these families and look forward to building more of these bridges.

In Delaware, the average renter earns $5.75 an hour, too little to afford the median rent of $1,096.

ABOUT JOE MYER

Joe Myer, executive director of the National Council on Agricultural Life and Labor Research Fund, is responsible for the overall management and administration of the organization's housing programs, which include technical assistance, direct housing services and lending for the Mid-Atlantic and Northeast regions. Under his leadership, NCALL has helped 8,000 families become homeowners.

ONLINE HOMEBUYER EDUCATION: A COMPREHENSIVE SOLUTION TO HOMEOWNERSHIP ISSUES

Kevin Smith, President and CEO

Community Ventures

Travel cost and time as well as childcare and work schedules challenge the ability of families to meet for traditional one-on-one counseling. Counseling agencies have limited resources, staff, and time. Rural housing agencies have to strategically locate where they can serve the most clients in a cost-effective manner, leaving some potential homebuyers without access to homebuyer education courses.

Community Ventures created eHome America in 2009, an online homebuyer education course that helps homebuyers make informed choices and achieve their dream of homeownership. Born out of the subprime lender crisis and originally funded by NeighborWorks America, eHome America is the most comprehensive online homebuyer education course in the nation. It is used by more than 450 housing agencies in all 50 states, Puerto Rico and Guam. eHome America benefits homebuyers and allows nonprofit partners to serve more clients at a lower cost. Its revenue-sharing model has brought over $7.5 million in shared revenue to partner agencies, allowing them to have a greater impact in the areas where they serve.

When first-time homebuyers start this daunting and confusing transaction, many are undereducated and exposed to the predatory lenders in the mortgage industry. The

CHALLENGE

Barriers to homeownership make it particularly difficult for low-to-moderate income families to achieve their goal. Homebuyer education helps people responsibly purchase a home and many lenders now require education courses for potential buyers. However, many homebuyers are unable to meet with local housing agencies due to time and money constraints.

We continue to restore the dream of homeownership, creating a stronger middle class and a stronger America.

housing crisis taught people that buying a home takes more than a dream and a few signatures.

New post-crisis regulations and higher expectations for compliance hit low-and-moderate-income families the hardest and many are disqualified from homeownership. With income, wealth and credit scores on average lower for minorities, access to mortgage credit for low-income borrowers will likely have major implications for the ongoing severity of wealth disparities.

Homebuyer education is proven to reduce the potential for foreclosures by 29 percent and counseled borrowers are 67 percent more likely to remain current on their mortgages.

Community Ventures President and CEO Kevin Smith realized how necessary home-buyer education is after meeting with a client who wanted the company to release his second mortgage. The client had a 30-year fixed-rate loan at one percent interest and was planning to switch to a loan with a lender who was offering $500 at closing. However, the fine print stated that this was an adjustable rate loan that could adjust up to a 14 percent interest rate.

"We were able to help this client, but I knew we were missing so many more," said Smith. "We had to do something to reach a wider audience so we had the idea to create eHome-America."

eHome America's online course gives people the option to take homebuyer education courses on their own schedule and at their own pace. eHome is approved and accepted by NeighborWorks, HUD, the USDA and 16 State Housing Finance Agencies.

As of June 2016, eHome has provided over 185,000 prospective homebuyers with high quality education. Broken into chapters so consumers can start and stop as desired, the program uses multiple adult learning techniques and has a completion rate of over ninety-five percent.

Through its revenue-sharing model of splitting the $99 course fee, with $74 going to agency partners and $25 to eHome America for administrative costs, eHome has funneled over $7.5 million to its nonprofit partners. The shared revenue is used for multiple services, including offsetting the high-intensity counseling that some customers require as well as strengthening core housing services.

eHome America also creates cost efficiencies because agencies are able to serve more clients at a lower cost. Among its administrative tools, eHome offers Spanish translation enhancements, an online chat feature and new counselor tools that are constantly updated.

For 42% of recent buyers, the first step taken in the home-buying process was to search for homes online.

Homebuyer education is a win for lenders, consumers and governmental entities. eHome America lessens the need for regulation, creates sustainable revenue for nonprofits, and raises financial literacy nationwide. Buyers receive a high-tech experience combined with one-on-one counseling, providing both convenience and personal guidance.

Overall, homebuyer education is expected to play a greater role in the home buying process in the years to come as lenders, consumer advocates and local governments recognize that education is a significant deterrent to foreclosure. Homebuyer education leads to better-performing loans made to better-qualified borrowers, builds consumer confidence and communities, strengthening the essential foundation of our economy.

"Working with our partners in eHome America, we can shape a housing market that is stronger and safer than before," said Smith. "In doing so, we continue to restore the dream of homeownership, creating a stronger middle class and a stronger America."

ABOUT KEVIN SMITH

Since 1993, Kevin Smith has led Community Ventures from a staff of one with $450,000 in assets to today's 70-member team in five regional offices managing over $121 million in assets. Smith has over 22 years of experience in designing, implementing and capitalizing nonprofit programs.

COMMUNITIES WIRED! EDEN HOUSING'S INITIATIVE TO ADDRESS A MODERN-DAY NECESSITY

Linda Mandolini, President

Jennifer Reed
Director of Fund Development and Public Relations

Eden Housing, Inc.

Two years ago, Eden Housing recognized that a majority of their residents, including 50 percent of families and up to 60 percent of seniors and those with special needs, had no access to broadband services. In many cases they did not know its importance, could not afford the monthly fees or did not have a reliable home computer. This put them at a huge disadvantage in today's world.

In response, Eden created Communities Wired! a portfolio-wide initiative that builds on over 30 years of experience providing residents with access to technology through on-site computer labs and training. This initiative provides those most in need, including low-income seniors and families, people with special needs and limited English speaking minorities; with computer training and low cost options for computer equipment and Internet service, with the goal of supporting them to use broadband access at home.

Over the past two years, Eden integrated Communities Wired! into our existing programs, building on the success of our "Digital Connectors" youth program (promoting digital literacy, leadership, community service and access to higher education) and our "Generation Exchange" program (youth teaching computer skills to seniors).

CHALLENGE

Low-income households, people with special needs and minorities with limited English often have little or no access to broadband services, making it difficult to monitor their children's school attendance and progress, access bus schedules, pay bills, search for work and access services in their local communities.

At one of their senior housing sites, Cottonwood Place, nearly 100 percent of the residents have access to the Internet.

Eden partnered with the California Emerging Technology Fund (CETF) and received $100,000 in funding for this initiative. We used the funds to assess current resident broadband adoption rates, obtain information on resident technology needs, develop promotional and educational materials, train staff, identify additional partners and provide technical assistance.

We also partnered with external providers to deliver technical assistance to residents. In 2015, we wrote grants and received commitments for $433,689 in funding from the California Public Utilities Commission (CPUC) to create the infrastructure to provide free Internet access at 11 housing sites – one farm-worker family housing site, four family sites and six senior housing sites. CPUC is also funding digital literacy programming at eight housing sites.

Eden worked with Digital Connector teen volunteers, senior resident leaders and local special needs service partners to develop a Communities Wired! Digital Literacy Tool Kit to use as part of the program.

Currently Eden offers free broadband at 24 sites, totaling 1,983 units. At one of our senior housing sites, Cottonwood Place, nearly 100 percent of the residents access the Internet as compared to the portfolio average of less than 40 percent for senior residents. In their apartments, residents must use their own computer or tablet, but Eden also offers a computer lab on site for use by all residents.

In addition to our efforts to acquire infrastructure and equipment, over the past two years, 756 residents subscribed to low-cost broadband services as part of the Communities Wired! program. Eden also reached 1,200 residents across the portfolio with their digital literacy training. Topics included help with email, searching the Internet, social media, Internet safety and online bill paying.

While implementing the Communities Wired! program we learned several lessons:

1) The monthly fees cause a severe hardship to many residents and in some cases a basic need could go unmet to pay the bill. We realized we need to find ways to provide free wireless access to residents.

58% of senior citizens use the Internet.

2) We needed to figure out how to address infrastructure and equipment costs. For new properties, we build this cost into the development of the community, but for existing properties, especially in rural and high-need areas, we are seeking funding from a variety of sources such as the CPUC. Eden is working to partner with local Internet providers to negotiate affordable fees to ensure long-term sustainability of the program.

3) We learned that we must provide residents with a minimum of 1.5 mbps of bandwidth because less than this doesn't provide enough speed for basic tasks and leads to frustration. We also learned that bandwidth needs to be allocated to each unit rather than as a shared pool. This is more equitable and prevents one resident from slowing the service for others.

4) We need to further expand our curriculum to assist residents using the Internet to support their daily activities. We are also developing tools to measure the impact of our technology efforts. Eden's goal is to find partners to help us provide wireless access at 100 percent of our properties. We believe this is a critical infrastructure necessity, like bringing electricity to homes in the 1930s, that will support residents' basic needs today and for years to come.

ABOUT LINDA MANDOLINI

Linda Mandolini, president of Eden Housing since 2001, previously served the organization as a project developer and director of real estate development. She oversees affordable housing production, resident support services and property management along with a staff of nearly 350 employees. Mandolini serves or has served on the boards of: The Housing Trust of Silicon Valley, Non-Profit Housing Association of Northern California, California Housing Consortium, National Housing Conference, Enterprise Communities' Community Leadership Council and International Housing Policy Exchange.

THE GOLDEN MOMENT: BUILDING ASSETS AND PARTNERSHIPS THROUGH FREE TAX PREPARATION

Lou Tisler, Executive Director

Neighborhood Housing Services of Greater Cleveland

Tax refunds can be crucial for low- and moderate-income families in this country. They consistently report using tax refunds to cover housing, utility and basic needs expenses. But families face obstacles to receiving refunds. First, tax preparers are often uncredentialed, costly and prone to errors in their filing. Their fees and loan products can eat up hundreds of dollars from a tax refund. Second, many families are unaware of how to file their taxes or how to use their tax refunds wisely. Additionally, roughly one in 10 families does not have a transactional bank account to deposit refunds, leading to long waits and fees associated with receiving and cashing a paper check.

The mission of Neighborhood Housing Services (NHS-GC) of Greater Cleveland is to provide programs and services to help families and individuals achieve, preserve and sustain homeownership. Greater Cleveland remains a challenged economy – still reeling from the Great Recession and an aging housing stock. More than 45 percent of people in Greater Cleveland are asset poor, creating a need for programs and services that promote economic development and bring dollars directly into neighborhoods.

The largest poverty relief program, the Earned Income Tax Credit (EITC), is delivered through the tax code and

CHALLENGE

Tax time is critical in building and sustaining assets for low- and moderate-income working families. They frequently use their refunds to make home, utility and basic needs purchases. But many families may face obstacles to getting their refunds because their preparers are uncredentialed, costly and prone to errors.

Combined with additional tax credits and deductions, a tax refund is often the largest paycheck for a working poor family all year.

provides community residents with real dollars to meet their basic needs and sometimes save for the future. In fact, combined with additional tax credits and deductions, a tax refund is often the largest paycheck for a working poor family all year. In the Cleveland area, the average EITC is slightly more than $2,400. The vast majority of EITC recipients who are NHSGC clients say that they use their refunds for housing, utility and food expenses.

But the full benefits of tax refunds continue to elude families in the Greater Cleveland area, who face obstacles – lack of tax code knowledge, expensive and unethical tax preparers, as examples – to receiving the funds to which they are legally entitled.

One NHS client, a single mother with two children, noted: "I spent so much last year on my taxes. I didn't know free was an option. I didn't know anything about the process, just that I needed help and my money."

Some families NHS of Greater Cleveland works with choose not to file taxes at all because they lack information. Other families – and about a quarter of NHSGC clients – do not have bank accounts, forcing them to endure additional wait periods and fees associated with cashing a paper check.

Problems in the tax refund delivery system drain resources from the community. For every dollar spent at a check cashing store or paid to a tax preparer, there are fewer dollars going directly into communities.

NHSGC is part of the Volunteer Income Tax Assistance (VITA) program, where trained and certified volunteers prepare taxes for free for low- and moderate-income tax filers. NHSGC is also a leading member of the Cuyahoga EITC Coalition, which provides free tax preparation services in Northeast Ohio.

Delivering tax filing assistance services requires substantial collaboration from community partners. Volunteer recruitment is essential. Board members, staff, local financial institutions, college students and friends of the NHSGC provide generous volunteer hours. VITA is an intense volunteer commitment, involving eight hours of training, testing and client meetings, but the return on the volunteer experience is powerful. One volunteer, a NHSGC board member, remarked: "Helping this family receive $3,000 and understand how direct deposit works has been the highlight of my year…what a major impact."

21% of Americans will use their tax refund to pay off bills and other debts.

Financial institution partners provide NHSGC not only with volunteers, but also with access to fair and safe transaction account products. Several financial institutions work with NHSGC to provide account opening at tax time, allowing clients to open low-cost checking accounts and use direct deposit for their tax refund. NHSGC further provides financial capability counseling and coaching before, during and after tax time.

After five years of offering free tax preparation programs, NHSGC continues to build success and partner with community groups to improve the financial health of northeast Ohio. On average, NHSGC serves 1,000 families annually, bringing in more than $2 million a year in refunds and savings to the community. NHSGC also use tax assistance programs to enroll clients in homebuyer and financial education courses.

Tax time is often the most important financial moment of the year for low- and moderate-income families. Having NHSGC act as both a preparer and a steward for clients greatly benefits the community. NHSGC continues to integrate the free tax program into a diverse offering of counseling and community development efforts.

ABOUT LOU TISLER

Lou Tisler has served as the executive director for Neighborhood Housing Services of Greater Cleveland for 11 years. The nonprofit's mission is to help families achieve, preserve and sustain the American dream of homeownership. Tisler serves as vice chair of the NeighborWorks America National HomeOwnership Steering Committee, as board member of Home-Matters and on the advisory councils for eHome America and Ocwen Financial Services.

FORECLOSURE INTERVENTION: KEEPING FAMILIES IN THEIR HOMES IN TIMES OF FINANCIAL CRISIS

Blanca Velez Beauchamp, Executive Director

Puerto Rico Neighborhood Housing Services

For the past 10 years, Puerto Rico has suffered an economic crisis. The U.S. territory's population is declining at an accelerating pace. The jobless rate is more than twice that on the U.S. mainland, poverty is three times higher and homes cost significantly less than they did 15 years ago. The Federal Housing Finance Agency index shows that home prices are the lowest since the end of 2000. Meanwhile, the same index for the United States as a whole is at a record high.

The number of foreclosures in Puerto Rico is up 19 percent, over a 50 percent of increase from 2008, according to data from the Commissioner of Financial Institutions of Puerto Rico. That's a troubling trend because residents used to do whatever it took to avoid losing possession of their homes. Now many are choosing to leave the island in search of steady work and a better future.

When the spate of foreclosures began, local commercial banks and mortgage brokers didn't trust Puerto Rico Neighborhood Housing Services (PRNHS) to help with the growing demand for education and counseling. However, traditional financial institutions weren't offering options to clients that helped match their mortgage payments with the new financial realities. Conventional banks in Puerto Rico were not interested to offer loss-mitigation tools or other programs to help families keep their

CHALLENGE

Financial uncertainty, high unemployment and a devalued real estate market have Puerto Rican residents afraid to invest money or buy houses. This has prompted some 500 families to leave the island every month.

Due to PRNHS success at helping families maintain homeownership, government agencies have begun to adopt our approaches to foreclosure prevention.

homes. Rather, local banks primarily dealt with mortgage-collection problems through repayment plans and forbearance, with the goal of keeping financial accounts current.

It was no surprise, then, that in the midst of Puerto Rico's mortgage crisis, demand for PRNHS services picked up. Loss-mitigation departments at banks noticed that their clients preferred to have PRNHS as a mediator in payment negotiations. In response, PRNHS created a "Working with Sensibility on the Crisis" workshop for collection and loss-mitigation professionals and real estate representatives. The workshop trains financial professionals to treat clients more humanely and sensibly, and how to provide foreclosure alternatives for distressed homeowners. Through the workshop, PRNHS also has developed alliances with the Puerto Rico Banks Association and Community Reinvestment Act officers, with the goal of easing the effects of collection and loss mitigation on families and communities.

The two-hour workshop includes actors who role play to demonstrate how to – and how not to – engage clients. "We teach participants how to listen effectively and create an atmosphere of mutual respect." The first workshop PRNHS held with the Puerto Rico Banks Association and Community Reinvestment Act officers drew 90 people. (Experience has shown that the ideal size is around 25 people.) Over the last year, PRNHS has held more than 15 "Working with Sensibility on the Crisis" workshops all over the island, with audiences that include staff of elected officials and government agencies.

Due to our success in helping families retain their homes even under difficult circumstances, government agencies have begun to adopt our approach to foreclosure prevention, as well as request our staff to coach their employees. For two consecutive years, the Puerto Rican government has invited PRNHS to depositions for the resolution of housing and financial disputes.

Our organization has made a difference by protecting many families from losing their homes. Since 2006, PRNHS has expanded our staff and developed in-house expertise in mitigating foreclosure risk. We used the NeighborWorks Ad Council campaign, "Nothing is Worse than Doing Nothing" ("Nada es Peor que no Hacer Nada" in Spanish) to build trust as an organization independent of any financial institution or government agency. In 2007, PRNHS created the first and only Foreclosure Prevention Center in Puerto Rico that focuses on mortgage intervention. Clients waited in lines around the block, and our staff worked well into the evening to accommodate everyone. Although that degree of enrollment is no longer the case, PRNHS has a steady demand for services.

The NeighborWorks foreclosure awareness campaign with the Ad Council resulted in more than $89 billion in donated media and 8 billion media impressions.

Financial counselors at our center are familiar with all the phases of Puerto Rico's foreclosure process. Our employees have also been trained and certified by NeighborWorks America in lending, financial counseling, first-time home buying and foreclosure risk mitigation. Also, staff members are recognized as Foreclosure Specialists by the National Industry Standards for Homeownership Counseling & Education. "Many of our clients have never developed a budget, and we are devoting a lot of time to help them to develop this critical skill. We have also started a new program for university students to teach them budgeting skills just as they are becoming adults, with an eye to preventing foreclosures and helping them achieve a better financial future."

ABOUT BLANCA VELEZ BEAUCHAMP

Blanca Velez Beauchamp is the executive director of Puerto Rico Neighborhood Housing Services, a nonprofit community-based organization whose mission is to promote and facilitate access to affordable housing in our communities, empowering and training them to achieve humane socioeconomic development.

KEEPING FAMILIES IN THEIR HOMES: STAVING OFF FORECLOSURES TO PREVENT DISPLACEMENT

Wayne Meyer, President

New Jersey Community Capital

New Jersey Community Capital was founded in 1987 to meet the capital needs of New Jersey-based community development groups. The organization's mission is to transform at-risk communities through strategic investments of capital and knowledge. With offices throughout New Jersey, NJCC provides innovative financing and technical assistance to critical community development efforts that strengthen neighborhoods and support low-to-moderate income populations. Since our inception, we have considered safe, healthy housing the bedrock of community development.

NJCC responded to the foreclosure crisis by launching ReStart, an innovative home preservation program, in December of 2012, with the purchase of 261 underwater mortgages split between the Newark region in New Jersey and the Tampa region in Florida. ReStart is our model for providing hundreds of families who are facing foreclosure a second chance to fulfill the dream of successful homeownership and economic stability.

The mechanics of ReStart work like this: We work with our private investors to purchase pools of distressed mortgages from Federal Housing Administration auctions at a steep discount, then offer homeowners the opportunity for one-on-one counseling and principal reduction to

CHALLENGE

New Jersey has the highest rate of homes in foreclosure. Many organizations, including New Jersey Community Capital (NJCC), offer financing and support for the development of affordable housing to help displaced families. But could NJCC help homeowners affected by the foreclosure crisis avoid needing affordable housing in the first place?

ReStart has enabled us to keep families in their homes, stabilize communities and rehabilitate vacant properties into affordable housing.

protect them from displacement. Meanwhile, we also work with local organizations to rehab vacant properties in the pool into affordable housing.

By the spring of 2016, we purchased 778 mortgages in Florida and New Jersey, resulting in 127 mortgage modifications. That is 127 families who are able to stay in their homes. Through the implementation of ReStart, we have learned how early intervention – foreclosure prevention and vacant property rehabilitation – can prevent negative long-term community consequences associated with concentrated vacancy, abandonment and blight.

Richard and Jacqueline are just one of ReStart's success stories. Richard works at a delivery company and his wife, Jacqueline, teaches high school Spanish. By 2005, the couple had saved enough to buy their first home, a duplex in Linden, NJ. The economic downturn hit the family hard, landing Richard and Jacqueline in a seven-year nightmare of predatory scammers and false promises. By 2014, they were ready to cut their financial losses and sell the Linden home.

Then Richard and Jacqueline learned from a local housing counseling organization that their mortgage had been purchased through ReStart. They were eligible for a modification and their payments would drop from over $4,000 per month to under $2,500. Richard and Jacqueline made their reduced mortgage payments through the required trial period and closed on a permanent modification. It took nearly a decade, but the couple finally feels hopeful again. Most importantly, Richard and Jacqueline – with assistance from ReStart – were able to stay in their home and in their community.

While ReStart has been largely effective at keeping families in their homes, not all families who participate are successful at making lowered mortgage payments, despite intensive financial counseling. These families receive support to transition to a stable housing situation, such as a lease-to-purchase agreement in their current home or affordable rental housing.

ReStart has enabled us to keep families in their homes, stabilize communities and rehabilitate vacant properties into affordable housing, but our work is not done. We continue to acquire pools of mortgages and work on a fee-for-service basis for other mortgage pool purchasers to manage their foreclosure prevention process for them.

Our success with ReStart in such diverse markets as New Jersey and Florida show that the program can serve as a national model for revitalizing distressed communities and jumpstarting housing markets across the country.

More than 1 in every 20 mortgaged homes in New Jersey remains in foreclosure.

ABOUT WAYNE MEYER

Wayne Meyer served on the board of directors before becoming president of New Jersey Community Capital in May 2009. An attorney and certified public accountant, Meyer brings to his position over 20 years of private sector real estate experience. Key accomplishments under Meyer include spearheading a new strategic vision, including creating a more comprehensive approach to revitalizing whole neighborhoods; helping shape a new model of community development that leverages the bulk purchase of troubled mortgages and foreclosed properties; increasing capital under management and guiding NJCC to chartered membership in NeighborWorks America.

NEW PARADIGM FOR A NEW MILLENNIUM

Kara Hay, President & CEO
Dana Ward, Loan Officer, MainStream Finance

Penquis

Waldo County, ME, is home to about 39,000 people and is perhaps best known for its appearance in Nathaniel Hawthorne's classic novel "The House of the Seven Gables." Penquis is one of nearly 1,100 community action agencies across the United States and one of 10 in Maine. Community action agencies were established under the Economic Opportunity Act of 1964 to fight America's War on Poverty.

We see the promise of community action this way: Community action changes people's lives, embodies the spirit of hope, improves communities and makes America a better place to live. We care about the entire community, and we are dedicated to helping people help themselves and each other.

In that spirit, Penquis formed MainStream Finance to serve as a community development financial institution. We offer educational and financial services to support homebuyers as well as residents who desire to start or grow a small business.

It made sense, then, for the county's Habitat for Humanity to come to us when it wanted to help a low-income couple build their first home. It had approached the local bank, but that institution didn't have a loan product that was appropriate and affordable, and instead recommended us. We were intrigued Habitat approached us with a proposal: a financing mechanism called a zero equivalent mortgage, or ZEM.

CHALLENGE
A Habitat for Humanity chapter in Maine needed help with obtaining a home loan for a low-income couple with limited credit. Getting creative with the financing would provide the homebuyers with a manageable mortgage.

We successfully made the case to our loan committee that the pair had established enough history through their rent payments to qualify.

This is the way a ZEM works: Rather than Habitat for Humanity lending the full amount of the loan to a borrower with no interest, a financial or community development institution lends just a portion of the building's appraised value at the prevailing interest rate, and Habitat holds a soft second mortgage on the difference. This allows Habitat to build more homes.

The proposal to partner with Habitat for Humanity on a ZEM was exciting to us because it matched our mission of serving lower-income residents. MaineStream Finance is a wholly owned subsidiary of Penquis, and a nonprofit community development financial institution. Our mission is two-fold: 1) serve low- to moderate-income residents with housing-related loans, and 2) provide technical assistance and commercial loans to startup and existing businesses, with a goal of increasing employment.

However, because ZEM is a relatively complex product, and the couple had limited credit, we were forced to think outside the box. Instead, we relied on an alternative form of credit: rental payments the couple had made for the last few years. We successfully made the case to our loan committee that the pair had established enough history through their rent payments to qualify for the ZEM arrangement, including the tax and insurance escrow requirements.

MaineStream Finance closed the ZEM in October 2015, three days before World Habitat Day. On that special day for Habitat organizations around the world, we attended an open house and ribbon cutting at the couple's new home.

Our partnership helped a deserving family secure a safe, energy-efficient home and enabled the local Habitat for Humanity organization to create additional housing opportunities for families in need. We encourage other nonprofit lenders across the country to consider partnering with Habitat for Humanity on zero equivalent mortgages to further help lower-income clients who seek to buy a home.

We offer two lessons we learned that others should consider: First, when presented with a challenging request, be careful not to dismiss it quickly as too difficult to achieve. Many obstacles can be overcome. Persist until either you can't possibly go any further or until a breakthrough is experienced.

Secondly, do not assume that just because a bank couldn't make a request work, it won't make sense for your organization. Yes, it may present challenges and require more time than usual, but at the end of the day, if you are able to help people in the communities you serve, then you have achieved your mission.

Community Action Agencies were established under the Economic Opportunity Act of 1964 as part of the "war on poverty."

ABOUT KARA HAY

Chief Executive Officer and President Kara Hay is a Maine native. She came to Penquis in 2009 as the deputy director and operations manager for the Penquis Child Development Department and was promoted to chief executive officer of Penquis in June, 2014. Kara collaborates with the board of directors to refine and implement the strategic plan while ensuring that the budget, staff, and priorities are aligned with Penquis's core mission. She provides inspirational leadership and direction enabling Penquis to achieve its long- and short-term goals and objectives. She ensures the delivery of high quality services while managing for current and future growth. She oversees the financial status of the organization including developing long- and short-range financial plans and sets financial priorities. She holds a Bachelor of Arts degree in Theatre from the University of Maine, a Bachelor of Arts degree in Psychology from the University of Hawaii at Hilo, and a Master of Arts degree in Marriage and Family Therapy from Argosy University, Hawaii. She has extensive experience working with children, families and communities. Previously, she worked as a mental health casework supervisor for the Maine Department of Health and Human Services, as a children's service coordinator providing direct services and support to families experiencing domestic violence, and she has also worked as a family therapist and a child development specialist. She has also worked as an independent consultant, providing training and consulting services to parents, mental health providers, early childhood specialists, and nonprofit and school staff.

GETTING YOUR HOUSE IN ORDER: FINANCIAL LITERACY BY COMMUNITY DESIGN

Peg Malloy, *Executive Director*

Portland Housing Center

The mission of the Portland Housing Center (PHC) is to provide access to homeownership through quality, education, counseling and financial services. While PHC services are available to all first-time homebuyers, particular attention is given to communities traditionally left out of home ownership, including African-Americans. African-Americans are among Portland Housing Center's target populations, with a homeownership rate in Portland of only 35 percent, compared to 65 percent for white households.

In 2010, we recognized a 50 percent decrease in the percentage of African-Americans who used our services to purchase a home compared to other demographics. At the time, the Obama Administration had instituted the first-time homebuyer tax credit, which drove increased homebuying for all groups served by Portland Housing Center – except African-Americans.

According to research by Brandeis University, a typical African-American household has accumulated less than one-tenth of the wealth of a typical white one. Over the past 25 years, the wealth gap between African-Americans and whites has nearly tripled. The main contributors to the wealth gap include homeownership, inheritance, college education, income and unemployment.

Concern over this increasing gap led to a series of focus groups with African-American customers and potential

> ## CHALLENGE
> In 2010, the Portland Housing Center saw a 50 percent drop in the proportion of African-Americans using our homebuying services compared to other demographics.
> We needed to find a way to bridge the gap.

"I used to have money nightmares; I was nervous and anxious about money all the time. Now I don't lose sleep over financial things."

— GYHIO graduate

customers to better understand the problem. When African-Americans participants asked for a more private forum to discuss culturally specific financial concerns, we started Getting Your House in Order, a culturally specific financial literacy class created by and for African-Americans. The class is now one piece of PHC's homebuyer preparation services, which also includes one-on-one counseling, homebuyer education, financial education classes, and down payment assistance for qualified households.

To develop the class, PHC contracted with experts in the African-American community and convened an African-American advisory committee who oversaw the creation and marketing of the class. During the four-week course participants learn how cultural, family and personal values and habits affect spending, steps for building a strong credit record and how to effectively move from a "paycheck to paycheck" mentality and save for specific goals.

In the early days of the project, we sought customers through a partnership with one of the largest African-American employers in Portland. By advertising the class as an employer benefit, we were able to reach participants for the early classes, and build momentum. The majority of new participants came from word of mouth referrals from friends and family.

Since starting the program, more than 230 households have completed Getting Your House in Order. Over the same time period, there has been a 69 percent increase in new African-American customers, and an 86 percent increase in African-American home purchases compared to 2011.

One of the most impressive outcomes for class participants was a 566 percent increase in households who "always" or "usually" keep an emergency fund after taking the class compared to before the course. Additionally, 100 percent of class participants maintained a budget at least "sometimes" after completing the course, compared to only 51 percent before the course. Participants also felt more in control of their finances with 96 percent of class participants feeling they can effectively manage their finances after completing the course, compared to only 34 percent prior to the course.

In a recent evaluation, we discovered that homeownership is just one positive outcome of the course. Getting Your House in Order has become a catalyst for new, positive financial behaviors. It has also helped participants build a personal connection to money and improve their financial confidence. Even those who have not yet achieved homeownership say they make better financial decisions and feel more empowered.

Since 2011, Portland Housing Center has seen an 86% increase in African-American home purchases.

For example, of the customers who had been out of the class for over a year, the number of respondents who said they "usually" or "always" contribute to savings or investment accounts, increased 150 percent compared to before the course. The number of survey respondents who reported "never" using a budget decreased from 49 percent prior to the class to zero at present.

I used to have anxiety attacks about money," said one of the participants. "I don't have those feelings any more. I don't feel out of control, or that I will be out in the streets. I don't lose sleep over financial things."

Top Lessons Learned:
1. Community engagement is key to successful outcomes.
2. Employer partnerships can be a valuable outreach tool in reaching target customers.
3. Evaluation is an important component of any program and should be planned early on.

PHC plans to use this successful model of engagement with the African-American community by training trainers in other community organizations to educate more African-Americans being left out of homeownership. Homeownership is about more than a house; it's about building and passing on wealth.

ABOUT PEG MALLOY

Peg Malloy is the executive director of the Portland Housing Center. Prior to joining PHC, Malloy she spent four years with the Seattle Housing Authority. She has worked in community development and lending in Portland, Seattle, and New York for over three decades.

FINANCING FISHERS' RECOVERY FROM THE BP OIL DISASTER

Lorna Bourg, President & CEO

Southern Mutual Help Association

The catastrophic 2010 BP oil spill in 2010 caused severe financial losses to many small-scale fishers along the Louisiana coast. Oyster fishers lost valuable stocks and shrimpers had to travel far to find safe products. They are vitally important to the Louisiana economy and culture and needed capital to restart their businesses, but the fishers lacked access to financial support.

The Southern Mutual Help Association (SMHA) has a long legacy of working to secure affordable housing and capital for underserved populations across coastal Louisiana. When the Deepwater Horizon offshore oil well exploded, we immediately realized that this would mean another devastating financial setback for an industry already underwater.

In the previous decade, fishing families along the Louisiana coast had suffered from hurricanes Katrina, Rita, Gustav and Ike, bringing destruction in their wakes. Furthermore, the small-boated fisher fleet, as small-scale fishers are known, had already suffered a multitude of economic pains as imported seafood flooded American consumer markets through the 2000s. Struggling fishing operations were barely hanging on by the time the oil spill hit.

Fishing families needed to restart their operations. As the initial disaster faded, so did the funds to pay fishing boats for helping with cleanup efforts. Fishers needed to do re-

CHALLENGE

Many small-scale fishers suffered severe financial losses after BP's 2010 oil spill in the Gulf of Mexico. They are vitally important to the Louisiana economy and culture and needed capital to restart their businesses, but they lacked access to financial support.

The honor loans were particularly successful because they were created specifically for a unique population of proud, independent people.

pairs, clean their boats, reseed and move oyster beds and get back on the water. Oyster fishers were hit hardest. Some beds were covered in oil while other stocks simply died. As oysters take between two and five years to mature, the impact was devastating. Fishers needed cash flow to restart their businesses.

SMHA needed to do something fast so we created an "Honor Loan" as a way to distribute capital quickly and easily. Louisiana's fishers often pride themselves as fiercely independent and self-sufficient people. Instead of developing grants, which fishers saw as handouts, we provided loans on their honor. Fishers only had to pay back 90 percent of the loan amount, if and when she or he was able, all with a simple handshake and a signature. Fishers saw repaying the loan as an opportunity to participate in the recovery of the fishing industry and an investment of the future of fishing cultures.

One oyster fishing family, headed by Croatian immigrants named Jure and Vedranka Slavic, had built a livelihood around oysters. The Slavics came to Sister Helen Vincent, a senior advisor to SMHA, shortly after the spill for financial assistance. The spill had destroyed much of the oyster stock. While they, and many others, knew BP would pay out for losses, they couldn't wait for the lengthy court proceedings.

The Slavics took an honor loan of $8,500 to reseed the beds and start anew. On a simple promise, the family committed to repay 90 percent of the loan amount at the earliest possible date. Within two years, Jure and Vedranka repaid the loan. They also gave Sister Helen an additional check for more than $1,500 dollars. They wanted to invest in the future of other fishers, and the future of fishing on the Louisiana coast. Today, the Slavics' son still operates the family oyster business. Dozens of other fisher families were also able to take the honor loans and quickly make necessary adjustments to their operations. Some fishers invested in crabbing when shrimping became difficult. Others invested in renovating their boats to fish farther from home – and farther from the spill – while simultaneously upgrading their operations with more efficient freezer technology.

SMHA eventually granted and loaned a total of nearly $1.4 million to fishers in southern Louisiana in the wake of the spill and hurricanes. The honor loans were particularly successful because they were created specifically for a unique population, all of whom were employed, and just needed help resuming operations. When the oil spill hit, these loans became a culturally sensitive way to get swift assistance to a group of people who did not want grants. Of all the loans we made, there was only a 4.04 percent loss rate. From the successes of the honor loans, SMHA is now working to create a sustainable source of affordable capital for fishers in Louisiana.

$1.4 million in honor loans were made with a simple handshake and resulted in only a 4% loss.

Many valuable insights were gained from this experience. Rather than providing only capital in the wake of disasters, it is important to find ways for victims to consistently invest in their enterprises, and to adapt to potential changes in the environment. As sea levels rise and storms increase in intensity, small-boated fishers recognize they need to change the way they do business. And that means investing in new models. SMHA's help can enable these fishers to remain a vital part of Louisiana's coastal culture and economy.

ABOUT LORNA BOURG

Lorna Bourg is co-founder, president and CEO of Southern Mutual Help Association, a 47-year-old nonprofit community development corporation recognized across the country for its entrepreneurial and innovative approaches to rural community and economic community development. Since its founding in the sugar cane fields of rural Louisiana, SMHA has developed over 1,400 units of new/rehabilitated affordable housing with an economic impact of over $425 million. A MacArthur Fellow and Fannie Mae Foundation James Johnson Fellow, Bourg is a visionary leader with a passion for justice.

CONNECT: CREATING A 'ONE-STOP SHOP' FOR FINANCIAL STABILITY

Ann Houston, Executive Director
Nancy Turner, Director of Resource Development

The Neighborhood Developers

Prior to the launch of CONNECT in 2012, The Neighborhood Developers offered financial education and benefits enrollment programming that, while valuable, was insufficient to move many families out of poverty. Our clients – primarily low-wage, low-skilled immigrants – needed a greater range of services than we could provide independently. While critical services were delivered locally, clients struggled to stitch different services together. Many reported feeling overwhelmed as they juggled the demands of work and family life.

In response, TND led the formation of CONNECT, located at our headquarters, which offers the services of five agencies working to improve the financial mobility of low-income families. The partnership includes two non-profits, a credit union, a community college and a career center.

We developed our program of bundled services by learning from national "one-stop financial opportunity centers" led by the Annie E. Casey Foundation, Local Initiatives Support Corporation (LISC) and the United Way. Once we decided on our services, TND set out to recruit partners whose services complement our own and who agreed to integrate services and work together at one site.

Our organization plays two roles at CONNECT. In addition to delivering financial capability services, we pro

CHALLENGE

To partner with other expert agencies to create a "one-stop-shop" to assist low-income clients with education, financial services, and benefits.

TND provides the 'glue' that binds the partners together. Initially this meant establishing a governance and accountability system that held each partner to shared goals and commitments.

vide the "glue" that binds the partners together. Initially, this meant establishing a governance and accountability system that held each partner to shared goals and commitments. We initiated monthly meetings with executive level managers in order to foster the buy-in from leadership that would be critical to our success.

We soon discovered that each organization had its own funding requirements, data-collection requirements and organizational culture. So, to avoid a culture clash, our first task was to make sure the partners understood each other's priorities, particularly regarding performance standards. Discussion – sometimes difficult – fostered better understanding and trust among stakeholders, leading to better outcomes for our clients.

While CONNECT began its early stage programming, TND invested in a facility expansion to add 2,800 square feet of classroom and programming space. We wanted to create a welcome environment that would keep client coming back. We also helped develop an adaptable database that allowed each partner to maintain their own data systems and avoid duplicating data entry. Eighteen months after launch, CONNECT was fully functioning with assistance and funding from the U.S. Department of Labor, NeighborWorks America, Boston LISC and the United Way.

When CONNECT's data went live, managers were initially surprised to see that in our first year of operation, only 12 percent of clients bundled services. We formed a task force to identify opportunities to overlay services. For example, we identified and spoke to clients engaged in semester-long adult education coursework about public benefits screening and financial education.

We held focus groups to better understand the client experience and developed new client brochures and messaging to reinforce that there was opportunity to move from one service to another. Frontline staff began weekly meetings to facilitate training, client flow and referrals. Early data on the effectiveness of bundling helped overcome staff resistance and incentivized change. The percentage of clients who receive bundled services at our location continues to increase, almost doubling from 12 percent in 2013 to 23 percent in 2015. The bundling goal for 2016 is 28 percent.

Through CONNECT's coaching and peer support programs, clients engage in financial goal setting delivered one-on-one or in a group setting. Coached clients tap into the greatest density of CONNECT's service offerings and are demonstrating impressive gains. In 2015, coached clients saw a median increase to net income of $716.50 per month. A coached client said of her experience, "I felt like I had a whole team there to support me."

Clients coached through CONNECT saw a median increase to a net income of $716.50 per month.

In mid-2015, after three full years of operation, CONNECT identified some areas for improvements. We are calling this effort CONNECT 2.0.

Clients now enter intake information directly into a computer that uses a series of questions to assess a client's needs and automatically maps the appropriate services. For example, families that have high debt, are unbanked or routinely pay late bill fees, will map into financial education or credit repair services.

For each client, the computer generates a "service map" that categorizes short-, medium- and long-term activities and considers service availability and the level of client interest. It notifies the CONNECT partner most appropriate to the service suggested and sends the client clear information about how to follow up. It even prescreens all clients for public benefits eligibility such as food stamps.

For The Neighborhood Developers, the launch of CONNECT has had a profound impact. The added staff, budget and facility have increased our reach and visibility and deepened our partnerships. We hope to take the lessons to other endeavors as we continue our mission to nurture those communities most in need.

ABOUT ANN HOUSTON

Since 2004 Ann Houston has served as executive director of The Neighborhood Developers, an organization that builds vibrant and sustainable communities using integrated investment strategies. Over the past decade, TND completed over $85 million of real estate development and it engages over 2,500 neighbors annually. CONNECT, a partnership of six co-located nonprofits, provides financial education and workforce development services to 4,000 clients annually.

FOSTERING FINANCIAL SKILLS IN RURAL ALASKA

Brian Shelton-Kelley, Deputy Director

NeighborWorks Alaska

For tens of thousands of years, Alaska's Native cultures have relied on a subsistence lifestyle and an affinity for community. But the state's economy is changing, and both urban and rural areas are reassessing their models for economic and community sustainability. Revenues from natural resource development, funding from the federal government, and investments from Alaska Native regional corporations have long supported the costs of building social and economic infrastructure in rural Alaska. The global decline of oil prices, retrenchment of the oil industry and decreasing availability of federal funds have created a perfect storm. Rural Alaskans, the majority of whom live subsistence lifestyles, are now trying to adapt. NeighborWorks Alaska has met this challenge by launching a program to help educate and equip rural residents with the tools for greater financial self-sufficiency.

Alaska is one of the most expensive states in the country. With a limited road system, shipment of goods depends primarily on air and barge throughout the year. In rural areas the result is prohibitively high prices for goods; in some villages bottled water is $30 a pack, and gas is $11 a gallon. Comparatively, the weekly grocery costs for a family of four in Portland, OR is $166, but in Dillingham it is $355. The lack of local banks in rural communities outside of the state's primary hubs has forced people to rely heavily upon multiple credit card accounts. Residents have to learn what it means to be credit-worthy and how to properly leverage personal wealth and asset management. This is especially true in rural Alaska where the cost of living is high and the opportunity for employment low. NeighborWorks Alaska moved to address the

CHALLENGE

Alaska's Native cultures span tens of thousands of years with a rich history of subsistence and affinity for community. However, the state's economy is changing, and both urban and rural areas are reassessing their models for economic and community sustainability.

The NeighborWorks Alaska way is and has always been to first listen and try to understand the needs of the communities we are working with before taking action.

problem by extending its Keep the Change program to these vulnerable remote communities. The program, first launched in Anchorage in 2014, equips residents with the tools for financial self-sufficiency. The goals are to increase credit scores, promote regular savings, reduce overall debt and create more opportunities for homeownership. To launch our expansion effort statewide, we partnered with Alaska Growth Capital (AGC), a subsidiary of Arctic Slope Regional Corporation (ASRC), a private, for-profit corporation specializing in energy support services and economic development. ASRC is owned by and represents the business interests of nearly 12,000 Iñupiat shareholders living in the eight villages of the North Slope.

The challenges have been many, ranging from accessing remote villages to creating culturally-relevant course materials. Travel on Alaska's North Slope is primarily accomplished via air and extreme weather can instantly disrupt a carefully planned itinerary. On several occasions our program manager had to walk through and to villages in "active" polar bear areas (without incident thanks to the kind help of local residents). These experiences reinforced the importance of collaborative communications with our partners.

The NeighborWorks Alaska way is and has always been to first listen and try to understand the needs of the communities we are working with before taking action. That's why we started by meeting with village sponsors, who are responsible for identifying their community's economic opportunities. We then developed a curriculum for financial education classes and forums and scheduled visits to all eight villages once a year over a three-year period. From those discussions, we agreed to focus our efforts at the household level to build proficiencies in budgeting, saving and credit management. We have since visited eight villages, attracted 42 participants, engaged 19 in counseling and received reports that most have reported improvement in their savings and credit management.

The Keep the Change program seeks to increase financial capability and help people manage their spending and saving behaviors. Smart financial practices strengthen stable housing opportunities, and stable housing strengthens the overall physical and emotional health of the entire community. The program has attracted positive interest, and we have developed close relationships with community leaders across the North Slope. Our partnership with AGC is part of our overall larger statewide strategy to support economic and social well-being by ensuring resource sustainability. We realize there are unique cultural aspects to this effort, and are moving very thoughtfully in this pilot program to build relationships with our regional sponsors and village leadership groups so the communities understand that our commitment to collaborate is for the long term.

Alaska is one of the most expensive states, with some villages pricing bottled water at $30 a pack and gas at $11 a gallon.

We recognize that methods of successful and culturally appropriate outreach and communication already exist on the North Slope so we want to ensure that we are not imposing an outsider's approach on places that are bound closely by very specific interpersonal traditions and processes that have worked for thousands of years. In the Arctic, the community – not the individual – is the center of the circle. For our program to be effective, we must make sure our goals and accompanying curricula are in alignment with this cultural context. The value of using relevant examples in our classes that reflect the unique challenges of subsistence living is a critical part of our outreach. Gaining a better understanding of these conditions will give us more effective tools and materials and will enhance our ability to connect with rural residents, enhance their financial skills and consequently the well-being of the community as a whole.

ABOUT BRIAN SHELTON-KELLEY

Brian Shelton-Kelley is deputy director of NeighborWorks Alaska. Prior to this role, he served as director of community development for the organization. NeighborWorks Alaska is dedicated to improving the quality of life for families and individuals by preserving homes, creating new housing opportunities and strengthening neighborhoods. Brian's background is in affordable housing and real estate.

BRIDGING THE BANKING GAPS

Bill Bynum, CEO
Ed Sivak, Chief Policy and Communications Officer

———

Hope Enterprise Corporation

Across the United States, there are 384 persistent-poverty counties where the poverty rate has exceeded 20 percent for three decades in a row. Fully one-quarter of the country's persistent-poverty counties are located in Arkansas, Louisiana and Mississippi. A deeper demographic analysis clarifies that persistent poverty is particularly acute in the Black Belt counties of these states. In 35 of 39 counties where the African-American population exceeds 50 percent, the poverty rate has been above 20 percent for the last 30 years. These counties are also home to some of the highest rates of unemployment and unbanked/underbanked households in the region. The intersection of poverty, race, unemployment and access to affordable financial services underscored the need for lasting community development solutions.

In 2015, Regions Bank announced plans to consolidate its operations in the Mississippi Delta and close its branches in the communities of Itta Bena and Moorhead. Both towns are located in persistent-poverty counties with populations of just over 2,000 residents – nine out of 10 of whom are African-American. In the absence of an alternative bank, local people would face the grim prospect of having to drive miles for basic banking services.

Building on their longstanding relationship, Hope Enterprise Corporation/Hope Credit Union (HOPE) and Regions Bank worked together to develop a solution. Regions donated its facilities to HOPE, provided information about HOPE to its customers and allowed HOPE to

CHALLENGE
Across the United States, there are hundreds of counties where the poverty rate has exceeded 20 percent for three decades in a row. In many of these counties, banks have moved to more profitable areas. As a result, residents lack basic financial services and face serious difficulties obtaining loans.

"HOPE's team treated me as if I had a million dollars in my pocket."

— Johnnie Lee Murry, Hope Enterprise Corp. Client

set up an in-branch presence to market the credit union's products and services. Finally, the bank also provided grant funding to support HOPE's start-up costs.

In November 2015, the former Regions locations re-opened as HOPE branches. Almost immediately, HOPE's local team members, a number of whom formerly worked for the bank, saw that things had changed.

First, HOPE was lending in the communities. In the years leading up to the transition, neither the Itta Bena nor the Moorhead branches originated loans. Bank customers were required to drive to branches in larger cities to apply for a loan. Second, HOPE reviewed loan applications through its community development lens. If a member was not ready for a loan, then someone from the HOPE team would sit down with the member to help them develop a plan to achieve their goals. Third, HOPE installed ATMs at both locations, where previously there had been none, to ensure that members and residents of the community could access cash even when the credit union was closed.

Johnnie Lee Murry's story underscores the dramatic change experienced in one of the communities. Shortly after HOPE's Itta Bena branch opened, Murry applied for an auto loan. Due to some past credit challenges, however, he did not immediately qualify. Rather than turn Murry away, HOPE's team developed a plan to improve his credit.

Murry took out a small-dollar loan in which half was set aside as a savings account. Over the life of the loan, he never missed a payment. After paying off the loan, his credit score went up and he was approved for the auto loan. Today, he is driving a new, reliable vehicle. "HOPE's team treated me as though I had a million dollars in my pocket," says Murry.

Murry is not alone. In the first eight months of operations, over 1,100 people have opened accounts with HOPE in its two new locations. The credit union also has originated $200,000 in loans. It will replicate this strategy in 2016 in two other rural Mississippi communities with persistent poverty and limited banking options.

Three important lessons emerge from HOPE's expansion in the Mississippi Delta. First, after a job, the single most important financial relationship an individual can have is the one with a financial institution. When one's financial relationship is with a depository, the path to ownership, for an automobile, a home or a small business for example, is much more direct than if that relationship doesn't exist or exists only with a high-cost alternative.

¼ of the country's persistent-poverty counties are in Arkansas, Louisiana and Mississippi.

Second, relationships matter and meaningful partnerships facilitate the deepest impacts. Bank and credit union partnerships are rare. However, the teams at HOPE and Regions had a long history of working together. The trust and social capital built up over the years between the institutions contributed to an environment of shared goals.

Finally, policy matters. All four of the branches were located in areas that were sensitive to Community Reinvestment Act (CRA) requirements by the bank. Undoubtedly, the CRA served as a catalyst for these innovative transactions illustrating that good policy broadens the reach of effective organizations.

ABOUT BILL BYNUM

Bill Bynum, CEO of HOPE (Hope Enterprise Corporation/ Hope Credit Union) a highly regarded community development financial institution and policy center that advances economic inclusion across the Mid-South, and influences related policies and practices nationwide. HOPE has generated more than $2 billion in financing that has benefited over 650,000 residents throughout Arkansas, Louisiana, Mississippi and Tennessee. For more than three decades, Bill Bynum has worked to advance economic opportunity for disenfranchised populations.

Nonprofit Excellence

Bill Ryan

The accounts that follow speak for themselves in making the case for investing in nonprofits' capacity for impact and innovation. Each one speaks to improvements in organization that helps them, in turn, improve their communities.

But investing in this capacity is a cause that still needs champions like NeighborWorks. True, the debates of 25 years ago – when many nonprofit leaders, board members, and funders questioned whether investing in these capacities was a good idea, or merely diverting scarce dollars away from programs – are pretty much over. Most within the sector now grant that nonprofits need leadership development, management training, and infrastructure investments if they are to develop new programs, execute them effectively, and evaluate their impact as they strive for continued improvements. But now the field faces new challenges, centered not on whether to offer these supports but how.

And on this question NeighborWorks can speak from the vanguard of new approaches to helping nonprofits build their capacity for impact and innovation. Its longstanding training institutes continue to equip individual leaders with new skills they can bring back to their organizations. But some of its newer programs are more ambitious, innovative and promising. Programs such as NeighborWorks Achieving Excellence Program (offered in partnership with Harvard Kennedy School) and Excellence in Governance (in collaboration with BoardSource) represent a new generation of hybrid approaches.

These programs combine familiar elements of professional development and organizational capacity building in new ways:

▸ Participants bring to the program a specific outcome-focused challenge – a trans formational issue that is critical to the organization's success. This keeps both learner and trainer alike focused, motivated and honest. These are real challenges that the program has to equip participants to address.

▸ As with any professional development program, trainers and educators design and deliver the content. But to ensure that participants actually make progress in applying the content to their organizations, they work with coaches between sessions. The coaches help them devise and stick to plans, while providing advice and troubleshooting problems in ways that convert learning to action, and action to results.

▸ Instead of teaching a single leader in a classroom and counting on him or her to educate colleagues at home, the Excellence in Governance program requires a team of four board members and the CEO to participate together, vastly improving the chances that new ideas will be applied.

▸ Additional elements – such as retreats and organizational assessments – blur the lines between training and consulting, exactly as we should if making real change in organizations is the goal.

This combination of approaches also raises the bar. Instead of focusing only on ensuring first-rate training in the classroom, everyone involved in designing and delivering the programs is focused on how to ensure the learning leads to success in the organization, equipping it in turn to help communities succeed.

NeighborWorks conducts longitudinal evaluations of these programs to ensure they are effective, and not just promising. For example, results from the Excellence in Governance program show participating boards making striking progress in improving their governing effectiveness, overall engagement, and partnership with their Executive Directors. That this enhanced effectiveness becomes "the way we do business" for nonprofit boards and outlives any one board member is the true sign of success. There will be much more to learn, and for NeighborWorks to share with others seeking similar impacts.

In the meantime, leaders on the frontline, like those featured in the chapters ahead, will be using these approaches and others to build better organizations and communities.

Bill Ryan *is a thought leader and expert in the way nonprofit leaders approach governance. In addition to helping nonprofits transform their governance, Ryan also spent 10 years as principal and research fellow at the Hauser Center for Nonprofit Organizations at Harvard University, where he now teaches executive education programs at the Kennedy School of Government.*

THE ENDICOTT HOTEL: REVITALIZATION AND SUSTAINABILITY

Rosemary M. Heard, President & CEO

CATCH Neighborhood Housing

CATCH Neighborhood Housing, founded in 1989, envisions a community where every person is confident of a home. The organization develops and rehabilitates affordable rental apartments, provides homebuyer and financial fitness education and offers property, asset and financial management services.

CATCH recognizes the need for supportive housing for low-income individuals with mental illnesses and worked with a local mental health service provider to rehabilitate the Endicott Hotel in Concord, N.H. into apartments targeted at this population. The mental health organization would provide case management services, while CATCH would manage the affordable apartments. Unfortunately, a lack of funding caused the other organization to withdraw from that arrangement, leaving CATCH with a property that was restricted to extremely low-income individuals.

Rents were kept low for affordability, but there was a gap in resources to maintain and update the historic building while meeting the needs of the building's residents and the community at large.

Adding to the challenge, the residents at the Endicott had extremely low incomes and many had mental health issues that would have made an interruption in their housing nearly impossible to handle. CATCH's Board of Directors realized the impact of construction and relo-

CHALLENGE

The Endicott Hotel, a historic landmark in downtown Concord, NH, needed rehabilitation and its residents needed services for individuals with very low incomes and mental health issues. CATCH developed a plan to restore the building, find appropriate housing solutions for residents and create a long-term source of funding for programs.

The Endicott was the first test of demand for downtown market-rate housing. Based on its success, the city government is hopeful that more property owners will follow suit.

cation could be disastrous for many residents, yet the only available choices were to relocate the residents and complete a gut rehabilitation of the Endicott or to continue with the status quo.

In the fall of 2010, CATCH completed construction on a new downtown rental development, Mennino Place, a Gold LEED-certified (Leadership in Energy and Environmental Design) building with 45 affordable apartments. Mennino Place offered an opportunity to provide accessible, affordable housing in downtown Concord while renovating the Endicott. After months of consideration, CATCH's Board of Directors voted to completely rehabilitate the Endicott Hotel into market rate apartments. The staff worked with local service providers to find new homes for the current residents.

The residents all found homes that were still affordable and in many cases met their needs better than the Endicott. Several moved into Mennino Place, some moved closer to family, while others were able to move into a facility that provided specialized care, such as a veterans' home.

CATCH purchased the first-floor commercial spaces in order to comprehensively restore the building. The Endicott Hotel has been on the National Register of Historic Places since 1987 and our renovations returned the building's storefronts to their historic beauty, refurbished the brick façade and restored the Endicott's distinctive oriel tower.

A few weeks after the last resident moved out, a restaurant on the first floor of the Endicott Hotel caught fire. The fire spread quickly throughout the eastern side of the building, but was contained by the Concord Fire Department. The damage from the fire itself was not extensive, though most of the building was saturated with water and smoke. However, if we had not decided to renovate when we did, the outcome could have been tragic. Though we had already planned to bring the building up to current code, this served as a reminder to always keep the well-being of our residents and their safety at the forefront of our decision making.

The Endicott provides a previously unavailable resource for Concord's downtown: market-rate housing. Because of zoning regulations, most of Concord's downtown storefronts have offices or vacant space in their upper floors. The Endicott was the first test of demand for downtown market-rate housing. Based on its success, the city government is hopeful that more property owners will follow suit.

The Endicott Hotel has been on the National Register of Historic Places since 1987.

The Endicott's apartments and storefronts provide a steady source of income for CATCH's mission-focused programs. Both apartments and retail spaces were quickly leased.

Through this redevelopment project we learned to be creative in our approach to long-term sustainability and hope to be a model for other nonprofits. Renting market-rate apartments in Concord's downtown fills a community need and allows CATCH to fulfill its mission for years to come.

ABOUT ROSEMARY HEARD

Rosemary Heard, CATCH's president and CEO for over 10 years, has guided the organization through economic fluctuations with an eye toward innovation and sustainability. CATCH provides 284 affordable rental apartments and 24 market-rate apartments at the Endicott Hotel; HOMEteam homebuyer education and financial fitness training through a partnership with NeighborWorks Southern New Hampshire and the Laconia Area Community Land Trust; and property management, asset management and financial services for affordable housing developers in New Hampshire and Southern Maine through our Alliance Asset Management program. CATCH Neighborhood Housing was founded in 1989 to provide opportunities for affordable housing in Merrimack County, NH.

LEVERAGING PARTNERSHIP TO REACH DISPERSED POPULATIONS

Scott Cooper, Executive Director

NeighborImpact

NeighborImpact, the community action agency serving central Oregon, is fortunate in having a partnership with our local television station, KTVZ, which is affiliated with FOX, NBC and CW networks.

KTVZ operates a unique partnership with NeighborImpact as one of five partner agencies focused on meeting the needs of children and families. The "21 Cares for Kids" campaign, in operation for more than five years, refers to channel 21, the UHF channel on which the station broadcast in its earliest days. Through the campaign, KTVZ allocates broadcast time during the day to its five partners to allow them to advertise their services. Because KTVZ's signal reaches across the entire geography of central Oregon, all residents with access to a television or the Internet can receive information about the services available to them through their community action agency.

Thanks to the KTVZ partnership, NeighborImpact airs approximately 6,000 commercial spots per year. At 30 seconds per ad, that's over 50 hours of TV airtime annually. The retail value of those spots is more than $54,000 per year – well above a service agency's typical TV advertising budget. KTVZ also provides pro-bono help in producing the service-oriented commercials, ensuring that they are professional broadcast quality and lending the voices of its on-air talent.

CHALLENGE

NeighborImpact is a community action agency with 14 major lines of business. Geographically, our region is approximately 7,000 square miles, covering eight communities. Approximately half the population lives in unincorporated areas. NeighborImpact's challenge is to effectively communicate across such a vast area.

Nearly all media stations have unsold advertising slots which can be used to promote social causes and television stations enjoy the opportunity to associate their talent with good works.

KTVZ's advertising on NeighborImpact's behalf showcase the agency's homebuyer education programs and its menu of financial coaching and other homeownership services. KTVZ offers further support to NeighborImpact by lending TV personalities to emcee agency events. Broadcast staff also help train NeighborImpact leadership on messaging and the "elevator speech."

In October of 2015, NeighborImpact commissioned the national survey firm USA Survey to poll residents of central Oregon. The poll found that when asked, "Have you ever heard of NeighborImpact?" 79 percent of respondents replied "Yes." Name recognition was consistent across income levels among those polled, with only slight variations based on age, gender and race.

Despite social media's popularity as a communications tool, NeighborImpact has learned through its partnership with KTVZ how traditional media still plays a significant and effective role in getting the message out regarding programs and services, particularly in rural areas. "Social media is a growing part of the communications landscape," says Sandra Visnack, director of communication for NeighborImpact, "but television remains the most universal way to reach an entire region."

NeighborImpact has learned that nearly all media stations have unsold advertising slots available on their schedule which can be used to promote social causes and services to viewers. Television stations enjoy the opportunity to associate their talent with good works. Working with advertising and marketing personnel at local television stations, along with news staff, can lead to productive and mutually beneficial relationships for both human services organizations and the media. Lack of budget to purchase paid advertising does not have to be a limiting factor for community organizations in designing an effective outreach program.

NeighborImpact, the community action agency serving central Oregon, is fortunate in having a partnership with our local television station, KTVZ, which helps our organization communicate across a wide, sometimes sparsely populated, geographic service area.

NeighborImpact's partnership with KTVZ has given it 50 hours of TV ads— valued at $54,000 annually.

ABOUT SCOTT COOPER

Scott Cooper is the executive director of NeighborImpact, the community action agency serving Oregon's geographic center. NeighborImpact serves about 50,000 people annually, with a $20 million budget and nearly 200 staff members. Programs include food provision, energy and weatherization assistance, housing support, early childhood education and financial capacity building. NeighborImpact's mission is to support people and strengthen communities.

CREATING EMPLOYMENT OPPORTUNITIES FOR THE HARD-TO-PLACE

Peggy Hutchison, CEO

The Primavera Foundation

The mission of The Primavera Foundation is to provide pathways out of poverty through safe, affordable housing, workforce development and neighborhood revitalization. Located in Tucson, AZ, Primavera serves residents in one of the most economically distressed large cities in the United States. In Pima County, home of Tucson, one in five people live below the poverty line, and the population of people experiencing homelessness is the highest in the state. Employment is critical and many rely on temporary day labor both for income and as a bridge to a more permanent solution – not to mention the self-esteem it builds.

However, day-labor contractors are not always the most ethical employers. As documented by a University of California-Los Angeles study, wage theft is commonplace and day laborers are frequently denied breaks, forced to work longer than agreed, or even threatened or assaulted by employers. That was true in Pima County in the 1990s, when Primavera staff and volunteers began hearing reports of scamming and abuse from the individuals living in our shelter and rental housing programs.

Our organizational strategy in response was two-pronged. We pressured the Department of Labor to investigate one of the perpetrators. This resulted in returned workers' wages and – in 1997 – the launch of Primavera Works. Our alternative staffing service provides temporary and temp-to-hire workers to residential, business and govern-

> ## CHALLENGE
> Establishing a reliable track record is critical for people with barriers to employment. Temporary employment can be a vital bridge, yet many residents in shelters and rental housing programs may be exploited by unethical day-labor businesses that pay less than minimum wage or charge them for supplies and transportation.

Customers seeking crews and individual workers come to us not only because they believe in our mission, but also because they want and get reliable workers who do a good job.

mental customers. It's a true win-win. People with significant barriers to employment – such as disabled or traumatized veterans, youth who have aged out of foster care, formerly incarcerated individuals and people who lost their jobs during the Great Recession – receive job-readiness and employment-retention training. They also are offered one-to-one employment coaching; assistance with housing, work supplies, clothing and transportation; and, of course, work for which they not only earn a fair wage which also builds experience and self-esteem. Our business customers get workers who already have been screened and are supervised by a reliable partner. Because the workers are on our payroll, we ensure employment eligibility and pay workers' compensation and FICA. And, unlike most day-labor contractors, we encourage customers to hire workers they like on a permanent basis.

Terence Atwood is an example of one of our success stories. He came to Tucson from Boston in December 2008, hoping to find work. He was previously incarcerated for 14 months, making it difficult to find employment. Atwood entered our men's shelter and was referred to Primavera Works for assistance in finding employment, as well as our New Chance program for homeless ex-offenders. Soon, he had obtained a monthly bus pass, acquired clothing appropriate for a job interview and earned a training certificate in food handling. He went on to obtain  full-time employment and housing. While he has experienced some challenges since leaving the shelter, including losing jobs and housing, Atwood continued to persevere, heeding advice from the Primavera Works Tools for Success Workshop to "never take no for an answer." In March of 2015, Atwood was promoted in his current job – including a pay increase.

After 18 years, Primavera Works is still is going strong and we recently developed a strategic plan for growth. Currently, many of our job placements (57 percent) are for manual work that requires relatively hard labor or long hours under the sun, such as landscaping and construction. That rules out many older people and those with physically challenging conditions. Thus, Primavera

Works is targeting and seeking to grow new sectors of the market, such as property management companies that need reliable crews to do apartment "turns" (preparing units for new occupants). Our growth plan includes hiring a business development manager to drive that growth, as well as the expansion of our water-harvesting service.

Expanding into new market sectors also means Primavera Works can serve more people needing work. While the first priority has been to ensure work opportunities for residents in our housing and shelter programs, our goal is to have so much business we can serve walk-ins from the larger community. Another emerging challenge in assisting people with lengthy gaps in their resumes or physical, mental and/or behavioral health challenges is assessing their skills and matching them to the needs of local businesses. Customers seeking crews and individual workers come to us not only because they believe in our mission, but also because they want and get reliable workers who do a good job.

In Pima County, home of Tucson, 1 in 5 people live below the poverty line.

Our growth plan for Primavera Works also requires the implementation of customer-performance-management technology that can quantify the value of business and residential customers as well as program participants. In addition, we want to better understand the impact of bundled services, such as housing plus employment, plus financial empowerment, plus community building and engagement. Which combination of services contributes the most to creating a successful work experience for both workers and customers? We want to know which efforts drive the highest performance with the greatest outcomes. This will enable us to direct precious resources to where we are having the greatest impact for individuals, businesses and our community.

Safe, affordable housing and economic opportunities go hand in hand. Without one, it's difficult to have the other. Primavera Works makes both achievable.

ABOUT PEGGY HUTCHISON

Peggy Hutchison serves as the chief executive officer of The Primavera Foundation, a nonprofit community housing development organization whose mission is to provide pathways out of poverty through safe, affordable housing, workforce development, and neighborhood revitalization. Primavera has a staff of more than 80 and a budget of $6.5 million. The organization serves about 7,500 people annually in Tucson and Pima County, AZ, through a variety of programs.

CREATING OPPORTUNITIES: COMMONBOND'S COMPLIANCE INTERN PROGRAM

Deidre Schmidt, President & CEO
Alyssa Andreska, Mary Coulter, Maggy Otte

CommonBond Communities

CommonBond, the largest nonprofit provider of affordable housing with onsite services in the Upper Midwest, relies on a number of funding sources and subsidies to operate our housing communities. In order for Common-Bond to remain in compliance with these sources and multiple monitoring agencies, such as HUD and the IRS, our documentation of the execution of financing requirements must be accurate and updated, a time-consuming and detailed task. CommonBond, like others in this field, employs compliance technicians to ensure funder requirements are met. However, because of the specialized knowledge needed to perform compliance tasks, there is a shortage of qualified compliance technicians.

CommonBond recently completed financing for a major refinance and rehabilitation of one of our largest housing communities, Seward Towers. As part of this work, 640 households were required to complete an income certification process. This additional work placed a significant burden on existing compliance staff.

In response, CommonBond used a technical assistance grant from NeighborWorks to establish a Compliance Internship program that trains individuals to complete resident interviews, review housing applications, complete eligibility certifications and maintain required compliance documents for funding sources and partners. Interns work 20 hours per week for three months. This program

CHALLENGE

CommonBond and other affordable housing providers have difficulty finding qualified candidates for positions involving affordable housing regulatory compliance. CommonBond residents and people of color are not frequently found in compliance positions and may face obstacles in obtaining skills needed to earn a living wage.

Through this program, CommonBond has expanded the pool of trained, certified and qualified compliance technicians and specialists.

was created to reach out to those communities we serve, both for CommonBond's benefit and to offer training and a paid internship to people who want to enhance their professional marketability.

The internship program offers Certified Occupancy Specialist training and certification, a nationally recognized certification that is applicable to all affordable housing programs that use the occupancy guidelines from the HUD manual. Ultimately, these trained interns could be hired by CommonBond and other organizations in order to better navigate the complicated regulatory landscape of the affordable housing industry.

Recruitment for the Compliance Internship program focused on local communities representing diverse populations. Helping individuals develop the specialized skills and knowledge of compliance can pave the way for stable, full-time employment.

Our primary source of candidates was our own residents, a pool of people who are familiar with affordable housing program requirements and are interested in professional development. Candidates came through our Adult Education and Advancement program, which provides support for residents in employment and career advancement, financial coaching and income support. The interns hired to date are CommonBond residents.

Two participants have completed the program so far, including Fekri, a married father of three who initially worked with an employment and financial coach to connect to maintenance training and a job he held for five years. Fekri decided to return to school to complete an accounting degree and, with the help of his coach, applied for the compliance intern program as it offered a new career opportunity. He participated in the program while continuing to finish his degree and recently began working with compliance in one of our housing communities. Our second participant, Hamza, lives with his brother and mother and, in spite of his degree in liberal arts and additional technology training, could not find a job. Hamza met with an employment and financial coach, recently completed the compliance program and hopes to join the CommonBond team.

Through this program, CommonBond has expanded the pool of trained, certified and qualified compliance technicians and specialists. We have lessened the severe shortage of qualified individuals able to understand, track and ensure compliance requirements. The compliance interns assisted in the certification process for Seward Towers' residents. Interns were able to translate, complete interviews and review certifications, which alleviated some of the burden on CommonBond's compliance team.

65.4% of the class of 2014 that completed a paid internship at a for-profit company received a job offer prior to graduation.

Through the intense income verification project alone, interns have acquired valuable customer service skills, training in accurate record keeping and skill in navigating the many regulatory layers involved with the affordable housing industry. These interns are ready to interview for and obtain compliance positions at CommonBond and other affordable housing organizations. One has already done so.

The lessons CommonBond learned while developing the Compliance Internship program include: 1) recognizing that our residents can benefit from professional training while we benefit from their internal knowledge of affordable housing and, 2) the skills learned in the internship program can be used for career advancement at CommonBond and at other organizations.

ABOUT DEIDRE SCHMIDT

Before joining CommonBond in 2014 as president and CEO, Deidre Schmidt was a principal at One Roof Global Consulting and executive director of the Affordable Housing Institute, a Boston-based nonprofit. She also worked in both for-profit and nonprofit sectors in consulting, project and enterprise management, real estate development, investment analysis and underwriting. Since 1971, CommonBond Communities has been building homes, hope and community. From its start as a small program of the Archdiocese of Saint Paul and Minneapolis, CommonBond now owns or manages over 5,400 units with 8,500 residents in approximately 100 housing communities in 50 cities and towns in Minnesota, Wisconsin and Iowa.

INVESTING IN EMPLOYEES PAYS OFF

Clemente Mojica, CEO
Tyler Wolfe
Public Relations and Marketing Coordinator
Jennifer Rivera, Fund Development Assistant

Neighborhood Partnership Housing Services

Neighborhood Partnership Housing Services (NPHS) is dedicated to improving the lives of residents in Southern California communities. To do so, we focus on growing, retaining and improving the lives of our greatest assets: our employees. We implemented strategies to reduce staff turnover rates and improve job satisfaction, which has led to improvement in the delivery of quality services. This has helped develop our organizational bench strength, which in turn improves our staff retention, effectiveness, and efficiency.

NPHS fosters interdepartmental collaboration through flexible, on-site work environments that promote synergy and cohesion by breaking down silos. Employees are often found working collaboratively in the board room or the training room or sharing new ideas in the company's innovation lab, a workspace designed to inspire creativity. Our CEO has an open door policy for all employees that encourages new ideas and promotes originality. Because communication with other staff and departments is so readily available, our employees are often informed and involved in projects that span multiple departments, increasing their knowledge, skill and overall strength.

Our employees are not only knowledgeable, but passionate about making a meaningful connection with their work in our local communities. One of NPHS' staff suc-

CHALLENGE

Talented staff at non-profits with limited budgets often leave for higher-paying jobs in private industry. To fulfill its mission to the community and stay competitive as an employer Neighborhood Partnership Housing Services needs to attract and retain diverse and talented staff, reduce turnover rates and improve job satisfaction.

NPHS encourages intergenerational information sharing to stay current with the needs of an ever-changing clientele.

cess stories involves Hitesh Kamble, who was hired through the AmeriCorps VISTA program. A recent graduate of Environmental Science at the University of California, Irvine, Kamble focuses on developing green policies and procedures. During his time at NPHS, Kamble has found meaningful ways to apply his passion and expertise to community economic development, making a major contribution to developing NPHS' new Sojourner Solar Financing Program.

"One of the first projects I worked on was helping NPHS receive its LEED gold certification," Kamble said. "The process was very eye-opening because I had not realized the extent to which policy and government regulation came into play when attempting to reduce energy consumption and waste."

As a subject matter expert on energy issues, Kamble further shares his insights as a millennial serving on NPHS' Millennial Advisory Committee (MAC).

NPHS encourages intergenerational information sharing to stay current with the needs of an ever-changing clientele. The MAC, a committee composed of millennial employees and executive leadership, was formed at NPHS to generate data and recommendations for targeting and servicing millennial clientele. Through routine development of surveys and community engage-

ment, the MAC assists NPHS in shaping its strategic direction to align with future consumers and employees. With a better understanding of millennial priorities and career concerns, NPHS can tailor its organizational culture to attract future leaders and continue to build bench strength by developing new products and services.

Through initiatives such as employer-assisted housing programs, NPHS implements creative methods to attract and retain talented staff while accomplishing its community mission. In helping employees become homeowners, NPHS fosters stability, employee loyalty and retention among its staff, while providing them the opportunity to experience the same life milestone they create for their clients.

In the last four years, NPHS has helped seven employees, including Curtis Miller, purchase homes with down payment and closing cost assistance.

"NPHS has provided me with the resources necessary to purchase my own home and build a family," says Miller. "For that I am forever grateful. I otherwise may not have been able to afford a home in the community that I serve."

By emphasizing an organizational culture rooted in creativity, inclusion and employee satisfaction, NPHS has developed effective ways to attract and retain qualified employees while fulfilling its responsibilities to the community.

In a 2015 Pathfinder Solutions survey, 76% of millennials said job advancement is not obvious in the nonprofit sector.

ABOUT CLEMENTE MOJICA

Clemente Mojica, president and CEO of NPHS, is a community and economic development executive with over 16 years of experience in housing policy, community revitalization and affordable housing development.

WHILE HELPING HOMEBUYERS, AN ORGANIZATION GETS A LIFT

Daniel Ellis, Executive Director

Neighborhood Housing Services of Baltimore

The LIFT program, a collaboration among Wells Fargo, NeighborWorks America and NHS of Baltimore, provides forgivable down-payment assistance loans of $15,000 to qualified borrowers. Before the program came to Baltimore, NHS was a low-profile organization. When NHS learned we would be responsible for administering 300 loans, a large number for an organization of our size, we knew our performance on this project would establish a reputation for the organization. We made a commitment to make it a good one. In the end, LIFT allowed us to make homeownership achievable for 300 families and individuals like Devin Lee, a truck driver and father of two. Without LIFT, Lee and the other LIFT buyers might have left the city to purchase homes they could afford; now they can remain here, invest in our city and raise their families in Baltimore.

The LIFT program came at the perfect time for NHS, just as we were poised for growth and when there were no competing programs in our area. It helped put us on the map in the lending and real estate communities and challenged us to stretch to meet the program's goals.

Over the 18 months that it took to close all the LIFT loans, we created economic growth through homeownership for 300 families in Baltimore, which in itself was a major accomplishment. The program had an additional benefit, however, in that it enabled NHS to improve our infrastructure, establish powerful partnerships and increase our bottom line.

CHALLENGE

Neighborhood Housing Services (NHS) of Baltimore, revitalizing neighborhoods through homeownership opportunities since 1974, recently increased its focus on lending as a line of business. The LIFT program – Let's Invest for Tomorrow – challenged us to deliver a high volume loan program and helped us meet a higher standard.

Without LIFT, buyers like Devin Lee, a truck driver and father of two, might have left the city; now he can remain here, invest in our city and raise his family in Baltimore.

In the past, our technology systems were adequate, but we needed improvements to handle the increased caseload, accounting and reporting. LIFT's operational funding provided us $25,000 to upgrade our systems – servers, computers, software – across the entire organization, which benefited us beyond the LIFT program; it enables us to function efficiently in the 21st century. In addition, LIFT provides tools such as the DataSafeCube, a database that allows people in the organization and our partners to see and share information on each loan and send alerts if action needs to be taken.

While NHS had never successfully applied for Community Development Financial Institution (CDFI) funding because it required a match and evidence that an organization could handle a robust volume of loans, the LIFT program changed our qualifications. We were able to consider the LIFT capital money for the match and had the loan volume to submit a competitive application. NHS was awarded $847,000 in our first round of funding and $1.5 million in the second. We now have tangible, measurable results to show, which we have leveraged for other successful grant applications.

LIFT also increased NHS' visibility among lenders and real estate agents. We are known as an organization that delivers and we're getting more referrals because our partners trust us.

We expanded our staff and now we see 1,000 homebuyer education and counseling customers a year, up from 300 pre-LIFT, because of the requirements of Maryland and Baltimore City homebuyer incentive programs for one-on-one counseling in addition to group education. We began charging for our classes, first $50 and eventually $100. We've seen no decrease in customers and now have an additional funding stream to support our counseling operation. This year, home-buyer education fees will result in $100,000 in revenue, directly attributable to LIFT.

The benefits of LIFT extend beyond the life of the program. For example, our financial coaching program, Fast Track, is now managed by one of the temporary people we hired for LIFT. Upon completion of the six-month Fast Track program, participants' credit scores increase by an average of 62 points and their average savings increase by $3,200. Sixty-four individuals have graduated from the program and have purchased or are in the process of buying a home.

Since 2012, LIFT programs have committed more than $220 million toward community revitalization, helping to create more than 12,000 homeowners.

Overall, LIFT is an extremely high-volume, fast-paced undertaking. At the launch event alone, 100 people had contracts on a home and were planning to close within 45 days. We needed to be equipped and ready to handle that volume.

The lessons learned through the LIFT program include: 1) technology upgrades are a necessary expenditure for program success, 2) partnerships can be leveraged to raise funds and expand the reach of our programs, and 3) expanding our capacity during LIFT made us more effective at what we do – helping people become homeowners.

ABOUT DANIEL ELLIS

Daniel Ellis has served as executive director of Neighborhood Housing Services of Baltimore since 2011. Ellis speaks on urban housing issues across the country, and has received numerous awards for his professional work. Ellis was named the 2015 National NeighborWorks Association Emerging Leader for his advocacy at the local, state and federal levels.

A SELF-SUSTAINING BUSINESS MODEL DELIVERS GREATER SUCCESS FOR CLIENTS AND ORGANIZATIONS

Mike Loftin, Chief Executive Officer

Homewise, Inc.

When purchasing a home, homebuyers must have the resources and information to make the process a success. In New Mexico, many low-income residents may not have the tools necessary to ensure long-term financial security. Solid financial habits and a good understanding about homebuying and owning are both key to affordability and stability.

Homewise, a nonprofit based in Santa Fe, NM, creates successful homeowners with a purchase model that integrates all of the services necessary to buy a home. The process begins with assessing the client's capacity to purchase a home. We then offer financial education and coaching to help clients find a home within their purchasing power and obtain affordable mortgage financing. To ensure alignment with the best interests of the client, Homewise employees do not earn a commission at any step of the process.

By offering their clients a single point of entry and a step-by-step process, Homewise removes the overwhelming confusion that can often be a barrier to homeownership. By offering the right services, tools and guidance at the right time, Homewise ensures that their clients are better prepared and more confident throughout the entire process.

CHALLENGE

Low-income residents throughout New Mexico face challenges that can prevent them from buying a home that will ensure affordability and stability. When long-term financial security is the goal, it is critical to buy an affordable home with low-cost financing and have solid financial habits and a good understanding about the process.

By aligning their own long-term success with their clients' success, Homewise achieves social benefits for their target market while securing their financial sustainability.

The Homewise target market includes low-income households throughout New Mexico, where the average median income is $38,950 for a low-income household of three. Clients in this market often face financial challenges to homeownership, including downpayment, affordability and credit. Homewise addresses all three challenges through a home purchase program as well as a self-sufficient business model to support the organization's long-term growth and success.

Downpayment: Based on the national savings rate, a family earning $35,000 annually would take over 20 years to save a 20 percent downpayment for a $175,000 home, according to the Center for Responsible Lending. For families without those funds, the main option is an FHA loan, which still requires at least $9,625 for downpayment and closing costs. The Homewise mortgage requires only a 2 percent upfront cash contribution for downpayment and closing costs or about $3,500.

Affordability: Median home prices remain out of reach for many in Homewise's target market, particularly in Santa Fe, where the median sales price is $304,000. The cost of mortgage insurance exacerbates this problem by reducing the amount a client can borrow and their ultimate purchasing power. The Homewise mortgage eliminates mortgage insurance, thereby increasing purchasing power and making it more likely for their clients to find a house they can afford.

Credit: Qualifying for a mortgage is a major barrier for families in their target market. Though Homewise's down payment requirements are low, their credit standards are not. Through their financial education and coaching services, Homewise helps clients improve their credit profiles to meet strict underwriting standards and qualify for a Homewise mortgage.

The Homewise model captures fee revenue that helps offset the costs of services- such as free financial counseling and homebuyer education which are critical to the buyer's success. They leverage equity to borrow additional capital to fund the Homewise mortgage, which generates revenue through origination and servicing fees and interest income. By selling the first mortgage on the secondary market and holding the second mortgage in their portfolio, they are able to help many more clients. By retaining the servicing of their loans, they stay engaged with the client, which contributes to their high-quality loan portfolio. Their 30-day delinquency rate is less than half the national rate for prime conventional loans. This strong portfolio builds their balance sheet and financial stability. The combination of revenue and assets makes them sustainable in the short and long-term.

The Homewise mortgage requires a 2% down payment, or about $3,500.

Another important outcome of the Homewise model is organizational self-sufficiency, achieved through the revenue they capture from lending, loan servicing, and real estate sales fees. The income earned from real estate sales commissions, loan originations and servicing generates additional revenue and ensures long-term supportive and high-touch relationships with the clients.

The self-sustaining revenue also allows Homewise to offer homebuyer education and financial fitness classes for free, unlike many nonprofits that charge for such classes. In addition, the leverage and revenue model means there is no artificial limit to the volume they can sustain, which would be the case if they relied on grants and donations to subsidize each transaction. As production grows, so does the revenue generated to support that growth.

Since Homewise's founding in 1986, over 12,800 households have attended the homebuyer classes. During that time, 3,500 of them have purchased homes. The strength of the Homewise business model has fueled growth, leading the organization to become the number one mortgage lender in Santa Fe.

The lessons learned through this project are: 1) the key to restoring the promise of homeownership is a smart home purchase process that aligns every step with the long-term financial interests of the homebuyers, 2) the process has a clear entry point that is followed by a direct, orderly progression of services – including help with the down payment, affordability and credit – that maximizes benefits to the potential homebuyer, 3) it is important to have self-sustaining revenue to ensure the financial stability of the organization and its loans and programs.

ABOUT MIKE LOFTIN
Mike Loftin, CEO of Homewise, has over 35 years of experience in community development. He is well known for developing innovative solutions for community issues, is widely regarded as an expert on affordable housing, and has created a nationally award winning model for self-sufficiency for affordable housing community development finance organizations. Prior to joining Homewise in 1992, Loftin was the founding organizer of The Resurrection Project in Chicago.

GROWING RURAL AMERICA

Marcia Erickson & Lori Finnesand, Co-CEOs

GROW South Dakota

The housing, community and economic development programs and services of GROW South Dakota have served the needs of residents, business owners and communities for 50 years. Seeing small rural communities' growing need for assistance with housing and economic development, the organization turned to the USDA Rural Community Development Initiative (RCDI) program and received their first funding award in 2006.

Since then, GROW South Dakota has offered technical and financial assistance to 14 rural organizations to support hiring staff, provide training and establish local offices. It now acts as an intermediary for RCDI funding and, through seven three-year grants, has shared $1.7 million in funding to spark capacity building in the recipient communities. Each community commits to a one-to-one financial match through fundraising, city or county funds or partnership support and creates a budget for future economic development priorities.

Each community has made tremendous strides in revitalizing their efforts and creating growth for their regions. They have been models for the value of the investment. For instance, with GROW South Dakota's support, the Glacial Lakes Area Development in Marshall County and Faulkton Area Economic Development in Faulk County have executive directors and Webster Area Development Corporation has spurred hundreds of new local jobs through manufacturing recruitment.

Hearing of these economic successes, people have begun to move to these communities. While they are delighted to have these new arrivals, the communities often do not have adequate quality housing for them. In response to

CHALLENGE

Images of small rural communities often show closing schools, abandoned homes, an aging population and a dying Main Street. Many of these communities have volunteer-run economic development and housing boards, but these boards need resources and leadership to keep working to revitalize rural areas.

Each community has made tremendous strides in revitalizing their efforts and creating growth for their regions. They have been models for the value of the investment.

this, GROW South Dakota created Grow Housing, which provides technical assistance to help rural communities develop more housing. Grow Housing works in five communities, four of which were in the original RCDI group.

After conducting a formal housing study, Grow Housing representatives and local leaders work together to ensure that the community's voice is heard. They hold public meetings to review the results of the study and begin a strategic planning process to establish priorities and ideas for housing solutions. After each community meeting, small teams of committed individuals meet with a Grow Housing coach to find and implement housing solutions specific to local needs. They often show resourcefulness in identifying new ways to accomplish tasks, such as a community painting day that drew on local volunteer labor and outside sources for funding and supplies.

The Grow Housing coach helps the local teams stay on task and brings them together regularly to share ideas, successes and challenges. An innovative example of this collaboration is the First Impressions Tour, in which all five community coordinators joined with the Grow Housing coach for a tour of each community to share successes and challenges.

In 2015 GROW South Dakota and leaders from Webster and Britton, two of the original RCDI communities, attended the NeighborWorks Community Leadership Institute to improve planning for specific projects. As a result, the Webster Vision Team hosted a one-day Housing Block Party in March 2016 to provide information on a variety of topics related to purchasing, building, remodeling or landscaping a property. An estimated 150 residents attended the event, visiting resource booths and attending home-related seminars. The Britton CORE Team worked with local civic and charitable organizations, government officials, school groups and youth groups to coordinate a neighborhood/community clean-up day.

GROW South Dakota is in the process of working with other South Dakota nonprofits that support similar housing programs to expand the Grow Housing concepts more broadly in the state.

GROW South Dakota learned three important lessons while working directly with these communities, each of which has its own unique character, priorities, organizational structure and challenges:

158 NeighborWorks organizations served more than 7,000 rural clients in FY15.

1) One primary obstacle is limited human resources. If staff exists, they are often stretched thin. The same group of volunteers is always at the table and while they may have skills, they often need time and direction to find the confidence to implement solutions. In addition to coaching, Grow Housing brings the credibility of GROW South Dakota to draw additional needed partners and sometimes new volunteers to the table.

2) Sometimes there is a hands-off approach to housing, with no entity taking responsibility for acting on housing issues. Grow Housing encourages communities to recognize that everyone has a role, from local government to employers to nonprofits to contractors and residents.

3) Sustaining engagement is a challenge. While some communities have maintained their initial energy, others suffer from different levels of involvement. GROW South Dakota's approach of funding the hiring of local staff and providing coaching is making a difference.

The task of solving housing and economic development issues can be daunting. However, with GROW South Dakota's help, communities are finding solutions, addressing development and housing issues and engaging in broad-based activities.

ABOUT MARCIA ERICKSON AND LORI FINNESAND

Marcia Erickson and Lori Finnesand are co-CEOs of GROW South Dakota, an umbrella that includes Northeast South Dakota Community Action Program, Northeast South Dakota Economic Corporation and GROW South Dakota. Erickson has been with the organization for 27 years, becoming the CEO of GROW South Dakota's 50-year-old sister organization Northeast South Dakota Community Action Program in 2005. Finnesand, who became CEO of Northeast South Dakota Economic Corporation in 2005, has 25 years of experience with the organization.

FILLING THE FUNDING GAP FOR HOMEOWNERS IN RURAL MONTANA

Maureen Rude, Executive Director

NeighborWorks Montana

Montana has one of the highest rural population rates in the country, spread across the fourth largest state in the union. About half of the residents also live at or below the median income, and many are in need of affordable housing assistance. But state and federal funding for such services recently dried up, and the only homeownership programs available for low-income residents were in the large cities, leaving a huge void in the vast rural communities.

NeighborWorks Montana (NWMT) was established in 1998 to support homeownership services across the state through partnerships. The goal was to funnel money raised on a statewide basis through grants and other sources to partners who would deliver homeownership services at the local level. NWMT would serve as an umbrella, thus having a single organization seeking funding rather than numerous agencies competing against each other.

Many organizations took part in the plan, including Rural Development, the U.S. Department of Housing and Urban Development (HUD), the Montana Board of Housing, Fannie Mae, local and regional financial institutions, Indian Tribal Housing organizations, city governments and several nonprofits interested in providing housing services. NeighborWorks America provided a manager to facilitate meetings. Approximately 20 education and counseling agencies began providing services across the state.

CHALLENGE

Montana is the fourth largest state in the nation and it has one of the highest rural population rates. Just over half of the residents live at or below the area median income, but funding cuts in 2001 virtually eliminated affordable housing assistance in rural areas.

The purpose was to serve as an umbrella: having one organization seeking funding for homebuyer education, counseling and lending rather than numerous organizations competing against each other.

Several grants were awarded to facilitate the launch of the new collaboration with service delivery partners around the state. Funds were raised from Rural Development and foundations, which were enthusiastic about contributing to the welfare of the entire state. Initially, the goal was to have one homeowner education class per month in each partner area. Funding was ultimately provided to each organization based on how many classes were held and how many graduated.

In 2005, the Montana Board of Housing (MBOH) successfully applied to become an intermediary for HUD Housing counseling funds. MBOH provided matching funds to support homebuyer education and pre-purchase counseling. Meanwhile, NWMT began building a lending team and providing down payment assistance through a statewide  partner network. In 2008, NWMT hired an operations director with significant lending and institutional knowledge to build the lending program and take the partner organization into the future. Grants from HUD and other sources continued to provide the basic funding for the partner organizations.

Everything went smoothly until 2011, when the federal budget eliminated Rural Conservation and Development Organizations, which commonly served rural areas. HUD housing counseling dollars were also zeroed out. As a result, NWMT had to reassess its approach and figure out new strategies for future sustainability.

To overcome the crisis, NWMT worked with the Montana attorney general's office to obtain funds from the National Mortgage Settlement, which was established in 2012 to provide relief for distressed homeowners and funding for state and federal governments. Then-attorney general Steve Bullock decided to put the bulk of the funds into counseling services and selected NWMT as the primary partner to distribute them to counseling organizations.

Homebuyer education is now available in every area of the state, either through live classes or a combination of eHome America and one-on-one in person or telephone counseling. Partnering with eHome America, an online homebuyer education program, has allowed NWMT and its collaborators to reach a much larger number of clients by reducing the need for travel. In 2015, the network provided a total of 94 homebuyer and financial education classes, serving 1,186 households. In addition, the network served 741 clients with one-on-one pre-purchase counseling and 270 rental and/or homeless clients. The foreclosure crisis has diminished, but NWMT was able to help meet the needs of over 7,000 Montana residents in need of foreclosure counseling.

In 2013, the median household income in Montana was $46,230.

NWMT looks very different today than it did in 1998 when it was launched, but at its core, it is still the effective umbrella visualized by its creators, with a solid foundation of experienced staff and strong board support. Building on our initial vision, we learned that we work best through partner organizations and that the state is better served by deploying locals to provide the services most needed in their unique areas. Testing new programs as pilots and knowing when to stop or revamp them is also key.

Finally, this is not a business where we can be complacent as conditions can change drastically. We must continually analyze both our processes and our programs to determine if they continue to stand up under shifting environments.

ABOUT MAUREEN RUDE

Maureen Rude became NeighborWorks Montana's executive director in 2016. Rude has been with the organization for over eight years, serving as director of lending and operations. She was previously employed as director of the Montana Fannie Mae Partnership office and executive director of the Montana Board of Housing.

DEVELOPING A RESOURCE

Merten Bangemann- Johnson, CEO
Dennis Bartlett, Director of Heartwood ReSources

NeighborWorks Umpqua

According to the American Housing Survey, problems with the quality of housing are most common in rural areas and central cities. That is in large part because poverty is high in rural areas, with 2012 data from the Housing Assistance Council showing about 17.2 percent of rural residents living below the poverty line in 2012 versus 14.9 percent nationwide.

Meanwhile, funds for rural housing provided by the USDA via the 502 Direct Loan program – one of the primary government-aid programs for purchasing or rehabilitating homes in rural areas – have decreased over the past few years, dropping from about $2.1 billion in 2010 to around $828 million in 2013.

Another dynamic is that rural America is "older" than the nation as a whole, with more than one-quarter of all seniors living in rural and small town areas. Most seniors wish to remain and age in their homes as long as possible, but rural elders are increasingly experiencing challenges with housing quality as well as affordability. In far too many rural communities, the only housing options for seniors are their own homes, which are often difficult for them to maintain, or nursing homes, which have their own set of problems (including affordability).

In addition, the vast majority of rural seniors live in single-family units built in earlier decades when there was less awareness of what's required to ensure accessibility for people with all levels of physical abilities. A recent study published by AARP estimated that more than 1

CHALLENGE
Two problems faced the community of Umpqua in the early 2000s. First, commercial builders were filling up the county landfill and county leaders were loath to impose fees that would be a political liability. Second, residents couldn't find enough low-cost home-repair materials. NeighborWorks Umpqua saw an opportunity.

After trying different strategies, the best one turned out to be word-of-mouth; people got to like what we were doing and they told others about it.

million older adults with disabilities live in homes that present barriers to meeting their daily needs. Rehabilitation is a way for family members to help them stay at home.

NeighborWorks Umpqua's Self-Help Housing Rehabilitation Program is designed to address these challenges. It is part of USDA Rural Development's 523 Mutual Self-Help initiative, which we have successfully redesigned to address the need for rehab, and financed in part by community development block grants and NeighborWorks America funds. We rehabilitated 70 homes in the last three years, improving the lives and preserving the assets of more than 150 individuals.

Our program provides low- or zero-interest loans to low-income families whose homes need health- and safety-related repairs and who cannot qualify for other financing. We replace leaking roofs, repair failed septic systems, install adequate heat sources and fix rotted flooring. Our program relies on the homeowners themselves to supply much of the labor: Many families put more than 40 hours a week into their rehab projects, often saving tens of thousands of dollars. Without our staff's tools and technical expertise, these health and safety repairs would not be feasible.

The bottom line: Homeowners, empowered with accessible financing and construction coaching, exit our program not just with a safe and durable home, but with skills and techniques that set

them up for success in future home repair and maintenance. Furthermore, they can leverage these same skills in the job market.

Mitchell Howard of Gold Beach, Oregon, is an example. "I knew the house needed some work when we bought it, and I had a plan for re-modeling the kitchen," he told my team. "But the [termite] damage was so much more extensive than we thought. It was scary. We would have walked away from the house if you hadn't helped [us]."

Another example is Bill from Roseburg's Green District. NeighborWorks Umpqua helped replace his roof, reframe a rotten wall, replace a foundation wall, and gut and repair a rotten bathroom. The home was completely re-sided and every window was replaced.

"I started walking months ahead to get in shape for this," said 74-year-old Bill. "I lost 20 pounds during the project!"

Bill did the vast majority of this work himself –with tools and technical assistance provided by NeighborWorks Umpqua – and saved an estimated $50,000 by doing so.

Since 2001, Oregon's economy has grown nearly 3 times faster than the national economy.

ABOUT MERTEN BANGEMANN-JOHNSON

Merten Bangemann-Johnson is CEO of NeighborWorks Umpqua. Prior to that, he worked with the Gilman Housing Trust in Vermont and served as special assistant to Mayor Mark Begich in Anchorage, AK, where he was CEO of the Anchorage Community Land Trust. He is on the board of the National Rural Housing Coalition.

INVESTING WHERE TRADITIONAL BANKS WON'T: BUILDING SUCCESS AND COMMUNITY IN INDIAN COUNTRY

Rollin Wood, Executive Director

Native Partnership for Housing

The Native Partnership for Housing (NPH) is the only NeighborWorks America network member focused exclusively on improving housing opportunities for Native Americans. It was created in 1996 as the Navajo Partnership for Housing to provide flexible homeownership financing opportunities for residents of the nation. Its founding goal was to empower Navajo families with the knowledge, skills and understanding needed to complete beneficial real estate transactions. The need was great then and is even greater today.

There are approximately 330,000 Navajos, of which 190,000 live on the Navajo Nation. Covering more than 27,000 square miles, or 17 million acres, the Navajo Nation is about the size of West Virginia. It encompasses large portions of northern Arizona, northern New Mexico and southeastern Utah. According to a recent study conducted by the Navajo Housing Authority, the nation needs more than 34,000 new homes, and an additional 34,000 homes require rehabilitation.

Furthermore, the concept of owning your own home, land and other property is a foreign concept to many Navajos. If raised in a traditional manner, a Navajo believes "Mother Earth, the land" cannot be owned. To compli-

CHALLENGE

The Navajo Nation covers more than 27,000 square miles. Seventy percent of those living in the Nation earn less than $15,000 per year. Many banks will not lend to residents of sovereign Native American Nations out of fear they will not be able to foreclose on delinquent loans. How can we develop and facilitate access to homes for members of the Navajo Nation – including homebuyer education and financial assistance?

Owning your own home, land and other property is a foreign concept to many Navajos. If raised in a traditional manner, a Navajo believes "Mother Earth, the land" cannot be owned.

cate matters, most of the land is held in trust, controlled by the Navajo Nation with oversight by the federal Bureau of Indian Affairs. It can take two to three years for a family to acquire a home-site lease.

Prior to our founding, there were no mortgage lenders willing to provide loans to Nation residents. Over the past 20 years, we have provided more than $50 million in loans and down-payment assistance, helping nearly 600 Native American families purchase their own homes.

In 2016, we changed our name to the Native Partnership for Housing to communicate our expansion of service delivery beyond the borders of the Navajo Nation and adjacent communities to members of other native nations in New Mexico, Arizona and Utah. The federal government recognizes more than 43 other tribes in New Mexico and Arizona alone.

In addition, most Native Americans don't live on reservations, and constitute a market that is equally important to serve. The name change is a step in that direction. When asked to describe NPH's new market, we now say "Native America!"

Central to our work is education – particularly related to homebuying. On average, we have learned that for every 30 clients inquiring about and beginning the homebuyer process, only two to three are ready to become homebuyers. Common issues are lack of funds for down payments and closing costs, poor credit and inconsistent income. NPH staff is dedicated to helping all clients facing barriers to homeownership qualify for a mortgage. Over the past 20 years, NPH's trainers have provided financial fitness and homebuyer education to 3,326 families.

To serve such a far-flung client base, we employ a combination of classroom and distance training through web-based systems. We expect that once our new marketing and online homeownership courses are fully implemented, the number of families who complete the NPH homebuyer education course will quadruple to 65 per month.

When Patrick Giago, an Oglala Sioux from Pine Ridge, SD, and his wife Lucy, who is Navajo, bought their first home after renting in Washington, D.C., and Arizona, they found NPH to be a great resource. They were looking for a home, not just a house, where they could retire after a lifelong career working for the Bureau of Indian Affairs. They found that home with our help.

Over the past 20 years, NPH has provided financial and homebuyer education to more than 3,326 families.

Patrick Giago describes his new neighborhood as the "Hollywood of the Navajo Nation." The house is beautiful, in stark contrast to some of the trailers and mobile homes in other parts of the reservation. He also credits our first-time homebuyer classes to his transformation into an astute and well-prepared homeowner. When his brother visited the Giagos' new house, he asked how they managed to buy such a beautiful home. We are so proud that their response was "NPH!"

Although NPH is one small player working in an area of vast need, we are expanding vitally needed services throughout Indian Country to enable residents to build, purchase or renovate their own homes.

ABOUT ROLLIN WOOD

Rollin Wood serves as the executive director of the Native Partnership for Housing, located in Gallup, NM. NPH is a 501(c) 3 nonprofit company and Native community development financial institution chartered under NeighborWorks America.

VOLUNTEER FORCE
FILLS A FINANCIAL VOID

Jesse Ergott, President and CEO

NeighborWorks Northeastern Pennsylvania

Financially strapped cities are battling blight in northeastern Pennsylvania, where residents are either too poor, too old or too sick to maintain their aging homes. Many of their houses are at least 70 years old, according to the most recent census data, which finds 59 percent of Scranton homes were built in 1939 or earlier, 58 percent for Wilkes-Barre and 44 percent for Hazleton, the three cities that make up the largest MSA in the NEPA market. As these homes fall into disrepair, their owners face health and safety hazards, while condemned or abandoned properties invite criminal activity and devalue neighborhoods.

For more than 30 years, the central mission of Neighbor-Works Northeastern Pennsylvania (NWNEPA) has been to preserve and improve communities such as these by providing assistance to homeowners in need. But its small staff and limited funding made it clear that NWNEPA would have to get creative. So, in 2010, instead of soliciting funds, the organization reached into the large, untapped pool of local volunteer labor. By forming fruitful partnerships across public and private sectors, NWNEPA developed a reliable force of hard workers ready to serve their neighbors while significantly expanding the organization's visibility. Over the next six years, NWNEPA partnered with universities, hospitals, health-care providers and corporations to deploy enthusiastic volunteer armies and contribute almost $1 million in donated labor to repair and beautify hundreds of homes.

NWNEPA first partnered with what is now GroupCares, a leading provider for Christian youth missions, to send

CHALLENGE

Northeastern Pennsylvania is home to many struggling communities, where high unemployment and low wages are compounded by a rapidly aging population, deteriorating houses and high taxes. Homeowners tend to be stalwart long-term residents, but maintaining their old homes is as challenging as it is essential to their social and economic stability.

In 2010, instead of soliciting funds, the organization reached into the large untapped pool of local volunteer labor, developing a force of hard workers ready to serve their neighbors while expanding the organization's visibility.

volunteers to Carbondale, where hundreds of youths labored alongside adult supervisors to rehabilitate more than 40 homes. The initially tentative relationship between residents and volunteers blossomed over the course of a week. The first day was fraught, with suspicious homeowners peering out their windows at the legions of strangers invading their turf. By the second day, the homeowners had grown more at ease, some even offering home-baked treats. By the third day, homeowners and volunteers were chatting freely and sharing lunch. When the week-long project concluded, the farewells were bittersweet for both sides.

After a similar project in North Scranton, Shirley Russell praised the volunteers who painted her home and worked on her garage and garden. "The work was outstanding," she said. "It is refresh-

ing knowing that people care, and it helps make you believe in people. I am so proud of my newly painted home."

Building on the successful volunteer strategy, NWNEPA formed a partnership with AmeriCorps VISTA for a "Paint The Town" campaign to beautify and repair the homes of senior citizens, people with disabilities and modest-income families in West Scranton.

As these high-impact home-improvement projects proved increasingly successful, NWNEPA next sought help from the all-volunteer Habitat for Humanity, local businesses and community groups in Lackawanna County. The response was quick and enthusiastic, with volunteer teams promised by banks, real-estate associations, churches and colleges. The teams were each assigned to an address and time slot, then provided with on-the-job training and supervision as they set out on their missions.

This model is simple but effective. NWNEPA now has its own locally-based, sustainable home-repair operation but continues to harness the power of volunteers. GroupCares signed on to contribute volunteers through 2016 and moved their troops to West Scranton, another vulnerable area. The efforts again proved hugely successful, attracting attention from the media, funders and government officials.

NWNEPA also launched bus tours of the completed projects for key constituents at the end of each week-long project, and those show-and-tell rides have become instrumental in securing financial and political support for the campaigns.

NWNEPA's volunteer recruitment, which employs the simplest of outreach techniques, has spawned more than a dozen long-term relationships with large groups. Between 2010 and 2016, 2,500 volunteer teams completed projects at 276 properties and logged more than 46,600 hours valued at almost $1 million.

Between 2010–2016, 2,500 volunteer teams completed projects at 276 properties and logged more than 46,000 hours—valued at almost $1 million.

These ventures have unveiled a surprising but fundamental lesson: hard labor can be a soft sell. Volunteers now come to NWNEPA unsolicited as word spreads through traditional and social media that they can make a difference that ripples through communities for years. NWNEPA has also learned that camaraderie and team building are key to motivating group efforts. Finally, moving ahead one small step is sometimes necessary to generate momentum. This has played out in several communities; when one house gets a makeover, the neighbors will follow suit – sometimes even without assistance. In other words: Think big, but don't be afraid to start small.

ABOUT JESSE ERGOTT

Jesse Ergott serves as the chief executive officer of NeighborWorks Northeastern Pennsylvania, a nonprofit working to improve the region's financial stability by providing effective homeownership services. With a staff of nine and a budget of $650,000, the organization serves hundreds of residents annually in Lackawanna, Luzerne, Monroe, Pike and Carbon counties. For nearly a decade, Ergott has been committed to building a better future for the area by improving housing and supporting homeowners through regional partnerships and the NeighborWorks America network.

TARGETING LOANS TO REVITALIZE NEIGHBORHOODS

Stephanie Preusch, Executive Director

Neighborhood Finance Corp.

Neighborhood Finance Corp. (NFC), now in its 26th year, is a nonprofit mortgage lender focusing on neighborhood revitalization in Polk County, Iowa. We were established in response to a declining housing stock. Through the leadership of the city, county, and neighborhood and business leaders, a study was commissioned in 1989 to examine neighborhood conditions and service delivery. The findings were used to develop a neighborhood revitalization program and to create an organization to provide local lending. The result was NFC, which serves neighborhoods selected by the city council and county board of supervisors. NFC's current lending area is approximately two-thirds of the city of Des Moines.

Since it opened, NFC has made more than $300 million in repayable and forgivable loans to more than 5,600 homebuyers and rehabbers. In 2014, NFC closed $16.4 million in loans and $2.3 million in forgivable loans. Through Sept. 30, 2015, the average rehab completed per loan was valued at $23,600.

Our work is made possible by partnerships with NeighborWorks America, the City of Des Moines, Polk County, the U.S. Department of the Treasury, local financial institutions and Fannie Mae.

What makes NFC's lending programs unique are the forgivable loans for home improvement that come with every mortgage loan. A subsidy (forgivable loan) of up to $10,000 can be obtained to help pay for property repairs and improvements when purchasing a home in an NFC lending area. Eligible homebuyers can also receive a sub-

CHALLENGE

Polk County, Iowa faced a challenge: People who had the ability to be mobile moved. Those who didn't were stuck in housing too expensive to maintain. When they couldn't do it anymore, absentee owners bought the properties up, converted them to small apartments and milked them.

Neighborhood trust, community connections and a strong track record of lending success have improved NFC's ability to attract lending capital.

sidy of up to $2,500 to assist with a down payment and/or closing costs on a purchase.

Our organization's emphasis on renovating existing structures has been a success. NFC's lending programs have attracted new buyers to Des Moines, helped people stay in their homes and increased property values.

Other customized, special-interest loan programs we offer include a partnership with Polk County and the Windsor Heights-Urbandale Sanitary Sewer District to provide financing for residents who need to replace or repair their sewer line as part of the Save Our Sewers (SOS) initiative. In

addition, for those residents who only need exterior improvements, our Front Porch Loan Program assists borrowers with lower credit scores than are typically approved for home purchases.

Meanwhile, through our limited liability corporation, NFC Properties, we purchase and rehab homes in need of repair. Once the rehab is complete, the property is listed for sale.

"Through NFC, I was able to refinance my mortgage and get a new roof, paint, furnace, A/C and water heater. Everyone at NFC was great to work with and I would highly recommend them." said Jennifer, an NFC client.

Recently, NFC tripled its commitment from Fannie Mae, from $5 to $15 million a year. In addition, NFC continues to receive annual support of at least $5 million from local investors. The continuous availability of capital is very important for NFC, and is possible due to our emphasis on quality control, compliance with Dodd-Frank regulatory changes, strong underwriting and low default rates.

As part of our 25th anniversary, we worked with a University of Iowa graduate student to complete a study of our lending and its impact on property values compared to core neighborhoods in other

Iowa cities. It found that Des Moines experienced a total average increase in property values of 61 percent during 1990-2010. The other three cities evaluated did not experience increases anywhere near this significant.

We have learned two valuable lessons from our work:

Neighborhood involvement – the importance of working with neighborhood organizations – cannot be overstated. Each targeted neighborhood goes through a comprehensive neighborhood planning process and develops a strategy that includes commercial development, corridor improvements, park enhancements, youth activities and residential development. We have learned to be sure our lending programs support the broader activities of the neighborhood.

Capital for lending – It is important to maintain momentum and the confidence of banks, since they are our sole source of funding for our home improvement loans and a partial source for our purchase and refinance products. We also must maintain the confidence of the city and county so they understand the value and impact of their annual contribution to our lending program.

Since 1990, NFC has assisted more than 5,600 homebuyers and homeowners with purchase and repair.

ABOUT STEPHANIE PREUSCH

Stephanie Preusch is the executive director of Neighborhood Finance Corporation (NFC) and has held this position since April 2014. Preusch has over 20 years of housing and mortgage experience and has been a leader in affordable housing policy and community collaboration initiatives.

COMMUNITY PARTNERSHIPS INCREASE SERVICE ACCESSIBILITY AND BRAND RECOGNITION

Colin Kelley, Chief Executive Officer

NeighborWorks Western Pennsylvania

NeighborWorks Western Pennsylvania creates greater neighborhood wealth through financial education, coaching and community leadership development. Throughout the early 2000s, the organization primarily provided homebuyer education services, and didn't serve communities beyond the city of Pittsburgh. Then, in 2008, the housing crisis rocked the nation's economy, followed by the Great Recession. Many western Pennsylvania residents faced foreclosure, and the unemployment rate in Allegheny County in February 2010 was 8.7 percent – admittedly a full point less than the national rate, but still not a number to be proud of.

NWWPA decided to expand its services not only geographically, but also into the offices of other service providers. Our goal was to increase access and to provide new services to residents in financial crisis. Temporarily, our focus shifted from promoting homeownership to keeping residents financially secure.

We brought services directly to clients' homes and workplaces and developed a "satellite model," in which we partnered with different community-based service organizations. We developed a partnership with the Pennsylvania CareerLink system, the statewide unemployment and job search center, which brought our services as far north as Crawford and Mercer Counties, and as far south as Washington County.

CHALLENGE
To expand the scope and geographical reach of housing services through partnerships with community development agencies across western Pennsylvania.

We brought services directly to clients' homes and workplaces and developed a "satellite model," in which we partnered with different community-based service organizations.

We also found ways to increase access to our services beyond our main office based in downtown Pittsburgh – a problematic location for some clients because transportation and parking are difficult. Therefore we identified redevelopment areas – Garfield, Homewood, Larimer, the Northside and South Pittsburgh – and co-opted trusted neighborhood organizations to help nurture brand-recognition in each community.

We sought to connect with those in need, provide counseling and ultimately help them stabilize their financial lives. Many of these clients were long-term residents who felt disenfranchised, and thus disengaged from the community development process. But in order to be truly successful in these communities, we knew we had to reach long-term residents. Consequently, our neighborhood partners had to meet certain criteria:

▸ Be a community-based organization or a resident-driven community development corporation
▸ Provide supportive services that complement credit, budget, and pre-purchase counseling services
▸ Have a longstanding history of community engagement

The Kingsley Association in Larimer, with whom we partnered in mid-2013 to serve residents of East End, is a perfect example:

▸ They have a history of service dating back to the late 1800s
▸ They provide additional social services, hosting a local Family Support Center and entrepreneurial support organization
▸ The Larimer Consensus Group, a high capacity community-based organization, calls the Kingsley Association home

Since partnering with Kinsley, NWWPA has gained the trust of long-time residents and Consensus Group members, most notably Betty Lane, a prominent community advocate and leader. We now provide financial education workshops and counsel a steady stream of clients.

Though the economy is improving, our clients continue to seek our help to repair credit as they rebuild their financial lives. At its peak, in the midst of the Great Recession, NWWPA provided counseling services in five western Pennsylvania counties and staffed as many as 16 satellite locations. Currently, NWWPA provides counseling and education at seven sites in Allegheny and Lawrence Counties, and at our HomeOwnership Center, and we continue to seek out new ways to serve those most in need in our community and beyond.

In 1968, Dorothy Richardson founded Pittsburgh Neighborhood Housing Services—which was the precursor to NeighborWorks.

ABOUT COLIN KELLEY

Colin Kelley is CEO of NeighborWorks Western Pennsylvania, a nonprofit that promotes homeownership and stable communities. Kelley has over 15 years of experience in the community development field, including program development, management, applied research, community organizing and leadership development.

ADOPTING TECHNOLOGY TO INCREASE EFFICIENCY OF INTERNAL OPERATIONS AND OUTREACH

Joan Carty, President & CEO
Suchana Costa, Innovations Analyst

Housing Development Fund

In 1989, the Housing Development Fund (HDF) was established to promote affordable housing through low-interest development loans in Stamford, CT. Today, HDF has expanded its services and products to include lending and advising services for developers and first-time homebuyers throughout the entire state of Connecticut and Nassau, Suffolk, Rockland and Westchester counties in New York. Over the past 27 years, HDF financed nearly 60 multifamily properties, advised and educated nearly 9,000 households and closed more than 2,000 loans. As HDF expanded, the need for innovative methods to keep track of our external and internal operations grew. In response, we implemented a series of technological upgrades, beginning with the NeighborWorks' Sustainable Homeownership Pilot in 2014.

Prior to these technology changes, potential first-time homebuyer clients called the main office, downloaded a pre-application form and gathered financial documents before they could sign up for a required group orientation session where they received an overview of products. Next, they met with a homeownership advisor to determine eligibility and create an action plan to become homeowners. Once they found a property, they down-

CHALLENGE

As organizations expand, manual systems that might once have been adequate can no longer keep up with the increased workload. Adopting new technology platforms improves speed and efficiency but it can be challenging to find the appropriate technology, motivate staff to embrace changes and work new technology into existing systems.

The movement away from redundant and laborious data entry has allowed HDF to focus on analysis of data to more accurately assess efficacy of programs and social impact.

loaded required forms and gathered documents before closing. Clients were encouraged to attend post-purchase events and complete paper surveys.

HDF maintained the list of attendees at each weekly orientation session in several locations:

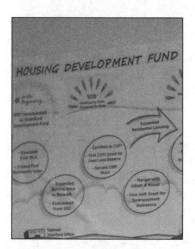

EventSpot (an online event manager), Counselor Max and Outlook, which meant that all three systems had to be updated for visibility and email reminders. There were also physical files with action plans, financial records and grant documents for each client that took staff time to maintain.

The new technological platforms allow clients to create an account on a customer portal site, update their personal and financial information, schedule appointments, share documents with staff, send emails and keep track of their own progress through their account. Clients can complete these profiles at their own pace, which helps us keep track of clients who are interested but not yet ready. In the past, only clients who attended an orientation session would enter their record system. Clients can now watch an orientation video, submit their financial documents through the portal and review an action plan during a virtual advising appointment without taking time off from work to visit an HDF office.

Salesforce, a customer relationship management system, allows advisors to interact with and track their clients. The Salesforce record can be updated by both the client and advisor at any time. Clients are automatically dispatched to their next step after completing a profile, such as financial fitness, homebuyer education or advising. The system generates a list of tasks associated with each client for advisors. All communications are recorded on the customer's profile, including auto-generated emails sent to them as they reach new milestones. All advisors have access to all client information, making transferring clients easy.

Via online surveys, we received overwhelmingly positive reviews on the convenience of the new process and customer portal. The implementation of Microsoft Azure (cloud data storage), Microsoft 365 (cloud email), Abila (grant and finance management), Encompass Banker Pro, ADP (time reporting) and Concur (expense reporting) further reduced paperwork and manual data entry. We can now obtain financial statements in five days rather than 30 days.

The movement away from redundant and laborious data entry allowed us to focus on analysis of data to more accurately assess efficacy of programs and social impact. For example, replacing spreadsheets with ADP for project-based time reporting and payroll allowed us to quickly determine how much time staff

> **In 2015, the median technology budget among nonprofits was less than 3% of the organization's total operating budget.**

spends on different projects. In addition to real-time analysis, we ran reports using historical data to identify external bottlenecks in our internal processes. Using Salesforce reports, we discovered that a majority of clients who did not complete a profile after being contacted by staff three times never became customers, so we reduced the number of required contact attempts by staff from six to three.

HDF's complete technological turnover has had challenges. We learned that while some changes, like the new Voice Over IP (VOIP) phone system, were seamless, others required training and patience as staff adjusted to completely new methods. However, any initial reluctance to learn a new system was quickly quashed as staff enjoyed completing previously time-consuming tasks in a fraction of the time.

By adopting new technology, HDF is able to better serve its mission. We can reach and maintain more clients in our system, work more efficiently and ultimately promote affordable housing in a more creative and effective manner.

ABOUT JOAN CARTY

Joan Carty, president and CEO of the Housing Development Fund (HDF) since1994, has grown its funding pool from $8.5 million to more than $140 million. HDF finances multifamily housing, first-time homebuyer acquisition and community development lending. It also provides one-on-one counseling and homebuyer education to low and moderate income households throughout its service area.

VACANT BANK BUILDING DONATION GIVES NONPROFITS ROOM TO GROW

Noel S. Halvorsen, Executive Director

NeighborWorks Green Bay

When Associated Bank, a regional banking leader, consolidated its various corporate offices into a single centralized location, it left a 15,000 square-foot building in downtown Green Bay, Wisconsin. Two leading area non-profit organizations, Brown County United Way and the Girl Scouts of the Northwestern Great Lakes, needed new office facilities, either because their current leases were expiring or their locations were no longer meeting their needs. Gail McNutt, the CEO of the Girl Scouts chapter, had long advocated for a collaborative nonprofit center in the community. A collective center for nonprofits can provide greater opportunities for collaborations with the other tenants and the community they serve. The vacated building in the government and corporate core of the city could deepen vital connections with officials and business leaders.

In 2013, McNutt initiated discussions with Associated Bank and United Way about the leasing space in the facility. Associated Bank decided to donate the building and chose NeighborWorks Green Bay (NWGB) as the recipient because of its nonprofit status and expertise in real estate development and management. The property deeded to NWGB in 2014 was the single largest donation we have ever received. Though we were not part of the initial discussions about the donation, clearly our strong, consistent community networking made us the best candidate.

CHALLENGE

When a big regional bank moved one of its departments to another site, it left a sprawling office building in downtown Green Bay, WI. Meanwhile, two leading nonprofits needed new offices, either because their leases were expiring or their locations were no longer adequate.

The tenants are saving thousands in rent and NWGB doubled its commercial real estate holdings.

Once on board, NWGB needed to work fast to bring make the building ready for its new tenants. We also needed to find a way to accommodate rules about donations, how to make leases affordable for the tenants and to maximize the donor's benefit. Of course, we also had to do this without losing money.

We created a so-called open book lease. All building tenants pay a pro-rata share of operating expenses and reserve contributions based on their portion of occupancy. NWGB adds an annual administrative fee to the cost. As expenses fluctuate, so does the rent. Each year, the tenants write a letter to the bank noting how much they are saving versus market rents thanks to its generous gift.

NeighborWorks Green Bay executed seven-year leases with the United Way and the Girl Scouts. Two other agencies, the First Tee (a golf-oriented youth development program) and the Bay Area Community Council (a nonprofit think tank) are also tenants. The tenants are saving thousands in rent, and NWGB doubled its commercial real estate holdings. We also have our name on a high-quality office building in the heart of the city.

The impact of the Associated Bank-NeighborWorks Green Bay Collaborative Center can perhaps best be described by the leaders of the organizations that occupy the building. McNutt said the new offices were a windfall for the Girl Scouts. "Not only does it improve our operating efficiencies, but more importantly, it brings us to a highly visible, central location in our community."

In addition to providing offices for the nonprofits, it also includes retail space where Girl Scouts and their leaders can buy uniforms, badges and other supplies. "I love popping into the Green Bay scout store and offices. There is something about the buzz downtown that makes the visit seem more important than just a stop for a badge in a mini-mall. The tree-lined streets afford shaded parking, and stepping up the stairs to the front door speak of a bygone era," says Trudi Wojtylaa, a parent and Girl Scout leader says.

The collective created many hurdles for NWGB. It took us longer to establish the routine of the annual rent adjustments relative to actual expenses than we anticipated. Also, one of the sites remains vacant, complicating the cost-sharing system for existing tenants.

But in addition to the boost in real estate holdings and visibility, NWGB has also benefited from the greater leadership role the donation provided, both with other nonprofit organizations and the downtown business community.

NeighborWorks Green Bay counseled and educated 627 customers in FY15.

The experience was also enriched by the wisdom that NWBG gained. We learned the value of continuously networking with other nonprofits and businesses, the importance of clear communication with donors about their expectations and acknowledging their generosity and learning how to effectively and affordably manage a multi-tenant office building.

ABOUT NOEL S. HALVORSEN

Noel S. Halvorsen has been serving as executive director of NeighborWorks Green Bay since 2000. Halvorsen has led the acquisition, renovation or development of 180 units of housing and 29,000 square feet of commercial space. During his tenure, NeighborWorks Green Bay has counseled more than 8,000 area households and helped more than 2,000 families to purchase homes. Halvorsen is active in other organizations including the Green Bay Neighborhood Leadership Council, the NeighborWorks Alliance of Wisconsin, and the National NeighborWorks Association.

A NEW BEGINNING

Jeffrey Eaton, CEO

———

Arbor Housing and Development

Arbor Development, a nonprofit housing agency previously located in Bath, NY, merged with a similar housing agency, Tri County Housing Council, based in Big Flats, NY, to form Arbor Housing and Development, a nonprofit agency serving the southern tier of New York and northern tier of Pennsylvania. To bring the two groups under one roof, a location in the City of Corning was identified as approximately midway between the two previous locations. A vacant Harley-Davidson dealership on a corner of Bridge Street, a main street in Corning, was available for conversion into an office space that could accommodate the new agency.

The City of Corning, our funders, the contractors and the agency itself had to work in perfect symmetry for a successful outcome for all parties. In May of 2014, Arbor Housing and Development moved into their new offices. Bringing the organization to Bridge Street has revitalized the area. We rented a portion of our building to Journey Fitness, an innovative fitness center that recently won the Corning Area Chamber of Commerce award for an emerging business. A new hair salon and chiropractic/wellness office have continued the revitalization of Bridge Street.

The relocation was not just about a building; that's just the visual piece of the puzzle. Relocation has made Arbor Housing and Development more visible within the city and able to form more partnerships that create housing options for the community. We are renovating and rehabilitating the largest housing complex in Corning, Meadowbrook Apartments, in a crime-ridden neighborhood with units that had fallen into disrepair. Similar to the partnerships we established to create our new office

CHALLENGE

The merger of two housing agencies into Arbor Housing and Development in 2011 created several challenges including finding a new location for the agency, tailoring that location to the needs of the new organization, transitioning the staff and securing funding to pay for the building and its rehabilitation.

building, Arbor and our partners will create a new home for the families of Meadowbrook. The Corning City Housing Study is another example of partnerships creating housing options that may not have been possible without our relocation. This collaboration will bring new homeowners to the community, rehabilitate homes in the city and provide incentives to owners to update and upgrade their homes.

Arbor's relocation created partnerships with other nonprofit and civic groups. For example, community events organized by the Corning Gaffer District around Bridge Street had been discontinued due to poor attendance until our presence brought new life to the community. At a new event this past summer, Arbor collaborated with a local restaurant and created our own little restaurant in our "Home Matters" courtyard. This holiday season, Arbor hosted the Northside Tree Lighting Ceremony. The new, more visible location of the tree was well received by the city and many residents commented on how great it was to cross the bridge and see the brightly lit tree on the corner.

In addition to the physical challenge of moving, our organization needed to merge two different employee cultures. Even though the organization merged three and one-half years before we moved into the new building, the separate staffs had their own culture, traditions and vibe. During the first year in the new space, we had to address which traditions to keep and how to handle different hours, dress down days and holiday celebrations. Now we have a new combined culture and have solidified our corporate structure; the "back room" logistics run more smoothly in the new central location. Two program departments were combined and overlapping programs were synced so clients receive services more quickly. Program staff from other areas were brought into the corporate office and now we have three programs within the building that serve some of the same clients.

The biggest lesson learned during our merger is the importance of collaborative efforts. As a nonprofit, it would have been difficult, if not impossible, to successfully complete a project of this magnitude. Collaborative partners included: Southern Tier Regional Economic Development Council; Empire State Development; Regional Economic Development and Energy Corporation; corporate sponsor Corning Enterprises; NYS Homes and Community Renewal; NYS Energy Research and Development Authority and Steuben County IDA. The Bridge Street headquarters building is a prime example of what is possible when private investors, corporate sponsors and economic development funds come together.

In a survey of 41 nonprofit mergers, 93% merged to increase service delivery.

ABOUT JEFFREY EATON

Jeffrey Eaton, CEO of Arbor Housing and Development for over 15 years, has nearly 40 years of professional experience in the public and private nonprofit sector. Arbor is a diverse multi-county housing and human service organization in the southern tier of western upstate New York and the northern tier of Pennsylvania. Eaton's experience includes delinquency prevention/diversion program development; community-based mental health and substance abuse programming; residential treatment programming; homeless and special needs housing development; senior/family affordable housing development and community revitalization/economic development.

WESTERN NEW YORK REGIONAL CONSOLIDATION: THE ROAD LESS TRAVELED

Matt Hjelmhaug and Laura Sweat, Interim CEOs

NeighborWorks Community Partners

The Rust Belt communities in western New York suffer from high poverty rates, abandoned buildings, and aging, deteriorating housing whose low market prices can't lure investments to rescue them. More than one-quarter of the populations of Rochester, Niagara Falls and Buffalo live below the federal poverty level. Meanwhile, the usual safety nets are increasingly fragile. Funding cuts for community development corporations (CDCs) over the past decade have severely curbed their ability to provide vital services like homebuyer education and counseling, lending, residential rehab and energy efficiency assistance. The dwindling funds also hinder neighborhood revitalization programs designed to strengthen communities which have seen plummeting investments. Moreover, small CDCs face escalating costs, increased regulations and complex business lines that require skilled workers, certifications and licenses. It has thus become ever more difficult to meet the urgent needs of underserved communities.

In response to this looming crisis, four independent CDCs in Western New York consolidated in 2015, using an innovative structure unprecedented in nonprofit mergers. NeighborWorks Rochester, West Side Neighborhood Housing Services (NHS), Niagara Falls NHS and Black Rock-Riverside NHS joined together under a new umbrella organization: NeighborWorks Community Partners. We have two locations in Buffalo, one in Niagara Falls and

CHALLENGE

Small nonprofit organizations increasingly struggle for survival in a time of shrinking funding and escalating demands for their services. Community development organizations (CDCs) are particularly hard hit, as traditional support from public agencies and private foundations shrinks and the need for their assistance expands.

What makes this merger different is a decentralized leadership approach combined with representative governance.

one in Rochester. Our umbrella organization based in Rochester supports the local affiliates serving high-need communities across 16 counties.

This partnership uses a unique structure that allows for a strong local voice to respond to specific community needs, while it standardizes some programs across the region to increase the number of people served. Unlike most nonprofit mergers, all four local affiliates entered into this partnership as thriving, productive organizations. Regardless of size, they come together as equals; the consolidation is a voluntary and proactive response to the imperative to do more with less. Under this new system, the affiliates aim to increase the number of residents they serve by more than 60 percent within five years, for a total of 12,600 families served and $176 million invested in the region by the end of 2021.

The consolidation is designed to provide the scale needed to support stronger back office support functions such as strategic direction, financing, human resources, technology and reporting. It also increases the ability to deliver highly technical lines of business like lending and energy services, while allowing for unique services tailored to the communities' needs. The strategy leads to increased impact in existing service areas as well as expansion into underserved areas throughout the region.

The partnership capitalizes on the network effect, allowing the organizations to draw on each member's strengths and expertise, creating a hybrid service delivery approach. By sharing administrative and leadership functions, we increase efficiency and cooperate more cost-effectively. The regional scale positions the organizations to attract new partners and greater support, ultimately enhancing long-term sustainability.

What makes this merger different is a decentralized leadership approach combined with representative governance. The regional organization has limited hierarchy and provides standardization where it adds value. This allows us to provide a platform of uniform offerings proportionately across a larger area while providing for the more specific needs of each community. Our new structure gives us the best of both worlds: capitalizing on our size where it makes sense, and leveraging our local advantage and responsiveness when that is needed.

Control of the organization comes from a regional board of twelve members, three representatives from each of the local organizations. Ultimately, this system is more complex and more challenging to develop than most nonprofit mergers, but it allows us to include each community's voice and needs in the foundation of our work.

NCP aims to increase the number of residents they serve by more than 60% in 5 years.

The corporate structure was intentionally built so that organizations can be added easily, allowing them access to a sustainable business model, while exponentially increasing the network's effect and overall strength. This is not about taking what the strongest organization does and replicating it across the network. Rather, this improves on what any one of the existing organizations brings to the consolidation.

As CDCs grow, they often lose their focus as they shift to a household-level approach from community-wide revitalization efforts. Our new structure builds regional programs that can be scaled effectively while retaining a more comprehensive approach, increasing our impact at both the household and the community level. Without this approach, these high-need communities would be in peril of losing the organizations that provide critical services. Much of what these CDCs offer is unique, and if they were to close, their communities would lose vital services and resources and many households would have nowhere to turn for assistance.

The list of lessons learned is long. Building an unprecedented structure such as this takes considerable effort, and making the change takes much longer than expected. Although it has been a challenging process, we are confident this new structure will reap benefits for decades to come and ensure the sustained delivery of critical services to communities across the region with high levels of need.

ABOUT MATT HJELMHAUG AND LAURA SWEAT

Matt Hjelmhaug and Laura Sweat are the interim co-CEOs of Upstate New York Community Partners, a new regional consolidation of four community development corporations, including the NeighborWorks organizations NeighborWorks Rochester, Niagara Falls Neighborhood Housing Services, and West Side Neighborhood Housing Services in Buffalo. The group's mission is to provide housing solutions as a foundation for individuals, families, and neighborhoods to build vibrant communities. With a consolidated staff of 38 and a budget of $3.7 million, Upstate New York Community Partners serves about 1,750 people in western New York State annually, and aims to significantly increase the number of people it serves through the partnership.

NONPROFIT TAKEOVERS: TOOLS FOR TOUGH TIMES

Steven Kirk, President

Rural Neighborhoods

Looming financial pressures and growing cracks in leadership marked the crises facing the Empowerment Alliance of Southwest Florida, Immokalee Housing and Family Services and Florida Non-Profit Services in late 2014. Much was certainly at stake, including more than 50 years of combined service, local know-how, land under development (and in debt) and rental apartments serving more than 400 low-income persons. Struggling with staff and board departures, these organizations saw that joining an experienced, well-capitalized, regional partner made more sense than trying to claw themselves back to limited impact.

Rural Neighborhoods involvement in Immokalee dates back a decade to the development of two successful rental communities totaling 171 units.

Salvaging troubled nonprofits is harder if a rescuer stumbles into such relationships rather than establishing a rationale with well-considered goals. Our two-year old strategic plan had carved out just such a blueprint, recommending that we seek out nonprofits that owned sound housing assets but had too little capital or trouble maintaining a volunteer board. Our strategic objectives for such an undertaking included: to improve asset and property management efficiencies, increase net cash flow, gain unrestricted capital and acquire new program skills.

It's not easy for small, decades-old housing and community development organizations to step aside, but creative exit strategies that offer new opportunities and honor organizational and personal legacies can bridge these senti-

CHALLENGE

In Southwest Florida, local groups asked Rural Neighborhoods to help preserve affordable housing developments and prevent the displacement of residents. Our organization needed to become a trusted neighborhood leader and to transform ourselves from a real estate project developer to a place-based, neighborhood stabilization activist.

Filling the void created by the simultaneous loss of several community-based nonprofits is a substantive challenge.

ments. In our Immokalee initiative, we celebrated partners' board and staff contributions through news coverage, building signage and recognition events. We provided organizations with legal assistance for their dissolution and contributions toward outstanding financial issues such as audits and severance pay. Recognition and assistance proved far better than having their past housing accomplishments deteriorate.

Filling the void created by the simultaneous loss of several community-based nonprofits is a substantive challenge. Our historic neighborhood role was limited to real estate development and property management, which positioned us as a peripheral stakeholder rather than a trusted leader. To emerge as a true neighborhood quarterback in the eyes of local residents required us to transform ourselves from a real estate project developer to a place-based, neighborhood stabilization activist. Hiring Dorothy Cook, former executive director of the Empowerment Alliance of Southwest Florida, as our neighborhood revitalization manager as she wound down her former group's corporate dissolution offered local continuity and deepened our neighborhood ties.

In this new role, Rural Neighborhoods established the EP2 Neighborhood Revitalization Plan by engaging 150 local households and 15 organizational stakeholders and inventorying housing conditions block by block. The plan includes resident priorities for the real estate assets associated with our merger and acquisition strategy and for broader neighborhood issues such as infrastructure, education, youth and healthy lifestyles. Resident engagement led to our ongoing sponsorship of semi-annual EP2 resident leadership academies, with more than 30 neighborhood graduates to date.

Highlights of Rural Neighborhoods' real estate production attributable to the Immokalee initiative include:

▶ Merging with Florida Non-Profit Services resulted in $5.3 million in new real estate assets including Esperanza Place, a newly built 48-unit multifamily rental community and three scattered-site rental homes.

▸ Takeover of Immokalee Housing and Family Services' title and $2 million in mortgage debt at Timber Ridge at Sanders Pines Reserve preserved affordable housing for its 75 households and will result in an additional $2.8 million in substantial rehabilitation improvements.

▸ Twenty-five acres of commercial, multifamily and single-family zoned land with more than $1.5 million in past public-private investment was preserved at one-tenth the cost and provides land for future development of more than 100 units of multifamily housing and 60 single-family homes.

The Immokalee initiative included $5.3 million in new real estate, $2.8 million in rehabilitation and $1.5 million in land investment.

The benefits of our takeover strategy and EP2 plan include expanding our Immokalee portfolio to 315 units, greatly improving our local property management efficiencies. Gross potential rent will grow by more than $1 million per year. The merged and dissolved entities provided a one-time contribution of $150,000 in unrestricted capital and retained personnel brought us new skills and aided our succession planning.

More than $12 million in neighborhood real estate assets were preserved, a pipeline of local housing developments endorsed by residents is in place and other parcels have been land banked for future investment. Our response to the local organizational crisis fundamentally changed our mission in Immokalee and led us to a place-based approach to our work.

ABOUT STEVEN KIRK

Steven Kirk serves as the president of Rural Neighborhoods, a nonprofit community housing development organization whose mission is to build livable places for working families through ground-breaking affordable housing, essential community facilities and creative placemaking. Rural Neighborhoods has 38 employees, a portfolio of 1,723 rental homes and apartments and annual revenue of $13.8 million. The organization serves 7,500 people in small towns and rural communities throughout Collier, Hendry, Hillsborough, Miami-Dade, Okeechobee, Polk and Saint Lucie County, FL. Under Kirk's leadership, Rural Neighborhoods fills a leading role in improving the lives of migrant and seasonal farmworkers.

Place-Based Investments

Mel Martinez

When I was a teenager, I arrived in the United States from Cuba as part of a Catholic humanitarian operation that brought more than 14,000 Cuban children to the United States in 1962, right after the Cuban Missile Crisis. I was alone and spoke almost no English, and a foster family was kind enough to take care of me until my parents arrived four years later. I've often said that America is not the country of my birth, but it is the country of my choice. That's one reason why the notion of place-making is so important to me: I learned at a young age how to make a place for myself, how to create a new home among people I didn't know, and how to become part of a new community. It's made all the difference in my life ever since.

Bringing people together is in my nature – and both as a United States Senator and as the Secretary of the Department of Housing and Urban Development, I worked hard to build consensus, find common ground, and build bridges instead of barriers. Increasing homeownership for all Americans and ending the scourge of chronic homelessness were particularly important to me.

But I also understood that place-making is about more than a roof over one's head. Place-making leverages a local community's assets as well as its potential for future growth, not just in terms of buildings and infrastructure, but in terms of intangibles like good education, access to healthy choices for exercise and nutrition, and even an inclusive attitude toward newcomers. The idea is to create welcoming public spaces that help make people safer, happier and healthier.

Early in my career, I headed the Orlando Housing Authority and served on the boards of a community bank and our local Catholic Charities organization – all of which proved to me the importance of a comprehensive approach to place-making. Collaboration between local nonprofits, financial institutions and housing organizations can make all the difference in the world when it comes to creating places of opportunity all over the United States.

As the architect Jan Gehl has said, "In a society becoming steadily more privatized with private homes, cars, computers, offices and shopping centers, the public component of our lives is disappearing. It is more and more important to make the cities inviting, so we can meet our fellow citizens face to face and experience directly through our senses. Public life in good quality public spaces is an important part of a democratic life and a full life."

Gehl is right – place-making is important to our democracy and to our well-being as citizens. It certainly was important to me as a 15 year-old boy arriving on our shores alone, not speaking the language, with only a suitcase in my hands. I found my place here, and I hope, through my work at JP Morgan Chase now, to help others find and make places to live fuller, better lives.

It's my pleasure to introduce to you NeighborWorks America and some of its tremendous network organizations working to create places that improve life – for all of us.

Mel Martinez is chairman of the Southeast U.S. and Latin America for JPMorgan Chase & Co. Martinez joined JPMorgan Chase in July 2010 after more than a decade of public service. Martinez was elected to the U.S. Senate from Florida in 2004. Prior to his time in the Senate, he served as the 12th Secretary of the United States Department of Housing and Urban Development (HUD). As the first Cuban-American to serve in a President's cabinet, he became known for his efforts to increase homeownership for all Americans and his aggressive efforts to end chronic homelessness. Martinez also served as mayor of Orange County (Orlando, FL) and he practiced law for 25 years. He received both his B.S. and J.D. degrees from Florida State University.

AFFORDABLE HOUSING AND DIVERSITY TRANSFORMING CHINATOWN

Norman Fong, Executive Director

Chinatown Community Development Center

Chinatown Community Development Center (CCDC) is a place-based community development organization serving primarily the Chinatown neighborhood since 1977. Our experience with developing and managing affordable housing using creative financing and acquisition tools led to our selection as developer for the Chinatown Cluster. Our strong ties to Chinatown placed us in a unique position to build the trust needed to accomplish this conversion.

The Chinatown Cluster, the largest in the Rental Assistance Demonstration (RAD) program, is the only one that includes family, senior and disabled residents. CCDC is unique in taking on a RAD cluster as a single entity, with five divisions: civic engagement/organizing, housing development, property management, resident services and the executive office. The work intersects with our role developing leaders and supporting tenant advocacy at Ping Yuen. We bring our community perspective to work through portfolio-wide RAD concerns and to develop policies addressing lease and house rules, temporary relocation, resident services, workforce/employment services, tenant engagement, tenant councils, waitlist and referrals and housing retention.

Through RAD, we gain access to private and public funding sources to pay for capital repairs and modernization and to ensure future maintenance and management. We

CHALLENGE

In 2013, HUD put the San Francisco Housing Authority on its "troubled" list due to the agency's financial problems and major management flaws. Continuing cuts in the federal budget left the agency unable to maintain or operate its public housing properties as decent homes for the city's poorest residents.

One-third of Chinatown's population lives in single-room occupancy homes, with families and seniors sharing a single room and common kitchens and bathrooms.

won additional local funding for on-site resident services to help tenants navigate these changes and for community engagement to bring their concerns and ideas to the table.

Our work with RAD correlates with our strategic goals: embracing diversity, increasing the impact of our affordable housing development work and strengthening Chinatown's infrastructure and vitality. We are confident the outcome will be improved housing, deeper services, high quality management and richer lives.

However, we realize that transition is difficult and some tenants are confused about their housing status. We work closely with residents to understand their concerns and incorporate their input into proposed changes and management choices. Our on-site property management and resident services staff is now a multi-cultural team that reflects the resident population and organizes activities that bring residents together and support the diverse tenant population. We also engage with African-American and Spanish-speaking residents.

Ping Yuen was constructed in the 1950s as housing for the Chinese population of Chinatown and historically the Ping Yuen Residents Improvement Association (PYRIA) reflected that population. While the association continues to be led by Asian residents, our goal is to ensure that its membership and leadership begins to reflect the ethnic diversity of residents in the buildings. The current ethnic makeup of Ping Yuen is about 30 percent non-Asian and we expect that trend toward diversity to increase. CCDC previously launched SuperNeighbors to begin outreach and leadership development beyond PYRIA and we hold small group discussions to build new bridges across ethnicity with all tenants at Ping Yuen.

"I love the Ping Yuen community, it really feels like one big family, a place where everyone can feel at home," says resident Barbara Thomas. "The key to everything is communication. We might not all speak the same language, but every resident can say how they feel and there is a sense that everyone's input is important."

Preservation of the units protects a critical resource for Chinatown, continuing the ability of low-income families to live here despite displacement pressures. One-third of Chinatown's population lives in single-room occupancy homes, with families and seniors sharing a single room and common kitchens and bathrooms.

In Chinatown, there was a 19.3% drop in the Asian population from 2000-2010.

The new units, which include accessible studios and one-bedrooms for seniors and disabled people and two-to-four-bedroom units for families, all with private bathrooms and kitchens, represent a major community resource for low-income households in Chinatown.

The three lessons we learned through this project include: 1) community-based organizations are critical in shaping affordable housing programs at federal and local levels; 2) embracing diversity within our own organization creates a strong foundation for building trust within diverse tenant populations; and 3) resident services and community engagement must be paired with high-quality property management to sustain healthy, safe, affordable housing communities.

ABOUT NORMAN FONG

Norman Fong serves as executive director of the Chinatown Community Development Center, a community development organization serving low-income residents in neighborhoods throughout San Francisco. Chinatown CDC develops and manages affordable housing; assists residents with support services, community organizing and engagement; conducts community planning and provides youth leadership development. Since Fong became executive director in 2011, he has nearly doubled the organization's budget to $10.8 million and professional staff to 160.

THE 'REEL' STORY: A LESSON IN NEW ECONOMIC DEVELOPMENT PRACTICES

Merten Bangemann-Johnson, CEO

NeighborWorks Umpqua

Food is an enormous asset in the Pacific Northwest economy and quality of life. That's why NeighborWorks Umpqua offers a range of programs designed to both encourage healthy eating and support this segment of our economy. Our initiatives include a farmers' market, a program that supports the planting of backyard gardens, a retail store that provides an outlet for local artisans and farmers to sell goods and allows food entrepreneurs to test and create value-added products in our licensed commercial kitchen, and a collaboration to develop edible landscapes in public parks and spaces where everyone has access to locally grown perennial foods.

Another major focus is our local seafood industry. You might assume that seafood ordered in a restaurant on the southern coast of Oregon is local. But you likely would be wrong. Communities on the Oregon coast have limited access to fresh, local seafood because the vast majority is exported to overseas markets by corporate buyers. Farm-produced seafood of lesser quality is then imported and sold to Oregon consumers at prices equal to local seafood.

People don't often ask for specifics about the seafood they eat, and some restaurants seem to think a local distributor means local fish. It doesn't. This can make it difficult for fishermen to differentiate themselves in the local market.

Lack of consumer knowledge is just the beginning of the

CHALLENGE

To revitalize the local fishing industry by bringing locally caught seafood back home to the Oregon southern coast, using technical assistance, training, consumer education and financial investment.

"The timing is perfect to take a hard look at the seafood value chain and explore interventions that both bring a higher value to fishermen and provide local fish for consumers."

— Leesa Cobb, executive director, Port Orford Ocean Resources Team

challenge. Small-boat fishermen are forced to pay many of the same fees as large-scale operations, which often monopolize permits and processing facilities. In fact, the lack of smaller, local processing plants has forced some ports to use larger out-of-state processors, sending money and jobs out of Oregon.

In 2015, NeighborWorks Umpqua became a beneficiary of WealthWorks, which works to advance a region's overall prosperity and self-reliance, strengthen existing and emerging sectors, and increase jobs and incomes for lower-income residents and firms – all at the same time. It describes itself as "a systematic approach that identifies enterprising opportunities in a region and engages a wide range of partners in turning those opportunities into results that both build and capture wealth. It can complement or incorporate traditional economic development methods, but intentionally focuses on creating more value that becomes rooted in local people, places and firms."

NeighborWorks Umpqua received a two-year grant from a WealthWorks Northwest arm called Rural Development Initiatives, which was formed in 1991 in response to the timber industry crisis facing the Pacific Northwest. NeighborWorks Umpqua partnered with organizations in Coos, Curry and Douglas Counties – all located on the southern coast of Oregon – to develop a plan. The result was the Southwestern Oregon Food System Collaborative-Seafood Project, bringing together residents and organizations involved in community development, education and natural resources.

The group worked to identify ways to help South Coast communities thrive on their own terms. One idea was to link the development of greater local fish-processing capacity to interactive port tours in which visitors could meet fishermen and watch them work. This would help not one, but two local industries: seafood and tourism.

More broadly, we are facilitating collaboration within the region to determine ways to address the many needs of the fishing community: ice-making equipment, distribution systems, access to public hoists, training, technical assistance and consumer education.

In 2014, U.S. fishermen landed 9.5 billion pounds of fish and shellfish, valued at $5.4 billion.

We also have made direct investments into local businesses. NeighborWorks Umpqua dedicated 30 slots per year in 2015 and 2016 for our Dream$avers program, a 3-to-1 matched savings program, to help fishing and other seafood-related enterprises build their businesses. Meanwhile, a notice to local businesses in the seafood sector received responses from six businesses, and we connected them to resources that can provide assistance on their business plans. It's expected that one or more of the six will receive WealthWorks funding of their own.

"The timing is perfect to take a hard look at the seafood value chain and explore interventions that both bring a higher value to fishermen and provide local fish for consumers," says Leesa Cobb, the executive director of Port Orford Ocean Resources Team.

On the policy front, the initiative has attracted new partners that focus on these types of barriers in the value chain. The Oregon Food Bank Policy Division is holding policy forums with local fishermen to test the idea of proposing legislation to increase access to their catch by niche buyers.

Most recently, the Seafood Project organized group "listening" sessions with leaders from six South Coast ports, more than 100 fishermen, owners of restaurants and grocers, and community members. We continue to expand, educate and learn, and remain focused on finding ways to revitalize local seafood businesses and the communities they support.

ABOUT MERTEN BANGEMANN-JOHNSON

Merten Bangemann-Johnson is CEO of NeighborWorks Umpqua. He has worked with the Gilman Housing Trust in Vermont, and served as special assistant to Mayor Mark Begich in Anchorage, Alaska, where he was CEO of the Anchorage Community Land Trust. He is on the board of the National Rural Housing Coalition.

NEIGHBORHOOD SUPERMARKET DEVELOPMENT IN A FOOD DESERT

Grady P. Appleton, President & CEO

East Akron Neighborhood Development Corp.

In 1993, East Akron, Ohio's local supermarket closed, leaving the low and moderate-income residents without a nearby place to shop for groceries and other goods. They also feared that the loss of the store would harm other businesses. Two of the banks in the neighborhood had already started having shorter workweeks and there was some concern that the banks would close altogether.

Since 1982, the East Akron Neighborhood Development Corp. (EANDC) has been serving individuals and families in Akron and surrounding areas. The mission of EANDC is to improve communities by providing quality and affordable housing, comprehensive homeownership services and economic development opportunities.

The loss of the supermarket/department store would undermine what the agency had been striving for year after year, a viable neighborhood with the necessary amenities. They held two meetings with F. Steven Albrecht, President of the F.W. Albrecht Grocery Company to persuade the owner to keep the store in the community. The meetings were attended by people from the area's private, public and religious sectors. At the meeting, the owner said that the store had been losing money for 10 years. He also said that the store had stayed far longer than other stores that had already closed and left. The store closed in September of 1993.

CHALLENGE

In 1993, a supermarket in East Akron, OH, closed, leaving the residents without a nearby place to shop for groceries and other goods. They also feared that the loss of the store would harm other businesses. How could the residents work together to ensure the viability of the neighborhood?

The Middlebury Plaza became a reality with Dave's Supermarket as the anchor business with related retail. It was the first new shopping center in Center City Akron in 40 years.

Then EANDC in concert with East Akron Community House, a community based settlement house, brought together a private, public, religious coalition to decide what to do about getting a supermarket in the neighborhood. They held a "Goal-Setting Conference" to reaffirm that the neighborhood wanted a supermarket. A supermarket coalition was established, representatives of which met with the owner of the closed supermarket in an attempt to get the supermarket back in the neighborhood, but the meeting was fruitless.

The city of Akron then asked EANDC to spearhead an effort to get a supermarket for the neighborhood. The City provided technical assistance and resources to EANDC to support this effort. One of their first steps was to hire an experienced consultant who had provided technical assistance to other nonprofits who successfully developed neighborhood supermarkets. The consulting

firm had studied supermarket development and had been commissioned by the Department of Agriculture to write a book on their research. Through his study, the consultant determined that the neighborhood could support a full service grocery store and related retail. Based on the study and successful advocacy by EANDC, an agreement was made with city government and the private sector to create a plaza with a supermarket as an anchor.

It was not an easy process. They faced barrier after barrier on the path to make the supermarket a reality. One supermarket chain agreed to be the anchor business and then backed out. It turned out that the site was badly contaminated and it took the EPA a long time to remediate the site. After very lengthy negotiations with the owner of the parcel of land, the city eventually had to acquire the site. Then the city of Akron and EANDC had to obtain other sources of funding, which was a monumental task.

But finally in 2004, after an 11-year battle, the Middlebury Plaza became a reality with Dave's Supermarket as the anchor business with related retail. It was the first new retail shopping center in Center City Akron in 40 years. In addition to providing vital goods and services to the neighborhood, there were many other positive economic impacts from the development, including: $9,000,000 of economic development, 60 full-time jobs and 120 part-time jobs, increased income tax and property tax revenues and additional private development. Currently, plans are on the drawing board for Phase III of the retail development of the outer parcel of the property.

After the nine year effort to develop the shopping plaza, neighborhood leader Ethel Chambers said: "This goes to show you that when we never quit clamoring and get together, our voices can be heard."

Of the 18 million people living in a food desert in 2010, only 1.4 million got a new supermarket in the past 4 years.

There were several critical lessons learned from this effort:
- By the time the community attempted to intervene to get the store to stay, it was already too late. Intervention should have begun much earlier when the store's quality was slipping and it was having a hard time being competitive with other grocery stores.
- EANDC had experience in housing redevelopment but no retail experience. Because of their lack of retail experience, EANDC should have locked in a 20-year fixed interest rate instead of using New Markets Tax Credits which only provided seven year financing.
- The project was costly to develop. EANDC used a number of financial resources available at that time including statewide loan funds, federal funding, city funds, TIF and its own capital (Neighborworks America). It would have made more sense for the city to have granted some of the funds instead of loaning the funds to EANDC. If the city had donated the land, the real estate tax abatement could have been a great help to the project.

ABOUT GRADY P. APPLETON
Grady P. Appleton serves as the president and CEO of East Akron Neighborhood Development Corp., an organization he helped to establish in 1982. Appleton has over 31 years of experience in the development of affordable housing and community development. Through EANDC, Appleton has effectively built over 500 new homes, several senior apartment buildings, contributed to the repair of 150 owner-occupied homes; created over 400 local, full time jobs, facilitated the start-up of over 100 new local businesses and weatherized over 2,000 homes.

BUILDING A SUSTAINABLE, HEALTHY COMMUNITY IN COMPTON

Lori Gay, President & Chief Executive Officer

Neighborhood Housing Services of Los Angeles County

After a grocery store closed 25 years ago, the property sat vacant and undeveloped, an eyesore. The Compton community also no longer had access to fresh, healthy food as there were few shopping options left. The site had the potential to be a transformative one, turning the intersection of Rosecrans Avenue and Dwight Avenue into a vibrant corner. The empty lot was located across the street from a tranquil park, adjacent to the Compton Creek and a few hundred feet away from a fire station, a neighborhood church and a senior center. Instead, the lot was a blighting influence, cutting off Gonzales Park from busy Rosecrans Avenue and effectively holding back the neighborhood from becoming the lively hotspot that it could and should have been.

Place matters. It matters to families, to children, to people looking for jobs and to people seeking to better themselves. Research tells us that a region's larger economy matters to individual outcomes, as do unemployment rates, school accessibility, health systems and transportation networks.

But what's on your block matters just as much. Children struggle in school if they have to walk by abandoned properties riddled with crime just to get to the bus stop. Teenagers will have a harder time finding work if there aren't any good, well-paying jobs in the neighborhood. Kids, adults and elderly people have more health problems and worse outcomes when they deal with the daily

CHALLENGE

Southern California is divided economically. Some areas boom with investment while others feature blight, vacant lots and limited access to healthcare, fresh food and transit links to job centers. It is an urgent priority to bring these needed amenities to underserved communities.

What makes a great community is more than just housing. It's more than just good transportation and walkable neighborhoods. It's more than access to jobs. What makes a community great is all of those pieces working together.

stress of living on a crumbling street that lacks amenities like fresh food, adequate transit and accessible green space.

When Neighborhood Housing Services of Los Angeles County (NHS) took a look at the corner, we saw an underused asset dragging down the surrounding area. We saw a partial explanation for why median income had stagnated in that census tract, declining from $52,800 in 2000 to $47,975 in 2014. We saw an explanation for why the child poverty rate in that tract had risen from 19 percent in 1990 to 25 percent in 2000 to 33 percent in 2014, and why unemployment in that tract had risen from five percent in 2000 to over 10 percent in 2014. We saw an explanation for why the homeownership rate in the surrounding area had fallen 20 percentage points over the last three decades.

At NHS, we have seen in Compton, in Los Angeles and in small cities throughout Southern California how booming regional economies can still leave many neighborhoods behind. Too many places that should have been diverse, walkable, sustainable neighborhoods were instead abandoned, blighted and depressed. But we also saw promise and hope in the Rosecrans property. The convergence of a park, a local fire station, a church, the Compton Creek and a senior center made the site a great location for placemaking. From this, the Center for Sustainable Communities was born.

What makes a great community is more than just housing. It's more than just good transportation and walkable neighborhoods. It's more than access to jobs. It's more than health. What makes a community great is all of those pieces working together. So we at NHS didn't seek to simply put up affordable housing at the corner. We sought to build an institution that would address the whole range of Compton's needs.

The center will offer the community an array of services. The building will include a community health clinic, a financial opportunity center to offer counseling and affordable loans, a small business development center and incubator, a job training organization offering workforce solutions and a healthy living cafe. Youth entrepreneurship and conservation programs will be offered through partner organizations, along with a 4,000 square foot community garden and a local farmers market that will provide the community with opportunities to grow and sell fresh vegetables and fruits. NHS plans to partner with the City of Compton to provide a Public Safety Center that will help reduce crime.

Incorporated as a city in 1888, Compton is one of the oldest communities in Los Angeles County.

Taken together, these services will improve options for the residents of Compton. Yet in a housing market like Los Angeles, with sky-high land values and rents and prices that the vast majority of residents cannot afford, new amenities and placemaking create a paradox. Will improving services exacerbate high housing costs and create gentrification and displacement of the very residents that those amenities are targeted to serve?

To address this, NHS plans to build an affordable development adjacent to the center, along with one less than a mile away on Compton Blvd., while also developing affordable townhomes just south of that. All the while, NHS continues to create and preserve affordable homeownership opportunities through financial education and lending services.

ABOUT LORI R. GAY

Lori R. Gay is the president and CEO of Neighborhood Housing Services of Los Angeles County, the largest nonprofit provider of affordable homeownership opportunities in Southern California. Gay has worked in the community development field for over 30 years, focusing her efforts on rebuilding impoverished communities and creating mechanisms for community empowerment and ownership. Gay is a co-chair of the NeighborWorks National Community Stabilization Task Force.

CREATING A CULTURE OF HEALTH USING ECONOMIC DEVELOPMENT TOOLS

Rosa Rios Valdez, CEO

Business and Community Lenders of Texas

Among U.S. metro areas, in a 2014 Gallup survey, San Antonio had the second highest rate of obesity, often a precursor to diabetes and other health problems. Diabetes is prevalent among low-to-moderate income households and people of color, including Latinos. To address this growing concern in Texas, home to a large Latino population, Business and Community Lenders of Texas (BCL) partnered with organizations and individuals to help change eating habits.

BCL strives to develop unique solutions to address the needs of our service area, which encompasses 94 counties. Our mission is to improve lives through economic development, to help individuals, entrepreneurs and families build assets and to help communities grow by creating jobs and increasing the tax base. BCL uses economic development tools to address social problems that are otherwise not directly tied to these services.

The founding of our social enterprise, Salud de Paloma, and our healthy foods business development efforts in San Antonio are a prime example of using economic growth to target social problems. We created jobs and promoted healthy eating by supporting a new, niche industry in Texas with an investment in an olive oil bottling facility. Collaborating with the National Association of Latino Community Asset Builders (NALCAB), BCL of Texas received a grant from the U.S. Department of Health and Human Services to form a business to bottle and sell olive

CHALLENGE
San Antonio had the second highest rate of obesity among U.S. metro areas in 2014. Obesity is often a precursor to diabetes and other health problems. Diabetes is prevalent among low-to-moderate income households and people of color, including Latinos.

We created jobs and promoted healthy eating by supporting a new, niche industry in Texas with an investment in the creation of an olive oil bottling facility.

oil. Salud de Paloma Extra Virgin Olive Oil, launched in 2013, received a grant from the Texas Department of Agriculture to become the first olive oil company in the U.S. to create sample packets specifically to disperse at health fairs, doctors' offices, charter schools, Dell Children's Hospital, diabetes awareness events and other locations.

We developed a network of healthy food providers and those working to promote healthy eating throughout their communities. A City of San Antonio redevelopment study recommended attracting a healthy eatery to its historic Plaza de Armas, so BCL partnered with a local entrepreneur to create O'liva Healthy Local Cuisine and Tasting Room, a seasonal farm-to-table eatery. The Plaza de Armas is located in a food desert and reaching these underserved customers is a priority for Salud de Paloma.

While the restaurant was under construction, BCL became a cofounder in establishing Mercado de O'liva, a farmers market located in the plaza of the Spanish Governor's Palace, near the O'liva Healthy Local Cuisine and Tasting Room and on the site of the first market in San Antonio. To further support the provision of healthy foods to those who need it most, BCL received a SNAP grant from the Texas Department of Agriculture to ensure we could reach underserved customers and accept Lone Star cards for payment. The Mercado de O'liva has since expanded into five additional food deserts in San Antonio. All are Go Texan Certified Farmers Markets by the Texas Department of Agriculture.

By selling a premium olive oil product at an affordable price, we expand access to this healthy food product and work toward our goal to create a culture of health within the communities we serve. Salud de Paloma distributed 16,000 samples to underserved customers who may be at risk of developing health conditions such as diabetes without proper eating habits. The opening of O'liva Healthy Local Cuisine and Tasting Room and the Mercados de O'liva provided momentum for the farm-to-table movement in San Antonio. In 2016 alone, we will have reached 2,000 underserved customers in food deserts through the Mercados de O'liva. The markets feature nutritionists and healthy cooking demonstrations, and the Salud de Paloma Extra Virgin Olive Oil is available online and at O'liva Healthy Local Cuisine and Tasting Room. Our combined efforts have resulted in an approximately $2 million in investments in healthy eating for San Antonio and the greater Texas area.

17.1% of the population of Texas is food insecure.

BCL learned several lessons through this project: 1) partnerships with entrepreneurs and nonprofits can result in economic development and solutions to social problems, 2) the role of economic development is broader than job creation and, 3) social enterprise is another tool nonprofits can use to further their missions while creating positive outcomes and an additional income stream for the organization.

ABOUT ROSA RIOS VALDEZ

Rosa Rios Valdez, CEO of Business and Community Lenders of Texas since 1997, has 30 years of experience in business development and commercial real estate lending. She manages a statewide $25,000,000 commercial real estate loan portfolio and is asset manager for a $4.5 million real estate portfolio. Rios Valdez serves on the Economic Development Board of the Capital Area Planning Council of Government, the Board of the NeighborWorks America Community Capital Corporation and is a past president of the National Association of Economic Developers and former chair of the Travis County Housing Authority.

HEALTHY BLOCKS: RESCUING NEIGHBORHOODS FROM THE BRINK

Matt Hjelmhaug and Laura Sweat, Interim CEOs

NeighborWorks Rochester

Rochester's neighborhoods are at a pivotal point. The city is the 5th poorest in the United States and studies show its poverty rate continues to rise. Many neighborhoods have seen property values decrease and vacancies dramatically increase. The population is shrinking as people leave the city.

The resident engagement and economic foundation of some neighborhoods can overcome the challenges of poverty and blight. Their success is intrinsically tied to the future of Rochester as whole. Although facing a growing level of economic and social challenges, these transitional neighborhoods still have enough of an asset base to leverage neighborhood reinvestment that can be sustained over time. Because of this, even modest investments and improvements have the potential to make a difference and add value.

NeighborWorks Rochester recognized an opportunity to rescue these teetering neighborhoods at a critical moment. In 2005, we launched the Healthy Blocks Initiative in our first transitional, weak-market neighborhood with the goal of working with residents and community stakeholders in order to transform it.

NeighborWorks Rochester's first Healthy Blocks revitalization project debuted in the Swillburg neighborhood, a neighborhood in southeast Rochester. In the 19th century, pig farms dominated the area, hence the name. Today,

CHALLENGE

Once a neighborhood has become overwhelmed by poverty, collapsed housing market conditions and high vacancy rates, it is difficult for it to fully recover. Although some Rochester, NY neighborhoods are stable, more are struggling. These transitional neighborhoods still have enough of an asset base that can help them recover.

NeighborWorks Rochester recognized an opportunity to rescue these teetering neighborhoods at a critical moment.

the small lots, modest, older homes and narrow streets give the neighborhood an intimate hamlet-like atmosphere.

But until Healthy Blocks began its work there, many Swillburg houses were starting to fall into disrepair and were beginning to show signs of disinvestment, discouraging potential would-be homebuyers and renters.

Working with Swillburg residents and community stakeholders, we first conducted baseline measurements that we could use to evaluate Healthy Blocks' impact. We tracked house sales data, including asking price, sale price and days on the market. We also conducted property surveys for each house, documenting their condition. Healthy Blocks also went door-to-door with resident leaders to ask homeowners and tenants to fill out a neighborhood confidence survey.

Healthy Blocks then offered each resident a decorative house plaque with the Swillburg logo and their house number. Most of the homeowners participated, as did many of the investors, quickly giving the neighborhood a unified, connected feel. We also branded street signs and installed gateway plaques at the neighborhood's two main entryways, creating a distinctive district feel.

Healthy Blocks organized group purchases that offered homeowners and landlords contractor discounts on driveway replacements. Because NeighborWorks Rochester is a Community Development Financial Institution, we were able to offer discounted interest rates on our home repair loans if work included House Proud exterior improvements. Healthy Blocks provided Welcome Wagon folders with information on projects and services that residents could distribute to new homeowners. Residents planned and organized the building of a gazebo in Otto Henderberg Park, now a popular venue for concerts and other events. The park was named for the man who led a campaign to stop an expressway from cutting up the neighborhood. He succeeded, but not before a block of homes was demolished. Some of that land is now home to the lovely park that has become a point of pride for the revitalized neighborhood.

When Healthy Blocks began working in Swillburg in 2005, the average house was selling for about $48,000. By 2010, houses sold on average for $82,000, bringing the neighborhood's value back up to where it had been before its decline. Property condition surveys documented an increase in House Proud scores for both owners and investors between 2005 and 2010. Most notably, House Proud scores for investor-owned properties improved almost 75 percent.

Rochester has lost 122,000 residents since 1950—more than ½ its current population.

The residents' overall confidence in the neighborhood improved as well, and the Swillburg Neighborhood Association membership rose by more than 40 percent. Resident participation in neighborhood social activities was also up and the survey found that in 2010 residents had a better feeling about the direction the neighborhood was headed and felt more connected to their neighbors.

When confronting Rochester's declining neighborhoods, NeighborWorks Rochester knew that a market-driven approach to stabilize property values and improve property conditions would be essential, if any impact was going to be sustained long-term. But we also knew that to get there we needed to have engaged residents whose confidence in their neighborhood was growing, leading them to reinvest both economically and socially.

Our most effective methods included implementing a unifier project (address plaques) and organizing social events on a regular basis. As we went door-to-door conducting our resident confidence survey, we were able to inform neighbors about how to get involved with Healthy Blocks and about the programs and loans available for home repairs and the grant funds we secured for public space projects. Concerts, picnics and other social events attracted residents usually reluctant to attend neighborhood meetings, helping to create a well-organized and connected community in the process. These efforts required only modest investments, but they led to big, long-lasting results.

ABOUT MATT HJELMHAUG AND LAURA SWEAT

Matt Hjelmhaug and Laura Sweat are the Interim Co-CEO's of Upstate New York Community Partners, a new regional consolidation of four community development corporations, including the NeighborWorks organizations NeighborWorks Rochester, Niagara Falls Neighborhood Housing Services, and West Side Neighborhood Housing Services in Buffalo. The group's mission is to provide housing solutions as a foundation for individuals, families, and neighborhoods to build vibrant communities. With a consolidated staff of 38 and a budget of $3.7 million, Upstate New York Community Partners serves about 1,750 people in western New York State annually, and aims to significantly increase the number of people it serves through the partnership.

PLACE-BASED STRATEGIES TO ADDRESS MULTIPLE COMMUNITY PRIORITIES

Gail Latimore, Executive Director

Codman Square Neighborhood Development Corporation

The mission of the Codman Square Neighborhood Development Corporation in Boston is to build a better, stronger community in Codman Square and South Dorchester by creating housing and commercial spaces that are safe, sustainable and affordable. We promote financial and economic stability for residents and for the neighborhood, and provide residents of all ages with opportunities and skills to improve their lives. We partnered with three abutting sister nonprofits to develop a vision for a transit corridor where a commuter rail line crosses several Boston neighborhoods with the highest concentration of low-and moderate-income and people of color in the city.

Our organizations set transit equity goals to transform the last section of the city without access to rapid transit with four new train stations to link local residents with jobs and services. Plans call for villages around the stations to provide green, affordable transit-oriented housing and commercial development as well as a greenway along the rail line to connect neighborhoods and provide opportunities for community stewardship of vacant land that could become green spaces and add to the quality of life for local residents. The vision gave birth to OASIS on Ballou, an urban agriculture and placemaking venture that became a key initiative to address a multitude of community challenges and was supported by a group of neighborhood residents known as the Friends of Ballou.

CHALLENGE
To address a lack of green space, limited access to healthy food and a significant number of previously incarcerated men whose past reduced access to employment and kept them disenfranchised from civic life.

Healthy food access, job training and urban agriculture were familiar to our organization but none were in our toolbox.

One objective of the comprehensive community planning effort was to engage area residents to identify community assets and challenges and arrive at a "community contract" around key strategies to pursue. Codman Square and local residents developed the idea of a neighborhood meeting place where youth could build skills, residents could share food growing and preparation expertise

and children could enjoy green space. The planning process highlighted groups to include, such as formerly incarcerated males who returned to our community and were challenged to integrate into family and community and find meaningful employment.

OASIS, named by residents, stands for Opportunity Affirmation, Sustainability, Innovation and Success. Research by academic institutions helped us understand that, in addition to green space benefits, the site could address food desert conditions prevalent not only in the Woodrow Mountain neighborhood, but in a major part of our service area. OASIS is located in the middle of a "cold spot" where residents lacked access to a full-service supermarket and were disproportionately exposed to venues that made access to unhealthy or expensive foods easier than going to a supermarket.

Green space development, healthy food access, urban agriculture, job training and employment were familiar to our organization but none were part of our toolbox. Without a partner to champion these priorities, we decided to take them on ourselves after neighbor support got us designated as the OASIS developer. Our community organizers recruited local men interested in supporting other men to succeed and created Men of Color/Men of Action.

The pilot year for OASIS, funded by Codman Square, began once permits were issued for our urban agriculture project. Recognizing the challenges facing men of after incarceration, the Friends of Ballou focused the farm's skills building training and employment program on that group. Other partners supported the recruitment and placements of these men, while a partner more experienced in urban farming provided training. Local residents can purchase affordable produce through a regular farm stand staffed by volunteers and at community building events. The produce generated by OASIS is also made available through our local health center.

Two lessons we've learned through the OASIS project include: 1) the importance of flexibility and shared stewardship with the community to meet pressing needs, 2) surrounding ourselves with allies and experts as partners has helped sustain hope when things seemed overwhelming, and 3) we've seen what small victories can do to leverage additional interest and support.

About 23.5 million people live in food deserts. Nearly ½ of them are also low-income.

ABOUT GAIL LATIMORE

Gail Latimore, a veteran of nonprofit management and development with over 25 years experience working in the public or nonprofit sector, has served as the executive director of Codman Square Neighborhood Development Corp since 1998. During Latimore's tenure, the NDC has expanded its service base to meet the needs of the community. A founding Board member of the Dudley Street Neighborhood Initiative, Latimore serves on several state, regional and local boards dedicated to responsible community development, including the Massachusetts Association of Community Development Corporations and the Four Corners Action Coalition.

STRATEGICALLY REVITALIZING A DISTRESSED DETROIT NEIGHBORHOOD

Timothy S. Thorland, Executive Director

Steve Palackdharry, Director of Communications

Southwest Housing Solutions

Southwest Detroit is an area about 14 square miles, home to about 90,000 people. It is the most diverse place in Michigan: About half the residents are Latino, a third are black and a fifth are white. More than 40 ethnicities are represented in the area.

Though it's considered one of the most viable areas of the city, there are issues of poverty, blight and disinvestment. The housing stock in southwest Detroit is generally weak and much of the quality is substandard. Nearly 30 percent of the 40,000 housing units are unoccupied and more than three-quarters of all the houses were built before 1959. Poverty, neglect, and foreclosure have taken a punishing toll.

Despite these issues, the area has a rich ethnic, historical, and artistic tradition. Vernor Avenue, one of the major arteries, has been called the "city's most viable commercial street," and Mexicantown attracts a million visitors a year.

Southwest Solutions is leading a community revitalization strategy for southwest Detroit that 1) identifies and holistically addresses residents' needs; 2) concentrates development on the two major corridors of West Vernor Highway and Michigan Avenue to create neighborhood activity centers, which serve as anchors for further development; and 3) engages residents in the decision-making about their neighborhood.

CHALLENGE

Southwest Detroit, MI, is one of the city's most viable areas, but it still suffers from poverty, blight and disinvestment. The housing stock is generally weak and its quality is substandard. Nearly 30 percent of the homes are unoccupied and more than three-quarters of all the houses were built before 1959.

Southwest Solutions facilitates more than 50 programs that help about 20,000 people a year.

Southwest Solutions facilitates more than 50 programs in everything from counseling and wellness, to early childhood and education, to workforce development and homeownership. These

programs help about 20,000 people a year, the majority of whom reside in southwest Detroit.

On the community development side, our primary objectives include: affordable housing, elimination of blight conditions, preservation of historic properties, creation of attractive commercial space, and preservation of existing housing stock.

The combination of human services, community and economic development and resident engagement form the basis of our comprehensive and place-based investment strategy to help revitalize and improve the quality of life in southwest Detroit.

Since 1998, Southwest Solutions has invested more than $100 million in southwest Detroit, much of it around three nodes, or "Neighborhood Activity Centers," that are essential to the area's revitalization. Two of the centers are along West Vernor Highway – the principal artery in southwest Detroit. These centers draw businesses, service agencies, and other assets that attract residents and visitors and create a positive sense of community.

One of the Vernor Highway centers is in the Mexicantown area. Here, Southwest Solutions has rehabilitated a dozen apartment buildings that were once a blight on the area. The buildings now provide quality, affordable housing.

"I still have a hard time believing that we are here, in a place this nice, this comfortable, and this comforting," says Bertha Huanosta, a tenant in an affordable townhouse developed by Southwest Solutions. "It's really made a big difference for me and my kids. It feels like a new start in life, and I feel confident that we will make the best of it."

Southwest Solutions has also built more than 150 units of new infill housing and repurposed three buildings key to the area's resurgence: an abandoned, historic, structure known as Lithuanian Hall; the former St. Anthony's church; and an abandoned police precinct building. These buildings now house organizations that make valuable contributions to the neighborhood.

This investment helped stabilize Mexicantown and has fostered its resurgence. New businesses, restaurants and nonprofit agencies have set up shop and new residents have moved in, all of which has caused a spike in property values.

Since 1998, Southwest Solutions has invested more than $100 million in Southwest Detroit.

Southwest Solutions learned valuable lessons from these efforts:

1. Evaluating the effectiveness of our strategy is difficult because of the number of variables. The staggering poverty rate in southwest Detroit continues to increase and families that are upwardly mobile continue to leave the area, often due to issues of public safety, education, taxation and the cost of insurance in the area. These are sobering reminders that a true revitalization is still a long way away, and that the devastating effects of poverty and broken families are a profound challenge.

2. The successful rehabilitation of abandoned apartment buildings in Mexicantown has caused mixed reactions. As new residents have moved in, property values have risen, city government has begun to operate more progressively, and the concentration of these affordable apartment buildings has drawn some backlash. Some have even questioned the value and appropriateness of affordable housing in the area, citing issues caused by some of the tenants in these buildings. In fact, Southwest Solutions was forced to scale back some affordable housing projects in the area, and we have been forced to reassess how best to serve those without a voice in this community.

ABOUT TIMOTHY S. THORLAND

Timothy S. Thorland is the executive director for Southwest Housing Solutions, a nonprofit housing corporation, in Detroit. He has more than 25 years' experience in urban planning and community development. He has served 10 years on the Board of Community Development Advocates of Detroit and serves on several other local and national boards.

BUILDING COMMUNITY AND FINDING STRENGTH IN A LOW-INCOME MARKET

Pilar Hogan Closkey, Executive Director

Saint Joseph's Carpenter Society

Fair housing advocates often argue that the best way to help low-income families is to move them out of their communities. Camden, NJ, particularly East Camden, is exactly the type of area these advocates like to pull from.

Camden, once a vital hub for industry and transportation, is now one of the poorest cities in the nation. The population of 89,000 is predominantly black and Hispanic. Forty percent of Camden adults lack a high school diploma, and unemployment is twice the national average.

But Camden has a rich communal history and strong family and social institutions as well. Nevertheless, some advocates insist that the best way to help low-income families in this type of area with housing is to push for vouchers and counseling to move them to "better" neighborhoods. It is in these "better" neighborhoods – the advocates say – that affordable housing should be built.

But at what cost? This strategy can tear families away from their core social groups, while the communities they leave behind are slowly robbed of cohesion and identity.

That's why, instead of moving people away from low-income areas, organizations such as SJCS try to bring job opportunities, public transportation, recreation centers, parks, food access, education and health care to those   areas in order to revitalize them for everyone's benefit.

CHALLENGE

To help low-income families in the historic, but struggling, city of Camden, NJ thrive in place, while revitalizing the city itself.

My family and friends kept telling me to move, but I didn't want to give up on my house. Instead of my house being the ugliest one on the block, it is now the most beautiful.

— Rosa Alicea, resident

Affordable housing is an essential component. It prevents displacement of low-income families, an excellent first step in neighborhood stabilization. SJCS's approach to affordable housing is unusual: We acquire abandoned homes that are a blight on the community, rehabilitate them and then sell them to neighborhood families. In so doing, we improve the physical quality of the area, discouraging crime and vagrancy. In addition, residents become more invested in their homes and more engaged in their community.

And we've been at it quite a long time. In 1985, a real estate market did not exist in East Camden, and there were abandoned homes everywhere. SJCS began acquiring and rehabbing these houses, pairing one house at a time with a family.

Creating a sense of community around homeownership was essential as well. Future homeowners met each other at required group education classes, and rehab areas were kept to just a few blocks, which compounded the positive effects, and created a sense of pride as the neighborhood improved before their eyes.

At first, houses were rehabbed by volunteer work teams and prices were low – initial houses sold for around $20,000. Today, houses are rehabbed by professional contractors, and sell for between $70,000 and $150,000.

Over 3,200 people have completed homeowner education classes and the vast majority of buyers are neighborhood residents or have some history within the city. Eighty-five percent of the original SJCS homebuyers, or their families, still own their homes, some for nearly 30 years. And, the foreclosure rate of SJCS buyers remains at 4 percent.

"This is a blessing. I never thought it would look this nice. My family and friends kept telling me to move, but I didn't want to give up on my house," says resident Rosa Alicea, who participated in a homeowner occupied rehabilitation program. "Instead of my house being the ugliest one on the block, it is the most beautiful one. This has raised my self-esteem."

Certain target neighborhoods now boast a building vacancy rate of 3 percent, compared to an overall city rate of 15 to 20 percent. In a recent Success Measures resident survey, 75 percent of residents were somewhat satisfied, satisfied, or very satisfied living in the community. Fifty percent said the main reason to live in the neighborhood was to be near family and friends.

Some neighborhoods in Camden now boast a building vacancy rate of 3%, compared to the city rate of 15–20%.

While housing was the starting point and will continue to be pivotal in East Camden's revitalization, SJCS hopes to focus on other aspects of neighborhood health, such as local businesses, park programming, street festivals, and pop-up parks.

ABOUT PILAR HOGAN CLOSKEY

Pilar Hogan Closkey is the executive director of Saint Joseph's Carpenter Society, a neighborhood-based community housing development organization dedicated to the revitalization of Camden, NJ, and surrounding communities.

UNITING FAMILIES–EMPOWERING COMMUNITIES: BETTER FAMILY LIFE'S PLACE-BASED INITIATIVE TO STABILIZE NEIGHBORHOODS

Malik Ahmed, CEO

———

Better Family Life, Inc.

Since 1983, Better Family Life's (BFL) mission has been to provide holistic family development in St. Louis through services for economic development, children and families, housing renovation, down payment assistance, cultural arts and community engagement. Over 80 percent of our residents are barely able to make ends meet for themselves or their family and suffer from low rates of high school graduation, substance abuse, problems with the criminal justice system, long-term unemployment and blighted neighborhoods.

BFL began with robust community outreach to understand local concerns, build a sustainable rapport and identify and train resident leaders in neighborhood stabilization. Our cultural thrust promotes self-worth and cultural pride to enable residents to recognize they could be community change-agents. This strategy built a cohesive group including residents, students and seasoned community activists who mobilized to implement systemic changes. We then persuaded stable families to move from affluent suburban neighborhoods to the city's 26th Ward, which spurred housing rehabs and new construction without government assistance.

CHALLENGE

More than 80 percent of the residents in north St. Louis are barely able to make ends meet and suffer from low rates of high school graduation, substance abuse, long-term unemployment and blighted neighborhoods.

We learned that we must be led by the people whom we serve, which means having the humility to realize "we are our customers and our customers are us."

BFL's $15 million renovation of a 60,000 square foot former elementary school into a community anchor and a hub for partnerships garnered new institutional and corporate support. For example, Washington University's Brown School of Social Work and Public Health became a tenant in the facility for cross-sector research and education. The Missouri Department of Social Services opened a Family Resource Center for Temporary Assistance for Needy Families (TANF). Accenture, a multinational IT consulting corporation, supported the establishment of a call center and GED program. They are currently operating their Skills to Succeed initiatives to help our customers get access to living wage jobs.

Partnerships with the city of St. Louis and the mayor's office strengthened our public safety, health and housing programs and joint community outreach efforts with the police department. The efforts achieved a 15 percent reduction in crime in the two most crime-ridden neighborhoods of the 26th Ward.

Our housing initiatives include over $1 million to repair homes for more than 50 senior citizens, $16 million in down payment and closing cost assistance invested in the city of St. Louis and help given to 700 first-time home buyers in the area.

Eleven programs reached 6,000 high school students in 2015 to spread awareness of the dangers of sexually transmitted diseases and teen pregnancy, while simultaneously increasing class participation and graduation rates. A federal Teen Health Empowerment study, which measured the effectiveness of our approach and curriculum, found that we had the most positive results among several national organizations.

More than 600 youth were placed in summer jobs by BFL as part of Missouri's Summer Jobs League in 2015. Our Missouri Work Assistance program served 6,000 TANF families in St. Louis County from 2010 to 2015 and our training and placement assistance helped 3,900 adults gain full-time employment. Our in-house training program, a partnership with the Daruby Nursing School, is highly successful with 114 out of 175 students trained as Certified Nurse Assistants and 22 out of 25 trained as Certified Medicine Technicians fully employed in their field.

In 2015, more than 600 youth were placed in summer jobs by Better Family Life.

Our Neighborhood Resource Center in Ferguson assisted 5,000 adults and children meet basic needs and become a positive force for civic engagement. A mural at our facility, the largest in Missouri depicting the cultural heritage of people of the Afrikan Diaspora, is anticipated to attract academics, artists and tourists.

We learned that we must be led by the people whom we serve, which means having the humility to realize "we are our customers and our customers are us." Residents of disinvested communities must receive holistic social services, workforce opportunities, affordable housing and commercial development. This requires pragmatic community leadership with the ability to shift the attention of stakeholders to the critical need to rebuild the inner-city and support under-served communities.

ABOUT MALIK AHMED

Malik Ahmed is founder and CEO of Better Family Life, Inc., a community development corporation established in 1983. As a Peace Corps volunteer in the 1970s, Ahmed spent three years in Mali developing a cost-effective sanitation program for the capital city of Bamako. He has received numerous national and international awards and serves on the NeighborWorks Strategic Planning Committee, the St Louis County Workforce Investment Board and the St. Louis Regional Chamber of Commerce.

REDEFINING A NEIGHBORHOOD THROUGH PLACE-BASED INITIATIVES

Kerry P. Quaglia, Executive Director

Home HeadQuarters

In Syracuse, NY, the SALT District is located in the Near Westside neighborhood, adjacent to the western edge of the city's downtown urban core. Although this neighborhood appears geographically central, it is separated by a six-lane highway on the eastern edge and an old railroad embankment on the northern border. Where once booming industries employed workers from this neighborhood, old abandoned warehouses line the gateway to the area. During the 1930's, the neighborhood was redlined, making it impossible for mortgages to be backed and stalling any additional investment in the neighborhood. For more than 80 years, the SALT District and the larger Near Westside neighborhood have suffered from severe disinvestment.

The SALT District is one of the city's most culturally diverse and economically distressed neighborhoods. According to the American Community Survey data, of the 1,887 residents, 37 percent are black, 39.9 percent are white and 44.9 percent are Hispanic. One-third of the population over the age of five speaks Spanish as their primary language. This is significant in because Hispanics make up only 8 percent of the city's total population. The median household income in the SALT District is $12,799 and the neighborhood's poverty rate is an alarming 65 percent, nearly double that of the city's rate.

The lack of wealth can be seen in the neighborhood's deteriorating housing stock where 12.8 percent of the housing units stand vacant. The latest Census data highlighted the

CHALLENGE

Nearly a century of regrettable public policies, including large-scale urban renewal highways that cut through urban centers, have impoverished the SALT District of Syracuse, NY. The area suffers from a transient residential population, high crime rates and entrenched poverty.

This project is centered on the idea that for it to thrive, an area of concentrated poverty has to transform to a neighborhood where families of a range of incomes are willing to live.

neighborhood's owner-occupancy rate at only 10.3 percent. Even with significant financial and human capital invested from Home HeadQuarters (HHQ) through real estate development subsidies, com-

mercial, first mortgage and home improvement financing and asset based planning activities and from their partners including, Syracuse University, the Near Westside Initiative and the Syracuse Center of Excellence in Energy and Environmental Systems (Syracuse CoE) residents continue to lag behind other parts of the city in economic prosperity and affordable housing opportunities.

Despite all of its challenges, the neighborhood has several key assets that are encouraging and spurring renewal and growth. The housing ranges from smaller one-story cottages, to large Italianate style buildings, to structures that offer mixed-use opportunities. The large number of vacant lots creates opportunities for new construction, increased yard space for existing residents, and/or off street parking. The Syracuse Housing Authority has an apartment complex with approximately 469 rental units. Small neighborhood businesses offer experiences and products that highlight the cultural roots of people who live in the area.

HHQ's project is part of a comprehensive neighborhood plan centered on the idea that for it to thrive, an area of concentrated poverty has to transform to a neighborhood where families across a range of incomes are willing to live. The project will bring two market rate units and two rentals at fair market plus six additional affordable single-family homes. This infusion of new residents from across the income spectrum will help de-concentrate the poverty in this area. The project is also designed to provide sustainable energy and other commercial services to improve the marketability and long-term health of the neighborhood.

In 2016, with their partners – Syracuse CoE and the Near Westside Initiative – HHQ will undertake its "resilient corners" project where they will build a geothermal district that will service eight new LEED rated single-family homes and a "green" community laundry facility that will use solar to heat the water. It will also build two new LEED rated single-family "Live-Work" homes and undertake the substantial rehab of a commercial building where they have two commercial units and two rental units. The goal is to create a mix of homeownership and rental opportunities that will attract diverse residents to the SALT District.

12.8% of housing units in the SALT district stand vacant.

This project will lead to immediate and long-lasting reductions in greenhouse gas emissions through the redevelopment of underutilized and vacant properties of three street corners in the SALT District. It relies on sustainable building practices already implemented in the neighborhood and uses smart planning principles including infill re-development, diversity of land use and proximity to employment, community assets and public transportation. It also encourages sustainable housing development including LEED housing design, the installation of green construction principles and green infrastructure improvements.

The SALT District is greener now than it was just five years ago, thanks in large part to the efforts of HHQ and their partners: the Near Westside Initiative, Syracuse University, the Syracuse Center of Excellence in Energy and Environmental Systems (Syracuse CoE), and the cooperation of neighborhood residents.

These community engagement efforts have created a vibrant road map for redevelopment and success in this neighborhood in particular.

This project illustrates the following lessons: 1) collaboration with many partners with different strengths and resources is key to the success of a project, 2) sustainable and green building practices greatly add to the quality of the development and the health and well-being of the neighborhood, and 3) bringing in new residents with a range of income helps to revitalize the neighborhood, which in turn increases its marketability.

ABOUT KERRY P. QUAGLIA

Kerry P. Quaglia serves as the executive director of Home HeadQuarters, a non-profit Community Housing Development Organization and certified Community Development Financial Institution whose mission is to create housing and related opportunities and services in central and upstate New York and to improve the lives of underserved people and revitalize the communities in which they live. HHQ has a staff of over 30 and a program budget of $11 million. In 2015, HHQ served nearly 2,500 people through education and counseling services throughout the region, provided $10.5 million in first mortgages, commercial investments, down payments and home improvement financing. It rehabilitated or built new 31 properties and demolished 70 vacant structures in the city of Syracuse.

A HOUSE BY HOUSE APPROACH TO REVITALIZATION

Bruce Luecke, President & CEO

Homeport

In the 1930s and '40s, the King Lincoln District in Columbus was a thriving African-American community with daily parades, bustling theatres and night clubs where the nation's top jazz entertainers, such as Miles Davis and Art Blakey, regularly performed. It was a thriving, self-sufficient neighborhood; everything needed was within walking distance, including grocery stores, doctor's offices, hospitals and schools.

Then, in the early '60s a highway development cut through the District and, as local businesses declined, residents began to leave the area. Homes and businesses were boarded up and crime rates soared. The once vibrant community became a place riddled with poverty, unemployment, and empty buildings.

King Lincoln District is the site of Poindexter Village, one of the nation's first public housing projects dedicated by President Roosevelt in 1940. In the late 1970s, President Carter later came to proclaim a revival of the area through new housing and stores, but the restoration was unsuccessful.

The key to successfully improving the area would be patience, a methodical approach and several partnerships. When interviewed about the neighborhood, former Mayor of Columbus Michael B. Coleman said, "The way to deal with bringing back a neighborhood is holistically. It's not a project. It's twenty projects. It's making an entire holistic effort of housing, commercial, entertainment, office, the works."

CHALLENGE

When a highway development cut through the King Lincoln District in Columbus, OH, residents of the formerly vibrant and culturally rich neighborhood were forced to leave the area for their needs and entertainment. Crime and poverty increased in the neglected community. An innovative approach was needed to revitalize the neighborhood.

The way to deal with bringing back a neighborhood is holistically. It's not a project. It's twenty projects.

— Michael B. Coleman, former Columbus mayor

The City of Columbus dedicated millions of dollars to reviving this historic area with a variety of improvements. City officials asked Homeport to handle improving housing in the area. Located in central Ohio, Homeport has been building vibrant communities and revitalizing neighborhoods since 1987. Homeport's place-based strategy for the neighborhood's development was to create a concentrated and critical mass of homeownership by stabilizing small portions of the neighborhood, block by block. We also began supporting the broader neighborhood through community

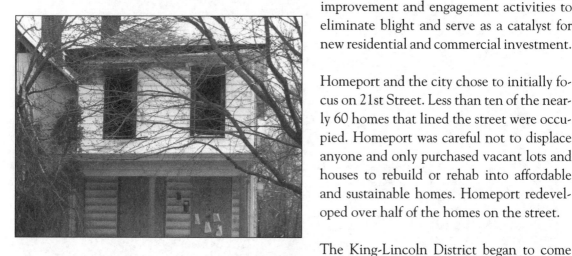

improvement and engagement activities to eliminate blight and serve as a catalyst for new residential and commercial investment.

Homeport and the city chose to initially focus on 21st Street. Less than ten of the nearly 60 homes that lined the street were occupied. Homeport was careful not to displace anyone and only purchased vacant lots and houses to rebuild or rehab into affordable and sustainable homes. Homeport redeveloped over half of the homes on the street.

The King-Lincoln District began to come alive again with city investments to attract businesses and revive local theatres and the construction of a new bridge connecting the neighborhood with downtown Columbus. Instead of just being a neighborhood that people drove through to get to other places, people began to move back into the area. As Homeport continued its work, private developers began investing in homes on other streets. Once a base of new homes and engaged residents was established on 21st Street, Homeport expanded the project to 20th and 22nd Streets. By concentrating block by block, then street by street, we began to revitalize the neighborhood.

From 2004 to 2015, Homeport had an impact on more than 100 homes through new construction, renovations, owner-occupied home repairs and community improvement projects, which includes building 69 new homes and condominiums and 30 repair projects on owner-occupied homes. We coordinated 15,000 hours of volunteer service in the neighborhood.

Homeport intentionally worked with partners to re-establish a mixed-income neighborhood that would continue to be affordable for existing residents. As the revitalization continued, buyers from throughout central Ohio began to identify "North of Broad" as a neighborhood of choice. Interest in its homes came from buyers at every income level, an indicator of the success of Homeport's revitalization efforts.

The Lincoln Theater, formerly known as Ogden Theatre and Ballroom, opened in 1928.

Homeport homeowners range from young professionals to retirees, mirroring the King Lincoln District's historic diversity. One homeowner was so impressed with the quality of his home and the values of the neighborhood, that prior to even closing on his home he began to encourage his mother to buy a Homeport home, which she did the following year.

The District may not return to being the same neighborhood it once was, but it is once again becoming a place to live, shop and work. While there are still more homes and streets to revitalize, people are moving back to the King-Lincoln District for the first time in decades. Businesses are beginning to develop and succeed. And the Lincoln Theatre, one of the main attractions when the District was in its prime, has been restored and now regularly hosts performances. The District has been transformed into a new neighborhood without losing the cultural richness of its original days.

The Homeport effort illustrates the following lessons learned: 1) successful revitalization takes a concentrated, place-based approach, 2) rather than focus on large projects, moving house-by-house, street-by-street, leads to a slow but steady rebuilding of a neighborhood, 3) by creating mixed-income housing, the neighborhood can be an affordable place for the original residents and welcome in needed new residents.

ABOUT BRUCE LUECKE

Bruce Luecke serves as the president and CEO of Homeport, a non-profit housing development organization whose mission is to create and preserve healthy, stable and affordable communities. Homeport, located in Columbus, OH, serves families, individuals and seniors through affordable rental communities, financial and homebuyer education and community revitalization. Luecke previously served on Homeport's board of directors for seven years, including two terms as the board chair, before becoming the interim president and CEO of Homeport in January 2016.

HISTORIC FACTORY MAKEOVER GIVES ARTISTS AND THE COMMUNITY A PLACE TO CREATE

Kevin O'Connor, CEO

RUPCO

The U.S. Lace Curtain Mill was once a robust job creator. The enormous factory produced Nottingham lace and was a vital hub for those who worked there and lived in the community. On average, 250 people – mostly women – worked the looms from 1903 to 1951, when the mill ceased operating. The building changed hands, warehouse boxes replacing the Jacquard sewing machines, and then it was abandoned. The crumbling, 70,000-square-foot building was shuttered, creating a major eyesore in the Midtown Arts District's west end for over 20 years.

RUPCO, a nonprofit promoting housing and community development in the Hudson Valley, specializes in housing for seniors, people with disabilities, working families and artists. We saw the defunct factory as the perfect opportunity to advance our mission. Bloomberg Businessweek had recognized Kingston in its Top 10 Cities for Artists in 2007. Six years later, Kingston launched its Business, Education, Arts and Technology initiative, designating a Midtown Arts District and appointing a council of artists, business owners and entrepreneurs. A quick survey revealed a strong presence of arts-related activity upon which the city could build. And so would RUPCO.

In 2013, RUPCO took over the Lace Mill and began working with 18 public and private funding partners to preserve the historic landmark recognized on both the

CHALLENGE

For decades, a boarded-up factory created an eyesore in Kingston, NY. It was considered a major blight to the area, where most of the old homes were falling into disrepair. The neighborhood, where a quarter of the residents are black or Latino, needed a boost to promote stability and economic opportunities.

The Lace Mill eliminates blight, establishes a thriving arts community and creates affordable housing.

New York State and federal registers. With the help of a local architectural firm RUPCO crafted an adaptive reuse plan with a $19 million budget.

The renovation plan was modeled on an emerging movement known as "creative placemaking," which is defined as the strengthening of the social, physical and economic fabric of a community through arts and culture. The repurposed building with 55 residential units would integrate afford-able housing – giving artists first dibs – with strict historic preservation standards and state-of-the art energy efficiency and building science. The plan won the blessing of the newly formed Kings-ton Midtown Arts council, the city government and the burgeoning arts community.

Today, the Lace Mill eliminates blight, establish-es a thriving arts community, creates affordable housing, and ultimately blends building science, energy efficiency and historic preservation to en-hance the district. The new residents brought di-versity, instant community and a local economy boost to an area poised for growth.

And the new space is beautiful. The dynam-ic loft-style living quarters feature soaring ceilings, stunning raw building elements including wood, concrete and steel, and huge windows to allow great lighting for the resident artists. An 8000-square-foot gallery provides a welcoming, airy space for exhibitions and community events. The Lace Mill also hosts BEAHIVE, a technical-marketing-entrepreneurial co-working space, and a monthly wellness clinic for Healthcare is a Human Right nonprofit. It also hosts Sunday afternoon music jams and collaborates on community projects like Made in Kingston, an artists' holiday showcase.

Energy efficiency and environmental sustainability were top priorities for this repurposing project. But equipping the Lace Mill with the best energy-efficient measures possible, while observing his-toric preservation mandates, posed high hurdles. RUPCO hired building science expert, Integral Building and Design, to assess the challenges posed by the early 20th-century brick-and-mortar factory and was ultimately able to implement many energy efficiency benefits.

To offset the building's common area electricity consumption, RUPCO installed Kingston's largest rooftop solar array. The mill's exterior brick walls were sealed to prevent energy loss and special insulation curbs moisture problems. Energy efficient LED lighting now illuminates 99 percent of the mill, and Energy Star windows replace the historic exterior windows to allow natural light inside. An HVAC system equipped with a 70-unit water-source water loop heat pump charges the boiler and cooling systems. Each apartment has heat recovery ventilation for 65 percent more efficiency, as well as EnergyStar appliances, premium water pumps, and electric storage water heaters.

About 650 textile plants closed between 1997– 2009.

Rubi Rose, a photographer, documentarian and visual artist, says moving into her Lace Mill apartment was life changing.

"I lived in a cramped apartment with low ceilings. The views were uninspiring and the windows did not let in much light. My creative energy did not flow easily. I had no room to spread out, which is crucial for working on any kind of creative project. I had little to no contact with my neighbors and often felt lonely," says Rose, adding that her appliances were energy hogs and her landlord negligent.

Now Rose's Lace Mill apartment is almost twice the size of her old one, her appliances are energy efficient and her geothermal system increases her comfort and lowers her electric bills. The lofty space and abundant natural light has also increased her productivity – and her earnings.

RUPCO learned three critical lessons in developing the Lace Mill. First, renovating vacant industrial spaces comes with surprises. Aging building quirks, federal requirements and energy standards may be high hurdles, but with the right assistance and determination they can be overcome. Also, creative placemaking is achievable with early and consistent community engagement. RUPCO involved the arts community from the ground up, receiving initial input on design and amenities.

ABOUT KEVIN O'CONNOR
Kevin O'Connor is the executive director and CEO of RUPCO, which has a staff of 61 and an annual operating budget over $6 million. RUPCO, a comprehensive housing and community development service in the Hudson Valley region, has over $15 million of real estate development and five business lines: real estate development, property management, rental assistance, community development and a NeighborWorks HomeOwnership Center. RUPCO provides nearly 2,000 units of rental assistance in Ulster and Greene Counties and owns/manages 411 affordable housing units.

THE MIDTOWN RENAISSANCE: AFTER THE HOUSING CRASH, A NEIGHBORHOOD REFORMED

Lori Hudson Flanery, President & CEO

Lisa D. Thompson
Executive Vice President and Chief Strategy Officer

New Directions Housing Corp.

This is the story of a tipping point – one that tipped in the right direction after a crisis. New Albany, Indiana, is only 10 minutes away from the metropolis of Louisville, and the local park is recognized as a gem. It also is treasured for its historic architecture. Although the city's fortunes first began to decline in the 20th century, officials resisted the "urban renewal" craze, preserving downtown buildings.

And then came the housing crisis. By Sept. 30, 2010, the average sales price for a house had dropped to $37,000 and the rate of owner occupancy had dropped to 40 percent. New Albany had reached a crossroad – either suffer continuing disinvestment or fight back and reverse the slide. The community chose the latter.

The first accomplishment came when the city secured one of the states' largest Neighborhood Stabilization Program grants, injecting $6.7 million of stimulus funding into Midtown. New Directions Housing Corp. was tapped to lead implementation of the Midtown Renaissance project.

However, it was good news/bad news at the time. We were awarded the grant, but by the time we got it, the deadline was just six months away. Within that timeframe, we had to identify and acquire properties and sign a contract for

CHALLENGE

The Great Recession and foreclosure crisis hit New Albany's Midtown hard, emptying 15 percent of the 900 homes in this Hoosier neighborhood. With too many highly leveraged landlords, Midtown felt the full impact when the housing bubble burst.

New Albany had reached a crossroad. Should it continue to suffer gradual disinvestment, or fight to hold onto and increase its share of residents ready to invest energy, capital and hope?

completion of the required renovations. So, we created a "bidder's list." As soon as we bought a property we'd fire off an RFP to the list. It was a struggle, but by the time the deadline arrived, New Directions had acquired 31 single-family homes and the Cardinal Ritter Birthplace. The latter will serve as a museum honoring Cardinal Joseph Elmer Ritter, a Catholic clergyman who desegregated the Saint Louis Archdiocesan schools during the late 1940s. The Cardinal Ritter Birthplace Foundation is working in partnership with New Directions to complete this project and will administer the facility–including a new community center – in the back of the museum.

Guided by a "healthy neighborhood" approach to revitalization, New Directions worked with residents to rebrand the neighborhood to attract investments by homebuyers and businesses. It did this in part by placing "coming soon' signs on each of the 31 properties targeted by New Directions for redevelopment and resale, while preserving the neighborhood's historic character. The cheery signs signaled to existing homeowners that their stake in their neighborhood was being "doubled down." It was so successful it won a coveted Rosemary Prentice Award from Indiana Landmarks.

Financial assistance to accelerate construction was secured from Fifth Third Bank. The institution became the project's lead bank – providing more than half of the mortgage lending needed by homebuyers. Other local institutions soon followed suit.

Overall, we turned around 31 highly blighted sites, built and sold 35 homes, developed a neighborhood center and community garden, and repaired or rehabilitated 46 homes, helping existing owners remain in the neighborhood they love. Other investors are now following the pace set by New Directions' lead in Midtown.

Vacancy is unusual now, and stakeholders are part of something special – a strong neighborhood.

One such stakeholder is Rebecca Futter. She grew up in New Albany. Creative and energetic, Rebecca didn't think homeownership was possible for her, until the Midtown Renaissance project.

"This program was a good opportunity for someone who is financially responsible, but who isn't making insane amounts of money, to actually own a home," she told us.

Rebecca's historic home is a restored American four-square overlooking the S. Ellen Jones Elementary School and Ritter Park. New Directions intentionally redeveloped 11 properties that border the park, which has become the heart of the neighborhood.

The Midtown Renaissance is well underway. Visit some time and enjoy a local wine or beer, walk the quiet streets and think about owning a home or business on what New Albanians call "The Sunny Side of Louisville."

New Directions tackled 31 highly blighted sites, built and sold 35 homes and repaired or rehabbed 46 homes.

ABOUT LORI HUDSON FLANERY

Lori Hudson Flanery is president and CEO of New Directions Housing Corporation, a 501(c)(3) provider of low-income and affordable housing, resident services, and sponsor of an owner-occupied rehab program known as Repair Affair. New Directions acquires, rehabs, and builds new single-family homes for sale to persons of low- to moderate-income. In operation for nearly a half-century, New Directions prides itself on a focus on neighborhood revitalization and community building, in addition to providing housing for more than 1,000 families in the Louisville, KY MSA. Lori comes to New Directions after a 25+ year career in public service with Kentucky State Government and with the quasi-governmental Kentucky Housing Corporation, which she served as Deputy Director and General Counsel. Lori served most recently as Secretary of Finance for the Commonwealth of Kentucky. She has assumed overall responsibility for an organization of more than 70 employees and an annual budget of over $11 million.

QUIRKY KENSINGTON LOOKS TO THE PAST TO REVITALIZE THE FUTURE

Sandy Salzman, Executive Director

New Kensington Community Development Corp.

In the 1950's Philadelphia residents began heading to the suburbs en masse, marking the start of the city's lengthy economic decline. By 1995, the city's Kensington-Fishtown area had lost about half of its peak population and was saddled with 1,100 vacant lots and hundreds of vacant buildings. Neighborhood blight eroded residents' quality of life, created an erosion of social cohesion and led to a loss in active civic engagement.

Since its founding in 1985, New Kensington Community Development Corp. (NKCDC) has approached neighborhood revitalization through real estate development, community engagement, housing counseling, vacant land management, neighborhood planning and economic development. NKCDC's mission is to strengthen the area's physical, social and economic fabric by being a catalyst for sustainable development and community building. Located in the Kensington neighborhood of Philadelphia, NKCDC draws on the strengths of the community to empower residents and promote resident-driven development.

Kensington has a long history as the working-class center of industry and production. The neighborhood's early workers consisted of ship builders and fish traders along the Delaware River. Later, workers from textile and weaving factories moved in.

Decades of urban decline and deindustrialization had a deleterious effect on Kensington, however, presenting NKC-

CHALLENGE
Philadelphia began a lengthy economic decline in the 1950's as residents left en masse for the suburbs. By 1995, the city's Kensington-Fishtown area had lost about half of its peak population and was saddled with 1,100 vacant lots and hundreds of vacant buildings.

Studies by researchers at the Harvard School of Public Health found that violent crime rates were significantly lower in neighborhoods where residents reported that they knew and trusted their neighbors.

DC with numerous challenges when the organization began its neighborhood redevelopment work.

Initially, NKCDC focused on rehabilitating vacant homes and providing housing counseling services to low- and moderate-income families. With neighborhood input, NKCDC over time expanded  its focus on larger quality of life issues in the neighborhood. The agency's priority became rebuilding Kensington's social cohesion, with an emphasis on arts and community. Studies by researchers at the Harvard School of Public Health found that violent crime rates were significantly lower in neighborhoods where residents reported that they knew and trusted their neighbors, and felt that neighbors were able to work together to solve problems.

Promoting the artist community and sustainability efforts are important neighborhood revitalization strategies for NKCDC, with evidence that they help encourage people to move in and invest in the neighborhood, improve neighborhood health and safety and put money in residents' pockets.

The Kensington name has been reappropriated through a number of economic development and arts initiatives led by NKCDC to support Frankford Avenue and its burgeoning arts corridor. Vacant lots have been turned into gardens and green space, homes are being built and repaired, the neighborhood's high school system has been reinvented and reformed and new residents and businesses – including a rapidly growing arts community – are moving in.

One of NKCDC's more successful arts integration projects began nearly a decade ago, as the community longed for a fun expression of local artistry and a resident-driven celebration.

Former staff member, Kathryn Doherty-Chapman, was an avid bicyclist who worked with local artists in her role as economic development assistant. She was familiar with "derby" events, and realized the opportunity to have one right in our neighborhood, with participation from bicyclists, welders and artists. Thus, the Kensington Kinetic Sculpture Derby was born. Part design competition, part parade of human-powered vehicle floats, the derby started in 2007 as an economic development initiative of NKC-DC to reintroduce the neighborhood to the larger region through an entertaining event highlighting the talents of local artists. From the derby's success, NKCDC has learned not to underestimate seemingly wacky ideas by staff members.

Another lesson the agency learned was to think big and start small. Initially, NKCDC wanted the derby to be a way to showcase local arts and creativity with a neighborhood celebration – and drew 500 attendees. As time went on, the agency recognized the derby's potential as a tool for business attraction, and encouraged private investment and commercial activity during the event, which now draws over 15,000 people into the neighborhood each year.

KENSINGTON KINETIC SCULPTURE DERBY

"Best Public Event"
– Star Newspapers
"Best Festival"
– Philadelphia Magazine

There are a lot of moving parts to this all-day event, such as organizing derby workshops, throwing happy hours with local businesses, and getting permits to close the streets for the day. Neighbors who participate in the event work together to develop creative ideas, and in doing so, strengthen Kensington's spirit of community. NKCDC has collaborated with the East Kensington Neighborhood Association's Trenton Avenue Arts Festival, which takes place concurrently with the derby. The festival highlights the artist community by lining the streets with local art vendors.

A true sense of community is put on display during Kensington's derby and art festival, which has gained notoriety and served as a place-making tool for the community. With over 52 zip codes represented, a large percentage of attendees come from outside the neighborhood and are seeing first-hand what strong community groups and local artists are capable of putting together. Kensington's homegrown celebration is now famous citywide; the derby was named "Best Public Event" by Star Newspapers and "Best Festival" by Philadelphia Magazine.

ABOUT SANDY SALZMAN

Sandy Salzman is a lifelong resident of Fishtown and is the executive director of New Kensington Community Development Corporation (NKCDC) in Philadelphia. She became active in civic affairs 20 years ago as a volunteer for the Fishtown Civic Association and soon thereafter became Director. At NKCDC, Salzman's work has garnered national awards from the U.S. Department of Housing and Urban Development, the National Neighborhood Coalition and the Enterprise Foundation.

A NEW FINANCING TOOL FOR AFFORDABLE HOUSING AND ECONOMIC DEVELOPMENT

Christopher Kui, Executive Director

Asian Americans for Equality

Low-income housing tax credits, referred to as LIHTCs, have been the primary financing tool for the development of affordable housing over 30 years. Demand for tax credits outweighs their availability and creates competition, while politics and federal priorities have made their future uncertain. In response, community development corporations (CDCs) have turned to creative financing alternatives to fill budget gaps.

Asian Americans for Equality (AAFE) developed the first LIHTC project in New York City with Enterprise Community Partners in the early 1990s. Like other community development corporations, the organization relied on the city's process of disposing of city-owned properties to developers who would build low-income housing and keep rents affordable as a result of the "free" land awarded to them, often for as little as $1. With no real acquisition costs, sponsors could make the projects work financially and offer deeply skewed rents with maximum affordability.

As the supply of city-owned property diminished and construction and land acquisition costs rose, AAFE thought creatively about how to finance affordable housing projects and large-scale community development initiatives. Simultaneously, the City of New York introduced an ambitious 10-year housing plan to create or preserve up to 200,000 units of affordable housing, emphasizing rezoning neighborhoods to allow for mandatory inclusionary

CHALLENGE

For more than 30 years, low-income builders have used housing tax credits as the primary financing tool for creating affordable housing. But demand for tax credits outweighs their availability and creates competition, while federal budget constraints have made their future uncertain.

As the supply of city-owned property diminished and construction and land acquisition costs rose, the organization thought creatively about how to finance affordable housing projects.

housing rather than conveying "free" land to build affordable housing. Our challenge was greater than anticipated: to fill funding gaps in our development projects to support market-rate land acquisition costs while keeping rents low.

The executive team and our small business lending arm, Renaissance Economic Development Corp., a community development financial institution, explored the EB-5 Immigrant Investor Program to finance our projects and fill our capital funding gaps through foreign private equity, while simultaneously creating permanent jobs. Job creation is a mutual goal for AAFE and the United

States Citizenship and Immigration Services, which created the EB-5 program in 1990 to stimulate the economy through capital investment by foreign investors. Under the program, foreign entrepreneurs and their families are eligible to apply for a U.S. Green Card if they invest in a commercial enterprise in the U.S. (at least $1,000,000 or $500,000 if in a targeted employment area) and create or preserve 10 permanent full-time jobs. In 1992, Congress enacted the Immigrant Investor Program, also known as the Regional Center Program, which sets aside EB-5 visas for participants who invest in commercial enterprises based on project proposals that promote economic growth and are associated with approved regional centers.

While the EB-5 program is primarily used by for-profit, private developers and municipalities to develop hotels, commercial buildings or stadiums, we explored using EB-5 to develop affordable housing and mixed-use developments that create low-income rental housing and permanent jobs. After researching other EB-5 regional centers nationally, we realized the program's potential for not-for-profit, CDC-led projects that need gap financing. Since the primary objective of EB-5 investors is to obtain a Green Card, returns on their equity investment are lower than other investment vehicles. The result is that interest rates on EB-5 loan funds are typically below market, making them attractive to not-for-profit developers.

In early 2016, with support from the Surdna and Garfield foundations, AAFE established its first EB-5 regional center in Flushing, Queens, known as the New York Renaissance Regional Center. The regional center introduces a new financing option for not-for-profit development by attracting foreign investment into mixed-use projects that promote affordable housing and community economic development. Our organization acts as an intermediary by vetting foreign investors and ensuring compliance with regulations and seeks to attract investments for our projects as well as citywide not-for-profits seeking below-market gap financing. Our EB-5 team has met with Chinese and other foreign investors willing to invest in projects that, from their perspective, carry less risk of non-completion due to their public purpose objective and often present government collaboration and/or partnership. Also, since many CDC projects are developed in low-income communities, they usually qualify for the lower-threshold targeted employment area investment amount of just $500,000, which also makes it attractive for a broader group of foreign investors.

The Renaissance Economic Development Corp. provided $28.5 million in affordable loans to 750 small businesses.

While the EB-5 program has met with its share of challenges due to interpretations around the targeted employment area boundaries or stalled capital projects, Congress extended the program until September 30, 2016 to develop reforms to benefit investors and developers. EB-5 financing is an alternative solution for financing our collective mission-driven work.

The EB-5 project illustrates several important lessons: 1) CDCs benefit from exploring new sources of financing for projects, 2) understanding regulations and opportunities can lead to partnerships that benefit the mission of nonprofit organizations, and 3) the missions of job creation and affordable housing can be compatible with investor interests.

ABOUT CHRISTOPHER KUI

Christopher Kui serves as executive director of Asian Americans for Equality (AAFE). AAFE was founded in 1974 to advocate for equal employment and has leveraged over $100 million in public and private funds to build and renovate over 800 units of affordable housing in addition to providing and leveraging over $244 million in mortgage financing for over 1,700 clients through its Community Development Fund. AAFE's Renaissance EDC has also disbursed $42 million in loans to over 1,200 projects and small businesses, creating and retaining nearly 5,000 jobs.

PARK FALLS, WISCONSIN: A CHRONICLE OF NORTHWOODS SURVIVAL

Brett Gerber, President and CEO

Impact Seven

Impact Seven, Inc. was founded in 1970 by residents from seven Wisconsin counties who were concerned with a waning economy, outmigration of youth, and high poverty. Over the past 45 years, Impact Seven has directly created or preserved dignified housing for tens of thousands of low-income households and generated thousands of jobs by supporting businesses ranging from microenterprises to major local employers. Today, Impact Seven builds capacity in communities across the entire state with integrated services and development in small business lending, affordable housing, and property management.

Impact Seven's business development programs provide flexible, affordable financing capital for expanding businesses. This was especially important during the 1990's after a series of disastrous layoffs at the local paper mill in Park Falls. In 1999, Impact Seven secured a $500,000 Community Economic Development grant from the U.S. Department of Health and Human Services Office of Community Services for the Forest Region Renaissance Initiative, which leveraged $10.5 million and supported the development of an 18-acre industrial park. Impact Seven also assisted in setting up a Tax Increment Finance district which was later instrumental in supporting the ongoing financing needs of the mill and of other area employers.

In 2006, despite best efforts to save it, the Flambeau Paper Company declared bankruptcy and closed the 100-year-old mill. Braced for disaster, state and local agencies began delivering relocation, education and mental health

CHALLENGE

For rural communities, economic decline is usually a one-way trip. As major employers disappear, so do other businesses. Housing and public services decline and young people move away for jobs. After decades of decline, a mill in Park Falls, WI, threatened to close leading to the loss of hundreds of jobs.

Altogether, Impact Seven investments directly contributed to the creation or retention of more than 100 permanent jobs in addition to mill-related jobs.

services for hundreds of displaced workers and their families. But just five months later, through the efforts of state government and private investors, the mill was saved and re-opened under the new name of Flambeau River Papers. Under new ownership, the mill hired back most of the workers with their same living wages and benefits.

However, the facility still needed upgrades to be competitive and compliant with federal regulations. In 2009, Impact Seven provided key financial support for a $2.3 million replacement of the 93-year-  old rock towers which blend water and gases into the acids that reduce wood fiber to paper pulp. Then in 2012, Impact Seven financed the acquisition of a warehouse complex to use for mill operations, and in 2014, it provided a $1.5 million loan funded from New Markets Tax Credits for boiler upgrades needed to meet EPA pollution requirements.

In an increasingly digital society, the paper industry's future is uncertain. For this reason, Impact Seven helped to diversify the Park Falls economy. They mobilized Economic Development Administration and Community Development Block Grant funds to construct speculative buildings that were later occupied by a major local employer, Weather Shield Manufacturing. Other businesses came into the area, including a manufacturer of custom racing products, a sporting goods store, and a metal manufacturer.

In 2010, Impact Seven was awarded another Office of Community Services - Community Economic Development grant to support the ambitious $270 million Flambeau River Biofuels project, an industrial facility to convert wood waste products into energy and create hundreds of jobs. Although changes in the energy market made this infeasible, the funds were used to set up a revolving loan fund for Park Falls businesses, including a $345,000 loan in 2015 to All Stone Solutions LLC, a startup producer of specialty locally-quarried stone. With no bank willing to make the loan, Impact Seven's financing package was critical for equipment purchases, building improvements, and to meet working capital needs.

Altogether, Impact Seven investments directly contributed to the creation or retention of more than

100 permanent jobs in addition to mill-related jobs, rounding out the Park Falls' employment base.

Small business lending is only one facet of Impact Seven's mission. In Park Falls, Impact Seven has developed and now owns and manages 54 units of safe, healthy, affordable multifamily housing for low-income families and seniors. This includes three 10-unit rent subsidized properties for low-income seniors.

In 2009, Impact Seven opened Lincoln School Apartments, a new 24-unit affordable family housing project. Developed in partnership with housing developer MetroPlains, LLC, this beautiful restoration and adaptive reuse of a vacant 1916 landmark used Low-Income Housing Tax Credit, HOME, and Affordable Housing Programs funds from Federal Home Loan Bank-Chicago. With 10 units set aside for incomes below 50 percent average minimum income and an additional 14 units for 60 percent average minimum income, the project preserved an important element of the community's historic fabric.

> **Wisconsin's paper industry employs more than 30,000 people, making the state the #1 paper producer in the nation.**

Over the decades, Impact Seven teamed up with many federal, state and local partners to build local capacity, leverage public and private resources, and to provide flexible, affordable financing to help the mill and many other small businesses grow and thrive. At times Impact Seven serves a leadership role, but usually a supporting role is also needed to provide just the right puzzle pieces. For its sustained work in Park Falls, Impact Seven and Johnson Bank were jointly recognized in 2009 with the first annual FHLB-Chicago Community First Partnership Award recognizing outstanding, ongoing partnerships that result in sustainable contributions to a community's quality of life.

Impact Seven's three-decade relationship with Park Falls illustrates important lessons: 1) successful community development requires sustained partnerships and long-term commitment, 2) a city's economic health depends on a multifaceted approach and diversified economic development, and 3) flexible, affordable financing capital is essential for expanding businesses.

ABOUT BRETT GERBER

As Impact Seven's president and CEO since 2011, Brett Gerber leads one of the state's largest community development financial institutions and nonprofit developers/managers of affordable housing. Impact Seven has overall responsibility for a $48 million loan portfolio and 1,500 units of affordable multifamily housing. Prior to Impact Seven, Gerber served as CEO of Indianhead Community Action Agency in Ladysmith, WI, and as the director of business services for Medford Area Public Schools. Gerber's leadership is grounded in strategic management, strong financial acuity, and responsible stewardship of resources while ensuring fidelity to the organizational mission.

REVITALIZING A NEIGHBORHOOD WHILE PRESERVING ITS CHARACTER

Robert Goldman, President

Montgomery Housing Partnership

The Long Branch neighborhood of East Silver Spring, MD, suffered from its failing commercial business district. A lack of investment, unsightly physical conditions, the perception of high crime and general neglect kept what should have been a vibrant economic corridor from thriving. Compounding the existing economic problems, Long Branch is slated for light rail construction and expects gentrification pressures to push out existing, largely minority-owned neighborhood businesses.

The mission of Montgomery Housing Partnership (MHP) is to preserve and expand quality affordable housing in Montgomery County, MD. Through subsidiaries, MHP has developed and owns more than 1,700 apartment homes around the county, in transit-oriented neighborhoods where low- and moderate-income residents are desperately searching for affordability.

To fulfill our affordable housing mission, MHP identifies and partners with various stakeholders in neighborhoods where we already maintain considerable affordable housing stock to strengthen the neighborhood as a whole. For example, MHP collaborates with civic associations, tackles traffic issues and deals with bulk trash complications in the communities it serves.

Long Branch, one of the poorest neighborhoods in Montgomery County, has been a focus of MHP's for many years. We currently own six multi-family communities in a five-

CHALLENGE

The Long Branch neighborhood of East Silver Spring, MD, struggled with a declining commercial business district. A lack of investment, blight, crime and neglect kept what should have been a vibrant economic corridor from thriving.

Only concrete changes would begin to reverse the atmosphere of discouragement and get both business owners and residents willing to start re-imagining what the area could be.

square-block area. We also operate several community centers and offer resident services. Many of our clients in Long Branch do not own cars. Over the years with support from public-private partnerships, MHP has invested more than $20 million dollars into acquiring and rehabbing properties in Long Branch.

MHP began working in Long Branch's commercial corridor more intensively some five years ago. Our goal was to revitalize the area as a whole, help individual businesses and preserve the character of the neighborhood. We wanted to beautify the area and increase business success without so gentrifying it that our success would undermine the feeling of being at home in the very community we have worked so hard to house affordably.

Early on, MHP decided that physical changes to the public face of the area were of central importance for two reasons. First, only concrete changes would begin to reverse the atmosphere of discouragement and get both business owners and residents willing to start reimagining what the area could be. Second, it was simply not plausible that new customers would start coming into an area that, in terms of its external appearance, pretty much shouted, "Go away!"

So we plunged ahead! Our subsequent success came from a combination of perseverance and good luck. We were lucky in that MHP was able to find selfless partners among small store owners on or near the busy Flower Avenue corridor who have proven willing, year after year, to stick with the program. Local businesses formed a partnership with MHP and our county colleagues and provided the nucleus of a Long Branch Business League (LBBL), which has become the voice and the face of commercial Long Branch. MHP was also lucky in finding partners in the county government who, over time, came to share our ethic and strategy.

MHP's strategy was, in short, to improve Long Branch by making cumulative small changes, oriented mainly to the arts and improved design. Equally important, we wanted to respect the neighborhood's existing minority-owned character, preserve affordability and improve the bottom line for businesses.

MHP's final piece of good luck was crucial: we secured a sympathetic hearing from the Morris and Gwendolyn Cafritz Foundation, and in 2014, it began to support our Arts Based Revitalization Program. Our goal was to achieve the integration of arts and culture into economic renewal efforts, and to do so in a way that demonstrates how low-income and mixed-income neighborhoods can thrive.

MHP's 2015 survey of 22 small businesses found 71% had seen an increase in customers.

Since then, MHP has commissioned and installed six vibrant and colorful murals on the sides of businesses within an area of just a few blocks. These murals reflect the rich culture and heritages of the neighborhood's residents, and were painted by local and national artists.

We have made other design improvements, such as a beautifully painted awning on a storefront, repainted store interiors, new glass on front windows and updated signs – some hand painted, some manufactured – for stores in the Long Branch commercial area.

"I am so impressed by how much your organization has done to transform the shopping center," says Nina Muys. "I have lived in the area since 1969 and have seen it go through many stages, but this is the best it has looked."

Our success in the design department attracted notice from local colleges and universities, and MHP and LBBL have forged relationships with the schools. Since 2013, the University of Maryland has held creative arts and dance events on Long Branch's Flower Avenue and helped create temporary art for a major festival.

What is MHP's measure of success in Long Branch? On the qualitative side, we find that people no longer toss trash casually in the neighborhood. The mood is more upbeat. Groups of men drinking from paper sacks no longer assemble on Flower Avenue. The atmosphere has changed.

Numbers also point in the right direction. Business success in Long Branch has improved. In 2015, according to a survey of 22 small businesses that MHP conducts annually, we found that 71 percent had seen an increase in customers compared with the previous year, and two-thirds had seen an increase in sales.

ABOUT ROBERT A. GOLDMAN

Robert A. Goldman has served as president of MHP for the past 15 years. This private, nonprofit real estate developer in Montgomery County houses people, empowers families and strengthens neighborhoods. MHP has a staff of 30 and a budget of $3.5 million. The organization was formed in 1989 to preserve and expand the supply of affordable housing, and serves more than 1,700 low- and moderate-income residents in transit-oriented neighborhoods around the county.

ACCELERATE BOSTON: GENERATING WEALTH THROUGH ENTREPRENEURSHIP

David Price, Executive Director

Nuestra Comunidad

Gentrification not only forces long-time residents out of Boston's changing neighborhoods; rising rents and property prices pose hardships for local entrepreneurs as well. Maintaining businesses and creating new ones can be fraught with insurmountable hurdles for these communities' residents, many of whom are low-income, immigrants and people of color.

To address this critical need for funding and support, Nuestra Comunidad, a community development corporation based in Boston's Roxbury neighborhood, joined forces with another nonprofit, Epicenter Community. Together they run Accelerate Boston, a program designed for entrepreneurs looking to launch a business supporting the creative economy.

The coaching program aims to promote economic growth through new businesses and investments in Roxbury and other Boston neighborhoods. The program, launched in 2012, helps more than 20 entrepreneurs a year to develop their concepts into business plans, secure financing and create marketing tools. A range of business owners, thought leaders and investors provide weekly training sessions over six months. The entrepreneurs then pitch their ideas to a panel of three judges and the winners receive $10,000 each to help start up or expand their enterprises. Successful owners of established businesses serve as mentors to help the startups get their businesses off the ground and begin growing.

CHALLENGE

As neighborhoods throughout Boston undergo revitalization, many locals struggle to survive or are driven out by rising costs. Starting a small locally-owned business is particularly difficult in these changing landscapes. Creative entrepreneurs often lack the essential funding, support and influence they need to thrive.

Accelerate Boston helps more than 20 entrepreneurs a year to develop their concepts into business plans, secure financing and create marketing tools.

"We can help people build businesses, especially in the creative and culture economy, that will preserve the heart and soul of Roxbury as well as be inviting to other communities," said Malia Lazu, co-founder and executive director of Future Boston Alliance.

Accelerate Boston has had 120 graduates over four years, and many of them have seen real success. Here are just a few:

Cassandria Campbell won the first Accelerate Boston pitch contest. Her Fresh Food Generation company is a food truck and catering business supplied by local farms producing delicious and healthy food inspired by Latin American and Caribbean cuisine.

Rica Elysee won the third Accelerate Boston pitch contest with BeautyLynk, which provides on-demand, at-home, state-of-the-art, licensed salon services. To meet the unique needs of clients, BeautyLynk deploys 22 make-up artists and hair stylists across Eastern Massachusetts and parts of Rhode Island.

Dr. Lesa Dennis-Mahamed, owner of Gallery Eyecare, was one of the first tenants to open in the new Bolling Municipal Building in Roxbury's main business district, Dudley Square. Gallery Eyecare marries an optometry practice and art gallery to create a holistic vision experience.

Tiffany's Transformations is a full service skin and nail care studio that uses only natural, non-toxic, cruelty-free and vegan products. Owner Tiffany White wanted to create an environmentally-friendly salon that is healthier for clients and workers alike.

Accelerate Boston is a vital component of Nuestra Comunidad's mission to prevent displacement and increase the number of small business owners of color in Boston. Some of the most effective elements of the program are: 1) assisting small startups to draft strong business plans, financial documents and forecasts, 2) providing technical assistance and analysis on an individual basis for microloan applications and funding proposals, and 3) partnering successful, established business owners with new businesses for mentoring and networking.

The 28 million small businesses in America account for 54% of all U.S. sales.

ABOUT DAVID PRICE

David Price is the executive director of Nuestra Comunidad, a community development corporation serving Boston's Roxbury community since 1981. Nuestra Comunidad educates first-time homebuyers, counsels homeowners facing foreclosure, strengthens the financial capability of low- and moderate-income residents and advocates for systems and policy change to improve community wealth and health. Price has been a leader in Boston's community development field since 1995, beginning as a volunteer for Mel King's campaigns for mayor of Boston in 1979 and 1983. Price was a real estate attorney at Goulston and Storrs in Boston prior to joining the CDC field.

GOSHEN: FOSTERING A SUSTAINABLE COMMUNITY

Tom Collishaw, CEO

Self-Help Enterprises

In the late 1950s, Lilia Jimenez lived with her husband and children in the rural community of Goshen, CA, in an uninsulated house that had no indoor toilet or city water. They were not alone – many in this farmworker community lived in similar conditions.

In 1963, together with pioneers from Self-Help Enterprises (SHE), the Jimenez clan, along with two other families, embarked on a journey to build the first three mutual self-help homes in the nation. Little did they know they were building the foundation for a better future for thousands of families across America.

Despite this auspicious start, Goshen continued to struggle for decades with substandard housing and a lack of essential public services. The community also lacked key infrastructure such as lighting, recreational space and medical services.

But in the 1990s, SHE started a major investment in the community to improve options for affordable housing, recreation and essential services. To chart their course, they engaged locally with the Goshen Planning Committee, Tulare County and the neighboring city of Visalia, among other local stakeholders.

By 2003, things were very different in Goshen. SHE had facilitated the construction of 45 mutual self-help homes, and a 64-unit apartment rental project (Goshen Village I). The organization also built a wastewater collection system, and helped residents connect to the community's sewer system.

CHALLENGE

Many residents in the farmworker community of Goshen, CA, lived in substandard conditions. Their homes had no insulation, indoor toilet, or city water.

Mortgages are structured so that they don't exceed 30% of the buyer's income, and apartment rent is based on what residents can afford, which helps keep the community financially stable.

In 2004, a prominent landowner who wanted to help approached SHE with some ideas about a youth recreation area. With a donation of 40 acres, SHE embarked on a multi-year strategy to help improve infrastructure, including a recreation area, housing, and a community center: Goshen Park Village.

Goshen Park Village was developed adjacent to SHE's existing affordable housing projects, and combines health, housing, and recreational space. It includes 77 mutual self-help homes, a 56-unit affordable rental housing development (Goshen Village II), an improved 10-acre community park and a permanent health clinic.

Each of the rental housing projects – Goshen Village I and II – feature a playground, basketball court, community center, after-school program and exercise classes. In addition, Goshen Village II is Build It Green rated, in keeping with SHE's commitment to sustainability.

The single-family homes are built by homebuyers, who provide over 70 percent of the construction labor. The three- and four-bedroom homes have energy efficient amenities, two-car garages and landscaped front yards. Today, there are a total of 122 self-help homes in Goshen.

The new, diverse housing options in Goshen help families save money. In addition, mortgages are structured so that they don't exceed 30 percent of the buyer's income, and apartment rent is based on what residents can afford, which helps keep the community financially stable.

Community stakeholders were essential to many parts of the Goshen project. For example, Peter Malloch Park was developed as a collaboration with Goshen Community Services District, and community residents participated directly in the design and planning of the park, the first public recreation space in the history of Goshen.

The park includes a playground, a trail, a picnic area with a grill, a baseball backstop and two full soccer fields. From opening day, it has been a gathering place for residents of all ages.

The design of Goshen Park Village also minimizes the need for motorized transportation. The medical clinic is operated by Family HealthCare Network, a long-time partner of Self-Help Enterprises, and is adjacent to Goshen Village II, offering affordable medical care within walking distance for much of Goshen.

17% of all hired farmworkers, both migrant and settled, live in employer-owned housing.

The success of Goshen Park Village has spawned a larger vision. SHE purchased 40 more acres next to Goshen Park Village and has plans to develop. In addition to more housing – 89 mutual self-help homes and 140 apartment units – there are plans for a fresh food market, commercial development and expanded transportation options. It is the next logical step in fostering Goshen as a sustainable community of opportunity.

ABOUT TOM COLLISHAW

Tom Collishaw is president and CEO of Self-Help Enterprises, a nationally recognized community development organization serving California's San Joaquin Valley. As the organization's fourth CEO in its 51-year history, Collishaw's efforts include expanding rental housing development, increasing the impact of water and sewer development activities, and creating large new multi-faceted developments in rural communities.

WINCORAM COMMONS - REALIZING A COMMUNITY VISION

Marianne Garvin, CEO

Community Development Corporation of Long Island

Blighted for a decade, a Long Island, NY community was concerned that an abandoned movie theater was bringing down property values and was a magnet for crime. Police, town inspectors and legislators received numerous complaints. Community Development Corporation of Long Island (CDCLI) saw the vacant building as an opportunity to revitalize the area with a neighborhood center, affordable housing, commercial space and public amenities.

CDCLI's mission is to invest in the housing and economic aspirations of individuals and families by providing solutions that foster and maintain vibrant, equitable and sustainable communities. The need for affordable rental housing on Long Island is severe, especially for non-age restricted populations. According to 2015 Census data 50 percent of area renters spend 35 percent or more of their incomes on rent, and median rents are in excess of $1,500 per month. This problem correlates closely to the fact that Long Island has a much smaller percentage of rental housing than most suburban areas. There is a limited availability of land for new construction. To compound matters, as one of the most racially segregated regions, we also face the daunting task of overcoming prejudices and misinformation regarding affordable housing and the families we want to help.

The 17-acre site that would ultimately become Wincoram Commons presented an ideal opportunity for CDCLI

CHALLENGE
To remove blight, reduce crime, increase affordable housing and create a new focal point in Long Island, NY through the demolition of an abandoned movie theatre, followed by the construction of a neighborhood center, affordable housing, commercial space and public amenities.

Blighted for a decade, the community was concerned that an abandoned movie theater was bringing down property values and was a magnet for crime.

to work with our partners and take a comprehensive approach to community development by educating the community, building affordable housing, providing commerce through retail, preserving wetlands and ultimately revitalizing the area.

The abandoned theater was identified in Brookhaven Town's 2010 "Blight to Light Plan" as a core project for the Coram community's renaissance. The plan called for redevelopment proposals to

include architectural quality, energy conservation measures, quality landscaping, pedestrian-friendly access, parking, community benefits and to be consistent with other visions for the area. An earlier recommendation called for a new roadway with storefront businesses in the community.

This high profile site needed an organization to leverage the investments necessary to design, finance and implement a redevelopment. In 2011, a Brookhaven Town official suggested that CDCLI take a look at the site and see whether we could transform it in accordance with the community's vision. For four years, CDCLI worked with the Coram Civic Association, elected officials from multiple layers of government, the Longwood School Board, the volunteer fire department, the chamber of commerce and other local organizations to understand the community's needs. We conducted a NeighborWorks Community Impact Measurement Survey of residents living in a one mile radius of the site, which indicated support for revitalization and especially the demolition of the movie theatre.

CDCLI interviewed private developers and selected Conifer Realty to partner with in the redevelopment of the site into a focal point for the community. The final design included 176 rental apartments and townhouses that are affordable to working families and seniors, a clubhouse with a fitness center and community space, a small downtown pedestrian plaza incorporating 9,000 square feet of office/retail space, reconfigured roadways, sidewalks and wetlands protections. The plan embodied the vision of local residents and their dream of a vibrant destination for the surrounding community.

"Wincoram Commons is the culmination of ten years of hard work by the community to create a vision plan and find a good developer to build our dream. CDCLI and Conifer understood exactly what we wanted to accomplish to create our vision of a hamlet center," says Erma Gluck, president of the Coram Civic Association. "For far too long we were frustrated that no one understood our vision. It's a wonderful feeling seeing our vision come to fruition."

50% of area renters in Long Island spend 35% or more of their income on rent.

Wincoram Commons received a $1 million grant from the Governor's Long Island Regional Economic Development Council due to its transformative nature, transit-oriented development, public plaza and importance to the local economy. In addition, CDCLI leveraged other public and private financial commitments, including low income housing tax credits, to finance the $56 million project, which created 150 construction jobs and 34 permanent jobs. More than 2,000 applications were received for the apartments, so a lottery was held in the spring of 2015 for the 176 mixed income apartments, which are energy efficient and developed according to New York's Green Building Standards. All units were occupied in February 2016.

We learned that developing affordable housing requires years of preparation, a skilled and experienced development team, a willingness to cooperate with and learn from local residents and elected officials, and a plan that incorporates solutions to multiple community issues. Time must be spent to meet with community stakeholders to understand their concerns and incorporate them into the development. The role of community development organizations like ours is to bring the community together for a lasting impact.

ABOUT MARIANNE GARVIN

Marianne Garvin serves as the chief executive officer of Community Development Corporation of Long Island, a regional non-profit whose mission includes increasing affordable housing and creating communities of opportunity. With a staff of nearly 90 and a budget over $75 million, the organization invests its resources, talents and knowledge in the people of Long Island, helping them to achieve their dreams of an affordable home in a vibrant community. Since its inception 47 years ago, CDCLI has assisted more than 181,000 Long Islanders and invested $1.2 billion into the communities in which they live.

BUILDING COMMUNITY IN THROUGH A SHARED SENSE OF IDENTITY

Samuel Sanders, Executive Director

Mid City Redevelopment Alliance

For 25 years, the Mid City Redevelopment Alliance (MCRA) has worked to develop and promote the growth and renewal of Mid City Baton Rouge by attracting new and retaining current residents and businesses. A central element of this effort is a focus on the arts, heritage and culture, with MCRA working to leverage these assets to spur additional investment.

To create a common vision for Mid City, MCRA embarked on a creative place-making initiative – dubbed CREATE Mid City – in partnership with the Mid City Merchants Association and the State of Louisiana Office of Culture, Recreation and Tourism. The collaboration coincided with the community's Cultural District designation.

CREATE Mid City's first deliverable was a creative place-making plan, funded by a grant from the Louisiana Creative Communities Initiative. An outgrowth was Mid City Studio, a nonprofit partnership with Louisiana State University's School of Architecture focused on creating opportunities for students to learn through practical community applications while serving residents.

In the fall of 2014, Mid City Studio began to address the challenge of creating a new identity for the Mid City region. With support from local businesses and residents, and fueled by social media, Mid City Studio launched the #IAMMIDCITY branding campaign.

CHALLENGE

Mid City is Baton Rouge's urban core, but the neighborhoods are a mix of experiences and conditions, most notably social and economic extremes. Poverty, crime and blight persist in some parts of the area. Elsewhere in Mid City, housing is in high demand and businesses thrive.

One of the valuable lessons MCRA learned has been about the power that a small grassroots campaign can have in creating a sense of inclusion in a highly diverse region.

Wooden hashtags with #IAMMIDCITY were produced and introduced at an art festival where photo booths were available for people to take pictures of themselves with the signs. Following the festival, the studio and MCRA distributed the signage to iconic and popular places around the area, with residents invited to take pictures with the hashtag throughout the community and post them on social media. During a Martin Luther King Day service project, an IAMMIDCITY mural was painted on the walls of MCRA's offices.

Since then, the #IAMMIDCITY branding campaign has continued to grow. Nearly 30 businesses now display hashtag signage and MCRA is selling branded coffee mugs and T-shirts through local merchants. One of the most creative extensions, however, was a project in which 180 third-graders from two elementary schools devoted a week to learning about the area's history, geography, culture and people. The students made maps and timelines and took photos to illustrate their most memorable impressions. The result was an art installation.

In 2016, the studio transformed an empty storefront in a local community radio station into a pop-up listening room and record shop. Its goals were to challenge public perception of abandoned spaces, bring people together and creatively use the station's extensive vinyl collection – combining public art with public space and commerce. The nonprofit radio station sells the donated records for $1 to support its operations.

To keep the social connection going, a "Coffee on the Porch" gathering is held on the last Friday of the month on front porches in different areas of Mid City Baton Rouge. Porches are natural forums for building community, and local sponsors range from the local art museum to a church to a deli shop.

One of the most valuable lessons MCRA has learned so far is the power that a small, grassroots campaign can have in creating a sense of inclusion in a highly diverse region. The #IAMMIDC-

ITY branding initiative brought the various neighborhoods together around a common theme, while allowing them to capture images that express their own uniqueness.

A second lesson learned was how to incorporate the creative output from activities such as #IAMMIDCITY into place-making efforts. We assigned a "place-maker" to assist in identifying common themes within the images collected by #IAMMIDCITY and how they reflect the focal areas of the master action plan.

In Baton Rouge, nearly 30 businesses now use the #IAMMIDCITY signage.

These shared themes are communicated to Mid City businesses, residents and organizations to incorporate as appropriate into their activities.

Innovation, engagement and inclusion are natural byproducts of working collaboratively with residents, businesses and organizations to develop creative solutions.

ABOUT SAMUEL SANDERS
Samuel Sanders is the executive director of Mid City Redevelopment Alliance, which provides housing and economic development services in a densely-populated and dynamic section of Baton Rouge, Louisiana.

About NeighborWorks America

Cultivating resident leadership

The core, defining mandate that sets NeighborWorks America apart flows directly from our roots – a resident-led campaign for better housing in Pittsburgh, Pennsylvania. Local resident Dorothy Mae Richardson formed an organization in 1964 to prevent urban renewal from destroying the character of her neighborhood. After many setbacks and delays, she recruited the support of city

bankers and government officials. By 1968, Richardson earned success: Sixteen financial institutions issued affordable-housing mortgages for her neighborhood and capitalized a revolving loan fund. They called their effort Neighborhood Housing Services, and the rest is history. Her work inspired our founding in 1978. Today, local residents are helping our nonprofit members lead positive change all across America.

Annually for nearly 25 years, NeighborWorks America has recognized the outstanding efforts of resident leaders who, like Richardson, create lasting, positive change in their communities. More than 175 individuals have been recognized since 1992 as recipients of our most coveted and prestigious honor, the Dorothy Richardson Award for Resident Leadership.

Meanwhile, to help develop today's generation of resident leaders, NeighborWorks America hosts a one-of-a-kind annual event: the Community Leadership Institute. The event went national in 2008 and annually welcomes close to 1,000 residents from cities, towns and neighborhoods large and small. Designed to strengthen the skills and amplify the voices of local residents of all ages, the three-day conference is attended by eight-member teams from up to 120

NeighborWorks network organizations. Participants attend workshops, share lessons learned, network and plan a project that will improve their home community – with implementation supported by a NeighborWorks America grant.

At NeighborWorks America, amplifying and responding to the voices of residents is part of our DNA.

Supporting front-line professionals

It's the professionals on the ground who must counsel homebuyers, coach individuals with limited budgets, preserve and re-develop communities and so much more. But they are only as effective as their expertise, energy and commitment. Each professional reaches within for energy and commitment; NeighborWorks America builds their skills and expertise.

Training is the foundation that makes it possible for nonprofit professionals to be effective and flourish. Without the necessary skills, knowledge, practice and connections, our members and other professionals who serve communities couldn't be as effective in their work or stay current in their fields.

NeighborWorks America offers a comprehensive spectrum of in-person and online courses, webinars, certificate programs and networking opportunities. At the leadership level, we are a pioneer in working with both senior staff and boards of directors to elevate their performance and that of their organizations to new heights.

For example, the NeighborWorks Achieving Excellence Program focuses on nonprofit executive directors and senior staff, guiding them as they choose a transformational project for their organization and work toward its completion over an 18-month period. Through our collaboration with Harvard University's Kennedy School of Government, an immersive experience is created that supports organizational leaders as they take their skills to a level they had not thought possible. A similar program, called Excellence in Governance, is offered for board members and their organizations' executive directors/CEOs.

To guide skill-building, we offer a comprehensive assessment service that helps organizations identify key areas for which professional development can build strength and efficiency.

And throughout all of our training and other types of organizational support, the question "What does success look like?" is central. That's why one of our core programs is Success Measures, an outcome-evaluation resource group created by and for nonprofits, intermediaries and funders across the country to document their impact for the people and communities they serve.

Making nonprofits effective, efficient and accountable

What makes NeighborWorks America unique? There are many answers to that question, but at the core is our national network of "boots on the ground." Today, member organizations number more than 245. We take pride in our commitment to diversity, equity and inclusion.

To assure that organizations in our network are strong and healthy in every facet of their operations – and remain that way despite the challenges they face – we conduct a rigorous assessment both before their acceptance into the NeighborWorks network and every year thereafter. We evaluate their:

Programs. Do they support the mission of the organization, incorporate best practices and positively impact the community?

Human capital. Do the organizations have tested, proven policies and procedures in place that assure a diverse, qualified workforce, professional development and accountability?

Resource management. Do they have the financial and other resources necessary to achieve their mission? Are checks and balances in place to assure ethical operations?

Systems. Do the organizations have the technical infrastructure required to monitor performance and ensure compliance with requirements of funders, regulatory bodies and partners?

Strategic planning. Do they have a blueprint in place to guide their activities and allocation of resources? And is that plan regularly updated and used to assess their performance?

Governance. Is there an effective partnership between the board and senior leadership that assures accountability and achievement of mission?

We like to think of NeighborWorks membership as the "Good Housekeeping Seal of Approval" in community development. This same assessment service is available to organizations outside our network to ensure that effective, efficient community development extends to the entire field.

Supporting local development with strategic grants

For more than 35 years, NeighborWorks America has deployed strategic grants to support nonprofit community development organizations across the United States. For the overwhelming majority of those years, our giving has focused on strengthening the organizations overall and helping them further their mission objectives. While we also provide program-specific funding, we believe it's essential that nonprofits have the flexibility to adapt to meet the often rapidly changing needs of the communities they serve.

In addition to these unlimited grants, we provide restricted grants for capital purposes, including real estate development and lending. The majority of these grants are made at the enterprise level with no other limitations, so recipients may use the monies as needed within their lines of service, including filling gaps and providing first-in funds to leverage other public-private investments.

The nonprofits we support undergo rigorous due diligence, because we are committed to being careful stewards of the money entrusted to us by the U.S. Congress, foundations and private businesses. Support for our network is predicated on a thorough analysis of each organization's financial, management and governance health. NeighborWorks America created a dedicated unit to assess the health of member organizations, helping us ensure that the money we invest in our grantees produces effective, measurable work. There also must be broad agreement at the outset of a grant on what metrics recipients will use to demonstrate impact.

Because of our strong track record in responsible grant-making and fiscal stewardship, NeighborWorks America has become the go-to intermediary for special-purpose grant programs, such as the National Foreclosure Mitigation Counseling Program, funded through a specific appropriation from Congress.

Through all our grant-making, NeighborWorks America's goal is simple – support organizations that create opportunities for people to live in affordable homes, improve their lives and strengthen communities.

THE NEIGHBORWORKS NETWORK

Alabama
Community Action Partnership of North Alabama, Inc., *Decatur*
Community Service Programs of West Alabama, Inc., *Tuscaloosa*
NHS of Birmingham, Inc., *Birmingham*

Alaska
Fairbanks NHS, Inc., *Fairbanks*
NeighborWorks Alaska, *Anchorage*

Arizona
Chicanos Por La Causa, Inc., *Phoenix*
Comite de Bien Estar, Inc., *San Luis*
The Primavera Foundation, Inc, *South Tucson*
Trellis, *Phoenix*

Arkansas
Crawford-Sebastian Community Development Council, Inc., *Fort Smith*
Universal Housing Development Corporation, *Russellville*

California
A Community of Friends, *Los Angeles*
Cabrillo Economic Development Corp., *Ventura*
Chinatown Community Development Center, *San Francisco*
Coachella Valley Housing Coalition, *Indio*
Community Housing Development Corporation of North Richmond, *Richmond*
Community Housing Improvement Program, Incorporated (CHIP), *Chico*
Community HousingWorks, *San Diego*
East Bay Asian Local Development Corporation (EBALDC), *Oakland*
Eden Housing, *Hayward*
LTSC CDC, *Los Angeles*
Mutual Housing California, *Sacramento*
Neighborhood Partnership Housing Services, *Rancho Cucamonga*
NeighborWorks HOC Sacramento Region, *Sacramento*
NeighborWorks Orange County, *Orange*
NHS of Los Angeles County, *Los Angeles*
NHS of the Inland Empire, Inc., *San Bernardino*
Peoples' Self-Help Housing Corporation, *San Luis Obispo*

Rural Communities Housing Development Corporation, *Ukiah*
Self-Help Enterprises, *Visalia*
Tenderloin Neighborhood Development Corporation, *San Francisco*
The Unity Council, *Oakland*

Colorado
Community Resources and Housing Development Corporation, *Westminster*
Housing Resources of Western Colorado, *Grand Junction*
Neighbor to Neighbor, Inc., *Fort Collins*
NeighborWorks of Pueblo, *Pueblo*
Rocky Mountain Communities, *Denver*
Thistle Communities, *Boulder*
Tri-County Housing & CDC, *Fowler*

Connecticut
Housing Development Fund, Inc., *Stamford*
MHA of Greater Hartford, Inc., *Hartford*
MHA of Southwestern Connecticut, Inc., *Stamford*
NeighborWorks New Horizons, *New Haven*
NHS of New Britain, Inc., *New Britain*
NHS of New Haven, Inc., *New Haven*
NHS of Waterbury, Inc., *Waterbury*

District of Columbia
Manna, Inc., *Washington*

Delaware
Interfaith Community Housing of Delaware, Inc., *Wilmington*
National Council on Agricultural Life and Labor Research Fund, Inc., *Dover*

Florida
Centro Campesino Farmworker Center, Inc., *Florida City*
Clearwater NHS, Inc., *Clearwater*
Corporation to Develop Communities of Tampa, *Tampa*
Housing Partnership, Inc., *Riviera Beach*
Neighborhood Housing & Development Corporation, *Gainesville*
NHS of South Florida, Inc., *Miami*
Orlando Neighborhood Improvement Corp., *Orlando*
Pensacola Habitat for Humanity, Inc., *Pensacola*
Rural Neighborhoods, Incorporated, *Florida City*

Tallahassee Lenders' Consortium, *Tallahassee*
Tampa Bay CDC, *Clearwater*
Wealth Watchers, Inc., *Jacksonville*

Georgia
Atlanta Neighborhood Development Partnership,
  Inc., *Atlanta*
NeighborWorks Columbus (GA), *Columbus*

Hawaii
Hawaii HOC, *Honolulu*
MHA of Hawaii, Inc., *Honolulu*

Idaho
NeighborWorks Boise, *Boise*
NeighborWorks Pocatello, *Pocatello*

Illinois
Hispanic Housing Development Corporation, *Chicago*
Joseph Corporation of Illinois, Inc., *Aurora*
Mid Central Community Action, *Bloomington*
NHS of Chicago, Inc., *Chicago*
NW HomeStart, Inc., *Freeport*

Indiana
LaCasa, Inc., *Goshen*
Pathfinder Services, Inc., *Huntington*
South Bend Heritage Foundation, *South Bend*

Iowa
Community Housing Initiatives, *Spencer*
Neighborhood Finance Corporation, *Des Moines*
NeighborWorks Home Solutions, *Council Bluffs*

Kansas
CHWC, Inc., *Kansas City*
Mennonite Housing Rehabilitation Services, Inc.,
  Wichita

Kentucky
Community Ventures Corporation, *Lexington*
Fahe, Inc., *Berea*
Frontier Housing, Inc., *Morehead*
New Directions Housing Corporation, *Louisville*
The Housing Partnership, Inc., *Louisville*

Louisiana
Mid City Redevelopment Alliance, Inc., *Baton Rouge*
NHS of New Orleans, Inc., *New Orleans*
Providence Community Housing, *New Orleans*
Southern Mutual Help Association, *New Iberia*

Maine
Avesta Housing Development Corporation, *Portland*
Coastal Enterprises, Inc., *Brunswick*
Community Concepts, Inc., *Lewiston*
Kennebec Valley Community Action Program
  Housing Services, *Waterville*
Penquis Community Action Program, Inc., *Bangor*

Maryland
Community Preservation and Development
  Corporation, *Silver Spring*
Cumberland NHS, Inc., *Cumberland*
Montgomery Housing Partnership, Inc., *Silver Spring*
NHS of Baltimore, Inc., *Baltimore*
Salisbury NHS, Inc., *Salisbury*
St. Ambrose Housing Aid Center, *Baltimore*

Massachusetts
Cambridge Neighborhood Apartment & Housing
  Services, Inc., *Cambridge*
Coalition for a Better Acre, *Lowell*
Codman Square Neighborhood Development Corp.,
  Dorchester
HAP, Inc., *Springfield*
Lawrence CommunityWorks, Inc., *Lawrence*
Madison Park Development Corporation, *Roxbury*
Neighborhood of Affordable Housing, Inc., *East Boston*
NeighborWorks Southern Mass, *Quincy*
NewVue Communities, Inc., *Fitchburg*
Nuestra Comunidad Development Corp., *Roxbury*
Oak Hill CDC, *Worcester*
The Neighborhood Developers, Inc., *Chelsea*
Urban Edge Housing Corporation, *Roxbury*

Michigan
Dwelling Place of Grand Rapids Nonprofit Housing
  Corporation, *Grand Rapids*
Habitat for Humanity of Michigan, *Lansing*
Kalamazoo NHS, Inc., *Kalamazoo*
Lighthouse of Oakland County, *Pontiac*

Metro Community Development, Inc., *Flint*
Southwest Michigan CDC, *Battle Creek*
Northwest Michigan Community Action Agency,
  Inc., *Traverse City*
Southwest Solutions, *Detroit*

Minnesota
Aeon, *Minneapolis*
CommonBond Communities, *St. Paul*
Dayton's Bluff NHS, Inc., *St. Paul*
Midwest Minnesota CDC, *Detroit Lakes*
NeighborWorks Home Partners, *St. Paul*
One Roof Community Housing, *Duluth*
Southwest Minnesota Housing Partnership, *Slayton*

Mississippi
Hope Enterprise Corporation, *Jackson*

Missouri
Better Family Life, Inc., *St. Louis*
Beyond Housing, Inc., *St. Louis*
NHS of Kansas City, Inc., *Kansas City*
North East Community Action Corporation,
  Bowling Green
Westside Housing Organization, Inc., *Kansas City*

Montana
NeighborWorks Great Falls, *Great Falls*
NeighborWorks Montana, *Great Falls*

Nebraska
NeighborWorks Home Solutions, *Omaha*
NeighborWorks Lincoln, *Lincoln*
NeighborWorks Northeast Nebraska, *Norfolk*

Nevada
Nevada H.A.N.D., Inc., *Las Vegas*
NHS of Southern Nevada, Inc., *North Las Vegas*

New Hampshire
Affordable Housing Education and Development,
  Inc., *Littleton*
CATCH Neighborhood Housing, *Concord*
Laconia Area Community Land Trust, Inc., *Laconia*
NeighborWorks Southern New Hampshire, *Manchester*

New Jersey
Affordable Housing Alliance, Inc., *Eatontown*
Housing and Neighborhood Development Services,
  Inc., *Orange*
Housing Partnership for Morris County, *Dover*
La Casa de Don Pedro, Inc., *Newark*
New Jersey Community Capital, *New Brunswick*
St. Joseph's Carpenter Society, *Camden*

New Mexico
Homewise, Inc., *Santa Fe*
Native Partnership for Housing, Inc., *Gallup*
Tierra del Sol Housing Corporation, *Las Cruces*

New York
Arbor Housing and Development, *Corning*
Asian Americans for Equality, Inc., *New York*
CDC of Long Island, Inc., *Centereach*
Chautauqua Home Rehabilitation and Improvement
  Corporation, *Mayville*
Home HeadQuarters, Inc., *Syracuse*
Housing Assistance Program of Essex County, Inc.,
  Elizabethtown
Hudson River Housing, Inc., *Poughkeepsie*
Ithaca NHS, Inc., *Ithaca*
NeighborWorks Rochester, *Rochester*
NHS of New York City, Inc., *New York*
Niagara Falls NHS, Inc., *Niagara Falls*
North Country Housing Council, *Canton*
Opportunities for Chenango, Inc., *Norwich*
PathStone Corporation, *Rochester*
RUPCO, Inc., *Kingston*
Troy Rehabilitation & Improvement Program, Inc.,
  Troy
UNHS NeighborWorks HOC, *Utica*
West Side NHS, Inc., *Buffalo*

North Carolina
Charlotte-Mecklenburg Housing Partnership, Inc.,
  Charlotte
DHIC, Inc., *Raleigh*
Durham Community Land Trustees, *Durham*
Mountain Housing Opportunities, Inc., *Asheville*

North Dakota
CommunityWorks North Dakota, *Mandan*

Ohio

East Akron Neighborhood Development Corporation Inc., *Akron*
Famicos Foundation, *Cleveland*
HOC of Greater Cincinnati, Inc., The, *Cincinnati*
Homeport, *Columbus*
Neighborhood Development Services, *Ravenna*
Neighborhood Housing Partnership of Greater Springfield, Inc., *Springfield*
NeighborWorks Toledo Region, *Toledo*
NHS of Greater Cleveland, Inc., *Cleveland*
NHS of Hamilton, Inc., *Hamilton*
St. Mary Development Corporation, *Dayton*

Oklahoma

Community Action Project of Tulsa County, *Tulsa*
Little Dixie Community Action Agency, *Hugo*
NHS of Oklahoma City, Inc., *Oklahoma City*

Oregon

NeighborImpact, *Redmond*
NeighborWorks Umpqua, *Roseburg*
Portland Housing Center, *Portland*
REACH Community Development, Inc., *Portland*
Willamette NHS, *Corvallis*

Pennsylvania

Housing Development Corporation MidAtlantic, *Lancaster*
NeighborWorks Northeastern Pennsylvania, *Scranton*
NeighborWorks Western Pennsylvania, *Pittsburgh*
New Kensington CDC, *Philadelphia*
NHS of Greater Berks, Inc., *Reading*
NHS of the Lehigh Valley, Inc., *Allentown*

Puerto Rico

Ponce NHS, Inc., *Ponce*
Puerto Rico NHS, Corp., *San Juan*

Rhode Island

NeighborWorks Blackstone River Valley, *Woonsocket*
ONE Neighborhood Builders, *Providence*
West Elmwood Housing Development Corp., *Providence*

South Carolina

Family Services, Inc., *North Charleston*

South Dakota

GROW South Dakota, *Sisseton*
NeighborWorks Dakota Home Resources, *Deadwood*

Tennessee

Affordable Housing Resources, Inc., *Nashville*
Chattanooga Neighborhood Enterprise, Inc., *Chattanooga*
Eastern Eight CDC, *Johnson City*
HomeSource east tennessee, *Knoxville*
United Housing, Inc., *Memphis*

Texas

Affordable Homes of South Texas, Inc., *McAllen*
Alamo Community Group, *San Antonio*
Avenue CDC, *Houston*
BCL of Texas, *Austin*
CDC of Brownsville, *Brownsville*
Fifth Ward Community Redevelopment Corporation, *Houston*
Foundation Communities, *Austin*
NeighborWorks Laredo, *Laredo*
NeighborWorks Waco, *Waco*
Nueces County Community Action Agency, *Corpus Christi*
Tejano Center for Community Concerns, *Houston*

Utah

NeighborWorks Provo, *Provo*
NeighborWorks Salt Lake, *Salt Lake City*

Vermont

Champlain Housing Trust, *Burlington*
Downstreet Housing and Community Development, *Barre*
NeighborWorks of Western Vermont, *West Rutland*
RuralEdge, *Lyndonville*
Windham & Windsor Housing Trust, *Brattleboro*

Virginia

AHC Inc., *Arlington*
Better Housing Coalition, *Richmond*
Community Housing Partners Corporation, *Christiansburg*

Washington
Community Frameworks, *Spokane*
HomeSight, *Seattle*
Low Income Housing Institute, *Seattle*
NeighborWorks of Grays Harbor County, *Aberdeen*

West Virginia
CommunityWorks In West Virginia, Inc., *Charleston*
HOC, Inc., *Elkins*

Wisconsin
Housing Resources, Inc., *Milwaukee*
Impact Seven, Inc., *Almena*
NeighborWorks Badgerland, *Kenosha*
NeighborWorks Blackhawk Region, *Beloit*
NeighborWorks Green Bay, *Green Bay*
NHS of Southwest Wisconsin, Inc., *Richland Center*

Wyoming
Wyoming Housing Network, *Casper*

REFERENCES

Below are citations for many of the statistics used in this book. For statistics not referenced here, information was pulled directly from the independent submission of each author.

Affordable Homes

Alamo Community Group
National Center for Veterans Analysis and Statistics. US Department of Veterans Affairs, 2014. *www.va.gov.*

CVHC
US Department of Agriculture Economic Research Service, July 2016. *www.ers.usda.gov.*

Frontier Housing
Trends and Information about the Manufactured Housing Industry. Manufactured Housing Institute, 2016. *www.manufacturedhousing.org.*

HAPEC
Achieving Excellence through Community Land Trusts. NeighborWorks America, Apr. 2016. *www.neighborworks.org.*

Low Income Housing Institute
What is the Tiny House Movement? The Tiny Life, 2015. *www.thetinylife.com.*

Montgomery Housing Partnership
Median Sales Price for New Houses Sold in the US. Federal Reserve Bank of St. Louis, Aug. 2016. *Alfred.stlouisfed.org.*

Mutual Housing California
Average Monthly Electric Bill by State. National Association of Home Builders, Mar. 2015. *www.eyeonhousing.org.*

Neighborhood Housing Services of New York City
Wealth Inequality, Hunger and Poverty a Critical Issue for City and State Residents. AM New York, Sept. 2015. *www.amny.com.*

Neighborhood Housing Services of South Florida
Income & Poverty in Miami-Dade County. Miami-Dade County, June 2015. *www.miamidade.gov.*

NeighborWorks Columbus
Policy Basics: Top Ten Facts about Social Security. Center on Budget and Policy Priorities, Aug. 2016. *www.cbppp.org.*

NeighborWorks New Horizons
State Register of Historic Places. State of Connecticut, Aug. 2016. *www.portal.ct.gov.*

NeighborWorks Southern Mass
National Coalition for Homeless Veterans, Mar. 2016. *www.nchv.org.*

NeighborWorks Umpqua
The Mutual Self-Help Housing Program. National Rural Housing Coalition, 2015. *www.ruralhousingcoalition.org.*

Nuestra Communidad
Gentrification in America Report. Governing the States and Localities, Feb. 2015. *www.governing.com.*

Pathfinder Services
Americans with Disabilities. US Census Bureau, July 2012. *www.census.gov.*

RUPCO, Inc.
Textile Industry Comes Back to Life, Especially in South. USA Today, Feb. 2014. *www.usatoday.com.*

Community Building

Beyond Housing
11 Facts about Education and Poverty in America. *www.dosomething.org.*

Community Action Partnership of North Alabama
NeighborWorks Quarterly Production Survey. NeighborWorks America, 2015. *www.neighborworks.org.*

Community Frameworks
What is the Tiny House Movement? The Tiny Life, 2015. *www.thetinylife.com.*

Community Preservation and Development Corp.
Broadband Progress Report. Federal Communications Commission, Feb. 2015. *www.fcc.gov.*

Housing Partnership Inc.
Community Leadership Institute attendance data. NeighborWorks America, 2015. *www.neighborworks.org.*

Hudson River Housing
Immigrants, Latinos Helped Drive Business Creation Last Year. The Wall Street Journal, May 2015. *www.wsj.com.*

La Casa De Don Pedro
NeighborWorks Resident Satisfaction Survey. NeighborWorks America, 2015. *www.neighborworks.org.*

Little Dixie Community Action Agency
NeighborWorks Week Survey. NeighborWorks America, 2016. *www.neighborworks.org.*

Mid Central Community Action
Building Community through Street Fairs: Identifying Community Assets. National Trust for Historic Preservation, Mar. 2016. *www.preservationnation.org.*

National Council on Agricultural Life and Labor Research Fund
National Neighborhood Watch, 2016. *www.nnw.org.*

Neighborhood Housing Services of New Haven
Garden to Table: A 5-Year Look at Food Gardening in America. National Gardening Association, Apr.2014. *www.garden.org.*

Neighborhood Housing Services of Southwest Wisconsin
Latinos in the 2016 Election: Wisconsin. Pew Research Center, Jan. 2016. *www.pewhispanic.org.*

Neighborhood of Affordable Housing
Surging Seas Risk Finder. Climate Central. *Riskfinder.climatecentral.org.*

NeighborWorks Blackstone River Valley
US High School Graduation Rate Hits New Record High. US Department of Education, Dec. 2015. *www.ed.gov.*

NeighborWorks Provo
How Much Does it Cost to Paint a Home Exterior? Home Advisor, 2016. *www.homeadvisor.com.*

NeighborWorks Salt Lake
Where Refugees to the US Come From. Pew Research Center, June 2016. *www.pewresearch.org.*

NeighborWorks Southern New Hampshire
Criminal Victimization. US Department of Justice, Sept. 2015. *www.bjs.gov.*

NeighborWorks Western Pennsylvania
The Nonprofit Sector's Leadership Deficit. The Bridgespan Group, Mar. 2006. *www.bridgespan.org.*

Orlando Neighborhood Improvement Corp.
NeighborWorks Annual Survey. NeighborWorks America, 2015. *www.neighborworks.org.*

PathStone Corp.
Puerto Rico Wants to Grow Your Next Cup of Specialty Coffee. NPR, May 2015. *www.npr.org.*

People's Self-Help Housing
US Department of Agriculture Economic Research Service, July 2016. *www.ers.usda.gov.*

Cross-Sector Collaboration

Atlanta Neighborhood Development Partnership, Inc.
Underwater Atlanta: Negative Equity Information & Resource Guide. Piece by Piece, Mar. 2015. *www.piecebypieceatlanta.org.*

Cambridge Neighborhood Apartment Housing Services, Inc.
Housing Costs and Financial Challenges for Low-Income Older Adults. Urban Institute, July 2015. *www.urban.org.*

Hawaii HomeOwnership Center
Hawaii's High Cost of Living. Living in Hawaii. *Aimforawesome.com.*

HomeSource east tennessee
US Department of Health and Human Services, 2010. *Longtermcare.gov.*

Madison Park Development Corp.
Map the Meal Gap. Feeding America, 2014. *Map.feedingamerica.org.*

Neighborhood Housing Services of Baltimore
Nightmare on Main Street: Older Americans and the Mortgage Market Crisis. AARP Public Policy Institute, 2012. *www.aarp.org.*

NeighborWorks Boise
Centers for Disease Control and Prevention, June 2014. *www.cdc.gov.*

NeighborWorks Green Bay
NeighborWorks Quarterly Production Survey. NeighborWorks America, 2015. *www.neighborworks.org.*

NeighborWorks Umpqua
NOAA Report Finds the 2014 Commercial Catch of US Seafood on Par with 2013. National Oceanic and Atmospheric Administration, Oct. 2015.

Neighborhood Housing Services of Chicago
Vacant and Abandoned Properties: Turing Liabilities into Assets. US Department of Housing and Urban Development, 2014. *www.huduser.gov.*

Nevada HAND
America After 3pm: After School Programs in Demand. The After School Alliance, Oct. 2014. *www.afterschoolalliance.org.*

North East Community Action Corp.
National Flood Insurance Program, Apr. 2016. *www.floodsmart.gov.*

Southwest Minnesota Housing Partnership
Green and Healthy Homes, 2016. *www.greenandhealthyhomes.org.*

Tenderloin Development Corp.
San Francisco Point-in-Time Homeless Count & Survey. Applied Survey Research, 2015. *www.sfgov.org.*

United Housing
How Many Seniors Really End Up in Nursing Homes? Nursing Home Diaries, Jan. 2016. *www.nursinghomediaries.com.*

Westside Housing Organization
Asthma and Schools. Centers for Disease Control and Prevention, June 2015. *www.cdc.gov.*

Financial Stability

AHEAD
FDIC National Survey of Unbanked and Underbanked Household. Federal Deposit Insurance Corp., June 2013. *www.fdic.gov.*

CATCH Neighborhood Housing
National Register of Historic Places. *www.nps.gov.*

Community Ventures
Home Buyer and Seller Generational Trends Report. National Association of Realtors, Mar. 2015. *www.realtor.org.*

Eden Housing
Americans' Internet Access: 2000-2015. Pew Research Center, June 2015. *www.pewinternet.org.*

Puerto Rico Neighborhood Housing Services
US Census Bureau. *www.census.gov.*

Neighborhood Housing Services of Greater Cleveland
NeighborWorks Consumer Finance Survey. NeighborWorks America, 2015. *www.neighborworks.org.*

The Neighborhood Developers
National Night Out 2016. US Department of Justice, Aug. 2016. *www.justice.gov.*

Nonprofit Excellence

Arbor Housing and Development
Stanford Social Innovation Review. Stanford University, 2014. *www.ssir.org.*

CommonBond Communities
The Class of 2014 Student Survey Report. National Association of Colleges and Employers, Sept. 2014. *www.naceweb.org.*

GROW South Dakota
NeighborWorks Quarterly Production Survey. NeighborWorks America, 2015. *www.neighborworks.org.*

Housing Development Fund
Nonprofit Technology Staffing and Investment Report. The Nonprofit Technology Network, Aug. 2015. *www.nten.org.*

Neighborhood Housing Services of Baltimore
Monthly Network Production Reports. NeighborWorks America, Sept. 2015. *www.neighborworks.org.*
Neighborhood Partnership Housing Services
Help Wanted: Millennials Need Apply. The Bridgespan Group, May 2015. *www.bridgespan.org.*

NeighborWorks Green Bay
Access to Healthy Food and why it Matters: A Review of the Research. The Food Trust, 2013. *www.thefoodtrust.org.*

NeighborWorks Montana
Montana Department of Commerce. *www.ceic.mt.gov*.

NeighborWorks Umpqua
Oregon Economy Continues to Be Top Performer. Oregon Center for Public Policy, Jan. 2015. *www.ocpp.org*.

NeighborWorks Western Pennsylvania
The Dorothy Richardson Story. NeighborWorks America, 2016. *www.neighborworks.org*.

Place-Based Investments

Asian Americas for Equality
Renaissance Economic Development Corp., 2016. *www.renaissance-ny.org*.

Business and Community Lenders of Texas
San Antonio Food Bank. *www.safoodbank.org*.

Chinatown Community Development Corp
Here's Why Chicago's Chinatown is Booming, Even as Others Across the US Fade. The Chicago Tribune, Sept. 2016. *www.chicagotribune.com*.

Codman Square Neighborhood Development Corp.
11 Facts about Food Deserts. *www.dosomething.org*.

East Akron Neighborhood Development Corp.
Grocery Chains Leave Food Deserts Barren. The Associated Press, Dec. 2015. *www.bigstory.ap.org*.

Homeport
The Lincoln Theatre. *www.lincolntheatrecolumbus.com*.

Impact Seven
Wisconsin Paper Council, 2016. *www.wipapercouncil.org*.

Neighborhood Housing Services of Los Angeles County
CityTownInfo.com, 2016. *www.citytowninfo.com*.

Nuestra Communidad
Small Business Trends. US Small Business Administration. *www.sba.gov*.

Self-Help Enterprises
States Struggle to Provide Housing for Migrant Farmworkers. The Pew Charitable Trusts, May 2016. *www.pewtrusts.org*.

INDEX BY AUTHOR

Adame, David, 275
Ahmed, Malik, 581
Ansley, Robert, 249
Appleton, Grady, 553

Bangemann-Johnson, Merten, 31, 503, 549
Biddle, Ludy, 123, 209
Blaze, Donna, 59
Bolding, Tim, 291
Bornstein, Julie, 23
Bourg, Lorna, 449
Bowman, Katie, 391
Burton, Cynthia, 161
Bynum, William, 461

Carty, Joan, 523
Casper, Janaka, 11
Chupik, Roland, 323
Claflin, Michael, 409
Collishaw, Tom, 621
Compher, Bud, 363
Conard-Wells, Sharon, 133
Cooper, Scott, 471
Corley, Robert, 79

Dahlquist, Mark, 205
Daly, Peter, 311
de Escontrias, Margarita, 221
Duvall, Mary, 39

Eaton, Jeffrey, 531
Ekstrom, Brent, 55
Ellis, Dan, 379, 487
Ergott, Jesse, 511
Erickson, Marcia, 495

Falk, Donald, 371
Farley, Sherry, 107
Farnsel, William, 43
Faust, Kristin, 327
Finnesand, Lori, 495
Flanery, Lori Hudson, 597
Fong, Norman, 545
Fowler, John, 145

Gagliardi, Peter, 307
Garcia-Duarte, Patricia, 87
Garciaz, Maria, 177
Garlick, Joseph, 245
Garvin, Marianne, 625
Gay, Lori, 557
Geer, David, 339
Gerber, Brett, 609
Giffee, Philip, 189
Goldman, Robert, 111, 613
Gonzalez, Jennifer, 83
Goodemann, Rick, 141, 299
Grenfell, Jim, 241
Guilfoil, Martina, 99

Halvorsen, Noel, 287, 527
Harvey, Linda, 119
Hay, Kara, 441
Heard, Rosemary, 467
Hipps, Alan, 27
Hjelmhaug, Matt, 535, 565
Hogan Closkey, Pilar, 577
Houston, Ann, 367, 453
Hugo, Linda, 237
Hutchison, Peggy, 67, 475

Ifill, Susan, 71
Iskow, Rachel, 127

Joab, Gerard, 19

Kelley, Colin, 169, 519
King, Jim, 95
Kirk, Steven, 539
Krehmeyer, Chris, 355
Kui, Chris, 605

Latimore, Gail, 569
Lawler, Mary, 225
Lee, Dawn, 331
Lee, Sharon, 103
Loftin, Michael, 491
Luecke, Bruce, 589
Lyons, Ken, 395

Malloy, Peg, 445
Mandolini, Linda, 425
Matsubayashi, Dean, 413
Mayo, Jackie, 315
McNamara, Patrick, 253
Meyer, Wayne, 437
Miller, Kimberly, 91
Miller, Ronald, 233
Mitchell, Stuart, 149, 343
Mitchell-Bennett, Nick, 63, 405
Mojica, Clemente, 483
Moreau, Walter, 303
Mosquera, Seila, 47
Mullin, Michael, 335
Myer, Joe, 157, 417

Nash, Roy, 75
Niederman, John, 15
North, Terri, 347

O'Callaghan, John, 271
Ocasio, Raymond, 257
O'Connor, Kevin, 51, 593
Ortiz Fisher, Gloria, 283
Oshiro, Dennis, 383

Padilla-Gonzalez, Jessica, 387
Paley, James, 181
Patrick, Don, 319
Pinado, Jeanne, 279
Pitchford, Michael, 217
Pollio, Gary, 185
Preusch, Stephanie, 515
Price, David, 35, 617

Quaglia, Kerry, 585

Reinke, Bill, 173
Renken, Michael, 213
Reynolds, Rebecca, 197
Rice, Sheila, 399
Rios Valdez, Rosa, 561
Robin, Sean, 137
Rude, Maureen, 499

Salzman, Sandy, 601
Sanders, Samuel, 629
Schmidt, Deidre, 479
Shank, Arden, 351
Shea, Frank, 295
Shelton-Kelly, Brian, 457
Smith, Kevin, 421
Sweat, Laura, 535, 565

Thorland, Timothy, 573
Tisler, Lou, 429
To, Tony, 229
Torpy, Brenda, 375
Totman, Dana, 359
Tourigny, Robert, 201
Tubbs, Michael, 261

Valliere, Daniel, 115
Velez Beauchamp, Blanca, 433

Walsh, Suzanne, 165
Warren, Gregg, 153
Webdale, Walter, 3
White, Deborah, 193
Wilde, Sharlene, 265
Williams, Cathy, 7
Wood, Rollin, 507

INDEX BY ORGANIZATION

Affordable Housing Alliance, Inc., 59

Affordable Housing Education
and Development, Inc., 409

AHC Inc., 3

Alamo Community Group, 83

Arbor Housing and Development, 531

Asian Americans for Equality, Inc., 605

Atlanta Neighborhood Development
Partnership, Inc., 271

Avenue CDC, 225

Avesta Housing Development Corporation, 359

BCL of Texas, 561

Better Family Life, Inc., 581

Beyond Housing, Inc., 355

Cabrillo Economic Development Corp., 221

Cambridge Neighborhood Apartment
& Housing Services, Inc., 311

CATCH Neighborhood Housing, 467

CDC of Brownsville, 63, 405

CDC of Long Island, Inc., 625

Champlain Housing Trust, 375

Chattanooga Neighborhood Enterprise, Inc., 99

Chicanos Por La Causa, Inc., 275

Chinatown Community
Development Center, 545

Coachella Valley Housing Coalition, 23

Codman Square Neighborhood Development
Corp., 569

CommonBond Communities, 479

Community Action Partnership of
North Alabama, Inc., 261

Community Frameworks, 237

Community Housing Partners Corporation, 11

Community Preservation and
Development Corporation, 217

Community Service Programs of West Alabama,
Inc., 161

Community Ventures Corporation, 421

CommunityWorks North Dakota, 55

DHIC, Inc., 153

East Akron Neighborhood Development
Corporation Inc., 553

Eden Housing, 425

Fahe, Inc., 95

Foundation Communities, 303

Frontier Housing, Inc., 107

GROW South Dakota, 495

HAP, Inc., 307

Hawaii HOC, 383

Home HeadQuarters, Inc., 585

Homeport, 589

HomeSight, 229

HomeSource east tennessee, 315

Homewise, Inc., 491

Hope Enterprise Corporation, 461

Housing Assistance Program of Essex County,
Inc., 27

Housing Development Fund, Inc., 523

Housing Partnership for Morris County, 387

Housing Partnership, Inc. 253

Housing Resources of Western Colorado, 391

Hudson River Housing, Inc., 137

Impact Seven, Inc., 609

Interfaith Community Housing of Delaware,
Inc., 185

Kennebec Valley Community Action Program
Housing Services, 165

La Casa de Don Pedro, Inc. 257

Laconia Area Community Land Trust, Inc., 119

Little Dixie Community Action Agency, 197

Low Income Housing Institute, 103

Little Tokyo Service Center CDC, 413

Madison Park Development Corporation, 279

Mid Central Community Action, 193

Mid City Redevelopment Alliance, Inc., 629

Montgomery Housing Partnership, Inc.,
111, 613

Mutual Housing California, 127

National Council on Agricultural Life and Labor Research Fund, Inc., 157, 417
Native Partnership for Housing, Inc., 507
Neighborhood Finance Corporation, 515
Neighborhood of Affordable Housing, Inc., 189
Neighborhood Partnership Housing Services, 483
NeighborImpact, 471
NeighborWorks Alaska, 457
NeighborWorks Blackstone River Valley, 245
NeighborWorks Boise, 363
NeighborWorks Columbus (GA), 7
NeighborWorks Community Partners, 535
NeighborWorks Great Falls, 399
NeighborWorks Green Bay, 287, 527
NeighborWorks Home Solutions, 395
NeighborWorks Lincoln, 213
NeighborWorks Montana, 499
NeighborWorks New Horizons, 47
NeighborWorks Northeastern Pennsylvania, 511
NeighborWorks of Western Vermont, 123, 209
NeighborWorks Pocatello, 205
NeighborWorks Provo, 265
NeighborWorks Rochester, 565
NeighborWorks Salt Lake, 177
NeighborWorks Southern Mass, 79
NeighborWorks Southern New Hampshire, 201
NeighborWorks Toledo Region, 43
NeighborWorks Umpqua, 31, 503, 549
NeighborWorks Waco, 75
NeighborWorks Western Pennsylvania, 169, 519
Nevada H.A.N.D., Inc., 335
New Directions Housing Corporation, 597
New Jersey Community Capital, 437
New Kensington CDC, 601
NHS of Baltimore, Inc., 379, 487
NHS of Chicago, Inc., 327
NHS of Greater Berks, Inc., 233
NHS of Greater Cleveland, Inc., 429
NHS of Los Angeles County, 557
NHS of New Haven, Inc., 181
NHS of New York City, Inc., 71
NHS of Oklahoma City, Inc., 323
NHS of South Florida, Inc., 351

NHS of Southwest Wisconsin, Inc., 173
NHS of the Inland Empire, Inc., 331
North East Community Action Corporation, 319
Nuestra Comunidad Development Corp., 35, 617

Origin SC, 339
Orlando Neighborhood Improvement Corp., 249

Pathfinder Services, Inc., 15
PathStone Corporation, 149, 343
Penquis Community Action Program, Inc., 441
Peoples' Self-Help Housing Corporation, 145
Portland Housing Center, 445
Providence Community Housing, 347
Puerto Rico NHS, Corp., 433

REACH Community Development, Inc., 115
RUPCO, Inc., 51, 593
Rural Neighborhoods, Incorporated, 539

Self-Help Enterprises, 621
Southern Mutual Help Association, 449
Southwest Minnesota Housing Partnership, 141, 299
Southwest Solutions, 573
St. Ambrose Housing Aid Center, 19
St. Joseph's Carpenter Society, 577

Tenderloin Neighborhood Development Corporation, 371
The Neighborhood Developers, Inc., 367, 453
The Primavera Foundation, Inc., 67, 475
Thistle Communities, 39
Trellis, 87

United Housing, Inc., 291
Universal Housing Development Corporation, 91
Urban Edge Housing Corporation, 295

West Elmwood Housing Development Corp., 133
Westside Housing Organization, Inc., 283
Wyoming Housing Network, 241

Essential Services and Tools to Optimize Your Impact

NeighborWorks used to be known for training around housing and community development. When you thought of Neighbor-Works, you thought of homes. Now, NeighborWorks training, tools and services offer everything you need to build and lead a better team, develop and implement a better strategy, and measure and demonstrate better outcomes, no matter what kind of public-serving organization you are. Basically, NeighborWorks helps you do more—BE more—from soup to nuts. And we still offer top-notch training to help you improve your community's housing and neighborhoods.

Organizational Assessments
Expert insight to strengthen organizational health and performance

Training and Professional Development
Knowledge and skills to power your work and your career

Leadership Programs
Curriculum and support to transform individual, organizational and board performance

Tools and Resources
What you need to make your work actually work

Gauging Outcomes and Impact
Evaluation tools and support beyond measure

We're here to help you and your organization perform at the highest level.
Connect with us at NeighborWorks.org